Of Sand or Soil

PRINCETON STUDIES IN MUSLIM POLITICS

Dale F. Eickelman and Augustus Richard Norton, series editors

A list of titles in this series can be found at the back of the book

Of Sand or Soil

GENEALOGY AND TRIBAL BELONGING IN SAUDI ARABIA

Nadav Samin

PRINCETON UNIVERSITY PRESS
PRINCETON AND OXFORD

Published by Princeton University Press,
41 William Street, Princeton, New Jersey 08540
In the United Kingdom: Princeton University Press,
6 Oxford Street, Woodstock, Oxfordshire OX20 1TR

press.princeton.edu

Cover art: With permission from ʿAbd al-Raḥmān al-Shuqayr, *Aṭlas Mushajjarāt Banī Zayd* (ʿAbd al-Raḥmān al-Shuqayr, 2015)

First paperback printing, 2019

Paper ISBN 978-0-691-18338-1

The Library of Congress has cataloged the cloth edition as follows:

Samin, Nadav, 1976-
Of sand or soil : genealogy and tribal belonging in Saudi Arabia / Nadav Samin.
pages cm.—(Princeton studies in muslim politics)
Includes bibliographical references and index.
ISBN 978-0-691-16444-1 (hardcover : alk. paper) 1. Tribes—Saudi Arabia. 2. Tribal government—Saudi Arabia. 3. Saudi Arabia—Ethnic relations. 4. Jasir, Hamad. I. Title.
DS218.S26 2015
953.805—dc23
2014044326

British Library Cataloging-in-Publication Data is available

This book has been composed in Linux Libertine O and Adobe Caslon Pro

For Lily and Selma

Contents

Illustrations

MAP AND TABLE

Acknowledgments

This book would not exist without the following people: Bernard Haykel, who combines two qualities—generosity and learnedness—uncommon in a single person; Michael Cook, whose mastery of both the grand and the intimate movements of history inspired this study; Isabelle Clark-Decès, who, by sharing generously her knowledge and time, made the process of writing this book a true joy; and Michael Laffan, who provided insightful feedback and support throughout the writing and editing of my early drafts. I would also like to thank Andras Hamori for helping me translate and interpret some of the poems included here, and Jonathan Chipman for his skill and patience in producing the map.

I thank the family of Ḥamad al-Jāsir for their generosity and openness with a stranger; Maʿan and May, I am in your debt. I also cannot forget my friends at the Ḥamad al-Jāsir Cultural Center, who greatly aided my research. I extend my gratitude to the King Faisal Center for Research and Islamic Studies, and to Prince Turki al-Faisal, Yahya b. Junayd, and Awadh al-Badi in particular, for graciously hosting me during my visits to the kingdom.

I acknowledge here the many Saudis who have advocated for my project, lent their expertise, or opened their homes and personal histories to me, including Nasir al-Hujailan, for his strong advocacy; Khaled Radihan, for educating me in the field; Fāyiz al-Badrānī, for his patience and generosity with a genealogical novice; ʿAbd al-Raḥmān al-Shuqayr, for his unparalleled support and kindness; Saud al-Sarhan, for his friendship and hospitality; ʿAbdallāh al-Munīf; Fahd al-Semari; Fahād al-Sahlī; Mushawwiḥ al-Mushawwiḥ; Aḥmad; the people of al-ʿUlā; and countless others.

I am sincerely grateful to Abdulaziz Al Fahad, Saad Sowayan, and the anonymous reviewers of the manuscript for their careful attention and valuable feedback. A number of other scholars lent their time and energies to book chapters or their precursors, including Steve Caton, Lawrence Rosen, Engseng Ho, Andrew Shryock, Dale Eickelman, Pascal Menoret, Amaney Jamal, Muhammad Qasim Zaman, and Cyrus Schayegh. This study owes a particular debt to the rich and innovative works of Andrew and Engseng, without which it would not exist.

I extend gratitude to Fred Appel, Sara Lerner, Dimitri Karetnikov, Juliana Fidler, and Bhisham Bherwani at Princeton University Press for helping guide this project to completion.

I thank my parents, Ami and Rena, and my sister, Bali, for their belief in me. Lastly, this book is dedicated to Lily, for your love, support and encouragement throughout the writing of this book, and to Selma, with whom we've now begun our own family tree.

My research in Saudi Arabia was supported by fellowships and grants from the Social Science Research Council Postdoctoral Fellowship for Transregional Research with funds provided by the Andrew W. Mellon Foundation; the Princeton Center for Arts and Cultural Policy Studies; the Project on Middle East Political Science; the Princeton Institute for International and Regional Studies; and the Near Eastern Studies Department at Princeton University.

Note on Transliteration

I adopt a modified *International Journal of Middle East Studies* (IJMES) system of transliteration. As this study is in many respects about names and naming practices, all Arabic names and most other proper nouns have been rendered with full diacritical markings. Exceptions are commonly invoked terms such as Saudi, Wahhabi, Salafi, Najdi, and Hijaz/Hijazi, as well as common Arabic terms that have entered the English lexicon (e.g., imam, Sufi, Shia). My transliterations of dialect poetry and other dialect terms from central Arabia and neighboring regions aspire less to linguistic precision than to establishing the visceral presence of Arabia's oral culture as a backdrop to this study.

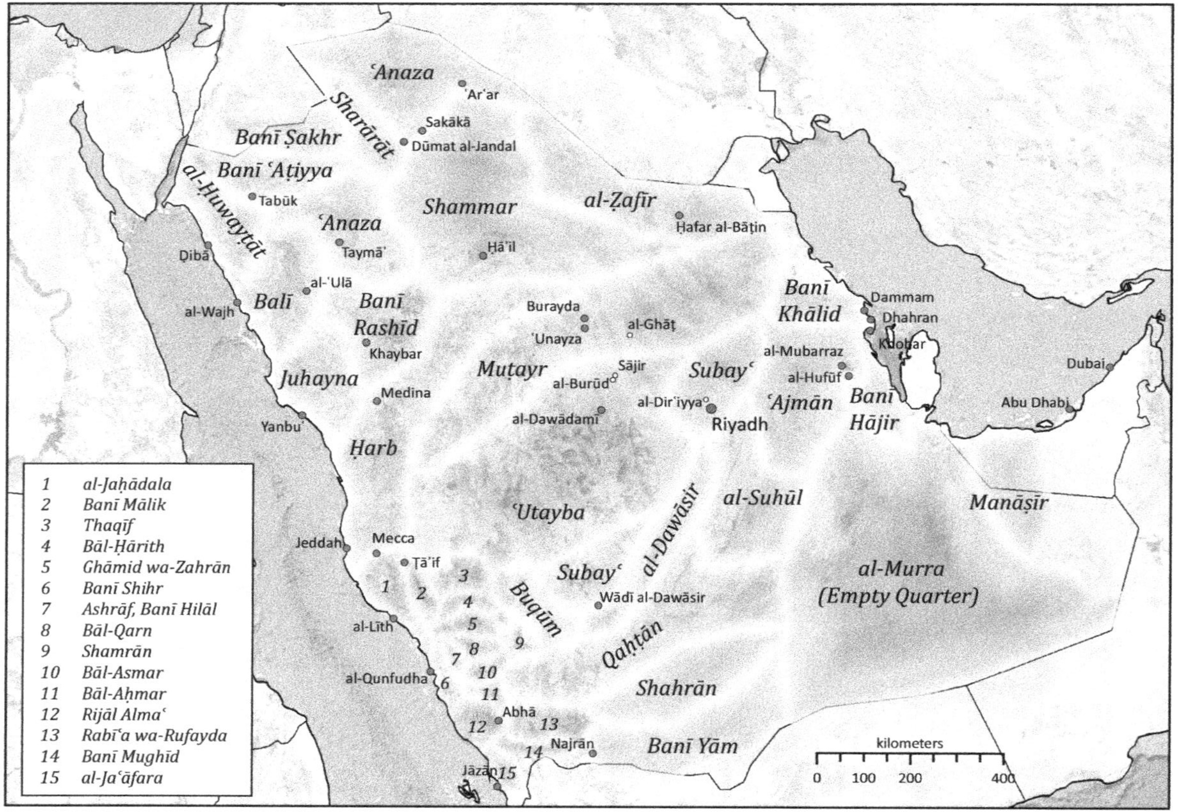

Map 1. Approximate boundaries of Arabian tribal territories before the establishment of the modern Saudi state, along with toponyms significant for this study.

Of Sand or Soil

Introduction

> It is not for the truth that men seek, but for that which is pleasant to believe. Poor, ill-clad, shivering truth stands pitiful by the way; for men have ever passed her by in search of that which they desire.[1]
>
> —*J. Horace Round*

Austere and fortress-like, the Saudi Ministry of Foreign Affairs in Riyadh was built to inhabit its central Arabian surroundings. Wrapped around the massive front gate of the Danish-designed building is a Quranic verse, 49:13: "O people, we have created you male and female," the inscription begins, ascending toward the right end of the lintel in flowing, golden script. Bearing left above the tall, recessed doorway, the verse's key phrase unfolds across the observer's field of vision: "and made you peoples and tribes." Descending to completion down the left side of the door frame, the inscription concludes: "so that you may come to know one another. Verily, the most noble among you is the most God-fearing."

Invoked in this context, verse 49:13 is a statement of bureaucratic purpose, reminding visitors that the Foreign Ministry's mission "to contribute to the formation of an international order based on justice and principles of common humanity" rests upon the Saudi state's pious foundations.[2] Immutable associations aside, it is to the peoples or nations of the world, not to its tribes, that the Foreign Ministry addresses itself. For an alternative reading of this verse, one might look to its presentation as a more figurative framing device for the thousands of genealogical trees that have been conceived and created by Saudis over the past half-century. Splashed across the top border of that quintessential Saudi art form is, quite often, verse 49:13. "O people, we have created you male and female, and made you peoples and tribes, so that you may come to know one another. Verily, the most noble among you is the most God-fearing." Positioned above a family tree, the verse takes on a radically new meaning. Its call for the mutual acquaintance of nations is muted, as is its apparent privileging of Muslim communion over the fractured and par-

Figure 0.1. Saudi Ministry of Foreign Affairs, front entrance. Courtesy of Henning Larsen Architects.

ticularist identities into which humanity has been arrayed. In this colorful and allusive statement of modern Saudi identity, the nations of the world, as its God-fearing people, recede into the background, and the Quran's indirect endorsement of tribal belonging becomes the central fact of the verse and its invocation.

This book intends to explain why tribal genealogies matter in modern Saudi Arabia. It addresses a specific question, one that connects intimately with verse 49:13 and the multiple contexts in which it is embedded in the kingdom: why, in a country so overwhelmingly saturated with public religiosity—its symbols, its laws, its functionaries—is this verse of scripture understood by so many Saudis as a license to assert their particularist tribal identities, while its ostensibly equalizing final clause is dismissed as an afterthought? What explains the compulsion to affirm tribal belonging in modern Saudi Arabia?

Despite the erosion of kinship ties resulting from almost three centuries of religious conditioning, and despite the unprecedented material transformation of Saudi society in the oil age, genealogy remains a central facet of modern Saudi identity.[3] A rising tide of interest in genealogies has appeared in the kingdom over the past half-century, embodied in the thousands of largely self-published books, articles, and family trees created by Saudis for the purposes of affirming their families' tribal lineages. At the heart of the kingdom's modern genealogical culture is the compulsion many Saudis feel to assert a tribal descent, that is, to prove their lineal attachment to a historically recog-

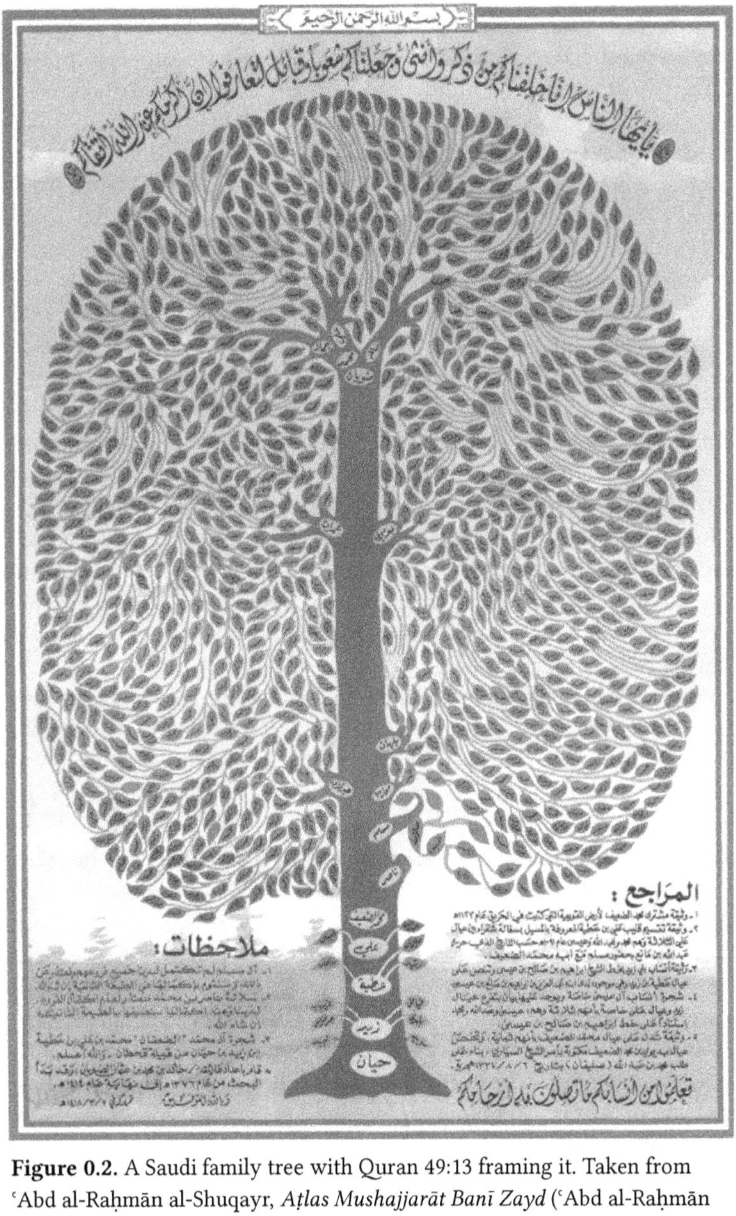

Figure 0.2. A Saudi family tree with Quran 49:13 framing it. Taken from ʿAbd al-Raḥmān al-Shuqayr, *Aṭlas Mushajjarāt Banī Zayd* (ʿAbd al-Raḥmān al-Shuqayr, 2015). Used with permission.

nizable Arabian tribe, and so establish their ancient roots in the Arabian Peninsula. At the social level, this compulsion reflects a transition from the predominantly oral culture of premodern Arabia to the new textually oriented, bureaucratically influenced society of the modern kingdom, where the capacity to identify or produce texts that credibly affirm one's tribal belonging has become an important marker of authenticity. At the political level, this compulsion is the outcome of a strategy of the Saudi state, which has sought to condition both its bedouin- and sedentary-origin populations toward a locally resonant and materially useful notion of national belonging.

For much of the period under investigation, which commences with the emergence of Wahhabism in the middle of the eighteenth century and concludes near the present day, the documenting of genealogies in central Arabia was a limited practice, confined to the recording of the lineages of the rulers and prominent families of the region's towns and nomadic tribes. It was only with the settling of Arabia's nomadic populations after the Second World War and the assimilation of both bedouin- and sedentary-origin Saudis into a new national enterprise that the documenting of genealogies emerged as a matter of intense social and political interest. Though central to the social and political life of the people of premodern Arabia, genealogies remained by and large unarticulated until the modern age, when they could no longer be taken for granted.

Few societies have undergone as rapid a material transformation as Saudi Arabia in the twentieth century. When the first Saudi state was founded in 1744, savory lizards and desert truffles were the known extent of Arabia's underground bounties. After Ottoman forces defeated the Saudis in 1818 and commenced their brief occupation of central Arabia, it was the scarcity of food and water, among other logistical constraints, that compelled them to beat a rapid retreat and leave the far-flung region to its own devices.[4] When American engineers were enlisted by the founder of the third and current Saudi state, ʿAbd al-ʿAzīz Ibn Saʿūd, to drill for fresh water reservoirs in the early 1930s, their attentions were drawn to the dark and viscous substance that would change the course of history.[5] The discovery of commercial quantities of oil in 1938 initiated a movement of populations and capital into and around the kingdom whose rapidity, particularly after the 1960s, has few precedents in history. This book explores an unexamined consequence of that transformation, namely, how and why a predominantly oral reservoir of social and cultural knowledge, Arabian genealogies, was transferred into print. With the emergence of the text as the authoritative pivot around which new Arabian identities were to be formed, novel categories of problems presented themselves to Saudis. In place of fuzzy genealogical conceptions of old that linked a person's extended family to an ancient or mythic tribal ancestor, lacunae in the genealogical record could now be imagined, and doubts about the origins of oneself or one's neighbors arose. These new categories of problems, at once historiographical and personal, commenced a scramble to assert belonging within the often disorienting spaces of the modern kingdom.

This book is primarily a study of the lineage claims of Saudis of sedentary origin, or Saudis whose ancestors originated in one or another of Arabia's scattered farming towns and villages. Such towns include the modern Saudi capital of Riyadh, which after the eighteenth century became a sizable population center, but also tiny and isolated hamlets where small clusters of date palms sustained no more than a few families. Though often generations removed from a direct connection to their root clans of origin, these sedentary agriculturalists believed themselves to descend from historically recognized Arabian tribes, most of which were nomadic, though a few, such as Banī Zayd and Banī Tamīm, were largely sedentary. The manner by which the modern, urban descendants of these peasant farmers conceive of their genealogical relations across space and time is one of the central concerns of this book. Unlike many studies of tribes and tribal identity,[6] this book is less concerned with what happens to nomadic groups when they come into contact with centralized states, as with what becomes of the sedentary social imagination when nomadic groups are brought into sedentary life. While I devote some attention to Saudi bedouin genealogies and questions of bedouin tribal identity, I do so mostly for the purposes of clarifying the sociological and historical backdrop against which sedentary genealogical claims are made. In tracking the bedouin-sedentary binary through the ebb and flow of modern Saudi history, I hope to demonstrate the dynamism and potency of kinship attitudes in the social and political imagination of the modern kingdom and, by extension, that of other societies experiencing rapid transformation.

What is the meaning of the tribe to which Saudis claim belonging? The concept of tribe, anthropologists have shown, can refer to peoples exhibiting a variety of economic activities, ethnic origins, or forms of sociopolitical organization.[7] Rather than fixed and unchanging entities, as we might be conditioned to consider them, premodern Arabian tribes are best thought of as processes of social formation and dissolution contingent on ecological and political circumstance. This changeability is apparent, for example, in the changing names of Arabia's tribal confederations, branches, and families over the centuries, most of which can be found blending into and out of oral and documented memory. Through the obscuring and illuminating of these names, one might trace an ecological, political, and social history of the Arabian Peninsula.[8]

Counterposed against this notion of changeability is a more durable construct that underpins the tribal system in its diverse guises: the ideology of patrilineal descent. The idea that the tribe achieves its definition through the principle of blood descent in an apical ancestor's paternal line has proven central to the conceptualizing of tribal systems by local actors and Western scholars alike. Yet if patrilineage is often the language in which social and political relationships are expressed, it does not, in and of itself, determine how these relationships are formed.[9] To explain the relevance of patrilineage to the modern Saudi genealogical story, and why tribal identity is so central to modern Saudi identity, I treat the ideology of patrilineal descent as one among a broad range of social, religious, and political discourses, each informed by a distinctively central Arabian material and historical context.

In modern Saudi Arabia, the steady expansion of the state into the traditional domains of the tribe, the provisioning of economic goods and physical security, has largely eliminated the tribal system's raison d'être. Yet the idea of the tribe and tribal belonging has persisted strongly in the Saudi imagination, beyond what might be justified by a personal desire to reattach oneself to one's newly unfamiliar homeland, or a historiographical concern with diminishing the span of the *inqiṭāʿ*, or rupture, that separates Arabia's oral cultural past from its documented present.[10] The role of the Saudi state must be accounted for in the emergence of the kingdom's genealogical culture. Through its practices, the state has breathed new life into tribal identity, rendering it one of the only meaningful forms of civic association permissible in the kingdom. It is ultimately this state's tacit glorification of the tribe that has compelled many in the kingdom to rediscover or invent patrilineal affiliations to prominent Arabian tribes through which they can authenticate their position in modern Saudi society. For the main subjects of this book, Saudis of sedentary origin whose tribal lineages are undesirable, uncertain, or suspect, the tribe is quite simply a normative aspiration, one that is as much a product of the biopolitics of the modern Saudi state as it is of the central Arabian social imagination.

Linking these threads together, the social and the political, is the individual whose life and work lie at the center of this study, the central Arabian (Najdi) genealogist and historian Ḥamad al-Jāsir (d. 2000). More than any other single person, al-Jāsir was responsible for ushering in the kingdom's modern genealogical culture, for defining its objectives and normalizing its methods. Born in 1909 in a central Arabian mud-brick village, this scholar rose to prominence during his lifetime as the primary authority on the history and heritage of central Arabia. When late in life al-Jāsir turned to the systematic compiling of the lineages of the kingdom's inhabitants, he was forced to confront the sparely documented record of central Arabia's past, and the predominant position of Arabia's oral tradition in the preservation and transmission of knowledge about this past.

In his influential study of modern identity formation, Benedict Anderson singles out three dimensions of the cultural life of the premodern world whose decline enabled the emergence of modern nationalism in Europe and other regions.[11] Among these was the dethroning of Latin as the unifying language of sacred and mundane authority, and its replacement by the Latin vernaculars that today comprise the national languages of many European states. In the modern Middle East, however, a countervailing process unfolded. In the aftermath of the European colonial project, the borrowed Latin and Germanic vernaculars of colonial administration ceded much of their terrain to Arabic, the sacred language of the Arabs, which was enshrined as the new language of Arab nationhood, albeit in modified form. In Saudi Arabia, which witnessed no such direct colonial handoff, the fusion of sacred and mundane languages was even more pronounced, and testified to the tight grip of Wahhabi religiosity on the Saudi political imagination. Public culture in Saudi Arabia, the culture of newspapers and books pioneered by Ḥamad al-Jāsir, was thus from the onset cast in a religious mold, its norms delimited by the constrictive priorities of the religious establishment and its royal backers.

When, in the 1950s, Ḥamad al-Jāsir staked his claim within this emergent public culture, he aimed to unsettle this fusion of the sacred and the mundane. Al-Jāsir's efforts to widen the boundaries of permissible knowledge and political engagement in central Arabia saw him condemned to death by the Wahhabi religious establishment and ostracized by the Saudi regime, events that compelled him to reorient his life toward the study of Arabian history and heritage. Of the many subjects al-Jāsir investigated, genealogy proved the most compelling to his readers, and the most fraught with controversy. Opening this unguarded door, the scholar was met with a rush of cultural matter unlike any he had encountered before. This was the force of Arabia's oral genealogical inheritance, which, with all its fluidity, contingency, and ultimate uncertainty, al-Jāsir sought to codify and fashion into documented "facts."

SAUDI HISTORY BETWEEN THE ORAL AND THE TEXTUAL

Investigating the oral cultural backdrop of central Arabian history, a primary concern of this book, is crucial for any understanding of modern Saudi Arabia.[12] While orality is without a doubt a contested analytical category, its utility for understanding the development of the modern genealogical culture of Saudi Arabia, and the kingdom's history in general, must not be understated or casually dismissed.[13] Several points combine to favor this analytical paradigm, among them the historical preponderance of nomadic populations in the territories that comprise modern Saudi Arabia;[14] the sparsely documented history of these territories, in particular central Arabia; and lastly and most significantly, the dominance in the modern kingdom of central Arabia, the region where nomadism was most widespread and where bedouin culture was most influential. Central Arabia's absence from the broad sweep of Islamic history is widely recognized.[15] Its marginal historiographical position would be less significant, however, if the region had not emerged as the center of power and authority in the modern kingdom of Saudi Arabia, a country that is today the only Arab member of the G20 group of wealthy nations, and is perhaps the single most influential state in the modern Middle East. Under this new dispensation, the once peripheral hinterland became the arbiter of culture and national identity, and Ḥamad al-Jāsir's position as its lexicographer and genealogist was crucial for giving voice to this transformation.

In treating the life and work of Ḥamad al-Jāsir as a connecting node between two distinct notions of genealogy, this study casts light as well on the politicization of the Arabian oral tradition. To understand what is meant by the Arabian oral tradition, I will briefly review the concept of orality and the sharp criticism it has sustained as a method of analysis. The notion of orality as a distinctive epistemology was developed by a diverse set of scholars with the goal of reconsidering the privileged position of texts in the interpretation of historical and social phenomena across a range of time periods and continents. Scholars who worked with the oral-textual binary elevated the concept of oral transmission as a privileged unit of analysis, focusing their attention on societies in which literacy was restricted to specific privileged groups (e.g., priestly classes, religious scholars) and oral forms of knowledge predominated. Textual literacy, the dominant mode of communication in the modern Western world, was measured by these scholars as the end state toward which non-Western oral cultures were transitioning.[16]

For Jack Goody, one of the first to look systematically at the influence of oral traditions in non-Western societies, the archetypal model of this end state was ancient Greece, where literacy was relatively widespread. Goody treated literacy as a causal mechanism that more than any other factor influenced the development of Greek civilization. The oral-textual binary was thus wedded from its inception to a notion of ancient Greek preeminence, which served in turn as a model against which to measure contemporary non-Western societies, whose failure to measure up was thus a feature built into the schema. For scholars of a more psychological bent, such as Walter Ong, orality and literacy were categories of consciousness whose parameters were fixed deterministically by the presence or absence of technologies of writing and textual reproduction in a given society. Though preoccupied chiefly with establishing new definitions of modernity, most scholars of orality and textuality gave little consideration to the role of the modern state in circumscribing oral culture or promoting particular forms of literacy. In the Saudi case, for example, the state and its validators within the Wahhabi religious establishment promoted religious literacy as the dominant form of engagement with modernity, leaving oral cultural forms subordinated and devalued.

As Brinkley Messick and others have demonstrated, oral transmission was an essential component of the production of literate knowledge in traditional Arabian societies.[17] In Yemen and Oman, as elsewhere, "recitational reproduction" was intrinsic to religious learning; Islamic knowledge was traditionally rooted in the oral transmission of texts, not the mere copying of manuscripts from one scribe to the next. Messick's approach, however, privileges a form of orality that was anchored in a textual referent, the Quran, and one whose purchase was limited to sedentary communities. The tradition of genealogical documentation investigated here is a far more slippery and subjective endeavor than the legal tradition Messick addresses, and thus opens the way for different considerations of the role of oral narrative and testimonial within it. As a sedentary figure narrating a history of sedentary lineages that for the most part excluded the bedouin, Ḥamad al-Jāsir fit into the cultural mold prepared by the dominant religious dispensation of his locale, Wahhabism. Yet despite his best efforts to transcend its localized constraints and imprecisions, the scholar remained beholden to an oral epistemology that had far less to do with Wahhabism than with the nomadic or otherwise nonliterate backdrop to Arabian settled life. The oral culture in which central Arabian genealogical consciousness was embedded was, at its nonliterate or nomadic source, at most only nominally attached to a textual-Islamic referent.

From the perspective of central Arabia's religious and political authorities, the oral culture at issue here was a dimension of the irredeemably syncretic and superstitious bedouin mode of thought, which would have to be disciplined by the delimiting authority of scripture if the sedentary project of Muḥammad b. ʿAbd al-Wahhāb was to succeed. This evolutionary reconditioning was thus imposed from within the central Arabian locale by central Arabia's own political and religious actors, and was not the solution to a problem that emerged from the application of Western-modeled yardsticks.[18] Genealogical consciousness survived this reconditioning, this book argues, and was drawn into settled life and transmuted by a confluence of social and political forces in the modern age. Following closely the thread of Arabian oral genealogical culture as it is absorbed into the textual life of the modern kingdom, I maintain, opens up new avenues for considering the sociology of Arabian societies, and allows us new insights into the interplay among a range of forces, sedentary and nomadic, religious and secularizing, institutional and personal.

I approach the influence of the oral cultural backdrop on modern Saudi history from two vantage points, one diachronic, the other synchronic. One of the primary concerns of this study is to examine changes in the nature of

Arabian genealogical authority over time. I mark the process by which the ability to produce authoritative statements about Arabian genealogies moved from the localized purview of town and tribal elders to the publishing and distribution networks of scholars such as Ḥamad al-Jāsir, who, as central Arabia's first newsman, was an important figure in the development of the kingdom's public culture. Al-Jāsir, who moved throughout his life in and out of the political orbit of the state—though never far from its patronage networks—was a transitional figure in the kingdom's modern genealogical culture. Although he was treated by many ordinary Saudis as an oracle who possessed arcane knowledge about their most intimate anxieties—their marital futures, their belonging within the nation—his personal charisma was ultimately insufficient to shield his genealogical project from the interested gaze of the state. Studying genealogical documentation as a historical phenomenon unfolding over time, it follows, allows us to move outside of the explicit truth claims of a particular set of genealogical texts such as those produced by al-Jāsir, and brings into focus the influence of an increasingly powerful centralizing state and the ideology of kinship it promoted. Studying Arabian genealogies in this way also allows us to track other unexamined dimensions of Arabian social and political life. A good example is the emergence of non-tribals onto the pages of Saudi history.

Non-tribals, Saudis whose lineages were historically believed suspect, are all but absent from the pages of premodern Saudi chronicles, yet are among the chief protagonists in the kingdom's modern genealogical culture. The intermingling of tribal and non-tribal populations in the modern kingdom as potentially equal citizens induced a reaction by Saudis of tribal origin to reassert the caste-like divisions that had existed historically in Arabian society. The denial of genealogical pedigree to central Arabia's non-tribal populations opened up social fissures that the scholar Ḥamad al-Jāsir took as his object to remedy. The effort by lineage-seeking, sedentary-origin Saudis to have their tribal roots affirmed in al-Jāsir's genealogical volumes is a characteristic development of the kingdom's modern genealogical culture, and investigating this effort forms an important part of this book.

THE ART OF SOCIAL CLIMBING: FROM SPANISH ANDALUSIA TO ARABIA

To consider the material backdrop against which the pageantry of modern Saudi lineages has unfolded, we might look to a time and place quite remote from modern Arabia. Between the sixteenth and seventeenth centuries, the Andalusian city of Seville was gripped by its own genealogical obsession, one that in important respects parallels our story. There, as in the Kingdom of Saudi Arabia, the exogenous inpouring of a new source of wealth—gold from the New World—transformed the social hierarchies of the city. The ranks of the patrician nobility, comprised mostly of Christians of recognizably pure lineages, became strained by an influx of newly wealthy merchants, many of Jewish and Muslim descent. These upwardly mobile merchants began seeking aristocratic title, the acquisition of which demanded the demonstration of pure bloodlines. As increasing numbers of merchants bought their way into the Sevillian nobility by fabricating their genealogies to obscure Jewish or Muslim connections, they were confronted by the *linajudos*, conservative genealogists who worked to expose their true origins. The *linajudos* represented the sharp end of the spear of the old Sevillian order, which objected to the social transformations brought on by the new transatlantic economy, and so worked to reverse them, often by devious means. The key element of their strategy was their obsession with the post-*Reconquista* social and ecclesiastical doctrine of *limpieza de sangre*, purity of blood, a standard that *converso* title seekers were shown to never quite attain.[19]

The story recounted in this book, though transposed to a massively divergent historical and political context, follows a similar group of social climbers and strivers. It is a story of how a once undifferentiated and socially unambitious peasantry came to covet lineal distinctiveness in a newly urban and literate context. The subjects of this study are by and large government clerks and middle managers, teachers and engineers, small and large businessmen, and newspaper and journal readers—newly literate strivers. These men—and they are almost always men—were born in villages that had yet to be fitted with electricity or running water. In their youth they had migrated, alone or with their families, to the kingdom's population centers where, for reasons to be discussed, a public discourse of tribal nobility and lineal prestige was taking root. With documentary evidence in hand, the strivers of the new Saudi economy sought to acquire a titular stake in that elusive status group, Saudis of pure (*aṣīl*) tribal origin. Their well-intentioned machinations and connivances will preoccupy us substantially in the pages that follow.

Well into the twentieth century, in places such as Yemen, Oman, and Morocco, the cultivation of elaborate genealogies remained a practice confined to the traditional religious or political elite. Martha Mundy, in her ethnographic study of a northern Yemeni village, found that the genealogical concerns of sedentary Yemeni agriculturalists were largely unambitious. Interest in tribal lineage amounted to a localized reverence for the land and "honourable occupations" of known ancestors, without any particular fixation on mythic antecedents. [20] In the circumstances described by Mundy we might discern what the Saudi genealogical imagination was like prior to the *ṭafra*, or inpouring of wealth, engendered by the oil boom. In a society of new material abundance, aspirants to social status enter into the lineage game. This is what is novel about the modern Saudi genealogical story, which has unfolded not among the landscaped cliffside terraces of an Arabian pastoral, but behind the high and bare concrete walls of Riyadh's urban middle-class villas.

AN ANTHROPOLOGY OF ARABIA

Narrating a social and cultural history of modern Saudi Arabia that moves beyond the privileged framework of the kingdom's religious culture—as was Ḥamad al-Jāsir's object and is the object of this book—demands that the historian serve double duty as an anthropologist. This is especially the case with modern Arabian genealogies, which are as much reflections of the kinship practices of Saudis as they are of the oral cultural backdrop against which these practices have been imagined and constructed. The study of kinship was anthropology's original project.[21] In working to uncover the kinship patterns of non-Western societies, Adam Kuper has argued, nineteenth- and early twentieth-century anthropologists believed themselves to be recovering traces of an essential humanity (chimerical, it seems) that was thought to have been trampled under the tow of industrialization.[22] Kinship studies took a battering among subsequent generations of anthropologists, for its close association with the colonial projects of Western empires[23] or for its biologizing of socially constructed facts,[24] and has still to recover its former luster. Still, in a society such as Saudi Arabia's, where over the past half-century kinship claims have come to be among the predominant cultural coins of the realm, the utility of the kinship paradigm for making sense of the kingdom's modern history should be apparent.

My study of how Saudi lineages have been represented over the past three centuries is informed throughout by anthropological theories of the constructed nature of kinship relations. Yet merely affirming one's allegiance to such an approach is not particularly meaningful; more interesting and pertinent is to detail how and by whom kinship relations are constructed and represented, and toward what ends. While I move with the weathered consensus that rejects classical conceptions of kinship structures as biologically determined units generative wholly of themselves or in close combination with one another, I am uneasy with the dominant postcolonial argument, that kinship networks are largely the invention of modern states. It is between the social and political imagination that modern kinship identity is formed, and though these two ways of conceiving kin relations might be deeply interwoven and difficult to separate from one another, they are not coterminous. Despite the ever-increasing reach of the Saudi state, I argue, how Saudis construct their kin relations is still conditioned strongly by the legacies of central Arabia's ecology and oral tradition.

The most important contribution of an anthropological approach is that it grounds us in a synchronic view of Arabian genealogies, which in turn helps restore a measure of equivalency between Arabia's oral and textual traditions. Placing these traditions on an equal footing affirms the importance of the paradigm of orality against claims that it is misguided or obsolete,[25] and serves as a rejoinder to the caveats of reform- or piety-minded Saudis, who see the demise of tribalism—and the challenges it poses to a secular or Wahhabi-inflected modernity—as being just around the corner. A synchronic view, moreover, reminds us of the continuing power, despite its apparent absence, of oral tradition in the modern kingdom. Removing this tradition from the frame of analysis, as too often occurs, radically changes the picture of Saudi history. The preponderance of scholarship on modern Saudi Arabia, driven largely by corporate and security service interests or the opposition to them, tends to overemphasize the religious and economic narratives that predominate in the kingdom's official culture, while dismissing as marginal those aspects of Saudi life whose vitality and centrality this book has set out to prove. In an Arabian environment dominated historically by a bedouin culture of oral preservation and transmission, I argue, conceptions of culture rooted in textuality—that is, modern Islamic conceptions—are inadequate for explaining the transformation of Saudi society over the course of the twentieth century. What's more, the disruption associated with the transition from oral to textual culture is a phenomenon with resonance far beyond Saudi Arabia, and is in fact a critical dimension of the transformation of Middle Eastern societies and polities in the twentieth century.

TRIBAL IDENTITY AND THE SAUDI STATE

This book is, finally, a study of identity formation in a developing society, and the complex role of the modern state in this process. In the premodern Gulf of coastal towns, oasis villages, and nomadic hinterland tribes, kinship networks played an important role in organizing social and political life. As the scope and reach of the modern Saudi state increased, the political power of the kinship unit was eroded, and kinship networks receded into the realm of symbolic expression. Yet in the process of normalizing the criteria for Saudi citizenship, I conclude, the idiom in which kinship was expressed—the tribal idiom—was appropriated by the state for the efficient ordering and sorting of its new subject-citizenry. Under the new Saudi order, tribal kinship was reified as an essential component of national belonging, creating a new inadequacy for those who could not credibly claim it.

In an illuminating article, Ceren Belge documents the history of resistance by Kurdish kinship groups to the atomizing policies of the early Turkish republic, whose strategies for dissolving Kurdish kinship solidarities and registering Kurds as deculturated citizens were undermined by the continuing potency of these solidarities and their capacity to weave through and undermine the state's program from within.[26] Belge's study is meant in part as a challenge to the idea prevalent in postcolonial literature that modern kinship networks and hierarchies were edifices built entirely by states,[27] their local constitution being a derivative outcome of far-off intra-bureaucratic debates or the managerial attributes of proconsuls. Considering the question of how modern kinship solidarities are constructed in Saudi Arabia is useful both for drawing out some of the dynamics of national identity formation in the kingdom, and for expanding the theoretical and empirical range of the debate over the politics of kinship more generally.

Despite nearly a century of policy prescription and experimentation, Saudi national identity remains deeply in flux. Some of this can be attributed to the lingering informality that continues to characterize Saudi political life. In the early days of the state, for example, national holidays such as Accession Day could be migrated down the calendar when a new king took power;[28] some sixty years later, holidays were still being declared at a moment's notice.[29] In part, it is the personalized and seemingly arbitrary exercise of power that obscures the process by which Saudi national identity has come into being. Yet the challenge in defining Saudi national identity, this book argues, has also to do with the relatively weak attraction of impersonal ties and the central place of ascriptive ones, genealogies, in the Saudi social imagination. Semantically, we might recall, "Saudi" refers to a lineage and not an ethnic, territorial, religious, or language group, the traditional root collectives out of which national identities have been constituted in the modern age. It is the distinctive nature of this building block of nationhood that the reader should consider as he or she progresses through this volume.

Rather than a republican citizenship collective endowed with rights and responsibilities, the Saudi state might be described cynically as a mechanism for distributing economic goods to its populace. As such, its will to intervene in the messy and potentially dangerous business of shaping citizen identities, in the way of the Turkish republic and many other modern states, has been relatively limited. The twofold needs of this state—to distribute goods and privileges on a mass scale and to efficiently police its burgeoning bedouin and sedentary populations—however, required that the criteria for citizenship, and the exclusion from its privileges, be standardized. The homogenizing of modern Saudi society was thus never in question—the choice lay in the criteria by which to proceed.

States cannot create societies wholesale. They can, however, make powerful use of the ethnographic knowledge they collect about their subjects and citizens. The Soviet Union, for example, used such knowledge to classify and sort the disparate ethno-national communities it had inherited from the Russian empire, so that they might be more neatly subordinated to a pan-Soviet nationalism and the transcendent socialist ideals it was meant to represent.[30]

In the Saudi case, progress toward forging the ultimate citizen was anchored deeply not in a techno-futurist vision but in a retro-gazing ethic that brought together religious and genealogical loyalties in a tense embrace.

While traditional kinship networks were certainly weakened in the process of state formation, most studies of modern Saudi Arabia fail to consider the extent to which genealogy, the ordering principle of the kin group, became the essential organizing principle of Saudi citizen identity. By normalizing citizenship on the basis of genealogical criteria, making lineal authentication a core function of substate political actors, and promoting an ideology of kinship meant to legitimate Āl Saʿūd family rule, this book argues, the Saudi state quietly established the grounds for a new form of political order. Under this new order, the idea of kinship was repurposed, and modern Saudi identity was transformed in ways whose meaning is still unfolding.

DESCRIPTION OF CHAPTERS

Chapter one introduces readers to the twentieth-century history of Saudi Arabia through the biography of one of its most notable but least recognized figures, the historian and genealogist Ḥamad al-Jāsir. More than any other single person, al-Jāsir was responsible for shaping the modern genealogical culture of Saudi Arabia. I document al-Jāsir's life from his birth in 1909 in a central Arabian village to the beginnings of his genealogical project in the 1970s. I review al-Jāsir's sometimes tumultuous relationship with his patrons in the Wahhabi religious establishment, his contributions to the development of the Saudi press and public culture, his views on Arabia's bedouin populations and on the Arabic language, and, finally, his turn toward scholarship and the documenting of Saudi lineages in the last third of his life.

In chapter two I examine how and why central Arabian genealogies were documented from the eighteenth through the twentieth century. I show how Saudi bedouin and settled populations conceived of their kinship relations through their own eyes and through the eyes of Western travelers. I draw attention to the caste-like status hierarchies that existed in central Arabia before the modern period, hierarchies rooted in Arabian political culture, and how the emergence of these hierarchies onto the pages of modern Saudi history represents an important transition in the kingdom's social and cultural life. It was the documenting of lineages and their mass circulation in print, I conclude, that helped transform Saudi genealogies from reflexive components of social and political life into coveted objects of modern Saudi identity.

In the next three chapters, I look closely at Ḥamad al-Jāsir's genealogical project and how it reflects social contestation in the modern kingdom. Proceeding from the intersection of anthropology and social history, chapter three follows the lives of Saudi lineage seekers as they weave in and out of al-Jāsir's letters and their own personal narratives and texts. I relate the story of one of al-Jāsir's lineage-seeking petitioners, whom I call Rāshid b. Ḥumayd.[31] Rāshid's story calls attention to the intimate and personal concerns that propel the modern Saudi search for tribal lineages, the uneasy interplay between oral and textual forms of genealogical knowledge, and the state's sometimes heavy hand in policing the boundaries of public culture in the kingdom.

Chapter four looks closely at marital patterns in Arabian history and demonstrates how knowledge of these patterns became a central dimension of Saudi Arabia's modern genealogical culture. The chapter commences with a review of new historical evidence from the central Arabian oasis town of al-Ghāṭ, which reveals the way marital patterns preserve knowledge about premodern status hierarchies. I then turn to Ḥamad al-Jāsir's use of marital patterns as a tool of lineal authentication, a practice epitomized in his study of a historically maligned Arabian tribe, Bāhila. I describe how al-Jāsir made use of Arabian marital patterns as a form of ethnographic data that could serve as a basis for rehabilitating the reputation of historically maligned tribes and advancing a nativist ethical blueprint for modern Saudi society in which tribal and religious values could cohere harmoniously against perceived external threats.

Chapter five calls attention to the role played by perceptions of racial difference in Saudi narratives of tribal authenticity. I examine how the intense pressure to claim affiliation with historically recognized Arabian tribes plays out in the western Arabian oasis town of al-ʿUlā. In their continuous cohabitation and close-knit solidarity, the people of al-ʿUlā, I find, are (ironically) constituted more "tribally" than many bedouin-origin Saudis who assert nominal tribal identities across the kingdom's atomized spaces, and who influence the sedentary discourse concerning tribes. By focusing on the histories of two parallel though disparate claimants to lineal origination within the Ḥarb tribe, Ḥamad al-Jāsir's tribe and that of many of the families of al-ʿUlā, I demonstrate the dynamic and contingent nature of tribal identity in modern Saudi Arabia.

In the concluding chapter, I situate the compulsion to claim tribal belonging in a set of institutional policies and techniques adopted by the modern Saudi state over the course of the twentieth century. Viewed as a whole, these policies and techniques combine to produce a genealogical rule of governance that underpins political practice in the kingdom. The position of Ḥamad al-Jāsir has by this point in the narrative diminished, as we open up to a consideration of the broader political context in which his project and worldview were embedded. I demonstrate how the Saudi state's efforts to standardize citizen identities according to genealogical criteria, promote lineal authentication as a core political function, and privilege kinship as a dominant symbol of Āl Saʿūd rule have made genealogy a pervasive aspect of social and political life in the modern kingdom.

Throughout this book, I make extensive use of letters and other documents preserved in Maktabat al-ʿArab, Ḥamad al-Jāsir's private library in Riyadh. Most have been cataloged with index numbers, to which I refer in subsequent citations. The letters examined here are part of a near-complete set of al-Jāsir's correspondence from December 1992 through September 2000. This set includes several thousand incoming and outgoing letters, many hundreds of which treat genealogical topics.[32] A complete set of outgoing letters from 1972 and 1973 was also available to me, as were scattered examples of letters from the period 1974–1991.[33] The whereabouts of the vast majority of al-Jāsir's correspondence from this important period remain unknown.

The recent quality of much of the narrative I present here, combined with the sensitivity of genealogies in the kingdom, has compelled me to make methodological choices that might displease scholars of a more purist disciplinary bent. Many of Ḥamad al-Jāsir's genealogical correspondents, those who in their letters to the scholar shared the intimate details of their private lives, are alive and well in the kingdom. As it is not my object to expose them to scandal, but rather to extract from their personal histories common themes that help shed light on the kingdom's genealogical culture, I have used pseudonyms and elected to disguise most details about their personal lives, as well as those of the other families and individuals whose genealogical stories are presented in this book.

One great advantage of studying the legacy of a recently deceased scholar such as Ḥamad al-Jāsir is the large number of biographies, articles, and oral histories that continue to emerge about his life and work. During my four stays in Saudi Arabia between 2009 and 2014, I had the good fortune of being able to interview a number of al-Jāsir's family members, disciples, and contemporaries, both admirers and detractors. Because of al-Jāsir's centrality to this story, I cite nearly all of his public and private writings for attribution, while removing from them information that implicates other relevant personalities as needed.[34]

While the affirmation of tribal genealogies is a ubiquitous facet of the modern culture of Saudi Arabia, the discussion of their absence in certain families remains a taboo, one I have not seen it fruitful to transgress. In making claims about the kingdom's genealogical culture or the tribal or nontribal status of individuals and families within it, I have sought to adhere closely to the textual evidence I have accumulated. While acknowledging the power of the oral tradition in reproducing knowledge about Arabian genealogies, I have also sought to problematize this tradition by reflecting on the malleability of central Arabia's oral heritage in the face of the ideological and material pressures exerted by the Saudi state. I have therefore looked to minimize my reliance in this book on the genealogical parlor chatter of the modern kingdom, while acknowledging the important role of this informal discourse in shaping perceptions about lineal affiliations.

In a study that deals primarily with representations of kinship, I have remained cognizant of, if disheartened by, what these representations include and what they exclude. Women especially are all but absent from Saudi genealogical charts and books. In the kingdom's genealogical culture, it is the ideology of patrilineage that predominates, such that the rich and significant world of matrilineal politics, and of the female genealogical imagination, is almost invariably obscured. I have been left therefore to draw inferences and make passing observations about the position of women within the kingdom's genealogical matrix, an outcome that, though inadequate, must for the moment suffice.

CHAPTER ONE

Ḥamad al-Jāsir: A Life in Context

Ḥamad al-Jāsir's death in September of 2000 was mourned on the pages of dozens of Saudi newspapers and magazines in hundreds of obituary columns and editorial tributes.[1] Even in a culture of praise such as Saudi Arabia's, the sheer volume of testimonials set the scholar apart as a unique phenomenon, an institution in his own right. Al-Jāsir's editorial and literary voice had no obvious precedent or equivalent, either within the kingdom's religious culture or its circles of political authority. There were certainly contemporaries who labored in the same pioneering mode as the scholar of Arabian history and genealogy; yet none achieved the same level of recognition.[2] How, then, did al-Jāsir establish himself among so many Saudi admirers as well as detractors? How did a half-blind, orphaned son of the Najdi soil make his way to the pinnacle of Saudi public life, influencing generations of Arab and Western scholars and multitudes of ordinary Saudis in the process?

Al-Jāsir's lasting legacy was to redefine the parameters of acceptable knowledge in the Wahhabi heartland. He did this by broadening the scope of the Islamic scholarly tradition in Saudi Arabia to encompass disciplines such as history and literature. These disciplines had possessed little utility in the scattered sedentary communities of central Arabia, where the production of knowledge rested in the hands of narrowly expert "ritual specialists."[3] In premodern Najd (central Arabia), history was little more than the terse and summary jottings of town or court scribes;[4] literature was oral poetry, which followed its own logic and purpose distinct from that of the textual tradition.[5] Underlying al-Jāsir's endeavor was the effort to attach a nascent Saudi national community to the legacy of urban Islamic civilization that had flourished for over a millennium in the distant metropolises of Baghdad, Damascus, and Cairo, a legacy to which the newly emergent oil power from the desert periphery now sought a claim. It is for this reason that Ḥamad al-Jāsir is revered by so many, because he connected Najdis to the broader, documented Islamic history that somehow eluded their region. He brought them a measure of literate culture where little existed previously. He fashioned a history for them.

Summarizing his influence in outsized terms, an admirer remarked:

> If the Shaykh al-Islām Muḥammad b. ʿAbd al-Wahhāb is an embodiment of the Islamic school of thought and Islamic history, and is distinguished and respected in the history of this Peninsula, then I believe that Shaykh Ḥamad al-Jāsir is the embodiment of the other school of thought, the intellectual and cultural school, and is distinguished and respected in the history of this great Islamic nation [i.e., Saudi Arabia].[6]

Ḥamad al-Jāsir's story is also that of the arrival of widespread literacy in central Arabia. Al-Jāsir was among the first to wrest textual authority away from the Wahhabi ʿulamāʾ. Ultimately, however, his challenge to central Arabia's learned establishment would see him ostracized by the same patrons who had first adopted him.[7] A biography of one of the leading Wahhabi scholars of the twentieth century, Muḥammad b. Ibrāhīm Āl al-Shaykh (d. 1969), conveys conservative sentiment toward al-Jāsir in characteristically Saudi terms. In a list of Ibn Ibrāhīm's most prominent students and disciples, the honorific *shaykh* is attached to all but one of these—al-Jāsir is listed as an *ustādh* (teacher). Intended perhaps to distinguish al-Jāsir as a practitioner of modern systems of knowledge, this is a downgrade, to be sure, in the reckoning of the pious.[8]

Al-Jāsir's frequent confrontations with Saudi religious authorities and his outspoken attitudes about history and culture have cemented for him a reputation among some as a secular-minded intellectual out of step with his own society.[9] While out of keeping with the devout public persona he maintained more or less consistently over seven decades of public life, there is a measure of truth to this criticism. At first a dutiful son of the Wahhabi establishment, the scholar would grow to challenge the reigning orthodoxies of his homeland. His attacks on the pieties of the Wahhabi ʿulamāʾ and their royal backers, subtle as they were at times, would eventually force the scholar to turn his gaze inward, away from political and social reform, and toward the history and culture of the society he inhabited. Yet, this inward turn would prove no less fraught with controversy, as his project of codifying the genealogies of the people of Saudi Arabia would later demonstrate. Al-Jāsir rose to prominence in the shadow of a modernizing court where the production of culture remained invested in the hands of an appointed few. Though influential in the development of modern education and the press in the Najdi heartland, the scholar's contributions to Saudi historiography were perhaps his most substantial. With his writings on tribal genealogies and Saudi history, al-Jāsir established a narrative foundation for a newly imagined Saudi nation and its central Arabian heartland.

This chapter examines the life and times of Ḥamad al-Jāsir from his birth through the launch of his genealogical project in the 1970s. I will discuss al-Jāsir's early dependence on and ultimate break from his patrons in the Wahhabi religious establishment; his effort to forge a history for Saudi Arabia commensurate with its rising influence; his growing sympathy for the nostalgic ideal of bedouinism; and, finally, his retreat from political activism and turn toward scholarship and the documentation of the genealogies of the families and tribes of the kingdom, an ostensibly benign pursuit that provoked a great deal of controversy and anxiety. By looking closely at the life of a central Arabian polymath and the documentary trail he left across most of the twentieth century, this chapter also introduces readers to the modern history of Saudi Arabia.

I divide al-Jāsir's biography into three stages, each of which corresponds to a distinctive intellectual and vocational turn in the scholar's life. The years 1909 to 1939 mark the period of al-Jāsir's education and early career under the patronage of the Wahhabi clerical establishment. Born into a family of peasant farmers, al-Jāsir's intellectual promise was recognized early by important Wahhabi scholars, and he became a valued participant in the expansion of Wahhabi influence throughout the Arabian Peninsula, particularly the Hijaz (western Arabia). It is during this formative period as well, most notably during intervals of study in Mecca and Cairo, that al-Jāsir was first exposed to the modern currents of thought that would propel much of the work of his mature life. As the scholar ascended the rungs of bureaucratic responsibility in the new state, his effort to synthesize the rival intellectual currents of his early life was impeded by his Wahhabi patrons, who resisted being displaced as Arabia's sole pedagogical authorities and arbiters of legitimate knowledge.

The second stage of al-Jāsir's life (1939–1966) marks the scholar's emergence as a public figure in Saudi Arabia. In the prime years of his productive life, he played a major part in the development of the kingdom's modern social and cultural institutions, particularly in Najd. He founded central Arabia's first printing press (Dār al-Yamāma), its first periodical (*al-Yamāma*) and first newspaper (*al-Riyāḍ*), and served as the region's first school superintendent. As a working man, al-Jāsir was, by the contemporary standards of his society, a reformist and progressive intellectual. It was during this second

TABLE 1. Chronology of Ḥamad al-Jāsir's Life

Year	Chronology of Ḥamad al-Jāsir's Life
1909	Born in al-Burūd
1926	Moves to Riyadh to live and study at Bayt al-Ikhwān
1929	Battle of al-Sibila (March)
1929	Appointed scribe in *hijra* of ʿArwā (July)
1930	Enrolls in al-Maʿhad al-ʿIlmī al-Saʿūdī (secondary school) in Mecca
1934	Appointed judge in Ḍibā
1939	Enrolls in Cairo University, College of Literature; leaves prematurely after outbreak of war
1944	Appointed monitor for Arabic language education at Aramco's Jabal School
1949	Appointed education inspector for Najd
1952	Appointed director of Arabic studies for religious high schools and colleges
1952	Founds *al-Yamāma* periodical
1956	Writes article welcoming Indian president Nehru to kingdom, fired from directorship
1959	Imprisoned by King Saʿūd for *al-Yamāma* article insulting religious establishment
1960	Departs with family for Egypt
1962	Departs Egypt for Beirut
1962	Stripped of control over *al-Yamāma*
1965	Saudi Press Institutions Decree enacted; individual ownership of newspapers outlawed
1966	*Madīnat al-Riyāḍ*
1966	Founds *Majallat al-ʿArab*
1968	*Abū ʿAlī al-Hajarī*
1968	Begins work on his geographical dictionary (*Al-Muʿjam al-Jughrāfī*)
1975	Son Muhammad b. Ḥamad killed in plane crash over Beirut; library destroyed
1975	Returns to Riyadh with family
1980	*Muʿjam Qabāʾil*
1981	*Jamharat Ansāb*
1990	*Bāhila*
2000	*Baldat al-Burūd*
2000	Dies in Boston, MA

phase of his life that the scholar developed a sympathy for the countercultural agenda of Arab nationalism, which would put him at odds with both the Saudi clerical establishment and the kingdom's political authorities.

Al-Jāsir was an Arab nationalist in a country where Arab nationalism was antithetical to political life. When his confrontations with the kingdom's religious and political authorities reached a climax, the scholar retreated to Beirut, where he would live for thirteen years (1962–1975), and where he would beat a second retreat, into the inner sanctum of historical knowledge. In the turn from political activism to Arabian historical arcana that marked the last phase of the scholar's life (1966–2000), one might consider simply that his Arab nationalism acquired a classical sheen, or was transmuted into something more benign. Yet to dismiss this inward turn as "sour grapes" is to miss out on the historical specificity of al-Jāsir's genealogical project and what it reveals about twentieth-century Saudi Arabia.[10] To fully understand this project, I contend in this chapter, we must first review the experiences and influences that preceded it.

For all of his liberalizing tendencies, ascribing Ḥamad al-Jāsir's thought to one clearly demarcated intellectual tradition is an unproductive proposition. As a columnist, al-Jāsir took pleasure in provoking the ostentatiously pious;[11] as a scholar, he made no secret of his preference for the historians and genealogists of the Islamic scholarly canon over its jurists and theologians (Muḥammad b. ʿAbd al-Wahhāb excluded); and as an activist, he sympathized with the dissident Free Princes movement of the mid-century. Despite these varied progressive credentials, it would be wrong to overstate the extent of the scholar's secular-modernist leanings. Al-Jāsir saw his project as thoroughly embedded in a wider program of Islamic revival, even if he seemed radically passive alongside other such revivalists whose reputations overtook his own during the course of the twentieth century (e.g., Abul ʿAla Maudoodi, Sayyid Qutb).[12]

It is a weakness of this biographical sketch of the first sixty years of al-Jāsir's life that we are forced to rely so much on the scholar's own recollections, particularly those captured in his serialized memoirs, *Min Sawāniḥ al-Dhikrayāt* (*Pleasant Memories*). Synthesizing these retrospective views with historical documents preserved among al-Jāsir's private papers, Saudi government archival records, and interviews with family members and close associates (and rivals) of the scholar, however, does much to corroborate al-Jāsir's own narrative.

AL-JĀSIR'S EARLY LIFE (1909–1939)

Ḥamad al-Jāsir was born around 1909 in the vicinity of al-Burūd,[13] a village in the Sirr region of Najd some 90 miles west of Riyadh.[14] Al-Sirr is a sliver of arable land set among several narrow, strip-like extensions of the Nafūd desert, which blankets large parts of northern Arabia with its distinctive red-orange sands. Like many of Najd's scattered settlements, al-Burūd was situated at the intersection of the territories of several major bedouin confederations, including ʿUtayba and Muṭayr. Al-Burūd is just west of the ʿUtayba bedouin settlement (*hijra*) of Sājir, famous as the birthplace of Juhaymān al-ʿUtaybī, the bedouin-origin army truck driver who founded the group that carried out the 1979 seizure of the Great Mosque of Mecca.

Before the age of trucks and planes, al-Burūd was a stopping point along the pilgrimage route to Medina. In Najdi historiography, it is recalled as the site of an eighteenth-century battle between the Sharifian rulers of Medina and the village's local Wahhabi loyalists. Al-Burūd's historical inhabitants trace their origins to that city as well. In village lore, branches of the Banī ʿAlī section of the Ḥarb tribe, al-Jāsir's paternal kin group, migrated to Najd from the outskirts of Medina around 1700.[15] Al-Burūd's sediment-rich soil made it a center of agricultural production in the area,[16] and its produce still circulates in the markets of Riyadh. It was into this small community of peasant farmers that the third son of Muḥammad al-Jāsir and Hayla bint ʿAlī b. Sālim was born.

Al-Jāsir's parents died when he was not yet a teenager, and he was placed under the care of his maternal grandfather ʿAlī b. ʿAbdallāh b. Sālim, the judge and religious leader of al-Burūd.[17] His sickly frame and partial blindness made him unfit for work in the village's date palm plantations, as was expected of his brothers and other village youth. Instead, he distinguished himself in the village Quranic school, where children were sent between harvests to acquire a basic education. In his memoirs, al-Jāsir recalled the harsh manner of the *muṭawwaʿ*, the village schoolteacher, whose persona he sought to emulate when appointed a teacher in al-Burūd by his grandfather several years later.[18]

To scrape out a living in the face of mounting debt, periodic drought, and locust infestations, Najdi peasant farmers required the full participation of the family in the work cycle, including children. Many of the young Najdi villagers who, like al-Jāsir, were sent off to Riyadh to study, were of no use in the countryside: the blind, the infirm, or those too poor for lack of gainful work. In 1926, escorted by his brother and guardian Jāsir, Ḥamad took up residence at the Bayt al-Ikhwān, a kind of boarding school for youth in Riyadh run by a senior Wahhabi scholar, Muḥammad b. Ibrāhīm Āl al-Shaykh.[19] Legally an orphan, he was taken into the care of the Arabian religious establishment,[20] on whose patronage he would be dependent for the next thirty years. Showing himself to be a formidable student, in July 1929 al-Jāsir was invited by Muḥammad b. Ibrāhīm to serve as a scribe for the latter's uncle, ʿAbd al-Raḥmān b. ʿAbd al-Laṭīf, who had been appointed a judge in the bed-

Figure 1.1. Ruins of al-Burūd, birthplace of Ḥamad al-Jāsir. Courtesy of author.

ouin *hijra* of ʿArwā.[21] It was Ibn Saʿūd's policy to disperse Wahhabi scholars among the recently sedentarized bedouin,[22] to teach them the rudiments of the Islamic faith in hopes of securing their loyalties.[23]

Al-Jāsir's teenage years coincided with a critical period in Saudi state formation. His appointment to ʿArwā came in the midst of the Ikhwān revolt, the last major challenge to Saudi rule in central Arabia, and constituted his first foray into the highly personalized world of Saudi politics.[24] In 1927, after two decades of service as the Saudi ruler's striking arm, Ikhwān leaders had become dissatisfied with their subordinate positions and began demanding a share of executive authority, including control over the newly conquered territories of the Hijaz. When their demands were rejected, they staged a series of revolts against their Saudi sponsors. To repulse this challenge, Ibn Saʿūd launched a series of attacks against the Ikhwān rebels.

ʿArwā, the settlement to which al-Jāsir had been dispatched, was the home of the ʿUtayba tribal leader Jihjāh b. Bijād, brother of the famous Ikhwān rebel

Sulṭān b. Bijād, who was captured by Ibn Saʿūd's forces during the decisive battle of al-Sibila (March 1929).[25] At the time of al-Jāsir's arrival, ʿArwā was the largest *hijra* in the kingdom; the Ikhwān hotbed of Ghaṭghaṭ had been destroyed,[26] and most of its inhabitants had been transferred there.[27] Al-Jāsir's close association with Jihjāh during his nine-month sojourn in ʿArwā gave him uncommon insights into the politics of the era. More significantly, it would help shape his views about bedouin culture, whose reform would become the object of many Saudi intellectuals in subsequent decades.

The most formative turn in al-Jāsir's early life came in 1930. After accompanying a raid against Ikhwān rebels in eastern Najd, al-Jāsir was convinced by his brother to bypass ʿArwā and go instead to Mecca on pilgrimage. While there, al-Jāsir met with the chief judge of the Hijaz, ʿAbdallāh b. Ḥasan Āl al-Shaykh, who invited him to enroll in the newly formed Saudi Scientific Institute (al-Maʿhad al-ʿIlmī al-Saʿūdī).[28] The Institute was one of the few secondary schools in Saudi Arabia at the time, and was considered the first modern school to be established in the Saudi era.[29] Founded, in al-Jāsir's words, "to spread the Salafi creed," the school was staffed by Salafi and Wahhabi teachers from Egypt, Syria, and Najd.[30] Exerting a more informal influence on al-Jāsir was the administrator of the Institute's dormitory, ʿAbdallāh b. Sulaymān al-Mazrūʿ, an erudite and intellectually curious Hijazi whom the scholar credited with encouraging his interest in secular subjects.[31]

Al-Jāsir's interactions at the Institute, particularly outside of the classroom, brought the young scholar into contact with non-Wahhabi currents of thought circulating in the Arab world of that period. Institute students would pass around worn copies of periodicals from Egypt and the Arab Levant—such as *al-Hilāl*, *al-Muqtaṭaf*, and *al-Fatḥ*[32]—and compete to have their poems and articles published in the two newspapers then in existence in the kingdom, *Umm al-Qurā* and *Ṣawt al-Ḥijāz*. One of al-Jāsir's earliest publications was a praise poem he composed on the occasion of the king's visit to the school, celebrating Ibn Saʿūd's recent victory against the Ikhwān at al-Sibila. Al-Jāsir graduated from the Institute in 1934 with the qualifications of an Islamic judge, and the expectation that he would utilize his new credentials as a religious functionary in roles to be determined by his sponsors.

In the same year as Ḥamad al-Jāsir's first apprenticeship under the Wahhabi ʿulamāʾ of Riyadh (1926), ʿAbd al-ʿAzīz Ibn Saʿūd's tribal conscripts were completing the capture of the Hijaz from the Ashrāf, nominal rulers of western Arabia for over a millennium. The Saudis would make Mecca the administrative capital of their new state, and Ibn Saʿūd would soon declare himself "King of Hijaz and Sultan of Najd and its Dependencies." Yet the physical conquest of the Hijaz was only the first stage in the expansion of Saudi hegemony over western Arabia, a process that would next proceed by non-coercive means.

In June 1930, while still a student at the Institute, al-Jāsir was asked by ʿAbdallāh b. Ḥasan Āl al-Shaykh to serve as the imam of the Abū Qubays mosque in Mecca. Abū Qubays, the highest peak in the vicinity of Mecca, held a number of important associations in Islamic history.[33] According to Meccan legend, it was at the foot of the Abū Qubays hill that the famous Quranic incident known as the splitting of the moon took place, when "Muhammad called the Moon to him and bade her to split herself."[34] Most significantly, Abū Qubays was an important locus of Sufi devotion in the Hijaz. "Ḥamad b. Muḥammad b. Jāsir al-Najdī," as he was described in the government's appointment letter, was asked to replace the previous supervisor of the Abū Qubays mosque, a "charlatan" who had exploited pilgrims passing through during the *Ḥajj* season with appeals to "superstition."[35] The dubious beliefs referred to in this decree and by al-Jāsir in his memoirs had for centuries formed an integral part of the religious and economic life of Mecca and other Hijazi cities.[36] At least until the end of the nineteenth century, the celebration of the birthdays of holy men and women, such as the Prophet's wife Maymūna or Mahdalī, were significant events on the Meccan calendar.[37] After the conquest of the Hijaz, the suppression of Hijazi religious beliefs and practices was made synonymous with the march of progress through Arabia.[38] The young Ḥamad al-Jāsir was a loyal foot soldier in this process.

In 1934, after four years of study at the Institute, al-Jāsir was invited to take a position as a primary school teacher in the Hijazi port town of Yanbuʿ. There, he clashed with teachers and administrators, partly on account of what a biographer described as their sympathies for Sufism, an orientation toward which the scholar would maintain a lifelong hostility.[39] Through calculated pressure and influence, al-Jāsir was able to push out his principal rival, though he soon found himself pressed reluctantly into another field of service, the judiciary.[40] Over his protestations, the scholar was presented by Muḥammad b. Ibrāhīm with two choices: to accept a position as a judge in the northern Hijazi village of Ḍibā, or face prison time. Unsurprisingly, Ḥamad chose the former.

Two years earlier, Ḍibā had been the site of the last violent uprising against Saudi authority in the Hijaz, the Ibn Rifāda revolt.[41] This rebellion by a bedouin leader against Saudi rule, which was supported from the outside by Ibn Saʿūd's exiled adversaries (the Hijazi Ashrāf), was quickly suppressed.[42] It marked the Saudi state's last use of coercive force in the Hijaz until 1979. Al-Jāsir's appointment in Ḍibā thus reflected the beginning of a new phase in modern Saudi history, the transition to non-coercive means of state consolidation.[43] As a small-town judge, al-Jāsir would contribute by legal means to the broader absorption of the Hijaz into a Ḥanbalī legal and Wahhabi creedal culture.[44]

In the scholar's conception, the transition to Ḥanbalī-Wahhabi norms was a move toward greater enlightenment and orthodoxy. Yet once established, the Wahhabi tradition was to become as contested as any other living code. This tension would be made plain in a murder case that spelled the end of al-Jāsir's brief tenure as a judge. Confronted with an accidental killing in a bedouin community, al-Jāsir awarded the standard Islamic legal remedy of one hundred camels to the victim's family as blood payment (*diya*). Considering the penalty excessive, the aggressor's family brought the case to the chief judge of the Hijaz, al-Jāsir's patron ʿAbdallāh b. Ḥasan, for appeal. The Wahhabi notable rejected al-Jāsir's ruling, stating that the upper limit of the blood payment should be fixed at the rate determined by the Council of Deputies (Majlis al-Wukalāʾ), which had decided on a substantially lesser penalty. Al-Jāsir objected, arguing that the Majlis's determination was pure whim, whereas his own ruling was delivered on the basis of a Tradition of the Prophet (Hadith). The scholar's retort was perceived as insubordination, and he was swiftly removed from his post.[45] While revealing here the first stirrings of an innately confrontational nature, this would be the last time al-Jāsir would be seen attempting to outmaneuver the reigning religious authorities on their conservative flank.

It was in the 1930s, as a student at the Saudi Scientific Institute, that al-Jāsir first confronted the contradictions engendered by central Arabia's new relationship with the broader Islamic world, when he was first confronted by the incongruence between his upbringing in the Wahhabi canon and the varied currents of thought circulating within the halls of his preparatory school. Though enthralled by modern science and literature, the young scholar was reflexively mindful of the Wahhabi axiom of his youth, that the only ideas of value were those inherited from the Salaf al-Ṣāliḥ, the Righteous Ancestors.[46] These rival dispensations, the culture of Wahhabism and the culture of the Western-influenced Arab Levant, seemed to be in agreement that the superstitions of popular religion, as practiced both by bedouin nomads and Hijazi town dwellers, had no place in a literate and God-fearing society. Yet from the perspective of the clerical establishment, which stage-directed much of al-Jāsir's young life, there could be only one sheriff in Arabia. By this measure, the pronouncements of astronomers were just as threatening as the chicanery of Sufis, since both siphoned attention away from God's word as echoed by his earthbound interpreters. For the first three decades of his adult life, al-Jāsir was content to help steward the Najdi ʿulamāʾ's advance through Arabia, seeing few alternatives open to him. Yet the outspoken and assertive young scholar seemed ill-fitted for the roles he was asked to assume by his ʿulamāʾ patrons. While remaining dutifully loyal to the anti-syncretic program of his Wahhabi patrons, al-Jāsir would come to emphatically reject their monopoly on mundane authority and obtuse responses to the challenges of modern science and technology.

By the end of the 1930s, al-Jāsir had outgrown the Saudi education system, and had set his sights on a more ambitious program of study. The culmination of the scholar's early life was his participation in the 1939 Saudi educational delegation to Egypt. The delegation was a government program designed to produce college-educated professionals abroad who would return to serve the administrative needs of the rapidly expanding state. Al-Jāsir's interactions with Egyptian teachers in Mecca and exposure to Egyptian publications had already left a deep mark on him, and he was eager to immerse himself further in the dynamic cultural life of early twentieth-century Egypt.[47] The young Ḥamad was the first Saudi to enroll in the College of Literature at Cairo University, whose outstanding personality at the time was its recently retired dean Ṭāhā Ḥusayn. The scholar recounted his interview with Ḥusayn as a nerve-racking affair, though one that ended favorably with an offer of admission.[48]

Writing of his experiences as a young man in Egypt, al-Jāsir contrasted the "splendors" he encountered there with the "repression and deprivation" that constituted his prior cultural life.[49] It is unlikely that the scholar could have mustered a harsher condemnation of the intellectual culture in which he had been reared. And yet, in subsequent years, he would turn his creative energies toward remedying this sense of deprivation, producing the rudiments of a modern Saudi historiography that moved beyond the annalistic accounting of the early Najdi chroniclers toward a kind of socio-historical engineering far more conscious of its purpose. The outbreak of World War II cut short al-Jāsir's stay in Egypt, but his brief sojourn there seemed to confirm in his mind the validity of the pursuit of diverse forms of knowledge. Al-Jāsir emerged from his Cairo experience a young man intent on using his education to instill a new type of consciousness in his compatriots, one receptive to non-Wahhabi sources of knowledge and authority. When, years later, he broke definitively with his first patron, Muḥammad b. Ibrāhīm, it would be over the question of the capaciousness of Saudi culture in the modern world.

AL-JĀSIR AS EDUCATOR AND JOURNALIST (1939–1966)

Back in Saudi Arabia, al-Jāsir bounced between teaching appointments in al-Aḥsā' and Jeddah, clashing with administrators and religious authorities over various issues. In 1941, he was approached by the powerful Minister of Finance ʿAbdallāh Sulaymān with the idea of establishing a school for the latter's children and those of his attendants.[50] Al-Jāsir spent three years on the project, and invited his boon companion from the Institute, the noted writer and political activist ʿAbd al-Karīm al-Juhaymān, to oversee its administration. In 1944, the king would direct al-Jāsir to take up a new position as an inspector at the Arabian American Oil Company's (Aramco's) flagship school.[51]

Aramco, which held the concession on oil exploration in Saudi Arabia and was rapidly expanding its operations in the country's eastern region, was interested in training Saudis to staff the lower and middle ranks of its workforce. As part of its deal with the Saudi government, the company sponsored a program of religious education for Saudi youth enrolled in its "trade preparatory schools," with teachers to be assigned by the Saudi government. Al-Jāsir's role was to ensure that Saudi students at the Jabal school in Dhahran received proper instruction in the Arabic language and basic religious concepts, against the wishes of Aramco administrators, who insisted that students be educated first in English so that they might interact better with their managers.[52] In a report to the king, al-Jāsir vented his anger over Aramco's unwillingness to implement any of his recommended curriculum modifications, and insisted that the Saudi Directorate of Education assume jurisdiction over the Jabal school's administration.[53] This anger was likely compounded by Aramco's discriminatory housing policies, which prohibited al-Jāsir and other Saudi employees of the firm from living in Dahran, where the company was based, thus requiring them to commute every day from nearby Khobar. Soon to prove a harsh critic of Saudi ʿulamāʾ obscurantism, al-Jāsir was here seen defending Islamic orthodoxy against encroachment by modernizers of a different, more alien stripe. With Aramco's growing importance to Saudi government coffers, however, his concerns were summarily brushed aside.

Al-Jāsir stayed in his Aramco post for almost five years, the single longest professional engagement of his still young life. In 1949, on orders from Crown Prince Saʿūd, Ḥamad was asked to take up the position of inspector of Najdi schools for the Directorate of Education. At the time of his appointment there were fewer than one hundred primary schools in the entire country, with the vast majority concentrated in the Hijaz.[54] The Saudi education budget was on the cusp of a major expansion, however, and al-Jāsir was tasked with assessing the state of central Arabia's schools and recommending means for their reform. The scholar performed site visits to a number of schools, where he encountered principals who waved before him signed rulings that prohibited the teaching of subjects like geography and engineering, on the orders of Muḥammad b. Ibrāhīm.[55] The report he produced for the court was deeply critical of the education system in Najd. It expressed the sum total of his experiences with the prevailing Saudi pedagogical authorities, the Wahhabi ʿulamāʾ. Al-Jāsir believed that the delayed spread of modern education in Najd was a consequence of the recalcitrant attitudes of these authorities. So long as pedagogy continued to be built on rote memorization and faithful transmission of the recorded expressions of the ʿulamāʾ, he reckoned, the Saudi educational system would be stuck in a reactionary posture. In a pithy retort to a critic of modern education at that time, al-Jāsir remarked: "whenever [an air conditioner] breaks down and you need it fixed, you call Aramco, you don't ask Shaykh Muḥammad [b. Ibrāhīm] to send one of his students."[56]

As part of his report for the court, al-Jāsir recommended that an elite secondary school be established where both religious and non-religious subjects could be taught. In 1950, the scholar was asked by the Crown Prince to assist Muḥammad b. Ibrāhīm in establishing a network of secondary and post-secondary religious schools in Najd. The administration was to be separate from the Directorate of Education and its growing public school system, and al-Jāsir was asked to manage its Arabic language studies division. Though profoundly disappointed by what he saw to be the government's surrender of education to the ʿulamāʾ, al-Jāsir accepted his assignment. The scholar would remain in this post until 1956, when his clashes with Muḥammad b. Ibrāhīm reached a boiling point and his appointment was abruptly terminated. These clashes come to light in al-Jāsir's career as a publisher and journalist.

From his earliest days, al-Jāsir's educational and professional advancement had depended on the patronage of the religious establishment, at the helm of which was Muḥammad b. Ibrāhīm. Ibn Ibrāhīm had been the driving force behind most of the scholar's academic and professional appointments, and would continue to exert a strong influence on his initiatives for decades to come. From 1939 until 1956, al-Jāsir served throughout the kingdom as a teacher and education administrator at the pleasure of Ibn Ibrāhīm and the royal court. During this same period, the scholar began participating actively in the newspapers and journals that were being established in the Hijaz. Living and working in Riyadh and Dammam, he published critical reviews, poems, and editorials in Hijazi publications such as *al-Manhal*, *al-Bilād al-Saʿūdiyya*, and *al-Madīna*. The disagreement between the scholar's journalistic and professional geographies would be remedied with his move to establish the first newspaper in Najd, *al-Yamāma*.

With the kingdom's center of political gravity shifting from Jeddah to Riyadh, al-Jāsir found a welcome patron for his newspaper project in Crown Prince Saʿūd.[57] In 1952, the Crown Prince authorized al-Jāsir's request to establish *al-Yamāma*, and supported its publication with an annual subsidy of approximately 5000 riyals.[58] Journalism offered al-Jāsir a way to circumvent the monopoly of ʿulamāʾ patronage, and an opportunity to pursue his reformist agenda in print. Yet the scholar's journalistic provocations would lead to numerous confrontations with the religious and political authorities. These confrontations proved to al-Jāsir the impossibility of politics in a society suffocated by royal patronage and religious policing.

When Ḥamad al-Jāsir founded *al-Yamāma* in 1954, the outward-looking culture of western Arabia's coastal towns had yet to achieve much influence in Najd.[59] Launched initially as a monthly magazine with a circulation that never exceeded 2,000, *al-Yamāma* was the first attempt by al-Jāsir to introduce elements of a modernizing Arab culture to a central Arabian audience. More central to his purpose in this second phase of his life, *al-Yamāma* was al-Jāsir's platform for pursuing social reform through journalism. To generate interest and minimize resistance to the publication, the scholar assembled a broad range of Saudi and non-Saudi Arab contributors, including a number of Najdi ʿulamāʾ.[60] Authors were invited to comment on the state of Saudi education, offer their opinions on the problem of bedouin integration, provide medical advice, or review recent publications in a wide range of disciplines. As al-Jāsir later described it, being an effective newsman required more than a taste for reform:

> You might say, dear friend, that I was not born a journalist. This is true. But even if I did not know all of the qualities that make a person a successful journalist . . . I believe that among the most important of these qualities is that he have a strong connection to the society in which he lives . . . such that he is able to immerse himself among the different classes of society, mingle with all of its members, and be included in such a way that he is able to understand the secrets of life in this society.[61]

While pursuing his own brand of advocacy journalism, it was between the lines of his overt agenda that al-Jāsir's identity as a bibliophile was taking shape. Exemplifying this turn is a review essay in the first issue of *al-Yamāma*, which the scholar devoted to correcting spelling and vocalization errors in several recently published classical texts, among them an edition of the prosopographical compendium of poets *Ṭabaqāt Fuḥūl al-Shuʿarāʾ* edited by the respected Egyptian scholar Muḥammad Maḥmūd Shākir. One set of corrections treated mistakes in lineage (*ansāb*), either misspelled names or false attributions.[62] Though mind-numbing by the standards of most magazine readers, Najdi or otherwise, al-Jāsir's essay was a demonstration of literacy at the highest level, a marker of distinction in the new Najd. Equally significant was the scholar's emerging interest in the study of lineages, a subject that, in subsequent decades, would come to define his life and work.

For the scattering of educated Najdis who congregated around al-Jāsir's enterprise, *al-Yamāma* was something novel and unique. One *al-Yamāma* author and al-Jāsir confidant described the *al-Yamāma* experience as follows:

> At that time . . . we were transitioning from one stage to another. We were taken with . . . the spirit of Arabism, of course, and the liberation

> of the Arab world from imperialism. We had, as a society, the zeal to return to the spirit, and we had desires as well. We had youthful words that expressed themselves frankly and clearly. The press was a spring.[63]

For the Saudi authors of *al-Yamāma*, Arabism was a synecdoche connoting progress in the broadest sense of the word, not a specific program for revolutionary political transformation on the basis of shared linguistic or ethnic heritage. Any conception that did not impinge on religious authority, creed, or other facets of Wahhabi knowledge was potentially embraced by Saudi progressives under the rubric of Arabism. Yet, for an audience of increasingly hostile government ministers and religious authorities, laboring to dissipate the energies of the Arab revolutionary movements of the 1950s, these nuances were largely irrelevant. The Saudi state remained tightly wrapped in the legitimating cloak of Wahhabism, and its appeal to Islam at the expense of Arab nationalism would only increase when the future of the state seemed in doubt. This shift in emphasis would prompt increasing suspicion of al-Jāsir's enterprise.

Al-Jāsir served as *al-Yamāma*'s editor-in-chief, publisher, and content director, in which capacity he was answerable to two separate censors, one dispatched by the newly established General Directorate for Radio, Press, and Publication, the other by Muḥammad b. Ibrāhīm.[64] This dual censorship regime, and the royal patronage that funded the enterprise, ensured a steady stream of heavily pietistic content and gushing loyalty to the state. Al-Jāsir's nod to local pieties, however, would be insufficient to immunize him from the fallout of his 1956 article welcoming Indian President Jawaharlal Nehru to the kingdom. "Welcome, Messenger of Peace," read the headline in *al-Yamāma*, an unforgivable provocation in the minds of religious conservatives such as Muḥammad b. Ibrāhīm, for whom the only messenger worthy of the title was the Prophet Muḥammad. In response, the scholar was summarily dismissed by Ibn Ibrāhīm from his position in the administration of religious high schools and colleges.[65] The firing marked al-Jāsir's definitive transition from state employee to scholar-proprietor. Yet even this quasi-autonomous status would not immunize him from further controversy.

Increasingly harried in his editorial position, and with a growing sense that the reigns of his newspaper were being surreptitiously removed from his grasp, al-Jāsir's frustrations grew more explicit. In the lead editorial of the May 3, 1959 edition of *al-Yamāma*, the scholar laid into the religious establishment as never before:

> In every group within a nation—any nation—there are those who mislead. In every nation there are those who are misled by the missionizers of deception (*duʿāt al-taḍlīl*) and are deceived by their falsehoods

> (*bāṭilihim*). The closer a nation is to its natural disposition and original essence (*al-fiṭra al-ūlā*), the closer it is to being misled, and the quicker it is to acquiesce to the missionizers of falsehood. . . .
>
> Among the most dangerous of these deceivers, the most influential in corrupting society . . . and extinguishing the soul's burning passion for reform, are those of this nation who ascend to the pulpits of spiritual guidance and instruction (*manābir al-irshād wa-l-tawjīh*), yet use their status as a means to obtain their private rewards. . . . We will not be deceived or beguiled, nor will we be among those whose assenting gaze blinds them to the recognition of the truth. . . . . [W]e will make of the truth itself evidence for determining the honesty of the one who calls for it, and not of the callers themselves a means of determining what is right. . . .[66]

Al-Jāsir's comfortable manipulation of religious rhetoric in this polemic was a reflection of the novelty of central Arabia's public culture, in which Wahhabism had yet to assume its unassailable ideological position. This stridency and relative fearlessness of tone was a common feature of the independent Saudi press of the 1950s, and was often surpassed in the short-lived *Akhbār al-Ẓahrān*, the newspaper run by al-Jāsir's schoolmate and fellow traveler, ʿAbd al-Karīm al-Juhaymān.[67]

Al-Jāsir's fulminations were greeted with rage by Muḥammad b. Ibrāhīm, who led other Najdi ʿulamāʾ in pronouncing a death sentence upon the scholar.[68] To escape this fate, the scholar was compelled to remain in Riyadh's Masmak fort under the protection of Crown Prince Fayṣal, who would serve as a crucial ally in the coming years. He was able to buy lasting immunity only after agreeing to pen an oath promising that neither *al-Yamāma* nor any future publication under his authority would ever print anything having to do with the kingdom's religious scholars.[69]

Despite retracting his public criticism of the ʿulamāʾ, al-Jāsir's sympathies for the emerging currents of Nasserism and Pan-Arabism would place him at odds with the kingdom's political authorities. Saudi relations with Gamal Abdel Nasser's Egypt began on a cordial note, but deteriorated in 1958 following the announcement of Egypt's unification with Syria.[70] Al-Jāsir's friendships with influential reformist prince Ṭalāl b. ʿAbd al-ʿAzīz and oil minister ʿAbdallah al-Ṭurayqī could only have added to the suspicions about his loyalties during the struggle for succession between King Saʿūd and Crown Prince Fayṣal that dominated this period.[71] Soliciting an article for *al-Yamāma* from Assistant Secretary General of the Arab League Aḥmad al-Shuqayrī, al-Jāsir expressed "the grand hopes" of the Arabs that the League would help "establish for the Arab *umma* a lofty place among the living nations of the world."[72] While al-Jāsir looked abroad to widen his contributor base, censors in the communications directorate were pressing the scholar to blacklist Saudi Arab nationalist writers and police his publication for pro-Nasser sentiments. Al-Jāsir steered his newspaper with a practiced hand, sometimes providing the real names of authors whose articles in *al-Yamāma* had irked the censors, such as the famous leftist activist ʿAlī al-ʿAwwāmī,[73] other times flouting their demands to keep blacklisted writers out of circulation.[74]

When pressured by the communications directorate to publish an attack on Arab nationalism by future Grand Muftī ʿAbd al-ʿAzīz b. Bāz (another of al-Jāsir's classmates at the Bayt al-Ikhwān), the scholar cleverly took cover behind the cloak of journalistic expertise. Ibn Bāz's article had been published elsewhere several days before, he told the head of the communications directorate, his former teacher Ibrāhīm al-Shūrā. "[We acted] on the journalistic principle known the world over . . . that you don't publish a single article on a single topic in more than one paper, especially if these papers are published in the same region."[75] In another instance, al-Shūrā could be seen pressuring al-Jāsir to steer *al-Yamāma*'s editorial attentions away from regional or international politics and toward the more innocuous arena of local affairs.[76] Whether proceeding by omission or commission, al-Jāsir's advocacy journalism betrayed his sympathies with the cause of broader Arab union, which would be interpreted by some as an expression of disloyalty to the Saudi state.

In 1960, seeking an escape from the political pressures bearing down on him, and possibly in sympathy with the dissident Free Princes movement,[77] al-Jāsir moved his family to Egypt and, two years later, Beirut. Like other Saudi dissidents who took up residence in Nasser's Egypt, he was greeted warmly upon his arrival in Cairo.[78] If al-Jāsir had been willing to provoke the religious authorities, however, he saw no profit in a public disavowal of the Saudi royal family.[79] Despite treading more cautiously than many other Saudi dissidents, the scholar's refusal to condemn Nasser's expansionist program grew into a major problem for the Saudi government, which was increasingly wary of the Egyptian leader's ambitions in the region, and specifically, his designs on its southern neighbor Yemen.[80] Al-Jāsir's continued dustups with government censors culminated in February 1962 with the seizure of *al-Yamāma* and subsequent handover of the paper to conservative loyalist Zayd b. Fayyāḍ at the recommendation of Muḥammad b. Ibrāhīm.[81] The scholar was in Beirut when he learned from reformist minister ʿAbdallāh al-Ṭurayqī that he was to be imprisoned, lashed, and sent to live in his hometown of al-Burūd.[82] He would remain in Beirut for the next thirteen years.

Fayṣal's 1964 accession to the throne following the deposing of Saʿūd would see the restoration of some of the scholar's privileges. Under the terms of the 1965 Press Institutions Decree (Niẓām al-Muʾassasāt al-Ṣaḥafiyya), al-Jāsir was reinstated as the head of a now reconstituted al-Yamāma Journalistic Institution, which would soon launch a daily edition of *al-Riyāḍ*, still today one of the leading newspapers in Saudi Arabia.[83] The decree stipulated that newspapers could no longer be owned by individuals, and would be required to be published by institutions governed by administrative councils. Despite Fayṣal's sympathies for the scholar, the forces of bureaucratic consolidation and state expansion were too powerful to permit the existence of influential fiefdoms such as al-Jāsir's *al-Yamāma*. The decree served to snuff out the autonomy of the newspaper editor, and with it al-Jāsir's enthusiasm for mainstream publishing.

In a 1966 interview, al-Jāsir shared his views on the uneven state of Saudi intellectual culture: "there are major efforts afoot, and no one can deny this, but they are limited to one dimension of this heritage, the religious dimension."[84] That same year, al-Jāsir petitioned King Fayṣal to establish *Majallat al-ʿArab*, a scholarly journal specializing in the history, geography, and genealogy of the Arabian Peninsula. *Al-ʿArab* was to function outside of the dictates of the press decree, and would steer as far as possible away from politics. Al-Jāsir's retreat inward coincided with his thirteen year self-imposed exile in Beirut, a move that would commence the most fertile period of his scholarly life. In Beirut he founded a new publishing house, Dār al-Yamāma li-l-Baḥth wa-l-Tarjama wa-l-Nashr (al-Yamāma Press for Research, Translation, and Publication), which would serve as his primary scholarly and intellectual hub from 1966 until his death in 2000.[85] In hundreds (if not thousands) of newspaper articles and over thirty self-published books, al-Jāsir directed the influence he had accumulated over the course of a professional lifetime toward shaping the emergent Saudi discourse on the history and genealogy of the peoples of the Arabian Peninsula. It was through these varied, late-career efforts that al-Jāsir acquired his famous honorific, ʿAllāmat al-Jazīra, "The Scholar of the Arabian Peninsula."

Despite spending much of his life in an oppositional pose, antagonizing the Wahhabi establishment or the ruling regime, al-Jāsir, like so many other Saudi intellectuals, was in many ways a creature of the court. He was ultimately dependent on the good will of royal patrons, or their sympathetic subordinates in various government ministries, to fund his creative endeavors. Receipts from subscriptions and sales of books to independent readers were never sufficient to underpin his publishing projects, and al-Jāsir was forced to rely on government subsidies to keep his new *al-Yamāma* printing house afloat.[86] While his scholarship was not always explicitly influenced by this dependency, in certain instances al-Jāsir's effort to aggrandize the Saudi role in Arabian history can be measured in relation to this vulnerability.

Al-Jāsir's contribution to the triumphalist accounting of Saudi history is exemplified in one of his earliest monographs, a 1966 history of Riyadh, *Madīnat al-Riyāḍ ʿAbra Aṭwār al-Tārīkh* (*The City of Riyadh through the Stages*

Figure 1.2. Ḥamad al-Jāsir. Courtesy of Maʿan al-Jāsir.

of History). Written early in the reign of King Fayṣal, after al-Jāsir's reconciliation with the Saudi regime, the book would have made an *adīb* (courtier) of the classical mold proud. In this narrative of Saudi origins, Ḥajr, the ancient town on whose ruins Riyadh was built, is described as the oldest settlement site in the early Islamic administrative province of al-Yamāma. By recasting Riyadh as the center of a vast province from the ancient Islamic past,[87] the scholar lends gravity and directionality to one of the book's central narratives, the rise of the Āl Saʿūd. The momentum of this narrative ebbs noticeably during periods of Zaydī (ninth to eleventh centuries) and Rashidi (1891–1902) control over Riyadh—the two embodying theological and political challenges to the Saudi-Wahhabi creed[88]—before culminating in the establishment of Saudi rule over the city in the twentieth century, when "goodness and good fortune returned to it."[89]

CONFRONTING THE RUPTURE

For Najdis, the dominant theme of central Arabian history is the *inqiṭāʿ*, the millennium-long rupture with the documented Islamic past. After the transfer of the Caliphate from Medina to Damascus in the first Islamic century, Arabian history recedes further and further into the background of Islamic historiography, rearing its head only to allow for the recounting of ancient heresies—the Najdi Musaylima's challenge to the Prophet Muḥammad's legacy during the Ridda wars, the tenth-century desecration of the Kaʿba by the Eastern Arabian Qarmatians and their bedouin auxiliaries. The ecological constraints on permanent settlement in central Arabia inhibited the development of a distinguishable textual culture until the eighteenth century, when the disparate populations of the region were unified under the Saudi arm and the Wahhabi creed. Eight hundred years of a dark age intervene, and the historian of Najd is left to cast his lantern toward either end of the rupture.

In 1968, al-Jāsir published *Abū ʿAlī al-Hajarī wa-Abḥāthahu fī Taḥdīd al-Mawāḍiʿ* (*Abū ʿAlī al-Hajarī and His Studies in the Identification of Places*). This volume of selections and critical commentary on the writings of a ninth-century Medinan scholar exemplified al-Jāsir's approach to history. Scrutinizing and reconciling two imperfect manuscript copies of al-Hajarī's work, *al-Taʿlīqāt wa-l-Nawādir*, al-Jāsir noticed that al-Hajarī had recorded genealogical information about the bedouin tribes around Medina not captured in the canonical genealogical works of the early Islamic period. More significantly, al-Hajarī had lived into the tenth century, nearly one hundred years past the foremost genealogist of the early and decisive period, Ibn al-Kalbī (d. 819). *Abū ʿAlī al-Hajarī* embodied the scholar's effort to diminish the span of the *inqiṭāʿ* (rupture) separating the Islamic past from the Saudi present.[90] With *Abū ʿAlī al-Hajarī* al-Jāsir attacked this *inqiṭāʿ* from the initial point of rupture. In subsequent volumes, he would approach it at the point of resumption, hoping to strengthen the modern Saudi connection to the recent past.

In historiographical terms, central Arabia's distance from the main action of Islamic history was compounded by the prevalence there of bedouin nomadism and the nonliterate means by which bedouin of the premodern age transmitted cultural and historical knowledge. Ḥamad al-Jāsir recognized this fact well,[91] and devoted much of the second half of his life to fashioning historical artifacts out of the variegated tribal and genealogical narratives of Arabian history. As Andrew Shryock has demonstrated with respect to Jordan, the modern effort to integrate oral tribal history into a literate cultural mold was confounded by the absence of a single, authoritative, and universally accepted narrative recounting of that history, even at the most local level.[92] While the Saudi story is laden with some of the same problems, al-Jāsir's difficulties assimilating the oral historical culture of Najd into an Islamic scholarly mold parallel a tension specific to the Saudi state-building experience, namely, the problem of bedouin integration into modern, Saudi society.

AL-JĀSIR AND THE NOSTALGIC IDEAL OF BEDOUINISM

The young Ḥamad al-Jāsir wrote some of his earliest articles under the byline "A bedouin of the Najd, al-Jāsir." Though perhaps playing off the exoticism of his Najdi background for Hijazi newspaper-reading audiences, "bedouin" was a sociologically inaccurate way for al-Jāsir to introduce himself to the reading public. Al-Jāsir was a member of the *ḥaḍar*, a sedentary oasis dweller of Najd, as had been his parents and generations of his ancestors before them. Al-Burūd, though surrounded by bedouin settlements and nomadic encampments, was inhabited entirely by peasant farmers.[93]

Before the modern Saudi state emerged to diminish the sociological distance between them, the relationship between the sedentary and nomadic populations of central Arabia was one of both cooperation and conflict. During times of relative material abundance and political stability, the complementary economies of these two social groups encouraged the exchange of goods and services between them. During cycles of drought and famine, however, the relationship took an adversarial turn, as sedentary and nomadic populations competed for scarce resources, and bedouin took to raiding sedentary community properties (e.g., livestock, date palms). For most twentieth-century *ḥaḍar*, the pre-state legacy of bedouin raids and involuntary protection taxes lingered on in the form of a suspicion of bedouin attitudes and a distrust of their fitness for settled life.[94] Yet, by al-Jāsir's reckoning, his suspicion was dispelled early on account of the intimacy of his experience at ʿArwā, where he lived like a bedouin himself for a time. Beginning in the

1950s, the scholar's writings would be distinguished by their sympathetic attention to the historical and contemporary conditions of the bedouin populations of Arabia. This emergent concern would have direct bearing on al-Jāsir's genealogical project, which, though addressed largely to central Arabia's sedentary populations, pivoted in important ways around a nostalgic ideal of bedouinism that emerged first during this period. More relevant for our purposes here, al-Jāsir's interest in bedouin life overlapped neatly with his dual identity as a reformist and a scholar, and thus provides a view into developments in his thinking over time.

In 1933, the bedouin population of Arabia, both recently settled and nomadic, was thought to comprise 55 percent of the kingdom's population, and roughly 60 percent in its two core regions, Najd and Hijaz.[95] The challenge of integrating the kingdom's bedouin populations into settled life was not the concern of the Wahhabi religious authorities alone, but was viewed also by central Arabia's emergent crop of intellectuals as a central mission of their advocacy. Al-Jāsir believed that the sedentarization of Arabia's bedouin was among the most significant developments in the history of the Peninsula, and that securing the gains of this achievement would depend on the integration of these newly sedentarized tribal communities into modern Saudi society.[96] As the original inhabitants of Arabia, the bedouin maintained a firm grip on their way of life, and were consequently a source of instability for the Saudi state, he reasoned in a special issue of *al-Yamāma*'s inaugural year devoted to the kingdom's nomadic populations. The initial advent of Islam had failed "to excise the roots of evil from the hearts of the bedouin." It was only with the arrival of Muḥammad b. ʿAbd al-Wahhāb and his victorious successor ʿAbd al-ʿAzīz Ibn Saʿūd that the beginnings of order were imposed on Arabia's restive populations. Al-Jāsir's emphasis on bedouin corruptibility was a common *ḥadarī* view that engaged tropes long embedded in urban Islamic civilization. The reconditioning of the bedouin was already a well-established state project, however, so the scholar's judgment was tempered by a recognition of the power of the state to reshape social outcomes.

Swayed by their demographic preponderance, al-Jāsir believed that the bedouin inhabitants of Arabia had rightful demands to make on the kingdom's towns and centers of governance. Toward that end, he enlisted *al-Yamāma* correspondents in the new bedouin settlements, who provided him with information about the needs of their under-served populations. He would then publish these correspondents' reports as news items in the magazine, calling the government's attention to unrecognized development projects.[97] After the government's confiscation of *al-Yamāma* in 1962, al-Jāsir's formal advocacy on behalf of bedouin causes ceased. In its place would emerge a new conception of the kingdom's bedouin population, one that reflected the scholar's shifting priorities, and equally, the social and political

Figure 1.3. *Al-Yamāma*, July 1954, "Special Issue on the Bedouin." Courtesy of Maʿan al-Jāsir.

transformation afoot in Saudi Arabia. To understand this transformation, a brief discussion of the history of bedouin relations with the modern Saudi state from the time of the Ikhwān rebellion is in order.

The Ikhwān rebellion of the early twentieth century was an effort by prominent bedouin tribes, primarily the ʿUtayba and Muṭayr confederations, to make their imprint on the *ḥaḍar*-dominated statebuilding project of ʿAbd al-ʿAzīz Ibn Saʿūd.[98] This effort was arrested under a hailstorm of British bombers and Wahhabi *muṭawwaʿūn*, the former checking the tribesmen's military advance, the latter conditioning their minds toward the sedentary loyalties of religion and state. As the state expanded and its institutions multiplied, Ibn Saʿūd enlisted a corps of foreign advisers and Saudi (often Hijazi) town dwellers to manage his newly inaugurated ministries, directorates, and agencies. Those bedouin who were to become dedicated members of the state-building project tended to be absorbed into its newly formed defense institutions, particularly the National Guard. The Guard was the successor to the Ikhwān forces, and its subordination to the royal family was reinforced by a command structure populated by senior princes of the Āl Saʿūd ruling dynasty. By and large, the bedouin inhabitants of Saudi Arabia had little formal input into the fashioning of the state's institutions, a circumstance that would breed disillusionment in certain quarters.

Bedouin resentment against the Saudi order was articulated in resonant terms in a series of pamphlets issued in 1978 by Juhaymān al-ʿUtaybī and his followers. Written or inspired by the former National Guard driver turned militant cult leader, the declining fortunes of the bedouin are evoked between the lines of the pamphlets' grandiose millenarian language. One such pamphlet comprised a collection of Prophetic Traditions that proved the imminent arrival of the Islamic hour of judgment. Bouncing unstably between hermeneutical exegesis and reflections on current affairs, Juhaymān paused to discuss the declining reputation of the Ikhwān movement within the National Guard. Before the 1960s, he explained, all Guard members were known casually as *Ikhwān* (brothers), there being nothing pejorative about the notion. Over the previous two decades, however, the notion of associating with the Ikhwān had fallen out of favor, and it had become a source of embarrassment to answer to that name.[99] The sole Saudi institutional identity that possessed some continuity with the recent bedouin past had ceased to be viable, he seemed to be arguing. Meanwhile, the bedouin were left to suffer under the weight of the government's failed economic policies.

According to a Prophetic Tradition, Juhaymān explained, the end of days would be imminent when herders of livestock were seen to be arrogantly building permanent structures. For Juhaymān, there seemed no better proof of this than the condition of the contemporary Saudi bedouin; already deeply impoverished, they subsisted on the rearing of livestock, until the government came along and showered them with loans to build homes, thereby sinking them deeper into debt.[100] In another pamphlet, Juhaymān and his followers directed their discontent at the Wahhabi pedagogical authorities. The Wahhabi ʿulamāʾ, they argued, belittled the bedouin for their inability to understand classical Arabic or access religious texts.[101] True, many bedouin were unable to comprehend sermons preached in classical Arabic; but this did not make their dialects illegitimate, the pamphleteers argued, as the message of God could still be conveyed if simply expressed for their benefit. In light of this evidence, the notion that the Salafi movement in which Juhaymān and his followers were embedded was predominantly a religious orientation that expressed itself in the rejection of *madhhab* (legal school) and other forms of ʿulamāʾ authority bears reconsideration. Instead, it seems more fruitful to consider Juhaymān's militant Salafism in terms of the ongoing contest between rural bedouin and literate townsmen, and the state authority the latter represented.[102]

Though painted in broad and erratic strokes, the sentiments captured by Juhaymān encapsulated the marginal position of the bedouin in the new Saudi Arabia. For Ḥamad al-Jāsir, however, who was born and raised not a stone's throw from Juhaymān's hometown of Sājir, the lack of status ascribed to them seemed unjust, and reflected a misapprehension of the bedouin role in Arabian history. In the transition from crusading newsman to historian and scholar, al-Jāsir developed a new understanding of the bedouin condition, one more sympathetic to the material forces that drove their behavior, yet ultimately divorced from the practical concerns that had driven his advocacy in earlier decades. This new understanding reflected less a concern for the welfare of the country's silent majority and more a sense of nostalgia for the pristine and irretrievable past they represented.

Echoing in certain respects Juhaymān's reading of the bedouin condition, al-Jāsir reconsidered the roots of the Ikhwān revolt in novel and sympathetic terms. Removed from the rehabilitative sentiments that colored his 1954 essay in *al-Yamāma*, al-Jāsir would come to see the bedouin as essentially innocent souls who were sometimes driven to nefarious acts by material necessity.[103] Embodying purity and innocence, they lacked only proper guidance.[104] Concerning the revolt itself, al-Jāsir laid the blame squarely on the shoulders of the *muṭawwaʿūn*, whose piecemeal understanding of Islamic teachings produced only discord and confusion when transmitted by rote to their bedouin pupils. The subsequent exposure of the bedouin to an imponderable *ḥaḍarī* town culture produced a religiosity of excess and exaggeration that in turn led to the Ikhwān revolt.[105] Before this "tremendous wave of religiosity" had swept over the bedouin, he maintained, their life was characterized by a kind of freedom. Najdi bedouin men and women mingled freely in weddings and social gatherings (*majālis*), and women kept their faces uncovered.[106]

In his sympathy for the bedouin, al-Jāsir seemed also to be echoing ideas embedded in the writings of the fourteenth-century North African historian Ibn Khaldūn (d. 1382). Like the Najdi scholar, Ibn Khaldūn considered the bedouin to be closer to the "original essence" (*al-fiṭra al-ūlā*) of human existence than town dwellers.[107] When al-Jāsir invoked this "original essence," as in his 1959 *al-Yamāma* polemic against nameless clerical opponents, he transposed it to apply to the whole of central Arabian society, both bedouin and sedentary. This formulation foreshadowed the emergence of a nostalgic ideal of bedouinism as a normative aspiration for Saudis, bedouin and sedentary alike, whose root matter was genealogical in nature.

Al-Jāsir's new emphasis on bedouin purity emerged in reaction to forces he saw massing within and around central Arabia, the forces of national and international integration. In a book review penned toward the end of his life, al-Jāsir elaborated on this sentiment:

> I believe, and am convinced, that the bedouin, and praise God for this, maintain their original essence, which God instilled in his creation. This essence has not been polluted in any way by the dirty stains (*awḍār*) known to civilized societies, nor by values and qualities considered alien to our environment, our Arab nature, our religion, and our *umma*.[108]

The reifying narrative of bedouin purity provided a convenient foil for al-Jāsir's burgeoning critique of Saudi modernity. *Ḥaḍarīs* had no basis for condemning bedouin, he reasoned in an article for the official National Guard magazine, as they are so caught up in material life that many of them have become incapacitated. "The bedouin is the source from which we derive," al-Jāsir explained to his undoubtedly approving National Guard readership.[109] For some, however, al-Jāsir's bias in favor of bedouin culture (*ʿaṣabiyya li-l-badāwa*) would do "great damage" to the fabric of identity in the kingdom,[110] as it was on the basis of this nostalgic ideal that al-Jāsir would build his taxonomy of the lineages of the kingdom's inhabitants. The tension inherent in al-Jāsir's attitudes toward bedouin culture is well encapsulated by P. Marcel Kurpershoek, a longtime student of Saudi culture:

> [T]he popularity of themes from the relatively distant past of the country's pre-modern age can be explained by the need to unite the Saudi state's contradictory versions of history and modernity, which emphasize the negative qualities of tribalism yet acknowledge the undiminished importance of tribal organization and the competition for prestige as measured by traditional tribal standards.[111]

Through his scholarly and popular writings, al-Jāsir repackaged traditional tribal standards for the symbolic life of the modern Saudi state, thus helping reshape the competition for prestige in the rapidly changing kingdom. If al-Jāsir's shifting approach to the bedouin question served double duty as a barometer of social change, his views on language were an even more potent indicator of the transformation of Peninsular life in the twentieth century.

AL-JĀSIR AND THE ARABIC LANGUAGE

One of al-Jāsir's preferred pen names was al-Aṣmaʿī, after the famous eighth-century Iraqi philologist Abū Saʿīd ʿAbd al-Malik b. Qurayb al-Aṣmaʿī (d. 828). This moniker was particularly suited for the kingdom's unofficial lexicographer. Al-Aṣmaʿī was well known for his interest in bedouin culture; stories of excursions deep into the desert to document bedouin speech and poetry add color to his biography, and cement his reputation as a pioneer in the study of the Arabic language.[112] The profile cut by this scholar-adventurer must have appealed to al-Jāsir's sensibilities. His early life was colored by a number of prolonged sojourns among the bedouin of Arabia, a fact that would set him apart from the typical educated Najdi town dweller. In 1927, fresh from his second educational tour in Riyadh, al-Jāsir was dispatched by his patrons to work as a *muṭawwaʿ* among a branch of the ʿUtayba tribe, not far from his ancestral home of al-Burūd.[113] Living and migrating with this bedouin group, he would later boast proudly, the scholar acquired an understanding of tribal dialects and an ability to discern differences among them. But as the twentieth century unfolded and al-Jāsir progressed up the status hierarchy of urban life, his embrace of linguistic diversity would give way to a vigilant defense of the Arabic language in its authorized, classical form. This ascent to the high cultural terrain of authoritative knowledge would have bearing on the difficulties the scholar would encounter when attempting to establish a definitive genealogical chart of Arabian origins.

In 1957, al-Jāsir was nominated to serve as a member of the prestigious Arabic Language Academy (Majmaʿ al-Lugha al-ʿArabiyya) in Egypt.[114] Modeled after the French Académie Française, the Academy was created in 1917 to serve as the preeminent authority for the preservation and development of the Arabic language in Egypt. With the Saudi government's promotion of his candidacy, al-Jāsir became the first person from the Arabian Peninsula to hold a seat there. The scholar would repay the honor, though, by activating philology in the service of an emergent Saudi nationalism. In meetings of the Academy, al-Jāsir would seek to demonstrate that much of the topography of pre-Islamic poetry had been misunderstood. By correcting transcriptions and vocalizations of ancient manuscripts, he sought to prove that the setting for the quintessential Arab art form—those obscure toponyms that pepper the landscape of ancient Arabic poetry—was in fact central Arabia.[115] Whatever the veracity of his methods, they were sufficient to convince noted Arab historians and colleagues such as Nāṣir al-Dīn al-Asad and Ṭāhā Ḥusayn, the latter of whom was said (apocryphally, it seems) to have conferred upon al-Jāsir his iconic honorific, ʿAllāmat al-Jazīra.

Al-Jāsir also used his newfound prestige as the kingdom's most high profile philologist to police the boundaries of the Arabic lexicon against neologisms and linguistic impurities.[116] His increasing aversion to linguistic syncretism is demonstrated in his attitude toward the study of dialects and popular poetry. Saudi Arabia is home to various Arabic dialects, from the Shia colloquial spoken in the villages of al-Aḥsā' and al-Qaṭīf, to the Egyptian-inflected Arabic of the Hijazi cities, to the tribal dialects in use across the vast expanses of rural Arabia. For al-Jāsir, as with al-Aṣmaʿī, the value in studying these dialects lay in the potential to extract from them traces of an original and unvarnished Arabic, an Arabic that, in the scholar's estimate of his era, had been buried under layers of alien accretions. Al-Jāsir believed that Arabic dialects spoken in areas formerly under colonial rule bore traces of the language of the colonizers, and had to be treated with great caution.[117] Meanwhile, Arabic dialects spoken in places such as Syria reflected as well the pre-Arab civilizations that inhabited those regions. In promoting the usage of these pre-Islamic or colonially infused dialects, Arabs were destroying their pure language.[118] What Saudis claim as their heritage is often nothing more than the cultural driftwood of Iran and South Asia, he considered. "We must be extremely cautious when examining what is called Arab heritage, [for] not everything that is heritable deserves to be called Arab heritage."[119]

At safe remove from the long arm of Western and pre-Islamic civilizations, and from the polyglot Persian Gulf and Red Sea coasts, however, was an Arabian heartland where pure, "unspoiled" Arabic could be found. Al-Jāsir elaborated on this view of Arabian dialects in a 1989 interview discussing vernacular poetry:

> . . . until recently, the dialects of the bedouin and of the city folk were not very different. Their dialect was closer to classical Arabic than the poetry [that has emerged] today. After the unification of the different parts of the kingdom, the intermingling of peoples and the communication ties between neighboring regions increased. This influenced every aspect of life in the country, not just language.[120]

Al-Jāsir's sense of anxiety about social transformation, discernible between the lines of the above assessment, was rendered even more explicit in the following xenophobic statement:

> Until around fifty years ago, popular poetry was closer to Classical Arabic. The tribes of the heart of the Arabian Peninsula did not mix with their neighbors from other lands. Their words were vernacular, but

> they were Arabic words. Then, mixing and blending with neighboring regions occurred, and "foreign words" entered with [foreign] dialects. The dialects of the [surrounding] regions are full of foreign words, and these [tribes] adopted them, and adopted many of the manners of these foreign peoples. This is what I fear. . . .[121]

Central Arabian dialects are riddled with Persian and other non-Arabic loan words, whose insertion into the lexicon one would be hard-pressed to date to any recent developments.[122] Yet al-Jāsir's sense of the linguistic map of Arabia is compelling in its own imperfect way. According to his conception, central Arabia, home to a once organic and largely unstratified culture of nomads and settled folk speaking a common language,[123] had in recent decades been plugged into a wider network of relations with neighboring regions. This linkage had eroded the purchase of pure central Arabian traditions and the linguistic bond between town dweller and bedouin.[124] Implicit in this conception is a need felt by the scholar to restore central Arabia's heritage to a recognizable and uncorrupted state, a project he would pursue first through geography and later through genealogy. In this way, al-Jāsir's scholarly project was not unlike that of the philologists of early modern Europe. Through textual, philological, and genealogical evidence, Patrick Geary has written, European philologists "provided . . . a means of projecting their nations into a distant, preliterate past." Like his European scholarly counterparts, al-Jāsir mustered historical knowledge to prove the existence of a discrete central Arabian linguistic community that possessed a proto-national social identity.[125]

In methodological terms, al-Jāsir's sense of the degradation of modern Arabian dialects caused him to reject modern vernacular (*Nabaṭī*) poetry as a source of historical knowledge. Previously a rich and unblemished source of oral history, he maintained, vernacular poetry had lost its credibility in the modern period.[126] The development of mass media had influenced the spread of poetical recitation as a sometimes lucrative trade and contributed to the mixing of local vernaculars with foreign dialect terms.[127] Popular poetry that was documented before the age of the contemporary narrators, however, could be a good source of history, he believed, in particular for knowledge about the Arabic language. Invoking the ancient Arab philologists, al-Jāsir claimed that those dialects preserved archaisms that reflected the language in a purer, earlier form.[128] "We must study the dialects of the tribes, because there are dialects in popular poetry that have been preserved from the earliest days, which we find documented in the [classical] books."[129]

When the living language of Arabia can be found corroborated in the documented records of early Islamic history, the nomadic interlude that looms throughout Arabian historiography becomes less uncomfortable to contemplate. Premodern vernacular poetry was a vehicle for restoring the linkages with this near-vanished past, even with an ur-Arabic. With a hint of false modesty and perhaps subtle disparagement, al-Jāsir once wrote to an aspiring poet: "I am sorry to say but I am not one whose tastes in poetry are deeply refined to the extent that I possess the ability to discern the way to properly judge the standing of a particular poet."[130] His passionate criticisms of Saudi vernacular poetry in the Saudi press would seem therefore to have served a broader non-literary agenda, namely, to articulate anxieties about a society transformed beyond recognition across the nine decades of his lifetime.

GEOGRAPHY VS. GENEALOGY

In the mythology of Ḥamad al-Jāsir, the story of how the scholar came to know the true identity of Jabal Raḍwā is recounted by his disciples more than any other. As a young substitute teacher in Yanbuʿ in 1934, al-Jāsir was instructing his sixth grade class on a poem by the famous medieval scholar Abū l-ʿAlāʾ al-Maʿarrī (d. 1057), explaining a reference to a mountain in the Hijaz on the basis of his knowledge of Islamic texts. When al-Jāsir announced that Raḍwā was in fact close to Medina and easy to traverse by camel, his students erupted in laughter. Through the open window, they pointed to a mountain southeast of Yanbuʾ—Raḍwā mountain, which was, they instructed, impossible to traverse by camel.[131]

The Mount Raḍwā story draws attention to an essential dimension of al-Jāsir's philosophy of history, namely, his insistence on the primacy of local knowledge. In practice, this philosophy had several implications. Methodologically, it meant that al-Jāsir was partial to particular classical sources, preferring Yāqūt over al-Bakrī for his geographical information, and al-Hamdānī over Ibn Ḥazm for his genealogical references. The simple reason for this bias was that Yāqūt and al-Hamdānī had visited the places in the Peninsula that they had written about (al-Hamdānī was a native of Yemen), while al-Bakrī and Ibn Ḥazm—from his distant perch in Andalusia—had not. More broadly, al-Jāsir's insistence on the primacy of local knowledge would find expression in his decades-long effort to document and classify the peoples and places of the Arabian Peninsula. His animating principle was that the most authoritative knowledge about Arabian toponyms and genealogical relations rested with the people most invested in these truths, the inhabitants of the kingdom's scattered towns and villages themselves. This erudite parochialism would make al-Jāsir the primary gatekeeper of Arabian history and geography for Arab and Western scholars alike. Yet in the course of time, his entrusting of history to its subjects would land the scholar in methodological hot water.

By his own estimation, al-Jāsir's embarrassed fumbling of the Jabal Raḍwa episode would provide the motivation for establishing himself as Saudi Arabia's foremost geographer. From Yanbuʿ and beyond, his peregrinations throughout the kingdom during the first sixty years of his life would prepare the ground for one of his most significant projects, *al-Muʿjam al-Jughrāfī li-l-Bilād al-ʿArabiyya al-Saʿūdiyya* (*The Geographical Dictionary of the Lands of Saudi Arabia*). By the measure of his scholarly disciples, and by his own accounting,[132] al-Jāsir's crowning achievement was this geographical compendium.[133] Written by a team of Saudi authors under his supervision, the *Dictionary* established al-Jāsir's identity as one of the kingdom's most authoritative scholarly voices.

Al-Jāsir's project was influenced by Saudi historian Muḥammad b. Bulayḥid's five-volume work on Arabian antiquity and geography, *Ṣaḥīḥ al-Akhbār ʿAmmā fī Bilād al-ʿArab min al-Āthār* (*The Authentic Reports of the Archaeological Relics in the Land of the Arabs*), which had appeared in the early 1950s.[134] While this project set the stage for his own, the scholar felt that the classical geographical volumes upon which Ibn Bulayḥid and others of his predecessors had relied were fundamentally flawed, as they conveyed information about the Peninsula at second hand, and were often mistaken.[135] Yet the primacy of local knowledge had its limitations. Tuning into radio broadcasts, al-Jāsir would be dismayed when listening to announcers mispronounce what he took to be the authentic names of towns and other toponyms within the kingdom. For the scholar, this free-for-all phonetic rummaging into the past reflected a lack of standardized knowledge about the kingdom's geography, an absence he would set out to remedy with his *Geographical Dictionary*.[136]

In 1968, with the approval of King Fayṣal and the Ministry of Information, al-Jāsir issued a call in *al-ʿArab* for researchers to join in preparing his geographical compendium. His primary aim was to establish authoritative vocalizations for the names of the towns, villages, and landscape features of the kingdom. This objective could only be achieved through fieldwork, he determined, to be carried out by a team of specialists from the regions in question, who would fan out across the country and document their findings.[137] From Beirut, al-Jāsir worked as a liaison with the Saudi court on behalf of the researchers compiling the *Dictionary*, and composed two of its volumes, one on the Eastern Province, the other on northwest Arabia. A major objective of the *Dictionary* was, in al-Jāsir's words, to "link the present with the past," one that would see him embark on the occasional flight of historical fancy.[138] Al-Jāsir focused his efforts on the compendium through 1979, by which point he had taken up a no less ambitious yet rather more fraught standardization project, the documenting of the genealogies of the peoples of Saudi Arabia.

"I composed works of history, geography, literature, and travel narratives," the scholar wrote. "Then I composed two books on lineage, *Muʿjam Qabāʾil al-Mamlaka* and *Jamharat Ansāb al-Usar al-Mutaḥaḍḍira*, and I noticed that interest in my work was based mostly on these two books."[139] Ironically, al-Jāsir's interest in Arab genealogies originated in the labors of Western Orientalists.[140] Al-Jāsir admired and respected Western scholars such as Werner Caskel and Évariste Lévi-Provençal for their efforts to edit and publish classic works of Arab genealogy (*ʿilm al-ansāb*), and made public note of their expressions of gratitude for his expert corrections and criticisms. His very method of work, compiling data on index cards until he achieved a critical mass of information on a subject, was influenced by a visit to the office of prolific Arabian travel writer and advisor to Ibn Saʿūd, Harry St. John Bridger Philby, and likely as well by the famous Italian Orientalist Giorgio Levi Della Vida, whom the scholar met in Rome in 1960.[141] Yet al-Jāsir remained puzzled by the fact that Western Orientalists were more interested in Arab genealogies than Arab scholars, repeating the claim as a sort of refrain.[142] A classical scholar by training and inclination, al-Jāsir recognized the essential connection between the study of history and the study of lineages. Genealogies were the first recorded elements of Arab history, and any effort to construct a modern historiography for Saudi Arabia would need to reckon with the deep and persistent significance of lineage in Arabian society.[143] In establishing himself as Saudi Arabia's foremost genealogist, al-Jāsir sought to reappropriate the study of genealogies from Western scholars and direct it toward his own localized ends.

Despite the tremendous attention generated by his genealogical project, al-Jāsir came to consider his bestselling work, the *Jamhara,* the least important of his scholarly contributions. Yet genealogy—when mingled with ancient history, a murky and imprecise discipline—seemed to ignite the imaginations of al-Jāsir's compatriots in a way that geography could not. For if the scholar had advanced in some place a dubious claim about the relationship between an ancient and modern toponym, that toponym was lifeless—it could not snipe back. At most, a refutation of al-Jāsir's geographical claims would find its way into a specialty journal, and die a peaceful death there. Genealogy, however, was something deeply interwoven into the identity of every family, clan and tribe in Arabia. Sifting through the scholar's correspondence in the last decade of his life, for example, one is struck by the number of genealogical queries directed by Saudis toward the scholar, and the relative silence on geographical matters. Al-Jāsir's documenting of the kingdom's genealogies was the most important such effort in the modern history of the kingdom. His genealogical project served as the textual representation of a society in formation, and thus constitutes the critical core of his oeuvre. The outlines of this project were tested first in the pages of *al-ʿArab.*

MAJALLAT AL-ʿARAB

Al-ʿArab marked al-Jāsir's turn away from explicit political engagement and toward sustained historical inquiry. From its launch in 1966 out of Beirut as a monthly scholarly journal, *al-ʿArab* was unlike any other Saudi publication. For one thing, with the exception of the first issue, the ubiquitous Islamic prefatory formula, the *basmala,* was absent from its pages, a decision for which al-Jāsir was roundly criticized by some of his more devout readers.[144] In the scholar's view, *al-ʿArab* was firstly a scholarly journal, as demonstrated by its continuous pagination and minimal advertising. Asked once to describe the magazine's subject matter on a government ministry form, al-Jāsir declined the choices provided ("political, economic, social, cultural, Islamic, sport, varied"), checking "other." If the proprietor of *al-ʿArab* was to be compelled to innocuousness by political and religious forces in his home country, he would be so on his own idiosyncratic terms.

The iconoclastic philosophy behind *al-ʿArab*'s founding is captured well in an essay marking the launch of its inaugural issue. There, al-Jāsir engages in a simulated exchange with a friend, who is shown to criticize the parochialism of Arabian culture. His anonymous foil is incredulous that obscure landmarks in the Arabian Peninsula could merit discussion while in the West the "Space Race" is raging and great advances are being made in the sciences.[145] Echoing contemporaneous critiques of Western materialism by Islamic intellectuals, al-Jāsir's rebuttal mobilizes religious philosophy in the service of cultural heritage. Man's ability to contemplate transformations in the material world, the scholar argued, is dependent on his consciousness, which is endowed by God and is unchanging. Once the primacy of consciousness is properly acknowledged, all material existence is equally valid and equally ephemeral. "Life in the age of the camel . . . was the same as it is in the age of the atom and the ascent to the moon," he concluded. While resonant with the critical Islamist discourse of his generation,[146] al-Jāsir did not seek solace in a state controlled by religious authorities or won through bloody revolutionary struggle. To the contrary, the scholar's escape from Western materialism and Wahhabi obscurantism was a culture of scattered Arabian landmarks, toponyms, and genealogies, which, in the pages of his journal, he would fashion into artifacts of modern Arabian identity.

From his office in the ʿĀzariyya building in downtown Beirut, al-Jāsir presided over *al-ʿArab*'s first decade in circulation. If measured by this circulation, *al-ʿArab*'s influence would seem unworthy of much attention. The average print run of the monthly and later bimonthly journal was approximately 5,000 copies, many of which were purchased by Saudi government ministries, as a form of hidden subsidy for the scholar. Rather, the significance of *al-ʿArab* was that it prefigured and later helped shape modern genealogical discourse in the kingdom, helping inaugurate a cultural phenomenon whose qualities are central to any understanding of modern Saudi Arabia. Before examining Ḥamad al-Jāsir's role in the emergence of the kingdom's modern genealogical culture, however, we must first establish the significance of genealogy in Arabian history. The following chapter looks at how and why the people of central Arabia documented their genealogies before the oil age, and how changes in the nature of genealogical documentation reflect transformations in Arabian social and political life.

CHAPTER TWO

The Dark Matter of Tribal Belonging

I swore that I wouldn't offer a sacrifice
in memory of a wretch[1]

a worthless man, who
bequeathed to me no beautiful
date palms

Rather, he bequeathed only the hammer
and the copperware

left me to fashion their cooking
pots and carry the axe[2]

—*Muṭawwaʿ Nafī*

Before the oil age, life was challenging in central Arabia. The year 1725 was particularly difficult, as recounted by the Najdi historian and genealogist Ibn ʿĪsā (d. 1924/5). In that year, a severe famine gripped Najd and the Hijaz, killing large numbers of people and forcing others to survive on emaciated animal carcasses. Heavy rains and flooding came next, followed by a severe winter chill that killed many of the cultivated plants. Soon after, locusts swarmed in, devouring large parts of the date crop, with still more being consumed by their wingless offspring. "We take refuge in God from his anger and punishment," Ibn ʿĪsā concluded from this unusual sequence of calamities.[3]

For much of its history, central Arabia was an isolated, insular, and remote outpost of the Islamic world, populated predominantly by nomadic tribes and scattered settlements about which comparatively little is known. In later centuries, trading and pilgrimage networks linked central Arabian settlements to the broader Islamic world through Iraq, Syria, and Egypt. Yet by and large, Najd was absent from the main action of Islamic history, sparsely populated and little acknowledged.

Central Arabia's most recognizable contribution to the broad sweep of Islamic civilization was Wahhabism, the religious revivalist movement that emerged in the middle of the eighteenth century and spread throughout Arabia as the ideological arm of oasis chieftain Muḥammad b. Saʿūd's (d. 1765) campaign to bring the Peninsula under his rule. Among other notable changes, the Wahhabi movement introduced religious literacy to the population on a wider scale than had existed before. The Swiss traveler John Lewis Burckhardt was impressed to learn of the magnitude of the Wahhabi educational mission during his visit to the Hijaz in 1814–15. ". . . [T]he Wahabys have established schools in every village, and oblige fathers of families to superintend the instruction of their children," he was told. "At Derayeh [the Saudi capital], many learned persons of the first class among eastern men of letters have collected very valuable libraries from all parts of Arabia, and some of their olemas have composed treatises on religious and judicial subjects."[4] Despite this reported efflorescence of text-based learning,[5] central Arabia remained well into the twentieth century a predominantly oral culture,[6] where oral persuasion and contest reigned as the dominant mode of communication, and textual learning was the province of a narrow elite who, moreover, were beholden to the expectations and practices of their nonliterate auditors.

The oral communicative backdrop of premodern Arabian society can be discerned in the early Najdi sources.[7] It is seen, for example, in the exchanges between Muḥammad b. ʿAbd al-Wahhāb and his opponents, who documented their religious views in epistles that were couriered to and from the various population centers of Arabia, where they were recited publicly and debated.[8] It is embedded in an early anti-Wahhabi polemic by the Basran scholar Aḥmad b. ʿAlī al-Qabbānī, who addressed his tract collectively to the people of eastern Najd (*yā ahl al-ʿĀriḍ!*), anticipating its public recitation.[9] In the nomadic context, the domain of near-unbroken orality, it can be seen in the title by which the poet was known among the bedouin of the ʿAnaza tribe, *ṣāḥib al-qawl* ("master of speech"), a title which implied a monopoly on such capabilities.[10] Alongside oral poetry, which could work like a telegraph spreading news of a political succession,[11] bedouin (and settlers) communicated via insignia (*wusūm*), which they might brand on their camels or etch into the sand to signal their presence in a given territory when unfamiliar groups approached.[12] For both bedouin and town dwellers in Arabia, the written word held magical properties. This is evident in magico-religious texts such as *Ḥirz al-Jawshan*, a book of incantations and numerological superstitions that circulated in Najd into the Wahhabi era, and in the bedouin practice of swallowing pieces of paper inscribed with magic formulas for curing illnesses.[13] The people of premodern central Arabia held the word close to their hearts, even if it was the word of a more crudely hewn god.

The Wahhabis promoted literacy as a means of spreading their vision of the ethical life throughout central Arabian society. Muḥammad b. ʿAbd al-Wahhāb considered it a man's duty to instruct his children and family in proper Islamic belief.[14] Yet the type of literacy promoted by the Wahhabis was not particularly expansive. It was a literacy designed to stamp out magical thinking and behavior, one in which theology and law were privileged, and disciplines such as history left largely unelaborated, except as related to the ideological needs of the court. ʿUthmān b. Bishr (d. 1871), the historian of the early Saudi conquests, lamented the state of Najdi history preceding his own efforts:

> . . . the people of Najd and their scholars, past and present, had no interest in the history of the important battles and polities [of Najd], or in those who built them, what occurred within them, and that which came and went from them. The exceptions are rare events recorded by the scholars, which are useless to me, because if they mentioned the year, they said such-and-such son of such-and-such was killed, but they did not mention his [full] name or the reason he was killed . . . We are aware that from the time of Adam until today, there have been only wars, but we would like to know the reality behind them, the reason for them, and the strange events and wonders that occurred within them. All of this is absent from their histories.[15]

Ibn Bishr proposed a clean break from the purposeless etchings of his predecessors, a goal made viable by his close association with the Saudi court and the mandate given to him to produce a history of the Saudi-Wahhabi conquests. Ibn Bishr's record of the Saudi-Wahhabi mission, *ʿUnwān al-Majd fī Tārīkh Najd* (*The Marker of Nobility in the History of Central Arabia*), was thus a history in the proper sense, a diachronic narrative of events with an implicit trajectory, however teleological its gaze.[16] Yet the building blocks of Ibn Bishr's history differed little from those that preceded *ʿUnwān al-Majd* in circulation. To take an example, genealogy, that catalog of clipped names to which Ibn Bishr refers in the above quoted passage, comprised one of the singular inheritances of central Arabian historiography. In a certain sense, early Najdi history is little more than a loosely stitched recitation of the prominent clans and lineages that populated central Arabia in the eighteenth and nineteenth centuries.

This chapter investigates Najdi historiography from a genealogical perspective. The purpose is not to retell the early modern history of central

Arabia, a task accomplished admirably by such scholars as Uwaidah al-Juhany,[17] Michael Cook,[18] Michael Crawford,[19] and Abdulaziz Al Fahad,[20] but to examine how genealogy was woven into the various facets of Saudi history and social life, so as to be able to explain why Ḥamad al-Jāsir's documenting of Saudi genealogies in the late twentieth century was so significant (and fraught) an enterprise.

I will demonstrate how from the early Wahhabi period to the twentieth century, genealogical signification in Saudi Arabia moved from a practice embedded in the workings of social life to a documented form, becoming objectified in response to sedentarization, the dispersion of kin groups, and the emergence of the text as the authoritative pivot around which a previously oral cultural life turned. The notion of objectification, taken here to mean the creation of a codified body of knowledge out of a set of reflexive, quotidian practices, has been explored with respect to Islam in the modern age.[21] Here, I propose to examine this phenomenon as it relates to a different facet of culture and society, genealogy. I will pay particular attention in this chapter to how genealogies have been textualized, and how genealogical representation reflects key aspects of social change in Saudi Arabia. One important dimension of social change in Saudi Arabia has been the transition from a mixed nomadic-sedentary society to one in which sedentarism has become the singular mode of living. Of interest here, however, is not sedentarism as a frozen sociological category, but sedentarization as a dynamic process, and not its material effects so much as its moral consequences, that is, how, and why, sedentarization and genealogical consciousness have combined to make tribal belonging a sought-after category in Saudi Arabia.

In central Arabia, as in the many other societies whose genealogical systems have been investigated by anthropologists and historians, genealogy served as a means of organizing knowledge about kinship relations.[22] The nomadic communities of central Arabia, and to a lesser extent its settled communities, organized themselves in kinship networks of varying sizes that might expand or contract depending on the circumstances in question. Considering briefly two important historical features of bedouin tribal systems, the tendency toward endogamous marriage and the belief in collective criminal liability, it is possible to demonstrate differences in the scope and therefore the conception of the kinship group.[23] With respect to marriage, the bedouin practice of *taḥjīr*, whereby a girl was vouchsafed for marriage to her closest permissible relative, usually a paternal first or second cousin, established a particular limit on how the kinship group might be defined.[24] When, on the other hand, a question of blood payment for an act of aggression committed by a kinsman arose, the principle of collective criminal liability activated a broader set of agnatic relations, for example, the collective offspring of a common fourth lineal ascendant (great-grandfather).[25] The same variation was true in central Arabia's settled communities, where, during times of local conflict, agnatic ties might be privileged and mobilized, despite a broader and more mundane tendency to cooperate with unrelated kin, particularly when it came to marriage.

The shifting boundaries of central Arabian kinship groups, and the way in which conflict could mobilize the genealogical solidarities of lineally diverse town cohabitants, is demonstrated in an episode captured in Ibn ʿĪsā's *ʿIqd al-Durar*. Ibn ʿĪsā composed this history of the events of the late nineteenth and early twentieth centuries at the request of King ʿAbd al-ʿAzīz Ibn Saʿūd (d. 1953). Written at the cusp of Saudi ascendancy in the twentieth century, Ibn ʿĪsā's volume is a kind of paramount premodern history, rife with genealogical information and details about commodity prices and the causes of their fluctuation.[26] The episode in question concerned Ushayqir, a prosperous town in the Washm region of western Najd, and a regional center of scholarship before its eclipse by Riyadh in the twentieth century. In 1874, Ushayqir was the site of a violent dispute between several families of the Wuhaba branch of the Banī Tamīm tribe. After members of two families of the Āl Bassām b. Munīf branch of the Wuhaba violently assaulted the *amīr* or governor of the town, a member of the *amīr*'s family (the Āl Nashwān) "went to [the town of] al-Ḥurayyiq and requested its aid, because the Āl Nashwān and the people of al-Ḥurayyiq are all one *ʿashīra* [i.e., tribal subbranch] descending from al-Mashārifa, from al-Wuhaba. . . ."[27] When conflict among cohabitants of the same tribal branch ensued,[28] in this case the Wuhaba, recourse to subbranch identities, that is, more proximal genealogical relations, was the solution of choice, traversing boundaries of space and township.

One finds a similar potential for the subordination of township and religious solidarities in the way genealogies were represented in the Najdi chronicles. Commenting on the death of a prominent scholar in 1865, ʿAbdallāh b. ʿAbd al-Raḥmān Abā Buṭayn, Ibn ʿĪsā described him as "genealogically an ʿĀʾidhī, religiously a Ḥanbalī, geographically a Najdi."[29] Ibn ʿĪsā represented the scholar's genealogical identity as primary to both his religious orientation and his locale, a formula echoed by Ibn ʿĪsā's near contemporary, the genealogist al-Mughīrī (d. 1945).[30] Taken together, these biographical notices testify strongly to the nomadic backdrop of central Arabian settled life, in which kinship attachments could be reckoned before attachments to locale and religious orientation.

GENEALOGIES IN THE NAJDI SOURCES

The integration of genealogical data into Najdi historical accounts reflects the extent to which knowledge about family and clan genealogies was embedded in the quotidian aspects of central Arabian social and political life. Heredity, for example, might determine a person's occupation, as well as reputation and character, both potential and actual. Within bedouin tribes, three key functions, that of the leader (*shaykh*), the military commander (*ʿaqīd* or *shaykh al-ḥarb*),[31] and the tribal judge (*ʿārifa*),[32] were all hereditary. In settled society, the scholarly vocation was often monopolized within prestigious families, a practice epitomized by the Āl al-Shaykh, the lineal descendants of Muḥammad b. ʿAbd al-Wahhāb. Yet the Wahhabis were not alone among religious authorities in adhering to a principle of heredity. When pressing the rhetorical assault on the enemies of his mission, Muḥammad b. ʿAbd al-Wahhāb would single out the itinerant holy men of central Arabia, among whom "Shamsān and his sons" came in for special opprobrium. As Ibn ʿAbd al-Wahhāb's letters make clear, it wasn't merely Shamsān with whom the Wahhabi leader was contending, but also Shamsān's lineal descendants, heirs to his impious calling.[33]

Practical concerns also drove the documentation and preservation of lineages among settled communities. These included affixing the division of inheritances among next of kin, upholding the stipulations associated with religious bequests (*awqāf*), determining the parties liable for contribution in the case of a blood payment (*diya* or *tha'r*), and regulating marriages.[34] From the perspective of the early (nineteenth-century) Saudi state, preserving knowledge about the genealogical networks in Najdi society was crucial for the muster system that underpinned the kingdom's defenses. The core of the state's fighting force comprised part-time warriors, who would be called up from the various towns of central Arabia to help defend a position or take part in a raid against non-compliant bedouin or town dwellers. The Saudi "muster-rolls" that the English traveler William Gifford Palgrave observed in Riyadh in 1862 would have been one of the only centralized genealogical records in the realm.[35]

In the context of Najdi historiography, the documenting of genealogies served the purpose of legitimating certain claims to political authority or property. Ibn Bishr's *sawābiq* are a prime example of this phenomenon. The *sawābiq*, or "events of the past" that preceded the Wahhabi mission, are a series of sketches by Ibn Bishr tacked onto the end of his history of the Saudi conquest of Arabia, *ʿUnwān al-Majd*.[36] On its face, the depiction of pre-Wahhabi history in Ibn Bishr's *sawābiq* appears less teleological than the story told of the subsequent age, in which history is progressive and driven, punctuated by Saudi-Wahhabi victories, interrupted by their defeats. There is a power in the *sawābiq*—the "Rūm" (Ottomans), the Sharīf (ruler of Mecca and Medina)—but it is removed from the scene. The *sawābiq* feel like a patch-up job, not an obvious court history, an almanac rather than an official record. Yet a genealogical view of the material demonstrates how purposeful it actually is.

The *sawābiq* begin in 1446 with the story of Rabīʿa b. Mānīʿ al-Muraydī's arrival in al-Dirʿiyya, the ancestral capital of the Āl Saʿūd. Rabīʿa b. Mānīʿ is the earliest known ancestor of the Āl Muqrin, the family from whom the ruling Āl Saʿūd descend. In *ʿUnwān al-Majd*, Ibn Bishr explained that Mānīʿ al-Muraydī, who lived in al-Durūʿ, a village near al-Qaṭīf in eastern Arabia, was invited by his kinsman in the town of Ḥajr (Riyadh) in central Arabia to settle nearby. Mānīʿ al-Muraydī established a farm in what came to be know as al-Dirʿiyya,[37] where his descendants eventually took over leadership of the town.[38] The *sawābiq* are in fact thoroughly invested in backdating Saudi antiquity in central Arabia, and the kinship ties that predated and motivated the family's arrival. Antiquity of residence seemed a prized element in legitimating one's position in central Arabian settled life,[39] and a prime vehicle by which to establish this antiquity was genealogy.

Ibn Bishr recorded another significant instance of the manipulation of genealogical knowledge in his *sawābiq*, though whether the author of the fiction was Ibn Bishr or his subject remains uncertain. One of the most inveterate opponents of the first Saudi conquest was the ruler of Riyadh, Dahhām b. Dawwās. Between 1746 and 1773, Dahhām and Muḥammad b. Saʿūd (and son) battled thirty-five times for control over the town.[40] As Ibn Bishr presented it, Dahhām's takeover of Riyadh was dubious from its onset. When Riyadh's last ruler, Zayd b. Mūsā, fled the city on account of conflict with its inhabitants, Dahhām assumed leadership.[41] He did so, Ibn Bishr related, "on the false pretense that Zayd's son was the son of his sister [i.e., Dahhām's nephew], and [Dahhām] claimed that he was [Zayd's son's] deputy."[42] It seems likely that Ibn Bishr included this detail to retroactively weaken the legitimacy of a historical enemy of the Āl Saʿūd. Whatever his reason for mentioning Dahhām's dubious genealogy, it is evident that genealogical claims were relevant to the way power was exercised and transmitted in Arabia, and making false claims or denying the legitimacy of other claims was an integral part of political discourse.

Thus did genealogical documentation enshrine power and power relations in central Arabia. This point is underscored when we examine the types of genealogies that were documented in the Najdi sources, and the types that were ignored. For the most part, Najdi historians and genealogists documented the lineages of the Najdi elite. The chronicles are rife with genealogical information about oasis leaders, religious scholars, and the occasional bedouin shaykh. Most of these individuals had been installed by the Saudis, or had found their preexisting local authority recognized in exchange for fidelity to the new order. Najdi historians were undoubtedly aware of the social hierarchies that prevailed within central Arabian society, hierarchies that were documented in sometimes great detail by Western travelers from the eighteenth century onward. Yet the chroniclers rarely acknowledged subordinate groups, for example, religious minorities, women, or non-tribals. Chroniclers such as Ibn Ghannām, Ibn Bishr, and Ibn ʿĪsā conducted their work in explicit relation to the Saudi court, producing what were by and large official histories, in which subordinate groups played no significant role. The chroniclers acknowledged only those who had attained a degree of prominence and could thus be integrated as antagonists or supporting cast members in the progressive advance of Saudi-Wahhabi hegemony. Their silence on non-elite genealogies was influenced as well by societal norms that pushed the subordinate ranks of both bedouin and settled society off the pages of history. The rationale for the subordinate status of Arabia's "low-caste" types was embedded in a conception of society that rewarded independence and self-defense, and punished dependency and vulnerability. In historiographical terms, the punishment for dependency was anonymity, or the withholding of glorification.

For example, non-tribals, inhabitants of Arabia whose origins among the prominent Arabian tribes were unproven or suspect, are all but absent from the Najdi sources. They are given fleeting mention in the Najdi chronicles by Ibn ʿĪsā. In 1842, Ibn ʿĪsā explained, Sulaymān al-Ghannām, the head of the ʿUqayl merchant guild of al-ʿĀriḍ (eastern Najd), was killed in Baghdad by some inhabitants of al-Qaṣīm. "He is from the people of Thādiq, and is a non-tribal (*wa-laysa bi-qabīlī*)."[43] By contrast, when examining the writings of Western travelers in Arabia over the centuries, we find detailed information about the various strata of Arabian society. In the travel literature of the assorted Western imperial agents, missionaries, scholars, and adventurers who traversed central Arabia's sandy expanse, the picture of premodern Arabian society at once broadens and contracts. Because of Western travelers' lack of intimacy with Arabian society, genealogical information in the strict sense of information about lineages and kin groups is more limited in the Western ethnographies and travelogues than in the Najdi sources. Westerners who documented Arabian genealogies limited their concerns for the most part to the lineages of the ruling houses of Arabia. At the same time, Western travelers documented details about Arabian social hierarchies that would be excluded from a strictly genealogical conception of history, details that help inform the way considerations of lineal exclusivity emerge and interact.

GENEALOGICAL STRATIFICATION IN WESTERN TRAVELOGUES

The age of expanding European influence and control in Africa and Asia witnessed the emergence of a particular sort of ethnographic literature designed to comprehend the range of behaviors and institutions of non-Western peoples.[44] In the Middle East, this emergent genre was best exemplified in the work of the British Orientalist Edward Lane, whose *Manners and Customs of the Modern Egyptians* (1836) proved influential for subsequent generations of scholars and colonial officers.[45] Even before Lane, travelers to the Arabian Peninsula had adopted a "manners and customs" approach to the classification of ethnographic materials, though one that was tailored to the distinctive social and political circumstances of that region.[46] In keeping with their empiricist orientations, the authors of these volumes aimed to comprehend the full range of Arabian social and cultural life, leaving no stone unturned. As such, Western travelers noted the presence of social groups about whom the Najdi sources were largely silent: slaves, non-tribals, women, youth, and others.

Significantly, the descriptions of social stratification in eighteenth- and nineteenth-century Arabia captured by these Western travelers constitute the only documented points of access to contemporary central Arabian attitudes and beliefs. As crucial as their observations are, we must at the same time acknowledge that Western travelers did not arrive as innocents in Arabia or as empty conduits for the objective transmission of information. They were often highly trained Arabists, missionaries, diplomats, surveyors, and many, including their most expert representative, the Czech Orientalist Alois Musil (d. 1944), were employed by European governments. Western travelers thus approached Arabia with an interested gaze, and the richness of their ethnographies or ethnographic-like descriptions is often subverted by their evident religious, national, or ethnic prejudices.

For the most part, Western travelers documented a high degree of stratification in Arabian society. In part, this reflected their sense that Arabia's bedouin and settler populations had hardly changed since Biblical times, their typological positions carved immutably into the imaginations of travelers by years of religious education. The Danish explorer Carsten Niebuhr (d. 1815) considered that being among the Arabs was like being "among the old patriarchs, with whose adventures we have been so much amused in our infant days."[47] Palgrave (d. 1888) was a Jesuit priest who donned the cloth in India only a generation after the departure of his influential coreligionist and fellow ethnographer, the Abbé Dubois (d. 1848),[48] while Musil was a Roman Catholic with a doctorate in theology.[49] The extent to which the impressions of Western travelers in Arabia were influenced by their religious convictions is an interesting question, but one that need not slow us down here. Though these travelers may have exaggerated or distorted the social stratification they observed or refracted it through their own pious preconceptions, they did not invent it outright. Used judiciously, their observations allow us a view into premodern Arabian society that cannot be obtained elsewhere.

Of the segments of Arabian society documented by Western travelers, one in particular would have resonance for the development of Saudi Arabia's genealogical culture in the twentieth century. Non-tribals are discussed frequently in the Western travelogues and ethnographies. The non-tribal or subordinate status of kinship groups in Arabian history was most often the outcome of political misfortune (e.g., defeat in battle), yet was perpetuated through an ethical prohibition against marriage into non-tribal or subordinate communities. This prohibition was upheld chiefly by Arabia's bedouin tribes and town elites, who attached racial or ethnic connotations to the hierarchies they policed, connotations which filtered into the observations of many Western travelers.

The relationship between political subordination and marital status was explained by Musil:

> No member of the Eben Sha'lān kin will take to wife a daughter of the Ḥwēṭāt or Beni 'Aṭijje tribes nor allow his daughter to marry any of them. Neither the Ḥwēṭāt nor Beni 'Aṭijje are by birth equal to the Eben Sha'lān, because they paid, as late as the first half of the nineteenth century, a tax for protection, [*khuwwā*], to the despised [Sharārāt] tribe and camped with them as their [*quṣarā'*], or protected neighbors.
>
> No Rwejli dares marry a member of the [Ṣluba], [al-Ḥawāzim], al-Fhejgāt, [Sharārāt], or ['Awāzim] tribes. All these are also called [Hutaym]. They have their chiefs and their social organization, they live in tents and breed camels just like the other Bedouins, and yet they are not held in esteem. The reason is that they pay a tax for protection, [*khuwwā*]; that they are neither able to protect themselves nor gain full independence. Being thus compelled to buy the protection of the more vigorous tribes, they are not allowed to enter into blood relationship with their protectors. They are [*khuwwān*], they pay [*khuwwā*] and their sons will pay too.[50]

At the micro level, non-tribal status was often the result of an abrupt change in kinship grouping. According to custom, any fugitive who wished to escape a punishment within his tribe could flee to another tribal group's jurisdiction and take refuge there indefinitely under the protection of its leader.[51] Fearing retaliation from one's agnates or other aggrieved parties, a fugitive might continue to disguise his original kinship identity until in subsequent generations it was forgotten.

In their discussions of non-tribal status, Western travelers tended to focus on another explanation: alien racial origins. Niebuhr, among the earliest of European visitors to Arabia, referred to non-tribals as "naturalized Arabs . . . a race debased by their intermixture with other nations." He commented on the contempt felt toward them by "genuine" bedouin-origin Arabs, who "value themselves so much on the purity of their descent," particularly the elite, who are diligent about preserving their genealogies. This social distinction was reinforced by the practice of prohibiting marriage with non-tribals, though the marriage rule could be relaxed, Niebuhr observed, in cases of economic necessity.[52]

Traversing Arabia in 1862–63, Palgrave appears to have been the first Western traveler to invoke the common Najdi pejorative term for non-tribals, "'Khoḍeyreeyah' or 'Benoo-Khoḍeyr.'" While the derivation of these terms is uncertain,[53] Ḥamad al-Jāsir believed their probable root to have a racial connotation. "Al-Khuḍra in Arabic is used for black people, and most of those in this category are black, generally speaking," he wrote in an article for the National Guard magazine.[54] In a letter to an inquirer, al-Jāsir explained that while he knew of no books that explained the meaning of the term *khaḍīrī*, he believed it to connote impure skin tone, with impure understood to mean non-Arab.[55] Pigmentation, or the perception of racial difference, was, then as now, seen as an intrinsic component of the distinctions that marked Arabian genealogical categories.

Like Niebuhr before him, Palgrave identified racial mixing as the factor underlying non-tribals' subordinate status. On account of relative Arab tolerance of blackness (relative to the English),[56] Palgrave wrote, "[newly emancipated slaves of African origin] can without any difficulty give their sons and daughters to the middle or lower class of Arab families, and thus arises a new generation of mixed race . . . like their progenitors they do not readily take their place among the nobles or upper ten thousand, however they may end by doing even this in process of time."[57] Notable here is Palgrave's sense that over time, non-tribals might sublimate their subordinate status and join the ranks of the central Arabian sedentary status elite, a group for whom genealogical status within a prominent tribal line of descent was only one among several criteria of prestige.

Musil, who traveled with the Rwala bedouin of southern Syria for several decades at the beginning of the twentieth century and was a clear partisan of nomadic life, advanced nonetheless a more nuanced view of the interaction between central Arabian social groups. Discussing marital patterns, Musil considered the way once-salient racial categories had the potential to collapse under the combined weight of town anonymity and the passage of time:

> If a black slave marries a white girl, the daughter of a *ṣāneʿ* [i.e., non-tribal artisan], and their son also marries a daughter of a *ṣāneʿ* again, the third and fourth generations are quite white, and yet they do not become free, *ḥorr*, but always remain slaves, *ʿabīd*. In the settlements—especially in the cultivated regions—the origin of such whites is sometimes forgotten, but never among the Bedouins of the desert. . . .[58]

Musil's observation underscores the contrasting meaning of genealogies for bedouin and settled communities in premodern Arabian society. Settled life, he seemed to suggest, tended inherently toward forms of solidarity that devalue kinship ties. Bedouin, on the other hand, remained forever cognizant of the lineal status of those around them. In the context of modern Saudi Arabia, however, bedouin historical memory would be challenged by the obliteration of bedouinism as a sociological category and the competition for prestigious origins that would ensue in the newly constituted urban spaces of Arabia.

The impressions Western travelers left of non-tribals are notable for two reasons. First, with the exception of Musil, all ascribed non-tribal status to mixed racial or ethnic origins (though how Western travelers defined race is never quite clear). As guests of tribal leaders or bedouin-origin oasis chiefs, Western travelers would have inevitably filtered their understanding of Arabian social hierarchies through the perspective of their hosts and bedouin guides,[59] who typically belonged to the dominant status group in Arabian society, that is, politically hegemonic families and clans whose dominance was articulated in part through a rhetoric of genealogical distinction. It was the political subordination of dependent groups to these dominant tribes, slaves and their emancipated descendants included, that gave rise to ideas of nobility and baseness. From notions of inferiority, it was not a long leap to the ascribing of foreignness or alien origins to non-tribal or even tribal groups.[60] A prime example of the latter would be the Ṣluba, an Arabian nomadic group of traditionally low social rank and unknown origin believed erroneously by some to descend from the Crusaders.[61] Second, Western travelers, Palgrave and Musil in particular, documented a certain degree of mobility between the categories of non-tribal and tribal, one which, despite relatively rigid marriage prohibitions and a prominent sense of social hierarchy, reflected a degree of fluid interchange within Arabian society. This prospect for reputational mobility would be meaningful in the twentieth century when kinship networks were dispersed across the Peninsula and genealogies were transferred from oral memory stores to mass-circulated texts.

BEDOUIN IN NAJDI HISTORY

Returning to the Najdi sources, we find another social category that is largely absent from the chronicles—bedouin. Bedouin, the nomadic inhabitants of Arabia, are very much in the background of the official central Arabian histories. They appear only as enlistees, auxiliaries in local Najdi skirmishes. There is a sense that their loyalties are temporary, their attention spans for fighting short.[62] Though bedouin often preyed on sedentary economies, they lived apart from sedentary culture, and appear only incidentally in its historical register. For the most part, therefore, Arabian historians ignored bedouin genealogies. The names of bedouin tribes, sections, and leaders are referred to frequently by Ibn Bishr, Ibn ʿĪsā, and others, but no further details are provided. Only those worthy of historical documentation are noted, that is, bedouin shaykhs who led warriors in combat with or against town dwellers. Though the founding myths of central Arabia's sedentary populations often connect them back to a bedouin origin, bedouin genealogies existed in a different space from those of town dwellers, in a pre-encapsulated oral tradition.

As might be predicted, Western travelers had far more to say about bedouin genealogies than their Najdi counterparts. Niebuhr, who traveled in Arabia from 1761 to 1765, recorded one of the first Western impressions of Arabian genealogies. Interestingly, Niebuhr found that bedouin knowledge of genealogies outside of the elite ranks was limited. He expressed this point with characteristic eighteenth-century prejudicial conviction:

> The Arabs are accused of being vain, full of prejudices with respect to birth, and ridiculously attentive to records of genealogy, which they keep even for their horses. This reproach cannot affect the great body of the nation, who know not their family names, and take not the trouble of keeping a register of births. Most of those, even in the middle station of life, know not who were their grandfathers, and would often be as much at a loss to know their fathers, it if were not regulated by custom, that the son shall join his father's name with his own.[63]

Niebuhr found that while the bedouin elite preserved their genealogies, lineal prestige among the bedouin was "incommunicable."[64] That is, it inhered in every prominent family, and could not be granted or rescinded by an extrinsic entity, for example, a sovereign or state. As the bedouin of premodern Arabia were largely autonomous of state authority, the valuation of prestige was not subject to the sort of state manipulations that became a characteristic feature of twentieth-century Saudi political life.

Musil refined Niebuhr's understanding of the limits of bedouin genealogical knowledge. Musil's ethnography was grounded in philology, and it was in the context of explaining the parameters of the bedouin concept of *ahl* (family or kin) that Musil articulated his view on bedouin genealogies. Musil reckoned that a bedouin maintained first-hand knowledge of his lineal ascendants up to his great-grandfather and out to his second cousin. Beyond these parameters, no obligation to protect one's kin existed, so genealogical knowledge quickly tapered off. "This conception of the kin explains why every Bedouin knows his great grandfather, whereas of his great-great-grandfather he is likely to be absolutely ignorant." [65]

Though of little interest to him, Musil had struck upon one of the most profound problems confronting Arabian genealogies in their transition from the oral register to the textual domain. As Musil implied, bedouin genealogical knowledge was of two kinds: practical knowledge, encompassing the living kinship collective and its recently deceased forebears, narrowly defined; and historical knowledge, encompassing the collective's mythic ancestor and the lore associated with his or her root clan.[66] There was the great-grandfather's clan, the smallest and most proximal kinship unit, and the Rwala root, the largest and temporally most distant. It is here that Musil's observations about bedouin lineages leave off, as do most tribal histories.[67] Yet how did these two unlike and distant nodes of a lineage combine? What were the intermediate linkages, the tribal branches and subbranches, by which they were joined? Such questions, which would prove central to Saudis investigating their lineages in the late twentieth century, had no salience in a bedouin society founded on trust, reciprocal obligation, and oral communication.[68] Intervening generations of pure-blooded relatives, joined via unilineal descent, were assumed to have produced the circumstances of existence; no further knowledge about these intervening generations was available or required.[69]

This opaqueness in the intervening generations of the mimetic lineage chart could lend itself to manipulation. As in most other societies, selective historical amnesia about the precise delineation of the bedouin kinship group could serve strategic ends. Musil recorded an example of this tendency in a remark—which he heard often among Rwala bedouin—that expressed skepticism about the genealogical position of a putative cousin: "His ancestor was not, at a remote period, our relation on the father's side; how could he now be our paternal cousin?"[70] Even more pronounced was a practice Musil documented whereby tribal leaders would establish fictive bonds of blood kinship between one another's clans, formalized in the expression: "Between us and you there shall continue the friendship of kinsmen as between kinsmen related by blood."[71] These facts demonstrate further that bedouin tribesmen distinguished between real and fictive kinship, that genealogy was not purely a form of received wisdom, but a craft requiring cultivation and refinement.

These perpetual refinements of genealogical knowledge were intrinsic to the process of combination and bifurcation that had characterized tribal affiliation throughout history; they were, in fact, its techniques. It was only when genealogies were textualized that the lacunae of the intermediate generations could be imagined, and doubts about genealogical authenticity could begin to surface. This was especially the case for long-settled town dwellers, *ḥaḍar*, whose origins were always suspect to bedouin and their recently sedentarized kin. The Najdi rupture with history, the *inqiṭāʿ*, is mirrored in the spotty genealogical record, whose importance emerges only after bedouinism, and its epistemology of oral reckoning, is obliterated as a sociological category. With the settling of the bedouin and the tethering of their value systems and intrinsically unbounded stores of knowledge to a textual culture of definitions and limits, the missing intermediate linkages in many Saudi family and tribal histories came to appear as reflections of an unfinished self. For modern Saudis of sedentary origin, these holes in the genealogical record resonated as giant fissures in their own lineal histories, and induced a scramble for scraps of knowledge by which to remedy their social deficiencies.

A WAHHABI VIEW OF BEDOUINISM

We are here converging on a consideration of one of the most important relationships in premodern Arabian society, that between bedouin and settler. The dynamics of this relationship are by no means unique to Arabian society, and figure as a significant theme in a number of other Islamic societies.[72] What renders the Arabian case unusual, however, is the strength and influence of the Wahhabi movement in reconditioning bedouin lifestyles and mores over the past three centuries. The nature of interaction between these often dichotomized social groups has been examined in rich detail by Saad Sowayan and in an influential chapter by Abdulaziz Al Fahad.[73] Here, we consider this relationship in terms of the development of Saudi Arabia's modern genealogical culture. The necessity of this approach arises from the profound influence bedouin life has exercised on the Saudi genealogical imagination. As al-Juhany explains:

> The attribution of a certain Najdi settled clan or family to its respective nomadic tribe depends solely on the oral tradition preserved and transmitted by the elders of that clan or family . . . former nomads, when settled, would associate themselves with fellow settlers of their village with whom they lived all year rather than with their nomadic kin who were always on the move. Their loyalty to the tribe was exchanged for that of the town or village. The connections of the settlers with their nomadic tribes were broken. One connection that remained intact, however, was the genealogical affiliation.[74]

Genealogical affiliation was thus an element of nomadic life that was carried over into town culture, where it took on a distinctive meaning that has resonance still today. To investigate this resonance, we must look at how genealogy informed the relationship between bedouin and town dweller in Arabian history. In Saudi popular culture, the historical relationship between the bedouin and sedentary populations of Arabia is often characterized in unnuanced terms, as tending toward either mutual affection or mutual distrust. Rather than to reconsider this relationship here, it is more useful to reflect on the ideological influences that shape the way this relationship is conceived.

The proverbial bedouin contempt for settled life was captured in apt terms by Musil. The offspring of a marriage between a bedouin and a town dweller was particularly contemptible, he was informed by his Shammar tribal guides. "He shirks raids and does not like to cultivate plants."[75] For bedouin, such a union reflected a disturbance in the order of things. Arabian vernacular poetry resonates with this sense of incongruity between bedouin and settled life, most poignantly in the laments of bedouin women whose guardians had given them in marriage to town dwellers:

I want nothing to do with Dārīn,
or with Qaṭīf
or with this Ḥilla[76]
and those who dwell there

I would rather be on pure white camels,
their rope reigns bouncing
as they're faster than the ropes
the sailors hang from the ship's mast

I would rather be gathering
desert truffles from clean earth
in an empty place, the scent of
whose bounties astounds you[77]

In this ancient trope of Arabic poetry,[78] the sedentary (or coastal) life is seen to weigh heavily on the hearts of new bedouin brides:

My eyes grow old from sitting
in this village
and from tying the cows down
by their necks

greetings to the bedouin girls
who graze in the wilderness
the scent of lavender and clover
in their camel's night milk[79]

More than a reflection of personal sentiments, the poetesses' distaste for settled life expressed a collective bedouin defiance of sedentary norms, one that would persist until the sedentarization campaigns of the twentieth century and beyond.

The attitudes of town dwellers toward bedouin as captured in the Najdi historical sources are by contrast more ambivalent. One finds the requisite complaints about bedouin perfidy and rapaciousness;[80] yet viewed through a genealogical lens, the sources convey as well a sense of bedouinness as a pristine virtue, to be tapped by town dwellers via narratives of shared origins. Illustrating this point is the origin narrative embedded in *Tārīkh Ibn Laʿbūn*. *Tārīkh Ibn Laʿbūn* is the earliest significant genealogical volume in central Arabia. Ibn Laʿbūn (d. 1844) was asked by his wealthy cousin to compose a work that would establish and preserve the lineage of their family,[81] the Āl Mudlij, Najdi town dwellers of ʿAnaza tribal extraction. The story of the Āl Mudlij, and how the family's founding ancestor, Mudlij, acquired his name, takes place in the town of Ushayqir. Ḥusayn Abū ʿAlī, a prominent Ushayqir farmer ("the first ancestor known by name to us," Ibn Laʿbūn wrote), provided hospitality to a group of bedouin of the Āl Mughīra tribe and their leader Mudlij,[82] who had encamped near Ushayqir after raiding a large caravan. As a reward for his generosity, the bedouin leader left Abū ʿAlī with a large share of the spoils. Impressed by Mudlij's actions, Abū ʿAlī and his wife named their son after him, and the Āl or "family of" Mudlij was thus born.[83]

The origin narrative presented by Ibn Laʿbūn reflects first a desire to tap some of the martial virtue associated with the bedouin through appropriation of a bedouin name. More generally, the narrative is grounded in a harmonious depiction of bedouin-*ḥaḍar* relations, despite the violent context of tribal raiding in which it is embedded. This point is significant, as tribal raiding was, after famine, the principal threat to settled life. Implied in the narrative is a system of reciprocity and exchange that helped stabilize relations between bedouin and town dwellers.[84] As will be demonstrated, this position is at odds with the emergent Wahhabi narrative of bedouinism, which brooked no such notion of equality between settler and bedouin. Ibn Laʿbūn's is not a court history, and some details of his life suggest an oppositional stance to the Wahhabi-Saudi mission. For instance, the author described a flight from his hometown of Ḥarma in 1779, after its capture by ʿAbd al-ʿAzīz b. Muḥammad b. Saʿūd, who ordered some of the town's homes destroyed and date palms uprooted.[85]

By contrast, the court historian Ibn Bishr refracted his understanding of bedouin-*ḥaḍar* relations through a Saudi-Wahhabi lens. Ibn Bishr promoted the view that it was the Saudi-Wahhabi mission that brought peace to Arabia and harmony to the relationship between bedouin and settlers, as a number of modern Saudi historians have also maintained. "Under this victorious (*qāhir*) rule the bedouin and the town dwellers became like kinsmen and brothers, and greeted one another in deserts and perilous places with a 'peace be upon you my brothers'. . . ."[86] This reconciliation transpired on account of the religious ethic that underpinned the Wahhabi mission, he seemed to believe. Interaction between the two principal groups in Najd could be legitimated on religious grounds alone.[87]

Najdi religious scholars beginning with Muḥammad b. ʿAbd al-Wahhāb were less sanguine than Ibn Laʿbūn about the organic harmony of Najdi society. Ibn ʿAbd al-Wahhāb saw bedouin recalcitrance, which he described as irreligious beliefs and practices, as the primary threat to his mission. Addressing his archrival Ibn Suhaym, whom he perceived as being overly tolerant of the bedouins' half-hearted religiosity, Ibn ʿAbd al-Wahhāb sketched a portrait of a sedentary Arabian civilization under siege by an inchoate and unruly dark matter:

> It is well-known that the people of our land [i.e., Najd] and the land of Hijaz who deny the Prophetic mission are greater than the number of those who affirm it, and those who know the faith are less than those who are unaware of it, and those who forego the prayers are more numerous than those who adhere to them, and those who prohibit the payment of *zakāt* more numerous than those who support it. . . . If ʿAnaza and Āl Ẓafīr and their likes from among the bedouin are the greater part of the population (*al-sawād al-aʿẓam*), and it has been the experience of yourself and your father that their adherence to the faith has been good, then show this to us.[88]

Ibn ʿAbd al-Wahhāb saw the bedouin threat as deriving from their noncommittal or even hostile relationship to the religious values of settled life:

> Everyone, both distinguished and common, knows about the situation of the bedouin, or at least most of the bedouin, as pertains to their beliefs. Even the obstinate and stubborn person would be unable to claim that the ʿAnaza, Āl Ẓafīr, and their likes, both their prominent sections and their followers, believe firmly in the Prophetic mission and have no doubts about it. He cannot say that they acknowledge that God's Book is with the town dwellers and have embraced it. They follow the innovations of their ancestors (*mā aḥdatha ābāʾuhum*) which they label the truth, preferring this so-called truth to God's law.[89]

Ibn ʿAbd al-Wahhāb's sense that the bedouin were once true Muslims who had been led astray by their ancestors is captured in his use of the fourth form of the Arabic root *ḥ-d-th*, meaning "to do something in a new way."[90] For the founder of Wahhabism, deviation from a once-perfected state is the only conceivable teleology of bedouinism. Ibn ʿAbd al-Wahhāb could never concede what Ibn Laʿbūn had implied, that the value system of the bedouin derived from its own coherent and legitimate basis.

The disciplining of the bedouin via Wahhabi textual culture became more sophisticated in the nineteenth century, even as the legal mechanisms instituted for this purpose were required to bend to the realities of bedouin social systems. Al Fahad discusses the introduction by nineteenth-century Wahhabi scholars of a legal principle of collective responsibility for crimes committed by individual members of bedouin tribes. "Collective responsibility would be the only way to ensure the application of the law through which security could be achieved," one prominent descendant of Muḥammad b. ʿAbd al-Wahhāb reasoned.[91] For the Rashidi dynasty of Ḥāʾil, which was the main rival to Saudi-Wahhabi authority in late nineteenth-century central Arabia, the strongly genealogical basis for state legitimacy ensured no such strict legal or conceptual separation between the sedentary al-Rashīd oasis leaders and their Shammar bedouin cousins and subjects.[92] Comparing Saudi-Wahhabi and Rashidi sedentary attitudes toward the bedouin underscores the role of *daʿwa* or missionizing creed in distilling the contrasts between these modes of life, while serving equally as a caution against presuming the inevitability of any single bedouin-sedentary dynamic.

Moving to the twentieth century, one finds echoes of Muḥammad b. ʿAbd al-Wahhāb's concerns about the bedouin in the writings of Wahhabi scholar Sulaymān b. Saḥmān (d. 1930). At his time of writing (1926/7), Wahhabism had become ascendant vis-à-vis the bedouin population, and its ʿulamāʾ expressed themselves with greater confidence. The bedouin value system of old was no longer a distinctive threat, as its legitimacy had been eroded substantially by forced sedentarization and prolonged interaction with the new literate order. The threat now arose from the excess of zeal with which the bedouin had absorbed their indoctrination at the hands of several centuries of Wahhabi scholars.[93]

In a series of responsa (*fatāwā*) published during the Ikhwān revolt of the 1920s, Ibn Saḥmān looked to temper the zeal of Ibn Saʿūd's tribal militias by reorienting their understanding of their religious obligations. Repeatedly, one finds the scholar denying the classificatory distinction between bedouin and town dweller. Before the Wahhabi *daʿwa* (mission), he explained, all of the inhabitants of Najd, bedouin and *ḥaḍar*, were guilty of unbelief (*kufr*), the *ḥaḍar* on account of their Sufism, worship of trees, and alcohol consumption, the bedouin because of their propensity toward theft and violence. Bedouin and *ḥaḍar*, therefore, are not legitimate categories, the only relevant distinction being between those who are "under the sovereignty of the Imam of the Believers" and those who are not.[94] By refusing to recognize a distinction between bedouin and town dweller, Ibn Saḥmān implicitly denied bedouinism a continued validity. Bedouin was a kind of pre-Islamic state of being, a pre-transitional condition.

Reflecting on whether migration to a settlement (*hijra*) was obligatory for a bedouin,[95] Ibn Saḥmān's worldview was fully revealed: "For one who is capable of asserting his faith and at the same time has immunized himself from temptation (*fitna*), migration to a settlement is something desirable but is not obligatory. Yet, who in the world is capable of this?" There, Ibn Saḥmān argued that although technically a bedouin did not have to live in a *hijra* if his faith was strong, in reality, it would be impossible for a bedouin living a nomadic lifestyle to be a correct Muslim, as he would inevitably succumb to the temptations of nomadic living, which would entail lax practice of the faith and distortion of the creed. Ibn Saḥmān's convictions regarding the destabilizing influence of the nomadic lifestyle convey most clearly a sense of the impossibility of bedouinness for Wahhabi religious scholars and the political order they represent.

A distinctive complexity of Wahhabism is that, while suppressing non-textual bedouin cultures, it at the same time provided the sole temporal framework for interpreting change in central Arabian social life, including the very process of bedouin deracination it had worked so hard to effect. Though the Wahhabis may have given short shrift to historical, literary, and philosophical studies, their introduction of a relatively uniform and temporally ordered textual culture to central Arabian society opened the way for consideration of such notions as chronology and progress. The dichotomy between pre-Wahhabi and post-Wahhabi times alluded to by Ibn Bishr,[96] which itself echoed Islam's initial rupture with the Age of Ignorance (al-Jāhiliyya) at its moment of inception, was a kind of historical sequencing that arguably prepared the grounds for chronological history. The bedouin system lacked any impetus for this sequencing, as, in part, no disciplining and temporalizing religious dogma had overtaken it. And yet, if Wahhabism brought the bedouin into history, they did not arrive as a clean slate.

LIVING THE (LINEAL) GOOD LIFE

Through the efforts of Muḥammad b. ʿAbd al-Wahhāb, Sulaymān b. Saḥmān, and the myriad of *muṭawwaʿūn* who were dispatched to bedouin communities over the centuries, the threat of bedouin tribal knowledge systems was gradually eroded. Oral culture was subdued and repurposed for a textual world, and sedentarism became synonymous with ethical living. As Ibn ʿAbd al-Wahhāb implied, to be settled was to be receptive to God's book, and to accept the teachings of the book was to be good and wise. The formation of this virtuous sedentary society in central Arabia, modeled on the Prophet's own experiences in Mecca and Medina, should by its own logic have entailed the subordination of narrow kinship ties to the broader interests of the newly formed ethical community of penitent Wahhabi Muslims. Yet the integral place of genealogical knowledge and identity in the lives of the bedouin, and, to a lesser though still potent extent, among town dwellers as well, complicated the workings of this new ethical dispensation.

For reasons both historical and political, there was one virtue of the bedouin past that was preserved and revered, one symbolic holdout from that precondition of settled life, genealogical knowledge and affiliation. Of the elements of the bedouin ethos—syncretic religious belief, an economy built on transience and raiding, to name a few—only genealogical consciousness survived into the modern age relatively intact as a dimension of culture that escaped traditional Saudi-Wahhabi reconditioning. Genealogical awareness was bequeathed by the bedouin to the settled communities of Arabia, who together brought an acute consciousness of kinship systems with them into the modern period. Today, the genealogical ethic is wedded to the Wahhabi ethic in the moral calculus of the Saudi citizen, but at the same time subverts it.

As a moral category, sedentarism in central Arabia was complicated by the taxonomical power of the genealogical vision of society, which distributed status unequally throughout the population. Under the dual influence of Wahhabism and this genealogical vision, being a full Saudi citizen came to mean being a proper Muslim, but also, being an Arab of *aṣīl* (pure) Arabian tribal roots. As will be demonstrated in subsequent chapters, by the late twentieth century, seeking tribal roots came to be synonymous with looking to complete one's moral position. This complication induced a scramble to achieve genealogical distinction and differentiation that would preoccupy a substantial portion of the Saudi population to this day.

THE BEGINNINGS OF MODERN GENEALOGICAL CULTURE

In their volume *Muslim Politics*, Dale F. Eickelman and James Piscatori discuss some of the key aspects of the objectification of religious consciousness in the modern Muslim world. An objectified notion of religion, they argue, is one in which a religious system, ceasing to monopolize the moral imagination,[97] is abstracted such that it is distinguishable from and comparable to other belief systems, and becomes a subject of conscious reflection and debate as opposed to an unexamined facet of consciousness and quotidian practice.[98] Transposing the notion of objectification to Arabian genealogies is useful, as it provides a conceptual apparatus for making sense of the shifting nature of genealogical consciousness in twentieth-century Saudi Arabia, and arguably other parts of the Middle East.

As noted above, genealogical consciousness had long been embedded in the broader cultural, religious, and political complex of central Arabian society. Yet the appearance of lineage as a glorified or coveted facet of Saudi national identity correlates with the emergence of a new form of genealogical consciousness in the modern period, an objectified genealogical culture rooted in declarative texts and authoritative documents. One important indicator of this development is the waning of nomadism as a sociological category and the glorification of the bedouin ideal as a symbol of Arabian heritage to be preserved in text, a phenomenon observable in the writings of Ḥamad al-Jāsir. A second indicator is the emergence of non-tribals as an explicit category of reflection in Saudi genealogical publications. A third indicator is the entry of skepticism about the tribal origins of Saudi citizens into the genealogical record. The emergent features of modern Saudi genealogical culture outlined here are discernible in the work of Saudi genealogist Ḥamad al-Ḥuqayl (d. 2008).

Ḥamad al-Ḥuqayl was born in 1919 in the Najdi town of al-Majmaʿa. Like many promising Najdi students of his generation, Ḥamad al-Jāsir included, al-Ḥuqayl was sent to Mecca as a young man to pursue his education. Trained there as a religious scholar, al-Ḥuqayl pursued a lengthy career as a judge in various Najdi towns, where he interacted frequently with bedouin and was influenced profoundly by bedouin culture.[99] Judges such as al-Ḥuqayl and Muḥammad al-Bayz (Ibn ʿĪsā's student) were often called upon to adjudicate disputes over land use and grazing rights between bedouin and *ḥaḍar*; familiarity with tribal genealogies would thus have been an intrinsic component of their job functions. Al-Ḥuqayl produced several influential volumes on the history, oral literature, and genealogy of Saudi Arabia, the most important of which was his *Kanz al-Ansāb* (*The Treasure of Lineages*).

While not the first modern work on central Arabian genealogies, Ḥuqayl's *Kanz al-Ansāb* was one of the most popular and, prior to the entry of Ḥamad al-Jāsir into the field, certainly the most significant. Published first in 1967 and now in its fifteenth edition, *Kanz al-Ansāb* prefigured the modern genealogical culture of Saudi Arabia in a number of ways. First, it was an early example of the textualizing of the tribal ethos. If in the era preceding the oil age, the Saudi state and its religious establishment saw the need to stamp out the bedouin ethos, its relegation to the margins of society activated a desire to revive the idea of the tribe as a symbol of heritage and authenticity. Yet as Jörg Determann has shown,[100] and as al-Ḥuqayl's work reveals, modern articulations of tribal pride tend not to be opposed to the Saudi-Wahhabi narrative of history, but are instead woven into expressions of fealty to state and regime.

While *Kanz al-Ansāb* is ostensibly an index of the genealogies and oral poetry of Saudi tribes, a substantial portion of its content is dedicated to information about the ʿAnaza, al-Ḥuqayl's tribe. Al-Ḥuqayl devoted a lengthy section to proving the descent of the ruling Āl Saʿūd family from the ʿAnaza tribe, a matter of some dispute in the Najdi historical records.[101] It is on this basis that he boasted of the ʿAnaza tribe's roster of distinguished members, who included "kings, princes, notables and warriors, courageous men, judges, poets and extraordinary people."[102] Al-Ḥuqayl concluded the section on ʿAnaza with a discussion of the tribe's extensive control over central Arabian territories in previous centuries.[103] There was nothing wrong with making maximalist historical claims on behalf of his bedouin tribe of origin in this passage, for if the Āl Saʿūd were ʿAnaza, then al-Ḥuqayl was not opposing the state with his pronouncements, but in fact glorifying it.

Second, al-Ḥuqayl's *Kanz* articulated an aggressive concept of tribal identity that was grounded both in religious discourse and Arab nationalist ideology, a conception whose obverse was expressed for the first time in the explicit disparagement of non-Arab origins. Al-Ḥuqayl's approach was anticipated in an earlier genealogical volume, *al-Muntakhab*, by ʿAbd al-Raḥmān b. Ḥamad al-Mughīrī (d. 1945). Al-Mughīrī, who grew up in a northern Najdi town along the pilgrimage route to Mecca and whose interest in genealogy was said to have derived from his encounters with the diverse persons passing through there,[104] explained that it was the prodding of others that led him to compose a work on the lineal origins of the Arabs. In apologetic mode, al-Mughīrī began his volume by extolling the virtues of documenting lineages, justifying his interest by quoting several Traditions of the Prophet as well as verse 49:13 of the Quran: "O people, verily, we have created you male and female, and made you peoples and tribes, so that you may come to know one another."

The need to justify an interest in the study of genealogies reflected the longstanding distaste of many Muslim religious scholars for the discipline of genealogy. This distaste extended back to the influential jurist Aḥmad b. Ḥanbal (d. 855), who was said to have despised the prominent ninth-century genealogist Hishām Ibn al-Kalbī for his favoring of genealogical and historical narratives over Prophetic Traditions (Hadith).[105] Al-Mughīrī worked to deflect this distaste in a manner novel to the tradition of genealogical documentation in central Arabia. It was novel first because of its appeal to Quranic evidence, something no previous Najdi genealogist felt it necessary to do.[106] Al-Mughīrī's defense was unique as well because it pivoted explicitly toward another category of detractor, those of presumably impure Arab stock. "Some witty people have said 'if you see a man who despises [the study of] lineage, know that his lineage is polluted by non-Arab blood.'"[107]

It is with the twentieth-century genealogists that the invisible ranks of Arabian society begin to enter the scene. If al-Mughīrī's reference to these ranks was oblique, al-Ḥuqayl addressed them directly in his *Kanz*. After noting the presence of subordinate tribes in Arabia, who were incapable of defending themselves and so sought protection from feared and formidable bedouin tribal confederations such as ʿAnaza and Shammar, al-Ḥuqayl stated:

> There are also in the Arabian Peninsula groups from within the social structure including *mawālī* [i.e., descendants of slaves] and those referred to by the Arabs as Banī Khuḍayr, who are present in every region. Some of them cannot trace their roots to an Arab racial element (*ʿunṣur ʿarabī*). Despite this, some of them participate in society, have become prominent, and have important positions in government and commerce. It isn't implausible that some of them, as they say, descend from Arab origins, but circumstances compelled them such that they declined in social rank by marrying a person who could not trace their descent to an Arab racial element, and they came to be judged as one of them. . . .[108]

Though al-Ḥuqayl adopted a tone of genealogical ecumenism in speculating about the roots of non-tribal Saudis (*mawālī* and Banī Khuḍayr), his acute sense of Arab preference was expressed elsewhere in the text. Only "refuse from the castoffs of nations," that is, those of impure stock, would deny Arab preference, he wrote, striking the same note as al-Mughīrī did a generation or two before him.[109] Arab preference, he explained, was embedded in the Arab tradition of marrying only those of pure Arab tribal origin, a concept enshrined in Islamic law under the rubric *al-kafāʾa fī l-nasab* (lineal compatibility in marriage). With al-Ḥuqayl's *Kanz*, the social categories so long invisible to Najdi historiography had crept onto the page, albeit as objects of disparagement or pity.

Lastly and most significantly, al-Ḥuqayl's *Kanz* reflected the fragmented nature of modern genealogical knowledge, and the entry of skepticism about the lineal origins of specific families into the documented record. As noted, al-Ḥuqayl devoted a good deal of space in his *Kanz* to detailing information about his own tribe, ʿAnaza. This would not be unexpected of a *nassāba*, or genealogist, whose traditional role was to preserve knowledge of genealogical relations extending outward from his own kinship group toward the increasingly opaque terrain of collateral relations and, ultimately, unrelated tribes. The textualizing of genealogies in al-Ḥuqayl's *Kanz* encapsulates this sense of the subjective nature of genealogical knowledge. About the affiliations of assorted families and branches with ʿAnaza al-Ḥuqayl had no doubts. It was only with respect to other tribes where the limits of his knowledge were felt, and a hint of skepticism about genealogical affiliation entered the record. Discussing the origins of an ʿAnaza tribal branch, al-Ḥuqayl noted: "The Āl Ṣuḥaym—in al-Majmaʿa, Manfūḥa, and Riyadh. Al-Ṣuḥaym is a branch of al-Qamaṣa, of al-Sabʿ al-Buṭaynāt, of ʿUbayd, of ʿAnaza. They live east of Ḥimṣ. There is [also] an Āl Ṣuḥaym who *claim* that they are from the Suḥama from Qaḥṭān [i.e., a southern Saudi tribe]."[110]

Al-Ḥuqayl's *Kanz* marked a shift in the textualizing of knowledge about genealogies in Arabia. Mass education and mass communication, those drivers of the objectification of culture identified by Eickelman and Piscatori, at once empowered the Ḥuqayls and al-Jāsirs of the world, and undermined their claims to authority. Mass culture empowered them because it gave them mass literate audiences for their writings, as well as the capacity to reproduce and circulate their publications in ways never before imagined. With the emergence in the 1950s of a public elementary school system and a nascent press culture, central Arabian society would be reconstituted around increasing textual literacy, and would witness the growth of a relatively unified field of intellectuals engaged in reflection and debate over the nature of modern religious and national life. With al-Ḥuqayl's *Kanz*, and more definitively with Ḥamad al-Jāsir's project, genealogy would become an integral component of this new textual tradition. In picking up their pens, modern Saudi genealogists were responding to the symbolic needs of a new class of social strivers and climbers, and their popularity only increased as the inpouring of oil wealth intensified. Yet sharing the stage with al-Ḥuqayl and al-Jāsir were now countless genealogical agents—guardians of their families' reputations—whose claims to lineal distinctiveness had to be accounted for in any documented reckoning of tribal genealogies.

By the late twentieth century, authoritative and localized genealogical knowledge of the sort advanced by Ibn Laʿbūn or Ibn ʿĪsā was becoming increasingly difficult to produce. The kinship networks documented in the works of al-Ḥuqayl and later al-Jāsir had been dispersed throughout the Peninsula. Successive land reforms by the Saudi state had wrested grazing lands away from their nomadic claimants, foisting a novel form of mobility onto a new category of bedouin laborer, who in the post-World War Two period would be integrated with long-settled *ḥaḍar* into a rapidly developing national labor market.[111] Al-Ḥuqayl's own professional biography, which saw him appointed to judicial positions in towns throughout central Arabia, attests to this fact. The entry of skepticism into the genealogical record was exacerbated by this dispersion of populations throughout the kingdom, and by the expansion of the genealogical field beyond the competencies of local knowledge.

"With the establishment of security and the spread of knowledge in this flourishing Saudi era, everyone has gone back to search for his roots and find the sections missing from his history (*mā inqaṭaʿa min tārīkhihi*)," wrote one genealogical inquirer to Ḥamad al-Jāsir.[112] By the age of al-Ḥuqayl and al-Jāsir, the genealogical field had been opened up to the inputs of geographically dispersed citizen claimants, on whose local authority the credibility of the scholars' texts came to depend. For al-Ḥuqayl, to say that a family "claimed" affiliation with a particular tribe was to hedge against these new circumstances of genealogical uncertainty. After all, while the new citizen genealogists had definite ideas about their tribal origins, the authority of their convictions often terminated at their own doorsteps. Lest it be imagined that genealogical uncertainty was a condition unique to the new genealogical agents found in al-Ḥuqayl's *Kanz*, the case of the lineage of the ruling Āl Saʿūd family helps clarify matters.

There is little agreement in the historical sources concerning the origins of the Āl Saʿūd family. Two dominant narratives exist, however: one local and Najdi, the other foreign in origin but earlier in time. Early Najdi sources such as Ibn Laʿbūn and Ibn Bishr ascribed the Āl Saʿūd lineage to Banū Ḥanīfa, a sedentary tribe from the Wādī Ḥanīfa area of Najd, home to the old Saudi capital al-Dirʿiyya. Ibn Bishr relied on an oral tradition that ascribed the Āl Saʿūd to this origin, though he was evidently uncertain about its veracity.[113] Ibn Laʿbūn stated that the Āl Saʿūd were remnants of a family later interpreted as belonging to Banī Ḥanīfa, who had displaced the ʿĀʾidh,[114] one of the old Najdi nomadic groups described by al-Juhany as being dominant in central Arabia until the eighteenth century. As al-Juhany points out further, the final mention of the ʿĀʾidh bedouin in the Najdi sources is the end of the seventeenth century, when they were eclipsed by newer nomadic elements such as ʿAnaza.[115]

Burckhardt, who recorded his findings around 1815 but who failed to visit central Arabia, preserved the earliest known textual conjecture concerning the Āl Saʿūd's origins. Burckhardt claimed that the Āl Saʿūd descended from a branch of ʿAnaza.[116] It is worth noting that ʿAnaza and al-Ẓafīr were the bedouin tribes mentioned explicitly by Muḥammad b. ʿAbd al-Wahhāb in several of his letters, as these tribes constituted the dominant central Arabian nomadic powers at the time of the Saudi-Wahhabi mission (the middle of the eighteenth century). That the Āl Saʿūd might have claimed an ʿAnaza origin in the eighteenth century is therefore unsurprising; doing so could have helped legitimate them in the estimation of one of the greatest threats to their authority.[117]

The political implications of the disagreement over the Āl Saʿūd's lineage will be revisited in the concluding chapter. It is sufficient here to acknowledge the basic incongruity at the very top of the Arabian genealogical pyramid, an incongruity that is emblematic of the entire genealogical enterprise. If the Āl Saʿūd, the dominant ideological and political force in modern Arabian history, have failed to produce a unified narrative of their origins, then the flux to be observed in the genealogical life of the Saudi everyman is hardly surprising. This conclusion emerges most cogently in the next three chapters, where we turn to Ḥamad al-Jāsir's genealogical project and what it reveals about the nature of social contestation in the modern kingdom.

CHAPTER THREE

The Oracle of al-Wurūd: Ḥamad al-Jāsir's Genealogical Correspondence

One looking to learn of a lineage
who's stuck in the muck of the matter
or some such perplexing connection
unsure where to exit or enter
To him I say, quit their conjecture
and find what you seek with al-Jāsir
You'll get from him what you'd expected
some word of your lost ancestors

—*Epigram for Ḥamad al-Jāsir*[1]

One summer afternoon in the early 1980s, in the Malazz neighborhood of what was then the new Riyadh, a man knocked on the door of Ḥamad al-Jāsir's home. It was around 2:30 p.m. Al-Jāsir had just finished eating lunch with his family, and was sitting in the sun. His daughter's husband opened the door, and the man who had been waiting said: "I would like to meet with Shaykh Ḥamad al-Jāsir about a very important issue." "He's tired, he's an old man," his son-in-law replied. "But I need to ask him a question. I received a proposal [for my daughter's hand], and gave my word [to the groom's father]. Then, I learned that I am marrying into a family that has a problem. This family—to which tribe do they belong?"[2]

During the final quarter-century of his life, Ḥamad al-Jāsir's fame as the kingdom's reigning genealogical authority would spread throughout Saudi society, eclipsing the numerous other personae (newsman, historian, geographer) the scholar cultivated during his lifetime. This unexpected afternoon visit would be the first of hundreds like it over the next several decades. By foot and by telephone, by letter and by fax, Saudis from every corner of the kingdom would reach out to al-Jāsir and press him for insights into their genealogical condition. In the twilight years of his life, as the proprietor of the kingdom's genealogical journal of record, *al-ʿArab*, al-Jāsir became something of an oracular figure, to whom Saudis young and old would turn for information about their families and tribes, hoping that he might unlock the puzzle of their identities, validate their social origins, or determine whether they were originally of tribal or non-tribal stock.

"I live in near isolation from the society that surrounds me," he informed one correspondent in 1994.[3] Yet from the confines of his high-walled villa abutting three residential streets in the al-Wurūd neighborhood of north Riyadh, al-Jāsir would preside over a genealogical awakening in the kingdom whose emerging contours were both unfamiliar and unprecedented. This chapter investigates Ḥamad al-Jāsir's genealogical correspondence, treating his letters as an entryway into the modern genealogical culture of Saudi Arabia, which emerged in the 1970s and has continued to develop into the present day. It examines the effort by Saudis of sedentary background to affirm their tribal origins against a bleak historiographical landscape; the role played by al-Jāsir's publications in this process of affirmation; how oral and textual authority are harnessed to affirm or deny genealogical claims; and, finally, the influence of the Saudi state as the final arbiter of genealogical legitimacy.

By the standards of the Islamic scholarly tradition, al-Jāsir spent most of his life operating on a high cultural plane. Trained first as a religious scholar and judge before gravitating to geography, history, and poetry, al-Jāsir inevitably found his way to that other fixture of the classical repertoire, genealogy (*al-ansāb*). In pursuit of comprehensiveness within the Islamic scholarly mode, though, the Scholar of the Arabian Peninsula dipped unexpectedly into the realm of popular cultural mythmaking concerning tribal roots and origins. This was an ironic turn for a man who styled himself at times as the scourge of linguistic and cultural syncretism—a bulwark of Arab classicism who opened the floodgates of popular genealogical culture in his country. Proceeding, as he believed, along the trail blazed by the ancient Arab genealogists—Ibn al-Kalbī, Ibn Ḥazm, al-Balādhurī—his genealogical project returned him instead to the realm of popular culture, where recourse to the textual authority of classical scholarship would serve as a feeble defense against the onrush of popular emotions and kinship-related assertions.

The locus of this commingling of "high" and "low" cultures, of the Islamic scholarly tradition with the popular lore surrounding Arabian tribal genealogies, was al-Jāsir's journal, *al-ʿArab*. It was within the pages of *al-ʿArab* that the modern Saudi genealogical conversation first began to take shape and that the genealogical conundrums articulated in thousands of letters to the scholar across three decades found their original motive force. Interspersed

Figure 3.1. Ḥamad al-Jāsir's home, al-Wurūd neighborhood in north Riyadh. Courtesy of author.

among *al-ʿArab*'s historical essays and serialized excerpts of publications forthcoming from his press, al-Jāsir would feature articles on tribal and family genealogies. It was this content, and the responses from readers it engendered, that constituted the materials out of which would emerge his two best-known genealogical volumes, the *Muʿjam Qabāʾil al-Mamlaka al-ʿArabiyya al-Saʿūdiyya* (*A Dictionary of the Tribes of the Kingdom of Saudi Arabia*) and the *Jamharat Ansāb al-Usar al-Mutaḥaḍḍira fī Najd* (*The Preponderance of the Lineages of the Settled Families of Najd*). Increasingly, the section he devoted to readers' letters, "With the Readers in their Questions and Comments," became a stage for debating these articles and subsequent monographs, where correctives to correctives could be issued, and barely concealed hostilities could be aired in sober scholarly tones. Below this refined surface, a new culture of genealogical inquiry and exchange was gestating, whose slapdash assemblage was finding its way to al-Jāsir's gated front door by various means.

The letters sent to *al-ʿArab*'s proprietor, particularly those left unpublished due to their personal or polemical nature, underscore the many ways in which genealogies matter in the modern kingdom. In the abstract, they attest to the oral cultural backdrop against which most genealogical claims in the kingdom are asserted. In more intimate terms, they testify to the gnawing anxieties of Saudis unsure of their own place within the genealogical matrix of the kingdom: whether they derive from tribal or non-tribal stock, whether their families are deserving of mention in al-Jāsir's genealogical volumes, whether they rank within the newly constituted hereditary nobility of the Saudi rentier state, whether they belong.

An anthropological look at the Maktabat al-ʿArab letters, and specifically the genealogical inquiries, affirmations, and denials dispatched to al-Jāsir for his expert judgment, reveals them to be a microcosm of the kingdom's diverse population.[4] The letters address, for example, affairs of state, printed on the crisp, clean, and sometimes gilded stationary of crown princes or influential ministers;[5] personal entreaties by half-educated young men, scribbled hurriedly on graph or loose leaf paper;[6] marital inquiries by Hijazi merchants, faxed to the scholar with apparent urgency;[7] testimonials by tribal leaders and elders attesting to the belonging of certain families to their tribes;[8] retractions of said testimonials by Interior Ministry officials;[9] lengthy polemics against rival genealogists accused of elevating or denigrating particular tribes or branches for suspect motives;[10] posthumous emails addressed to the Ḥamad al-Jāsir Cultural Center requesting recognition in the scholar's genealogical compendia;[11] and so forth.

Some letters are unsigned and undated, a fact to which al-Jāsir would draw sharp attention in his customary replies. Some include notes scribbled as afterthoughts, urging the scholar to refrain from publishing a letter's genealogical information in *al-ʿArab* on account of its sensitive or personal nature. Others are prefaced with requests to broadcast their claims as widely as al-Jāsir's influence would permit. There are letters written in a florid high Arabic that won al-Jāsir's praise, and others riddled with grammatical mistakes and colloquialisms for which admonishment was their author's sole reward.[12] A few letters meant for publication in *al-ʿArab* contain al-Jāsir's handwritten edits in red ink—ceremonious prefaces and codas clipped, their genealogical meat readied for publication. The letters often include the contact information of their authors: phone numbers, fax numbers, mobile numbers, and email addresses, tracing by their chronology technological changes in styles of communication.

The letters originate from Riyadh, Mecca, Medina, Jeddah, Ṭā'if, Yanbuʿ, Abhā, Dammam, Dhahran, al-Hufūf, al-Mubarraz—in short, all of the population centers of the kingdom, as well as many of its smaller towns. A number of private genealogical queries are penned on the letterhead of government ministries, reflecting the state's dominant role in the labor market, and suggesting possible uses for bureaucratic idle time. Some letters include modest hand-drawn diagrams of kinship relations intended as visual complements to family histories. Others are accompanied by elaborate genealogical trees meant to legitimate grander assertions of tribal belonging. Attached to some letters are testimonials of lineal affiliation stamped with a battery of government seals or authenticated (in lieu of a literate hand?) by a tribal elder's thumbprint. There are letters issued by sons on behalf of fathers, by individuals on behalf of tribes, by deputies on behalf of their ministries. Al-Jāsir's correspondents included high school students and middle-aged men, ministers and paupers, even the rare female inquirer. In short, the *al-ʿArab* letters provide documented entry into a deeply significant facet of Saudi society, and their contents have important implications for Saudi history, politics, and social life. They reflect significant transformations in the life of the kingdom's inhabitants, and are articulated in an idiom that possesses enduring historical resonance, a genealogical idiom. Making sense of the latter will be the objective of this chapter. To do so, we must first capture the confusion in the picture these letters present.

The sometimes bewildering disorder of modern Arabian genealogies is expressed in several letters addressed to al-Jāsir in the final years of his life. An engineering student in Riyadh contacted al-Jāsir in the year 2000 after discovering disagreement about his family's tribal affiliation across three modern genealogical texts. *Imtāʿ al-Sāmir* ("Delighting the Companion"), a now discredited volume believed to be a modern forgery, indicated that the family belonged to the Qaḥṭān tribe and originated in Sudayr, a region several hundred kilometers northwest of Riyadh. In his own *Jamhara*, al-Jāsir wrote that the family belonged originally to the Banī Ḥanīfa tribe, one of the first tribes to settle Najd. A third book, by the son of al-Jāsir's contemporary Ḥamad al-Ḥuqayl, maintained that a family by that name from the same region was affiliated with the Banī Tamīm, another long-settled tribe.[13] The discrepancies in these volumes allude to the volatility at the core of Saudi genealogical culture, where commonly accepted truths are scarce, and few authoritative texts exist to stake truth claims upon.

Similar confusion reigns in another late letter to al-Jāsir. The disagreement is here situated in the domain of oral culture, from which the aforementioned volumes are in any case not far removed. A religious scholar in Riyadh wrote al-Jāsir criticizing the *Jamhara*'s attribution of his family to the Muṭayr tribe.

In the process, the author drew attention to the extent of disagreement within his family over their lineal origins. While the author's father claimed that the family belonged to the Ẓafīr tribe, recently deceased family elders believed that the family descended from al-Saʿdūn. Meanwhile, another relative was convinced that they belonged to Shammar. "We don't know anyone who associated this family with Muṭayr lineally except your noble book [*sic*]."[14] The family's tribal history seemed to be held together by only one fact—that it was not as constituted in print by al-Jāsir.

THE *JAMHARA*

Despite a perceived misattribution of its origins, the religious scholar's family name was privileged enough to have a place in al-Jāsir's *Jamhara*. In the pre-Internet era, when monopolies on the printed word still existed,[15] the *Jamhara* played a substantial social role. First, it served as an index of the "well-known" sedentary families (*al-usar al-mashhūra/maʿrūfa*) of central Arabia, by which al-Jāsir meant families of known tribal origin that possessed a quantity of branches sufficient to root their presence in premodern Najd.[16] Such a distinction permitted the symbolic differentiation of these *aṣīl* families not only from non-tribal Saudis, but also from the hundreds of thousands of non-Saudi foreign laborers and businessmen who began pouring into the kingdom beginning in the 1960s and at an accelerated pace after the first oil boom of the 1970s. In another respect, it served to recodify a social division that Wahhabism had sought to erase, that between central Arabia's bedouin and sedentary populations. When a rare pair of bedouin-origin petitioners wrote al-Jāsir asking that their family name be included in the volume, the scholar rejected their request on the grounds that their family did not possess a critical mass of sedentary branches, as it had not been settled before the book's cut-off date, the period in the early twentieth century when the first bedouin *hujar* settlements were founded.[17] Lastly, the *Jamhara* helped delineate the range of prospective marriage partners for sedentary Najdis. Its use as a reference volume by Najdi families contemplating marriage for their children was a well-established fact of the culture. In a word, mention in the *Jamhara* was symbolic affirmation of a family's inclusion within central Arabian sedentary society, by one of its most well-placed and authoritative arbiters.

In this respect, the religious scholar's family stood on firmer ground than many of al-Jāsir's other Saudi inquirers, whose deeply opaque family histories made it unlikely that they would ever enjoy the honor of having their tribal roots authenticated in so ceremonial a fashion. These other inquirers might be termed collectively "lineage seekers," on account of their common objective in writing Ḥamad al-Jāsir, namely, to identify their *nasab*, or, lineage. Their story goes something like this:[18]

> To the Esteemed Shaykh, the Scholar of the Arabian Peninsula Ḥamad al-Jāsir,
>
> There is a question that has "nagged at me"[19] "for many years,"[20] a question that has left me "confused"[21] and "perplexed."[22] I turn to you, Shaykh Ḥamad, as "a last resort,"[23] out of "extreme necessity."[24] The question concerns "my family's belonging (*intimāʾ*)."[25] "We have lost our *nasab*,"[26] and we hope that you might "clarify for us where we came from and how we lost our origins."[27] "Your magazine is my only hope—after God—for learning about [my] family." "The absence of knowledge causes me hardship from certain people who ask, 'what is your descent (*ayn tarjaʿūn*) within [the tribe], and who is your tribal leader (*amīr*) or elder (*kabīr*) who can verify your identity (*taʿarruf bikum*)?"[28] "This has its effects upon us, no doubt, as does the difficulty we face with our children when they ask about their *nasab*."[29] "We hope from your grace the favor of helping us to know to which tribe we affiliate lineally . . . so as to eliminate confusion and the plethora of questions and difficulties we have faced in certain matters."[30]

The motion of the Maktabat al-ʿArab letters is guided by an implicit force, a dark matter of tribal belonging that determines one's place in Saudi society. To be able to claim an expansive clan identity is to be reassured of one's normalcy within the impersonal modern spaces of the kingdom, and, if fortunate, to make credible claims of belonging to the dominant status group in central Arabia—*ḥaḍar* of pure tribal origin. Without this ability, the cultural work reflected in the queries of the lineage seekers begins.

LINEAGE SEEKERS

The stories conveyed to al-Jāsir by lineage seekers trace paths of migration around and about the Arabian Peninsula. Unlike the diasporic Ḥaḍramī communities, whose lengthy and sinuous historical memories were investigated by Engseng Ho,[31] the recollections of these individuals often fall short. Allusions to internal migrations driven by assorted hardships are often the most they can muster from the collective recounting of their families. Beyond that is the *inqiṭāʿ*, the rupture in historical time that blots out their memories. The stories they tell have all the gravity and vagueness of Biblical exile plots, further underscoring the oral cultural backdrop against which they operate. The absence of definitive information is especially distressful for some of al-

Jāsir's younger inquirers, who turned to the scholar after despairing of their parents' apathy concerning their family origins, or out of frustration with the limited genealogical knowledge of their clan elders.[32] For others, the severance of the oral link upon the death of a parent or guardian meant that knowledge about their origins, or implicit comfort with the absence of such knowledge, had disappeared, and the need for compensatory reserves of social authority came to be felt acutely.[33] Working against them in their thirst for clarity is the dismaying opaqueness of history, which casts a shadow over even the most emphatic genealogical claims.

What is often affirmed in the letters is that the author's ancestor (e.g., father, grandfather, great-grandfather) was thought (or known) to have lived in a small town in the vicinity of a large population center (e.g., Riyadh, Mecca, Jeddah, Dammam). He worked as a cultivator, a merchant,[34] a craftsman, a pearl diver,[35] or a religious scholar,[36] and, at some point in the past (typically fifty to 150 years earlier) had migrated to a city where, through intermarriage or for other reasons, his lineage had become obscured. The protagonist of the lineage seekers' stories was invariably a *ḥaḍar*, a town dweller, whose descendant was now seeking by various designs to attach his ancestor to an indistinct tribal past.

Efforts by lineage seekers to deny this process of lineal dissolution and assert a pure tribal origin appear frequently within the letters. In 1995, the owner of an engineering firm in Medina wrote al-Jāsir with a question about his origins. His ancestors, he implied, were bedouin of the ʿAnaza tribe who had settled in the northwestern Hijazi oasis town of al-ʿUlā. After settling, "commerce overcame them," by which he meant that necessity drove his nomadic ancestors to adopt an economic pursuit historically stigmatized by bedouin. His father became a well-known merchant, and married into multiple well-established Hijazi tribes, he noted, marital exchange being an important legitimator of tribal origin. Alternatively, he explained, documents in his possession indicated that his family descended from the Ashrāf, or Descendants of the Prophet, of Medina. As descent in Arabia is measured in patrilineal terms,[37] the author's reach for two alternative explanations of his origins suggested confusion. Diluted on account of their bifurcation, the author's claims failed to pass muster with al-Jāsir, who replied skeptically: "it is possible that the information you presented clarifies things for you more so than for others."[38]

Other efforts to assert bedouin tribal roots by denying town origins appear in the *al-ʿArab* letters. A Saudi economist wrote al-Jāsir from Jeddah to announce his discovery, after a lengthy investigation, of the true origins of his family and its legitimate descent from the Shammar tribe.[39] He explained that the "current" surname attached to his family[40] was said by certain elders of the Shammar tribe—whom he had queried—to derive from the name of a market in the northern city of Ḥā'il. Yet this onomastic association with commercial origins could not be correct, he insisted, as "it is impossible for a man to derive his lineal affiliation from a market. . . ." Such an affiliation would be tantamount to denying the man tribal origins, a fact that was impossible by his reckoning. His unusual name was instead attributable to such factors as "sedentarization, attachment to land [i.e., agriculture], isolation from the tribe and clan, the need for sustenance, marriage, societal compulsion, as well as ignorance and forgetting." Now, he had "arrested his erring" and discovered his family's tribal origins, which were depicted in the enclosed family tree and were awaiting only al-Jāsir's blessing. Lineal affiliation to toponym,[41] to locale, town, or market, with its allusions to racial admixture and impurity, is a stigma that Saudi lineage seekers work to shake off in both the textual representation of their genealogies and in practice.

The most suspect of these toponymic affiliations, in the eyes of al-Jāsir and the Najdi culture he embodied, was the Hijazi city of Mecca. While Mecca and its sister city Medina are the birthplaces of Islam, by central Arabian standards they are the final resting grounds of genealogical purity.[42] Writing in the late nineteenth century, Dutch scholar and traveler C. Snouck Hurgronje described Mecca as partly "a town of foreigners" whose "many-tongued mass of humanity . . . feels itself there quite at home."[43] Absent from this mass was a notable central Arabian presence, about which Snouck remarked:

> It is strange how few of the natives of Central Arabia choose the town for their permanent dwelling. Those who do are almost all merchants, the rest come only as pilgrims and soon return homeward. They revere . . . the holy ground as much as any other pious Moslim . . . ; only Mekka *society* seems to them corrupt. On the holiest soil, a most unholy Babel has, according to their view, arisen.[44]

A polyglot society would naturally be genealogically diverse, making Mecca a problematic venue in which to affix pure tribal origins. This emerges in a letter to al-Jāsir by a young Meccan man resident in Jeddah. The young man wrote al-Jāsir to inquire about the likelihood of his belonging to a tribe discussed recently in *al-ʿArab*, and with whom he shared a surname. "I heard from my grandfathers that we are nomadic bedouin (*badw ruḥḥal*), and we fled from wars [in Wādī Sirḥān] to Mecca," the author stated without elaboration.[45] Al-Jāsir explained in reply that the young Jeddan had failed to provide adequate evidence for his claims of affiliation, and that "one would first need to know the village from which you came to Mecca, as numerous families from many lands migrated to Mecca, may God ennoble her."[46] The scholar's subtle pressing of the author to provide more conclusive evidence of his tribal origins resonated beyond the scope of his genealogical project to encompass long-standing Najdi skepticism regarding the Arabian origins of the populations of the Hijaz. In that respect, far from being an impartial observer, al-Jāsir's own attitudes helped reify the categories through which social stratification was to be articulated in the new Saudi Arabia.

Despite these sometimes elaborate protestations, the story of the lineage seekers was fundamentally a *ḥaḍarī*, or sedentary, one. The sedentary background of the lineage seekers is affirmed further when we consider how the quintessential embodiments of Arabian settled life, religious scholars, are represented in the *al-ʿArab* correspondence. One letter in particular stands out in this regard. It concerns a family from the Eastern Province, a member of which approached al-Jāsir to request his expertise in affirming its tribal status. The author explained:

> What caused us to lose our *nasab* is the fact that our ancestors were well-known for their deep knowledge of Islamic sciences. . . . They were well-known in Dammam, and people used to [seek their counsel] from Riyadh, and from the north, south, and west of the kingdom. . . . We went to [a shaykh] in the al-Aḥsāʾ region, and when we met him, he said "you are known to the people of the region and the scholars within it" but he didn't know our *nasab*. . . . Our elders informed us that . . . in the past, when people would ask about our *nasab*, [our forefathers] would say, "don't concern yourself with such things," before quoting the Quranic verse . . . "verily the most noble among you is the most God-fearing."[47]

That Saudi religious scholars and ritual specialists often derive from non-tribal origins is a fact firmly tied in with our story. The former Grand Mufti of the kingdom, ʿAbd al-ʿAzīz Ibn Bāz (d. 1999), was of non-tribal origin. Ibn Bāz, who was al-Jāsir's schoolmate, was taught by the Qāḍī (chief judge) of Riyadh, Saʿd al-ʿAtīq (d. 1930), whose family of prominent religious scholars, the Āl ʿAtīq, were known historically to be of non-tribal origin.[48] Social prominence, however, even of the respected religious variety, does not equate to tribal roots. There is undoubtedly a strong tension between the religious and tribal *daʿwa*'s of modern Saudi life, between the egalitarian ethic of religious communion and the particularist pull of tribal belonging. For this author from Dammam, the very act of inquiring with al-Jāsir affirmed that his ancestors' capacity to deflect uncomfortable queries about their origins with appeals to a genealogically neutral faith was no longer valid.

In letter or in spirit, al-Jāsir would himself often invoke the aforementioned Quranic verse (49:13) when wishing to draw attention away from his inability to verify a *nasab* seeker's origins. "Genealogies are among the concerns that are not founded on a sound scientific basis, and God has made them unnecessary through Islamic brotherhood . . . 'verily the most noble among you is the most God-fearing'," he informed one such inquirer.[49] In another letter, al-Jāsir praised the Āl ʿAtīq's scholarly lineage as a genealogical trump card that required no authenticating narrative of pure Arab roots, citing the following lines of a well-known poem about the family: "Ḥamad built greatness for you,[50] O Āl ʿAtīq, / not by might or nobility / but rather by knowledge, which elevates those who command it / above every man, even one whose ancestor is Muḍar [i.e., the ancient ancestor of the Arabs]."[51]

The transcendent appeal of religious solidarity is invoked frequently throughout the *al-ʿArab* genealogical correspondence. And yet, beneath the patina of religious affirmations is an undeniable compulsion on the part of al-Jāsir's correspondents to deny or sublimate their non-tribal origins. This compulsion is exercised by appealing to al-Jāsir for a form of oracular wisdom beyond that which religion can provide. This and other letters like it are therefore significant, as they demonstrate instances in which religious discourse is subordinated to the typically unspoken communal dictates of Saudi society.

DENIAL AND CONTINGENCY

Within the hard borders of the Saudi state, the soft boundaries of genealogical identity are perpetually collapsing and expanding, reflecting a true dynamism in Saudi society that is typically concealed behind the brittle rhetoric of religious exhortation and rentier economic speak. As emerges from the letters, the genealogical dictates of this society were not in any way unidirectional. Just as there are letters containing affirmations of correct lineal origins, there are letters denying the claims of others to tribal belonging. The *al-ʿArab* contributor who claimed to be a member of a subbranch of the ʿUtayba tribe and had used this pretense to assert his genealogical authority in an article for the magazine, al-Jāsir was told in one letter, was actually a former slave from al-Qaṣīm who was seeking to insinuate himself into the tribe and stir up trouble from within.[52] Some *al-ʿArab* genealogists, went another argument, worked through insidious means to undermine the reputations of well-established tribes, denying their claims to ancient continuity around a strong core branch, weakening them by emphasizing their lineal heterogeneity.[53]

In one late letter (1999), a young genealogist from ʿUnayza warned al-Jāsir against the dangers of *al-ʿArab* being co-opted by non-tribal pretenders. As observed in this excerpt, his insistence on plain and fixed truths, simple dichotomies that permanently affixed the status of Saudis as tribal or non-tribal, captured in fervently youthful tones the accumulated weight of the

Najdi social inheritance and the anxiety engendered by its public airing in al-Jāsir's novel forum:

> I hope that *al-ʿArab* returns to its brilliance and strength, and does not become a pulpit for every *nasab* claimant who wishes to prove something out of nothing. This is something I've seen beginning to infiltrate our beloved magazine of late, from people who had achieved every worldly delight and had nothing remaining to acquire apart from [tribal lineage]. They think that a seal-embossed paper from one who worshipped the *dīnār* or the *dirham* confirms the matter, and negates what is known about these claimants for long years—that they are nothing [i.e., non-tribal]. A person, a family, is not an innocent seedling that appeared suddenly, when nothing was known of it before.[54]

Such virulent affirmations of the caste-like fissures running through Saudi society testified to a broader culture of genealogical affirmation and denial emergent in the new print culture of the kingdom. Al-Jāsir was a central pivot of this culture; yet his role within it was conflicted. Unlike the *linajudo*s of seventeenth-century Seville, who were driven often by jealousy and greed to expose the impure origins of newly arrived noble families through blackmail and other nefarious means, al-Jāsir's social jiggering proceeded often by omission, by excluding families from his publications, for example, or by denying the veracity and soundness of their lineal claims. Al-Jāsir had risen from peasant farmer to join the ranks of the elite, sedentary tribal families of central Arabia, and his *Jamhara* was in many respects a defense of that order and the social privilege it hoped to maintain through the upheavals of the oil era. By promoting the study of genealogies as an interactive pursuit and a legitimate scholarly discipline, al-Jāsir helped rearticulate social distinctions between tribal and non-tribal Saudis in modern, textual terms. And yet, the genealogical method he favored privileged a particular quality that dulled the sharp edges of these boundary lines—the quality of contingency.[55]

The notion of genealogical contingency, which al-Jāsir drew in part from Ibn Khaldūn,[56] was chiefly a means of reconciling the documented legacy of early Arabian history with the divergent reality of modern Arabian society, in which very little continuity in the names of tribes, branches, and families could be observed.[57] As the scholar explained to a lineage seeker: "I don't believe that the ancient books of genealogy are useful for the lineages of contemporary families, on account of the ruptured connection (*inqiṭāʿ al-ṣila*) between these families and the times in which those books were composed."[58] Contingency explained how those originally of pure Arab tribal origin had lost their lineages,[59] and how modern Arabian tribes came to be what al-Jāsir termed "disparate thickets" (*alfāf mutafarriqa*),[60] heterogeneous collectives constituted of branches of diverse tribal origin, instead of blood kin descending from one ancestor, as was sometimes popularly imagined.[61] It was even embedded in the rhetorical tools al-Jāsir used to describe genealogical relationships. For example, as al-Jāsir noted in the introduction to his tribal dictionary (*Muʿjam Qabāʾil*), when describing the nature of the relationship of a specific clan or branch to a particular tribe, he favored the preposition *fī* ("belonging to," "part of") over *min* ("deriving from"), avoiding the latter on account of its connotation of unequivocal blood descent.[62] It was contingency that permitted an inclusivist view of Arabian genealogies to coexist with the innately particularist and potentially divisive practice of genealogical inquiry.

When a professor from the Islamic University of Medina wrote al-Jāsir to complain about the tendency of "the common people" to doubt the pure and direct descent of certain well-established branches of the Ḥarb tribe, al-Jāsir could do no better than concede their point, if for distinct reasons. To this denial of lineal purity, he asserted his well-rehearsed theory of genealogical contingency, which held that Arabian tribes "comprise a mixture of numerous branches not joined by one father, but rather, joined together under a name by way of alliance (*ḥilf*), lineage (*nasab*), adjacent residency (*al-jiwār*), and other things."[63] Notably, the absence in al-Jāsir's formulation of what David Schneider termed "a single rigid rule of recruitment" governing genealogical affiliation and his rejection of a standard of genealogical authentication based on unilineal descent in favor of an emphasis on the importance of marital exchange and geography reveal the scholar's conceptions to be aligned with prevailing understandings in anthropology today that emphasize the dynamically constructed nature of kinship identities.[64] To be sure, his was not a theory of constructedness intended to undermine a waning academic consensus, but one designed, in a sense, for sacrifice to a higher purpose, an Arab-Islamic ideology of state in which the fractious particularism of the tribe was to be ultimately dissolved and sublimated. Setting aside for a moment its grander purpose, what is clear is that al-Jāsir's theory of contingency had an important influence on those who flocked to his banner in search of prestigious lineal origins.

Al-Jāsir's theory of contingency was epitomized by the aborted third installment of his genealogical project. Its intention, as he announced in the 1981 edition of his *Jamhara*, was to "affirm the lineages of families whose *nasab* might be considered unknown, or to clarify the now-obscured lineal origins of certain families."[65] This would be the most important of his genealogical works, he speculated, and would constitute a feat of social engineering unprecedented in central Arabian history. For those waiting in the wings to intimidate him or deny him the right to attempt to reorder prevailing social hierarchies, he had this retort: ". . . fear of those characterized by [ignorance] will not impede me from the publication of this study after its completion, for it elucidates aspects of our social life that are worthy of investigation and will eliminate divisions that are objectionable to both our pure religion and our noble Arab values."[66]

Al-Jāsir's determination to proceed with his endeavor waned considerably when the full weight of the culture of genealogical denial was brought to bear on his enterprise. This culture of denial spread beyond the confines of his readership to encompass even his own claims of origination from the Ḥarb tribe.[67] Contingency was simply unpalatable within a textually biased genealogical discourse that demanded ontological certainty and, under the influence of an emergent, media-driven religious culture, tended toward absolutist conceptions of tribal identity. Criticizing the title of a volume by a young genealogist, al-Jāsir urged its author to back away from the precipice of excessive certainty and consider the shaky nature of the entire genealogical enterprise: "I wished that your book had a title other than *The Most Trustworthy Proofs [of the Lineages of Several Tribes]*. They may well be the most trustworthy proofs by the measure of what you yourself know, but they aren't the most trustworthy with respect to what those other than you may think."[68]

Having grasped boldly at the third rail of central Arabian society, al-Jāsir was unprepared for the ensuing shock. This proved a disappointment for some of his lineage-seeking readers. "Years have passed, and this study has not seen the light of day," a man from Riyadh wrote the scholar. "Myself and many others are awaiting the emergence of this study with endless patience, on account of its great importance. It is an effort that will affix [your name] throughout the generations. . . . who else can do it but you?"[69] It was the virulence of the lineage deniers, who, like their affirming counterparts, petitioned al-Jāsir by letter, fax, phone, and personal audience, that ultimately dissuaded him from pursuing his project.[70] "I saw that it would stir sensitivity in some hearts, so I left it alone."[71]

Despite the abandonment of his lineal restoration project, the conceptions that underpinned it exercised a profound effect on his readership. At the level of the individual lineage, or the unilineal descent unit, the contingency al-Jāsir proposed was interpreted by lineage seekers in relatable terms, that is, as social or economic twists of fortune. The stories outlined above capture this point well. Al-Jāsir's interpretation of Arabia's recent genealogical history gave lineage seekers hope that they might reverse the whims of chance and reclaim what had been lost to contingency by their forefathers, namely, tribal origins. In light of this contingency, the proximity of the rupture with their origins seemed tantalizingly close, discernible, explicable. Yet this same contingency, being synonymous with things unknown and unknowable, was also the basis upon which the denial of genealogical claims thrived. Those misalignments of chance invoked by al-Jāsir to account for the "correct" Arab origins of the historical inhabitants of central Arabia, were introduced contrarily by skeptics as the best evidence for denying lineage seekers the authentication they sought. "He who has lost his *nasab*, claims he is from [tribe x]," goes a popular and confusing saying in Saudi Arabia, confusing because the tribe named in the proverb is never the same. The jumble of genealogical affirmations and denials that defines the *al-ʿArab* correspondence cannot therefore be explained on the basis of this methodological nuance introduced by al-Jāsir. Rather, our attention must turn elsewhere, outside of the explicit discursive frame, to the oral cultural backdrop against which genealogical claims and denials are asserted, and to the shifting nature of genealogical authority in the modern kingdom.

RĀSHID B. ḤUMAYD'S STORY

If, as argued earlier, the story of the *nasab* seekers is a *ḥaḍar* story, it is also a paradoxical one, at least when measured against patterns of social change envisioned by theorists across continents and centuries—Ibn Khaldūn, Henry Maine, Ferdinand Tönnies, to name a few.[72] It is a story of town dwellers who, having abandoned knowledge of their lineal origins at some point in the distant past, felt themselves compelled to recover them in the modern age, an age in which tribal group feeling had purportedly given way to urban solidarity, status to contract, *Gemeinschaft* to *Gesellschaft*, and so forth. For this paradox to be unwound, for the dark matter of tribal belonging to be illuminated, we must train our focus on two divergent points: one distant, comprehending a broader swathe of *al-ʿArab* correspondents than has previously been considered; the other proximal, taking in the history of a particular individual who corresponded with Ḥamad al-Jāsir, Rāshid b. Ḥumayd. By weaving between the generalized and the particular, I hope to draw out the broader resonances of the modern Saudi genealogical story. From the lineally challenged and their challengers, therefore, we turn to Rāshid b. Ḥumayd and others like him who sought validation of their *nasab* claims from al-Jāsir, whether through inclusion in his *Jamhara* or by other means.

Al-Jāsir began to conceive of the *Jamhara* in the middle of the 1970s. The first hint of its eventual contours would appear in an advertisement on the back of the March/April 1976 issue of *al-ʿArab*, announcing the impending release of several new volumes from al-Jāsir's imprint, the al-Yamāma Press.[73] See figure 3.2.[74]

For a staid and sober scholarly journal, this marquee-like advertisement announcing the imminent decoding of the *Origins* of the tribes of the Arabian Peninsula and the *Origins* of the settled families of Najd had a very showman-like quality to it. Its implicitly curative message would not have escaped the notice of his genealogically invested readers. In September 1981, shortly after the publication of the *Jamhara*, a public servant in Riyadh by the name of

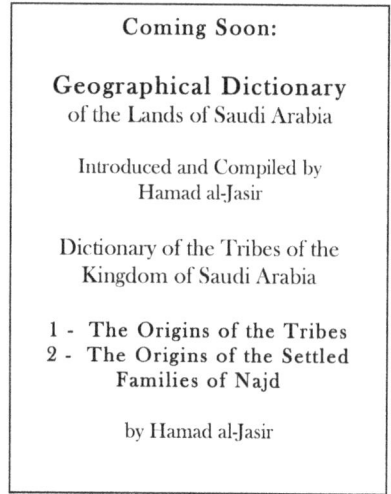

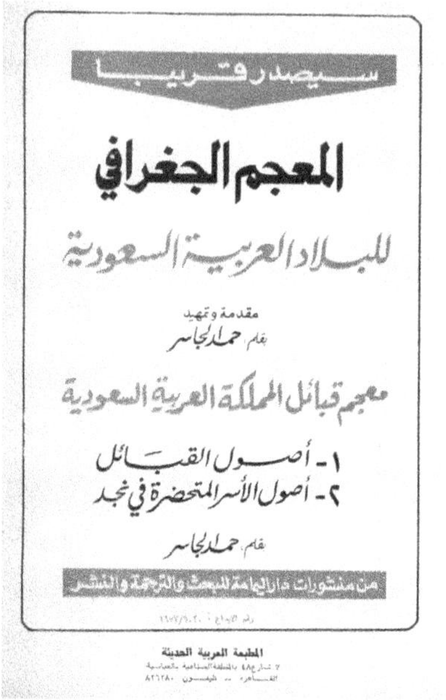
سيصدر قريبا
المعجم الجغرافي
للبلاد العربية السعودية
مقدمة وتمهيد
بقلم حمد الجاسر
معجم قبائل المملكة العربية السعودية
١- أصول القبائل
٢- أصول الأسر المتحضرة في نجد
بقلم حمد الجاسر
من منشورات دار اليمامة للبحث والترجمة والنشر
المطبعة العربية الحديثة

Coming Soon:

Geographical Dictionary
of the Lands of Saudi Arabia

Introduced and Compiled by
Hamad al-Jasir

Dictionary of the Tribes of the
Kingdom of Saudi Arabia

1 - The Origins of the Tribes
2 - The Origins of the Settled Families of Najd

by Hamad al-Jasir

Figure 3.2. *Al-ʿArab*, March/April 1976, back cover. Courtesy of Maʿan al-Jāsir.

Rāshid b. Ḥumayd wrote al-Jāsir expressing a desire to see his family's name documented in the volume. Rāshid was born in 1944 in a village outside of Sakāka, a city in northern Saudi Arabia. In 1965, he moved with his family to Riyadh, where he began a long career as a civil servant in one of the kingdom's burgeoning government ministries, while moonlighting as a prolific writer on cultural and historical affairs. His biography mirrors closely that of other modern Saudi strivers, but his effort to achieve lineal distinction stands out for its rich and prolonged resonances.

Rāshid explained to me the motivation behind his 1981 letter to Ḥamad al-Jāsir:

> We are like others . . . we are like the others, like the ones [al-Jāsir] published about [i.e., tribal-origin Najdi *ḥaḍar*]. He would say, give me any [genealogical information] you have that is new. So on the basis of this, we gave him something new. Because he requested of us [i.e., the readers of *al-ʿArab*] that we give him new and correct (*ṣaḥīḥ*) things, so we gave him what [information] we had about [our family] . . . based on his request.[75]

As early as 1969, al-Jāsir had been encouraging *al-ʿArab* readers to contribute to the public register of central Arabia's bedouin tribes and sedentary tribal families he was in the process of compiling.[76] Rāshid responded dutifully to this call—yet Rāshid had a problem. Rāshid's cousin, a Riyadh businessman with whom I became closely acquainted, explained to me the nature of this problem:

> COUSIN: Rāshid is my father's cousin. Yet we pretend that we are from another tribe, from ʿAnaza. He is from, he alleges that he is from ʿAjmān.
>
> NS: Which is interesting. So, two cousins are pretending that they are from different tribes?
>
> COUSIN: Yes. What we have is allegations. I mean, we are not sure about ʿAnaza.
>
> NS: You don't believe it?
>
> COUSIN: No.
>
> NS: But other people in your family do?
>
> COUSIN: Yes. And they don't want anybody in the family to say it is [merely] an allegation . . . they want to say it is [something] sure, sure, sure.[77]

Rāshid's problem, as his cousin explained it, was that his tribal origins were suspect. From the starting line of status determination in the new Najd, there seemed a mad dash underway, a sprint to reach the closest credible tribal affiliation and hang on for dear life, even if this meant inviting the most profound sort of contradiction, disagreement over descent among closely related kin.[78]

Though Rāshid may have desired public affirmation of his tribal origins, his attitude toward the bedouin tribal culture from which he claimed to derive was ambivalent.[79] Bedouin contempt toward settled trades and crafts, he argued in one of his published writings,[80] resulted not from their noble nomadic heritage, as the romantic notion favored by many Saudis would suggest, but out of an insecurity derived from ignorance or incapacity to master these professions. Settled life in Arabia, on the other hand, was characterized historically by a "spirit of competition," a spirit that for Rāshid foreshadowed the meritocratic, productive society he hoped the kingdom might embody: "the nations that don't care about these things [i.e., tribal lineages], that care about industry, economy, and such, have surpassed us, while we sit around and say, such-and-such, son of such-and-such, son of such-and-such," he complained to me.[81] If Rāshid was here downplaying the value of genealogical affirmation, it was because of his own difficulty in achieving it. Rāshid's embrace of modernizing ideologies makes broader sense in light of his problematic efforts to assert a place for himself as a sedentary Najdi of tribal origin. His experience, moreover, is not unique to Saudi Arabia, and can be found, for example, in the anti-tribal, Islamist and Arab Nationalist positions asserted by many of the inhabitants of the Taʿizz region of south Yemen.[82]

In reply to Rāshid's 1981 letter, al-Jāsir promised that he would include the latter's family in a subsequent edition of the *Jamhara*.[83] Yet when a revised edition with hundreds of new names appeared in 1988, Rāshid's family was not among them. Over the course of that decade, Rāshid had struck up a professional acquaintance with al-Jāsir, visiting the scholar on occasion at his home, discussing with him the fine details of northern Arabian topography, and writing articles and correctives on geographical and historical subjects for publication in *al-ʿArab*. Yet, the sting of al-Jāsir's failure to address the matter of his family's belonging clearly lingered with Rāshid, who explained:

> I requested, I requested, with respect to what concerns our family, I requested [a mention in the *Jamhara*], and nothing came of it. . . . If [al-Jāsir] had published the *Jamhara* with [all of his readers' corrections and additions] it would have been six volumes instead of two. . . . All of the people who sent responses to him had a personal connection to the material. For example, a man gives him [genealogical] information about a family [i.e., his family]. This information comes *directly* from that person. [Al-Jāsir] must accept this information and publish it. When a person gives you information [about his family's lineage], no matter who it is, he must publish it. But, God have mercy on him, he didn't publish anything or do anything.[84]

Twelve years passed from the date of Rāshid's first letter. In December of 1993, a man from al-Qaṣīm, another of Rāshid's cousins by the name of Muḥammad b. Sālim, wrote al-Jāsir with an intricate tale of lineal affirmation. Muḥammad's story had much in common with the stories of the lineage seekers outlined above. It aimed to set straight an incomplete historical record, by reaffirming the connection of Muḥammad and Rāshid's ancestors to a family of ʿAjmān tribal origin, ancestors who had "disappeared" from the reckoning of the latter family's known subbranches. Muḥammad's story derived from the narrations of two deceased shaykhs, one of whom was Rāshid's direct ancestor. Bloody conflicts forced two brothers to flee their town of origin in al-Qaṣīm four hundred years earlier, the narrations explained. "When they were far from the town, they came upon a caravan destined for Iraq. [One] decided to accompany this caravan, and requested that his brother accompany him to Iraq. The other decided that he would head to [a town in northern Najd]. . . . So the two brothers went their separate ways in that place."[85] Via a vague and tortuous narrative route, Muḥammad arrived at his key conclusion, that Rashid's family and his own family were paternal kin, and that both descended from the same prominent central Arabian family of well-established ʿAjmān tribal origins.

By al-Jāsir's reckoning, Muḥammad's story of lineal affirmation was "not suitable for publication in *al-ʿArab* Magazine." The lack of a single credible documented source, the reliance on uncorroborated statements made by deceased individuals, and the quantity of linguistic errors in the text combined to condemn Muḥammad's story to the obscurity of the Maktabat al-ʿArab archive.[86] Without some other method of authentication, Rāshid's desire to be included in the *Jamhara* and Muḥammad's hope of affirming his family's belonging to the ʿAjmān tribe would remain submerged in an increasingly discredited oral narrative framework.[87]

GENEALOGY BETWEEN THE ORAL AND THE TEXTUAL

While the *Jamhara* may have been al-Jāsir's most popular book, it was hardly a bestseller. "There are still copies of it piled up in its warehouses that haven't been sold," al-Jāsir told a fellow publisher in 1999. "Heritage books, as you know, are not in great demand."[88] For those seeking entry into its pages, however, the dust collecting on its covers must have seemed of the gold variety. "I hope you might take notice of this unintended neglect [of my family's name] and publish it in the next edition of [the *Jamhara*], God willing, as adding my family and the remainder of Najdi families would constitute the perfection of the desired promise of its composition, and the fulfillment of the intended meaning of the book's title,"[89] wrote a prominent farmer from the town of Thādiq. Writing from Burayda in the same vein, a family patriarch requested "the honor of a mention in your great book, which has achieved widespread interest and is broadly read by all classes of readers in our beloved kingdom."[90]

The jockeying for entry into the *Jamhara* captured in these letters and scores of others like them calls attention to another crucial dimension of the genealogical story, namely, the relationship between documentation and authority in the new Arabia. The potency and reach of Saudi religious discourse, together with a post-9/11 Western scholarly orientation that has positioned Islam as a singularly privileged field of analysis,[91] has diverted attention from a crucial fact, that Saudi Arabia was historically, and in significant ways remains, a predominantly oral culture. That Saudi Arabia is also today a modern authoritarian state with a thriving commercial sector and a robust bureaucratic apparatus, that it is, in short, buried in paperwork, merely adds luster to the paradox I am seeking to unravel here.[92]

Ḥamad al-Jāsir, who had surveyed central Arabia's historiographical terrain more extensively than most others of his generation, was the first to acknowledge the paucity of documented sources and the corresponding potency of the oral tradition.[93] Other prominent Saudi historians echoed al-Jāsir's assessment. Rāshid b. Ḥumayd, however, was not convinced:

> RĀSHID: I visited [al-Jāsir] . . . and said, Shaykh Ḥamad . . . I want to get into the subject of the history of Najd . . . its history isn't known. I mean, the Hijaz, its history is known. Yemen, its history is known. The Eastern Province, its history is known. This Najd, it isn't known. He said, "My son, this topic is . . . what do you hope to find? I didn't find anything. We [i.e., al-Jāsir's generation of historians] didn't find anything."
>
> NS: Meaning, there are no sources?
>
> RĀSHID: He said there aren't any. So I went to Shaykh—all of them have passed—ʿAbdallāh b. Khamīs,[94] and I asked him the same question. He said, we haven't found anything, we haven't found anything, and what you would like to do is difficult. So I went to Shaykh Ibn Junaydil, Saʿd b. Junaydil,[95] and he said to me, you won't find anything. I told him that I wanted to risk it. . . . So I went into the subject, and I published [a] book.
>
> NS: So how did you find all of these materials when these distinguished scholars couldn't find them?
>
> RĀSHID: I found them, thank God, I found them, right or wrong, I found them.[96]

Rāshid's intensive (though unannotated) efforts acknowledged, the assertions made by al-Jāsir concerning the scarcity of historical source materials and the corresponding power of the oral tradition are echoed, consciously or unconsciously, by those who sought his counsel on genealogical matters. Examining the *al-ʿArab* letters in terms of this oral cultural backdrop is therefore crucial for understanding their full significance.

Al-Jāsir favored textual evidence over oral narration, and in a country becoming increasingly permeated with textual authority, he found favor. Yet, as anthropologists of tribal culture such as Saad Sowayan and Andrew Shryock have demonstrated, and as al-Jāsir discovered through his own ethnographic endeavors, the effort to document history in a place like Saudi Arabia can be a Sisyphean enterprise. Documenting history in a tribal context often means imposing a definite casing on scattered oral narratives that are incomplete and unending.[97] This is especially true of so fractious a field as genealogy, where every individual in society is a prospective repository of conflicting, intimate truths. The uneasy interplay between the oral and the textual is why the codifying of genealogies has proven so tremendously problematic in Saudi Arabia.

In working to impose order over Arabian genealogies, far from being the master of his scholarly domain, al-Jāsir discovered himself to be the prisoner of an oral tradition.[98] Yet, for al-Jāsir's correspondents, both those seeking to discover and those looking to affirm their lineages, being prisoner to this tradition meant something different. In an age of documentation and textual authority, in a Gulf society dominated by textual protocols and bureaucratic formalisms, being captive to an oral culture meant asserting one's genealogical identity in terms of the new standards demanded by that society. Al-Jāsir set the stage for these many individual assertions, introducing Arabian genealogies in a new form, as mechanically circulated artifacts of identity. It was for his correspondents to prove that they too could produce these artifacts and integrate them into the newly privileged textual modes of circulation. Adopting a synchronic view of the story recounted here becomes crucial, as it underscores the manner by which the oral underpinnings of the kingdom's genealogical culture and the new textual embodiment of this culture came to mutually inform and perturb one another.

The most elementary tension in the relationship between oral genealogical culture and its textual embodiment concerned names. The names of al-Jāsir's correspondents were often a central issue in their inquiries. Two facts might be known to a given inquirer: for example, that his fourth and last-known ancestor was named ʿAlī, and that he belonged to the Ḥarb tribe. That al-Jāsir might connect for him branch to root was the central hope of his inquiry,[99] notwithstanding the scores of nameless generations that intervened to render such feats impossible.[100] Hardly deterred, the lacunae peppering unilineal descent chains were seized upon by many lineage seekers as prospective openings into which they might insert themselves and their families.

One of the easiest ways for non-tribal families to lay claim to a tribal affiliation was by taking advantage of the vast overlap in Arabian family names (*al-tashābuh fī l-asmāʾ*). The *al-ʿArab* letters are rife with claims by individuals asserting common origins with known tribal families on account of the similarity (or identity) of their respective names.[101] Al-Jāsir believed that "the mere presence of names similar to the names of families does not imply true linkages between them,"[102] and insisted on grounding a genealogical authentication in three interrelated aspects of a family's history—its lineage, its original domicile, and its marital history.[103] Despite these requirements, policing the boundaries of lineages proved nearly impossible, so much so that a good deal of the controversy observable in the codification of modern Arabian genealogies can be attributed to the perceived dilution of the group identity of Gulf tribal families by non-tribals who had 'infiltrated'—or been welcomed unwittingly into—the new textual genealogical records.[104]

At a more tactile level, the tension between oral and textual culture involved the rendering of vernacular names into classical Arabic. Names were one of the few robust inheritances of the Arabian past. In settled areas, names were recorded for practical purposes, in commercial contracts (typically land sales or purchases), marriage contracts, *awqāf* (religious bequests), wills, as well as documents known as *wathā'iq al-aḍāḥī* (sacrificial bequests honoring deceased ancestors).[105] Among nomadic groups, names were committed to memory, forming a mimetic passport that eased transit through towns and across sometimes unfamiliar grazing lands. Stacked up alongside one another, these sedentary and bedouin names encompassed the entire phonetic range of vernacular speech, a range that the rigorously outlined rules of classical Arabic could not accommodate. As a one-time youthful apprentice of al-Jāsir explained:

> There are a great many problems with the vocalizations of names, for example: as-Slaym, as-Slīm, as-Slaymī, as-Sulmī, as-Slayyim, as-Sallūm, as-Sallūmī. All of these are *different* families, and when there is a family as-Slīm, and you pronounce it al-Sulaym, or as-Slaym, they get angry ... Ḥamad al-Jāsir would always [document according to classical Arabic conventions], for example, "al-Sulaym, in 'Unayza" ... ; written, it was al-Sulaym, but spoken, it is as-Slaym ... when you write [al-Sulaym] it is unnatural—and incorrect, to an extent, because what is commonly known is Slaym. According to the laws of Arabic grammar, you don't begin [a word] with a *sukun*,[106] but [in the vernacular] until today, it is pronounced ... with a *sukun* at the beginning. This is ... one of the things that causes confusion in writing.[107]

This confusion was echoed in a letter by a young man from Riyadh, who complained to al-Jāsir about the damage inherent in codifying the oral catalog of Arabian names:

> There are many families who are named according to dialect names, and if you wanted to correct their names according to the rules of the language then the meaning would change completely, while if you wanted to find a classical Arabic expression for the meaning, it would change the vernacular pronunciation completely. It is very difficult to say to some family "correct the name of your family according to the rules of the classical Arabic language, and accept the change in meaning."[108]

The contorting of vernacular names into predetermined classical shapes was emblematic of the larger genealogical project launched by al-Jāsir, and the opportunities and pitfalls it presented. On its surface, the taxonomy of tribal affiliations al-Jāsir established in his genealogical indices bore the sober look and feel of authority. Names were organized alphabetically in dry, list-like fashion, the text loaded with citations to earlier genealogical volumes. Belying this cool, clinical exterior, however, was the fundamental restlessness of the content it encapsulated.

In the epilogue to his *Jamhara*, al-Jāsir cautioned the casual reader to refrain from independently accessing the genealogical reference volumes he drew upon for its composition. This was because of "the large quantity of fictions and mistakes they contain, which only scholars with an interest in the discipline of genealogies can recognize."[109] Despite this disclaimer, which served to affirm the mystique of genealogical expertise, al-Jāsir would live to regret drawing on the genealogical information transmitted in some of these volumes. One example is Muḥammad al-ʿUbūdī's never-published manuscript, *Muʿjam Usar al-Qaṣīm* (*Dictionary of the Families of al-Qaṣīm*). Al-Jāsir relied heavily on this manuscript for the first edition of his *Jamhara*, but excised from the second edition much of this content, he explained, because it became the focus of strong criticism from genealogists in the Qaṣīm region.[110] Al-ʿUbūdī's own manuscript was eventually refined into a study of a single city within al-Qaṣīm, Burayda, and published in 23 volumes. Like practically every other genealogical work published in modern Saudi Arabia, it proved controversial on account of some of its questionable lineal attributions.[111] A Saudi writer characterized al-ʿUbūdī's project to me in the following way:

> Burayda is a city of around 200 years old. Non-tribals and tribals live there intermingled. Muḥammad al-ʿUbūdī, a non-tribal from Burayda, wanted to write a history of the place. So he mailed a survey to Buraydan families asking them to send him their genealogies. Many non-tribal families sent in information claiming tribal ancestry for themselves. In this way, there seemed a "conspiracy of non-tribals" afoot between the author and the families to establish tribal lineages for themselves.[112]

Another controversial volume that al-Jāsir drew upon for his *Jamhara* was *Imtāʿ al-Sāmir bi-Takmilat Mutʿat al-Nāẓir* (*Delighting the Companion with a Supplement to [the Book] The Pleasure of the Observer*).[113] This prosopographical volume, which presented itself as a 1946 composition but which first appeared in Saudi bookstores and library catalogs in the mid-1980s, purported to present historical and genealogical details about famous personalities from the country's neglected southwestern region, ʿAsīr. Its author, Shuʿayb b. ʿAbd al-Ḥamīd al-Dawsarī, signed the volume "Commander of the First Artillery Unit, Abhā, Government of Āl ʿĀʾiḍ," a reference to the formerly independent chieftains of the southern city of Abhā, and a seeming deliberate provocation against the reigning Saudi historiographical narrative, in which the recollections of the conquered have no recognized place. Initially embraced by scholars, the book was later determined a forgery, its genealogical data discredited, at least in Najd. Al-Jāsir would also question the validity of important early authorities on Arabian genealogies, for example, Ibn Laʿbūn, whose *Tārīkh* he described in a letter as "not reliant upon dependable historical evidence."[114] As the shaky foundations of the genealogical enterprise emerge in relief, the spirited reactions to al-Jāsir's genealogical classifications suggest that the *Jamhara* and, to a lesser extent, its sister volume, the *Muʿjam*, are in many ways no more than the amalgamation of an innately contentious oral record transferred wholesale to print.

For those seeking to affirm their lineal origins, the absence of credible documentation created both opportunities and challenges. A member of the Majlis al-Shūrā looking to authenticate his tribal origins took up the challenge in a letter to al-Jāsir.[115] His purpose was "to document the reports that have been narrated concerning the lineal affiliation of [my] family, and by way of this document, to *emerge from the oral narrative framework and enter the domain of written narrative*."[116] According to numerous oral narrations, he explained, his family was originally a tribal family. However, the family's founding ancestor had migrated from his ancestral homeland in the al-Aḥsāʾ region of eastern Arabia and settled in a town near Riyadh. There, he married a woman who was disapproved of by his tribal relatives, he implied, on account of her perceived non-tribal origins. Furthering his claims to tribal status, the author noted that, according to another oral narration, "some units (*buyūt*) of this family still maintain their previous social status [i.e., are tribal], and were not transformed [i.e., became non-tribal]."[117]

The social categories alluded to by the author, tribal and non-tribal, existed long before al-Jāsir's genealogical project. They were, within the thousands of microcommunities of Saudi Arabia, things "commonly recognized" (*mutaʿāraf ʿalayh*), yet undocumented and unspoken. In creating a documented, authoritative, public record of these social categories, al-Jāsir's genealogical project reshaped the way these categories were conceived and their boundaries enacted. With the privileging of textual claims to tribal belonging over inconsistent and often inconvenient oral narrations, it becomes clear how the transition from an oral genealogical culture to a textual one could be harnessed by some as a move from non-tribal to tribal status. Picking up the story of Rāshid b. Ḥumayd, we can observe further how these dualities interact to produce the new "paper truths" of Saudi genealogical culture.[118]

THE SHIFTING WINDS OF GENEALOGICAL AUTHORITY

One can imagine why Rāshid b. Ḥumayd wanted his name included in the *Jamhara*. Glancing at the first edition of the text, one finds Āl Ḥumūd, Āl Ḥumayyid, Āl Ḥumaydān, and multiple Āl Ḥumayds. Why should Rāshid's Āl Ḥumayd not be included among them? After all, he explained, "we are like other people, we know our origins, we know our situation, we know everything."[119] In January 1994, one month after his cousin Muḥammad's submission was rejected by *al-ʿArab*, Rāshid wrote al-Jāsir announcing an important development in his twelve year mission to achieve publicly documented affirmation of his tribal origins. Rāshid had obtained authentication of his family's genealogical history from a prominent ʿAjmān tribal leader, and was submitting the evidence to *al-ʿArab*:

> This letter is in reference to the promise you made in your letter of [September 1981], a copy of which is attached, concerning the publishing of the lineage of our family in your book *Jamharat al-Usar al-Mutaḥaḍḍira fī Najd* [*sic*].
>
> For this reason, I enclose a summary of our family's history from our first ancestor's migration from [al-Qaṣīm] to the present, with the endorsement (*ta'yīd*) of the leader (*amīr*) of the [ʿAjmān] tribe concerning our belonging to this tribe.
>
> I hope that you might publish this summary along with the text of the *amīr*'s resolution in *al-ʿArab Magazine*, in preparation for its publication in the [*Jamhara*] upon its reissue, and in implementation of your aforementioned promise.[120]

The family history enclosed by Rāshid was the very same story that had been submitted to *al-ʿArab* by his cousin Muḥammad and roundly rejected for its lack of internal coherence and failure to adhere to minimal evidentiary standards. Rāshid's submission was nearly identical, but for a crucial new element. His history had been formally endorsed by a prominent ʿAjmān tribal leader,[121] whose testimonial had in turn been authenticated by the deputy administrator of the Riyadh Governorate, Prince Salmān b. ʿAbd al-ʿAzīz's deputy, ʿAbdallāh al-Bulayhid. Rendered credible by these endorsements, al-Jāsir published Rāshid's family history in *al-ʿArab*, as well as a testimonial by the same tribal leader testifying to Muḥammad's belonging to the tribe.[122]

Why had Rāshid waited twelve years to press his case? Could Rāshid have been swept up in his cousin Muḥammad's own lineal affirmation claims, and seen fit to make common cause with him? Rāshid's motivations for reactivating his campaign to achieve recognition in the *Jamhara* are uncertain. The turn in his fortune, however, draws attention to another important dimension of the Saudi genealogical story, one that concerns the nature of genealogical authority and the changes in how it has been exercised in modern Saudi history. Examining these changes through the letters and publications of Ḥamad al-Jāsir, one can observe the progressive receding of oral cultural authority and its gradual encapsulation by the bureaucratic state. As early as 1973, al-Jāsir was establishing a principle, derived from a statement by the classical Muslim jurist Mālik,[123] that would guide his genealogical inquiries going forward, that "the people are the most trustworthy concerning their lineages."[124] In the absence of sufficient documentary evidence, this seemed the only constructive route for establishing genealogy as a viable discipline in modern Saudi Arabia. When genealogies began to migrate from oral accountings to print via the medium of *al-ʿArab*, however, the local authority that underpinned them was severely challenged.

In al-Jāsir's hands, Arabian genealogies were transformed into mechanically circulated artifacts of identity. They were documented in typeface, reproduced in identical form, and distributed as products of an emergent mass media. Normalized in this way, made to conform uneasily to print, they were gradually excised from the oral accounts of their local preservers, whose collective memories came to be challenged by the new authority embodied in mass-circulated texts. Naturally, this process did not proceed without a countervailing challenge from below, from individuals whose genealogies had been entered problematically into the new public record. These challenges, which would draw the attention of the Saudi state, can be observed in several letters complaining to al-Jāsir about erroneous tribal affiliations.

In one such letter, which seems to have gone without reply, a man chastised al-Jāsir for mistakenly attributing his father's lineage to Bāhila.[125] Bāhila,[126] a sedentary tribe whose reputation was maligned in Arab history, was the subject of a 726-page apologetic monograph by al-Jāsir. Written at the request of prominent figures within the Bāhila tribe, al-Jāsir's fascinating volume proved controversial, so much so that a prominent person within the tribe who was particularly sensitive to its reputation purchased the entire print run of the book and allegedly had it burnt in a bonfire.[127] In his letter of complaint, the aggrieved man's son complained that al-Jāsir had asked the wrong people about the family's lineal affiliation, and that, as a general rule he should only transmit information from members of the family in question. "It would be better if one were to open up a Riyadh phone book and call up one of the [members of this family]—and, praise God, they are plentiful . . .—to obtain such information from them," he concluded reproachfully.[128]

In a similar case, a man requesting anonymity wrote al-Jāsir from Ḥā'il on behalf of a family whose reputation had been injured by the scholar's misattribution of its tribal lineage. The family had deep roots in Ḥā'il, the author explained, and was linked by marriage to most of the families in the city, a sure indication of its proper tribal origins. Yet in his *Muʿjam*, al-Jāsir had assigned the family to the Ṣluba, described in the previous chapter as a formerly nomadic group of unknown origin who were reckoned inferior in the tribal status hierarchy. A great deal of chatter ensued in Ḥā'il, and the reputation of a "noble and well-respected family" was damaged as a consequence. The family's true affiliation was with the Shammar tribe, and al-Jāsir was asked to note this fact in *al-ʿArab*.[129]

The contrast between Shammar and Ṣluba origins is captured in a once-popular *sālifa*, or evening conversation piece, in which Shammar and other prominent tribes are portrayed according to the classic bedouin tropes of generosity, ferocity, and courage,[130] while the Ṣluba are associated with sheep herding, an economic activity more closely associated with sedentarism and thus inferior to camel herding in the bedouin historical imagination:

A person from the Ṣluba tribe invited a Qaḥṭānī to be his guest. The Qaḥṭānī asked the Ṣlubī: "To what tribe do you belong?"

> "To a tribe whose clothes are silk (*qazz*) and whose attack is piercing (*khazz*)."
>
> "Those are the ʿAnaza, and you aren't one of them."
>
> "To a tribe whose plates (*ṣuhūn*) are large and whose attacks (*ṭuʿūn*) are vast."
>
> "You aren't from those, as they are Shammar."
>
> "To a people whose field of play is massive (*baʿīd*), and who dress in iron (*ḥadīd*)."
>
> "Nor are you from those, the Ẓafīr." . . .
>
> "From those whose swords (*suyūf*) are wet, and who are generous to guests (*ḍuyūf*)."
>
> "Those are Subayʿ, and you aren't Subayʿī."
>
> "[Those] unfearing of lambs (*al-ṭulay*), who cut the tips off puppies' ears (*al-juray*)."
>
> "You speak the truth, you are a Ṣlubī."[131]

Though a survival of an earlier age of economic and political differentiation,[132] the potency of this status distinction lingers on in the Saudi historical imagination, becoming inflamed when cast, truthfully or otherwise, in print.

With so vast a range of lineages to document, the occasional misattribution of tribal affiliations by modern genealogists seemed inevitable. Yet scholarly misstep was an insufficient excuse for the denial of a symbolic patrimony. As demonstrated, al-Jāsir's project generated intense reactions among Saudis, and helped instigate the emergence of a new class of censors in the kingdom. For the Saudi state, whose censoring gaze was ubiquitous from the 1950s onward,[133] the rise of genealogical citizen censors was unexpected. Of the many subjects prohibited by the early Saudi censoring authorities, tribal genealogy was not one.[134] Censors of an earlier generation could not have foreseen how combustible a subject tribal genealogy would prove to be when transferred to print, or how threatening to the social and political fabric of the country. Saudi Arabia was too atomized, too regionalized for the notion of a nationwide public discourse on tribal heritage to have any valence at that early stage. Yet by the middle of the 1990s, the Ministry of Information was beginning to heavily censor all tribal-related media, and al-Jāsir was once again caught up in the state's disciplining grip. Notably, Rāshid and Muḥammad's lobbying of al-Jāsir seems to have played a significant role in this turn of events.

In 1996, al-Jāsir received word from the Interior Ministry that the tribal leader who had authenticated Rāshid and Muḥammad's lineal belonging to the ʿAjmān tribe had changed his mind. A letter to al-Jāsir from ʿAbdallāh al-Bulayhid at the Riyadh Governorate indicated that the ʿAjmān shaykh had "corrected a mistake . . . pertaining to [his testimonial]," namely, that "the affiliation of these families to the [ʿAjmān tribe] was not proven before him."[135] As al-Jāsir explained to an inquirer, agitated on account of his dual manipulation at the hands of genealogically interested citizens and government agencies:

> Some people called the magazine a little while ago claiming that they were from [the ʿAjmān] tribe, and presented an authentication of this from . . . one of the famous shaykhs of the tribe. But the magazine didn't publish it until after it was verified by the Riyadh Governorate. When it published [the claim], a decree came from the Governorate stating that what had been published about that matter was based on a mistake by [the shaykh] which he had retracted. They issued a warning and cautioned against publishing anything like it that relates to the tribes.[136]

Why had the ʿAjmān shaykh changed his mind? What had motivated him to retract his testimonial, denying Rāshid and Muḥammad the authenticated tribal origins they sought? Had his affirmation been credible to begin with, or was it, to quote the young genealogist we encountered earlier, no more than the "seal-embossed paper" of a titular tribal leader, who today "worshipped the *dīnār* or the *dirham*," issuing genealogical edicts for transactional gain? Rāshid's cousin, the businessman, thought so:

> . . . some shaykhs, people come to them, families, requesting lineal affiliation with the tribe, and say, we are lineally affiliated with you. You

> are the shaykh of the tribe. I come to you, I say, I want to be lineally affiliated with your tribe. And I come to you with a big present, a gift. Sometimes it is money, sometimes it is camels, sometimes cars, sometimes very precious things. They take these things and they, say, yes, you guys are one of us, and we will give you papers, and so forth. Then subsequently, after they have consumed these things, they disavow what they have said . . . it is a kind of buying and selling, a business.[137]

Al-Jāsir seemed to think so as well. Discussing the case with a trusted genealogist friend from ʿUnayza, al-Jāsir noted that Rāshid and Muḥammad had presented him with a credible certificate from a tribal leader, and he had no reason to doubt its authenticity or the motives behind its issuance. "Lineal affiliation (*al-intisāb*) might occur not on account of actual lineal connection (*al-ṣila bi-l-nasab*), but for other reasons, which you understand," he conceded obliquely.[138] While the trade in lineages was but one aspect of the modern genealogical culture al-Jāsir had helped legitimate, it had the power to undermine the credibility of the entire enterprise.

After this and other episodes of governmental interference,[139] al-Jāsir's distaste for the subculture he helped spawn seemed to crystallize. The discussion of genealogies had grown especially sensitive in recent years, he lamented, with "numerous, ignorant people rising in protest of all matters published about their tribes, truthful or false, and causing problems for the magazine and its owner."[140] The scholar began informing inquirers that the media had been permitted by the Saudi government to publish only the most unassailable genealogical claims, and that he had been threatened with financial penalties if failing to adjust to this Kafkaesque standard.[141] It was apparent that by the end of the twentieth century, genealogy in Saudi Arabia had moved from a problem of heritage, identity, and history to one of social order and organization, that is, from the purview of men such as al-Jāsir to the purview of the state. If not a catalyst for this development, Rāshid and Muḥammad's story was at the very least symbolic of the larger shift in the nature of genealogical authority in the kingdom.

The shifting winds of genealogical authentication can be examined further when contrasting two exchanges of letters across the decades of al-Jāsir's genealogical correspondence. In April 1972, a traffic policeman from Medina wrote al-Jāsir requesting information about a subbranch of the Banū Rashīd tribe. Al-Jāsir referred the policeman to his geographical volume, *Fī Shimāl Gharb al-Jazīra*, which contained information about the tribe. About his sources, al-Jāsir explained: "I got the information from a man of your [tribe] who rode with me in the car from Khibr until the crossroads. I've forgotten his name, but he appeared to know about the tribe and its domains."[142] Al-Jāsir's manifestly casual, even lackadaisical, approach to the issue of source veracity was the product of an earlier era, an era in which tribal affiliation had yet to acquire the competitive, almost commodified aspect of subsequent decades,[143] one in which the word of a local hitchhiker could be taken as fact. By contrast, a 1994 exchange between al-Jāsir and a genealogical petitioner demonstrated clearly the waning of the sort of oral genealogical authority that had been privileged throughout Arabian history and was implicit in al-Jāsir's traditional method of genealogical collection.

The case involved a family whose tribal affiliation had been noted incorrectly in the *Jamhara*. The author wrote al-Jāsir to request that the family's true affiliation with the ʿAnaza tribe be registered in *al-ʿArab* magazine and a future edition of the *Jamhara*, so that the public record of its origins could be corrected. Supplementing his letter, the author explained, "the *nassāba* (genealogist) of ʿAnaza" had written al-Jāsir with independent corroboration of his testimony. In support of his claim, the author enclosed a sworn testimonial by several "supreme shaykhs" (*mashāyikh al-shumul*) of a subbranch of the ʿAnaza tribe in Ḥāʾil, who testified that the family in question "are our paternal cousins, and their blood comes from our own blood."[144] A verbal attestation to the joining of the two families at their fifth or sixth ancestor was the most that could be mustered from these tribal leaders, however, one of whose signatures was a thumbprint.

Al-Jāsir responded skeptically to the letter. "In reference to your letter . . . concerning [your family's lineage], and your reliance on the words of one you call 'the *nassāba* of ʿAnaza . . . ' ," he wrote, subtly casting doubt on the notion that the vast and scattered network of ʿAnaza families and subclans could be comprehended by any single authority within the tribe. "I will refer to what you have mentioned in your letter upon the reprinting of the book *Jamharat Ansāb al-Usar al-Mutaḥaḍḍira fī Najd*, God willing, even if I am not fully trusting of everything our brothers from the sons of the bedouin say, as I have known a great deal of this [i.e., manipulation of genealogies]."[145] Despite his evident skepticism, al-Jāsir's hands were tied, as by the new standards of genealogical legitimation in the kingdom, the document had been rendered definitive; that is, it had been affixed with the seal of the Interior Ministry, Riyadh Region, stamped and authorized by the son of one of the testifying shaykhs, who happened to be the government liaison (*ʿumda*) for a Riyadh neighborhood.[146] These seals, which are distributed by the Interior Ministry to designated tribal leaders, serve to link through text and imagery two formerly distinctive forms of authority, bureaucratic and tribal. In the scholar's view, the authority of the seal seemed the only thing weighing in favor of this lineage claim.

As the standards of genealogical authentication shifted, al-Jāsir's favored methods of lineal authentication—establishing a family's place of origin together with its patterns of marriage with other unrelated families—began to conflict with those favored by Saudi petitioners themselves. Along with documents such as the ʿAnaza testimonial, which bore government-issued tribal seals of authentication, genealogical *ṣukūk*, or testimonials notarized by Saudi Islamic judges,[147] came to play an important role in the process of lineal authentication.[148] According to al-Jāsir, these documents proved so problematic that, sometime in the late 1990s, state officials ordered the Presidency of the Saudi Judiciary to instruct its judges that they would no longer be permitted to issue them.[149] The prohibition on Saudi Sharia court involvement in the politics of lineal authentication revealed the Saudi government's extreme distaste for public recognition of genealogical claims and their attendant controversies. Such adjudications were thought best reserved for the opaque and inscrutable precincts of the Ministry of Interior. In fact, after having instructed al-Jāsir to publish the ʿAjmān shaykh's repudiation of Rāshid and Muḥammad's claims, an Interior Ministry missive arrived subsequently to inform the scholar in cryptic prose that he should pretend as if a correspondence on the matter between himself and the Ministry had never occurred, and that *al-ʿArab*'s retraction, should it be issued, would need to come of its own initiative.[150] By the end of the scholar's life, the unseen hand of oral genealogical transmission had been replaced by an even more opaque presence, the security apparatus of the Saudi state.

A new, strict threshold was now in play for the publication of lineage claims, al-Jāsir told one petitioner. To be fit to print, any such claim required authentication by the relevant tribal shaykh through shariah-compliant means.[151] With the authority to make lineage claims now formally relocated to the emergent nexus of tribal and bureaucratic authority, the position of Ḥamad al-Jāsir, who was neither a state official nor a tribal leader, was disadvantageous. The oral or personal record, discredited largely on account of its manipulation at the hands of moneyed interests, was no longer the basis for credible genealogical reporting. For al-Jāsir, to surrender to the will of the state was in a sense to abandon his own claims to genealogical authority. And yet, aged 86 and bedridden, this battle seemed hardly worth fighting. Citizen dependency on the Saudi rentier state had come to encompass the most intimate details of social life, and al-Jāsir could hardly stand in the way of its embrace. In assuming the unequivocal power to authenticate or revoke lineage claims, however, the state would be forced to confront the fractious culture of genealogical affirmation and denial it had helped to instigate.

RESURRECTING KINSHIP TIES

The jockeying for genealogical position observable throughout the *al-ʿArab* letters reflects what has always been a dynamic process of affiliation and detachment, unification and bifurcation, among Arabian tribal segments and kin groups. Today, in an urbanized, literate, and commercialized Saudi Arabia, this dynamic is proceeding by other, sometimes transactional means, and all under the watchful eye of the state. We should not lose sight of another fact as well, that in genealogical matters, the line dividing an authentic historical claim from a naked political gambit has never been precise. This is as true of European or Asian history as it is of the Arab Middle East.[152] What is arguably fascinating about the *al-ʿArab* letters is that they provide a window into the sausage-making of modern genealogical politics, in a country where, for complex economic, social, and political reasons that will be the subject of this study going forward, genealogies matter. They are fascinating because they divulge the techniques, claims, and counterclaims through which Saudi genealogies are defined and redefined. Lastly, they are fascinating because they allow us to step outside of the inherited framework of Saudi history, which, in privileging phenomena such as religious culture or rentier economics, make of our destination, the study of how and why tribal lineages are constructed, a mere way station.

The dynamism of Saudi genealogical culture is epitomized by the phenomenon of family reunification. This phenomenon is woven implicitly into a number of the stories and letters we have reviewed. Most notably thus far, it can be observed in the effort by Rāshid and his cousin Muḥammad to promote a joint narrative of origins that affixed them credibly within a tribal genealogical framework.[153] Underlying this and other unification narratives to be discussed in subsequent chapters, moreover, is a growing sense of the breakdown of kinship networks, and the need to actively counteract the socially disruptive effects of national integration. Ḥamad al-Jāsir's personal history is relevant here, as his own reunification with his family and home country came at a particularly significant time in his life.

Al-Jāsir's thirteen year sojourn in Lebanon was cut short by two tragedies that struck in the span of several weeks in September–October 1975: the death of his first born son Muḥammad in a plane crash over Beirut,[154] and the destruction of his library by shelling following the outbreak of the Lebanese Civil War. These events hastened his return to Riyadh, a city in the throes of convulsive growth, and one increasingly foreign to his aging eyes. In a 1977 interview, al-Jāsir reflected on his sense of the creeping atomization of Saudi life: "Today, our families have come apart, [both] families and society (*al-nās*). A person might get together with his son or relative once a year. Certain things have been lost to us . . ."[155] It would be tempting to locate the impetus for al-Jāsir's genealogical project, announced formally just six months after his return from Lebanon, in the confluence of these personal, intellectual, and social upheavals, in a desire to restore the familial, social, and intellectual connections that had been undone by war, personal loss, and disorienting economic growth. At a broader level, the restoration of kinship ties, real or perceived, was an aspiration shared by the vast majority of al-Jāsir's correspondents, and was undoubtedly the impetus behind one of the most interesting letters preserved in his library.

In October 1996, Aḥmad b. Kamāl al-ʿUrayr al-Sulamī wrote Ḥamad al-Jāsir from Mecca to report on a development in his family. Aḥmad prefaced his letter with two religious references, Quran 49:13, followed by a popular Tradition of the Prophet that reads: "learn of your lineages enough to maintain ties of kinship."[156] Fifteen years earlier, he continued, a man from the Āl Ghulūb family of ʿUnayza, in al-Qaṣīm, had contacted his father requesting from him a testimonial that affirmed the lineal connection of the Āl Ghulūb to the Āl ʿUrayr, Aḥmad al-ʿUrayr's tribal branch. Aḥmad's father gathered a number of the branch's elders in Mecca, who deliberated over the matter and decided that the petitioner's family, the Āl Ghulūb, were in fact their kin. "He is one of us if he is from the Āl Ghulūb," they said, "as they [i.e., the Āl Ghulūb] are from us (*hum minnā*). When the caravans of Qaṣīm used to pass through our lands, and their crier would cry out '[We know] your cousin, Ibn Ghulūb', they would pass in peace."

How did two families from distant regions of Arabia knowingly share a common ancestor, yet come to lose sight of this fact in the fog of time? According to the author, their shared ancestor, Ghālib al-ʿUrayr, lived in the vicinity of Mecca around the beginning of the nineteenth century. As a member of the Sulaym tribe, Ghālib helped ʿAbd al-ʿAzīz b. Muḥammad Āl Saʿūd besiege Mecca in 1805. When in 1813, Muhammad Ali's Egyptian armies overwhelmed the Saudis and their loyalists, Ghālib refused to pledge his allegiance to the conquerors and betray the Saudi leader, choosing instead to flee Mecca for the central Arabian town of ʿUnayza. With a simple stroke, Aḥmad's narrative of genealogical origins was woven seamlessly into a profession of historical fealty to the Saudi political project.[157] The very legitimacy of his lineage seemed to depend in his mind on the side his putative progenitor took during the early Saudi conquests. In a country designed around, by, and in many respects, for a single ruling lineage, no other sort of narrative of origination could be expected.

The testimonial provided by the family members in Mecca commenced the process of reunification between the Āl Ghulūb and the Āl ʿUrayr, now fused together into the parent al-Sulaym tribe. This process involved reciprocal visits by family members in Mecca and ʿUnayza. In August of 1996, the Āl ʿUrayr were invited to ʿUnayza to deepen their acquaintance with their Āl Ghulūb cousins. A party was held to celebrate the occasion, for which Aḥmad al-ʿUrayr, the author of the letter to al-Jāsir, composed a poem. Aḥmad's *qaṣīda* is rich in allusions to the genealogical dynamics encountered throughout this chapter:

Gratitude is due to you, O Lord, and thanks and blessing
you have granted reunification, and the break has been repaired

For our cousins have returned to us after an absence
as the hawk returns from a distance to its nest

An arrow has reverted to the quiver of our people
and what time had divided has, by God's grace, returned

Āl Ghulūb belongs to Sulaym through common lineage
and there is glory in mentioning them

Your ancestor is one of us, a leader, who settled in ʿUnayza
for a reason decreed by God

We have no worldly need
of you, nor you any designs on us

All of us live amid peace and bounty
and protection by the ruler, and gratitude is due to the Creator

But we and you, all of us
descend from a noble ancestor, without boasting

So welcome, O people of ours, upon your arrival
for you are for us a point of pride, and a treasure

You are welcome as long as lightning flashes from the Tihāma
and the plains and rugged country flow with its downpours

as long as it glimmers from Najd, and the east wind blows
and the heavenly spheres and radiant stars proceed on their course

as long as the light of the sun radiates every forenoon
and the night is covered in darkness or dawn appears

Bless us, O Lord, in our coming together
and guide our steps toward you, O Singular, Merciful one

In closing, God's prayers and peace
upon he through whom Muḍar was elevated among the people

Muḥammad the guide, his family, companions
and followers, as long as rain falls upon the earth.[158]

Aḥmad's welcoming of the Āl Ghulūb back to the Āl ʿUrayr lineage is particularly notable. While the poet invokes bedrock themes of greeting and hospitality, it is the Āl Ghulūb of ʿUnayza who are in fact providing hospitality to the author's family, the Āl ʿUrayr, on the occasion of the poem's recitation. The new genealogical discourse of the kingdom appears in this instance to stand the ubiquitous "bedouin values" of Arabia on their head. Noteworthy as well is Aḥmad's poetical disclaimer, in which he rejects out of hand the notion that "worldly need," or material motives, could lie behind the reuniting of the two families. His disclaimer mirrors accusations of such impropriety observed in this chapter, in which lineages were seen to be purchased from tribal leaders and used to assert false claims. That Aḥmad finds need to reserve a space within his celebratory verse for such a disclaimer is emblematic of the fraught environment in which genealogical claims are today advanced in the kingdom.

CONCLUSION

Taken at face value, the Āl ʿUrayr narrative and others explored in this chapter attest to a desire to strengthen associations within an increasingly atomized society, via one of the only meaningful routes permissible, tribal association. They also put paid to the notion of the tribe as a fixed, unchanging entity. By their pronouncement, they show the tribe to be a dynamic social collective whose boundaries shift with every convincing genealogical affirmation and denial. This growth and contraction correlates to a cultural and social vitality that is otherwise thought to have evaded Saudi Arabia. Though integrated within a pervasive religious discourse and a narrative of fealty to the state, the affirmations of tribal belonging and communion demonstrated here attest to a more intimate and deeply entrenched source from which the cultural and social norms of modern Saudi Arabia derive.

Exclusivity and denial occupy the obverse side of the kingdom's new genealogical coin. The destructiveness of these sentiments reveals a society grasping for a symbolic corollary to the explosion of wealth that has made billionaires of paupers, yet one that has delayed a reckoning with its own history, a history in which racial discrimination and xenophobic distrust of outsiders figure centrally. In the following chapters I will look to examine both sides of this genealogical coin, reflecting on how the conflicting sentiments captured in the *al-ʿArab* letters interact to produce the modern genealogical culture of the kingdom.

CHAPTER FOUR

Marriage and Lineal Authentication

Behind the anxious inquiries of Ḥamad al-Jāsir's petitioners was, more often than not, a problem of marriage. Al-Jāsir's daughter May would field phone calls night and day on behalf of her elderly father, often from women investigating the tribal backgrounds of their prospective suitors:

> CALLER: May God preserve you (*Allāh ykhallīkī*), can you ask your father about something?
>
> MAY: What is it?
>
> CALLER: It's about [a certain] family. Is it tribal or non-tribal?

"If the family was tribal," said May, "[my father] would say so, but if it was not, he would say 'tell them I don't know'. He would never say that it is a non-tribal family."

> ANOTHER CALLER: I have a very important question. Such-and-Such son of Such-and-Such, is he tribal or non-tribal?
>
> MAY [to FATHER]: Father, Such-and-Such son of Such-and-Such, tribal or non-tribal?
>
> FATHER: I don't know.

"He would say 'I don't know', and I knew what that meant. Or, he would say, 'no, no, they are tribal'. And you would hear the relief over the telephone, or the disappointment."[1]

The dramatic emotional swings of Ḥamad al-Jāsir's callers, their marital futures often hanging in the balance, underscore the perceived importance of pure tribal lineages for affirming one's social position in modern Saudi Arabia. More significantly, they reflect a society in which the networks of local knowledge that once governed marital practices had begun to break down, and the accepted parameters of endogamous marriage—town, tribal, or familial—were being contorted beyond recognition. In modern Saudi Arabia, tribal lineage was only one of a set of qualities that made for a desirable marriage partner, the lack of which could in some cases be mitigated by wealth, piety, or personal status deriving from proximity to the ruling family or the higher offices of the state.[2] Yet for many Saudis of sedentary origin, the disorienting effects of modern life in the kingdom made the assertion of pure (*aṣīl*) tribal lineages into a kind of anchoring force, one that might counteract the imbalances of their new social and economic environment. For Saudis of marrying age and their parental guardians, the anonymity of the urban landscape necessitated a resort to novel and external sources of authoritative knowledge about the constituent elements of their society. For non-tribal families and their like, stuck with historical reputations that limited their marriage prospects, the breakdown of these networks offered the chance to reinvent themselves as respectable members of a protean national community. Weighing against their claims, however, was the central Arabian oral inheritance, which carried and preserved often precise knowledge about the lineal status of the region's inhabitants.

As a central node in this new matrimonial exchange, Ḥamad al-Jāsir developed a distinctive method for dealing with his petitioners, one that utilized the historical marriage patterns of Arabia's families as a technique of lineal authentication.[3] As artifacts of local knowledge, these marital patterns carried the potential to violently rebut the aspirations of social climbers. From the scholar's vantage point, however, marital patterns were an essential tool for recovering knowledge about a rapidly evanescing central Arabian way of life. Such knowledge was useful for counteracting some of the destabilizing tendencies of modern Saudi life like the development of a national labor market and the centrifugal forces it unleashed, but also transformative changes in other facets of life, including the kingdom's religious culture. In numerous writings, especially his late-career apologetic on behalf of the Bāhila tribe, al-Jāsir would make use of Arabian marital patterns to counteract the deficit of trust arising from the dispersion of kin groups throughout the kingdom, overturn dominant perceptions about Arabia's maligned tribes, and formulate a locally resonant, nativist blueprint for an Arabian virtuous life.

This chapter looks closely at marital patterns in Arabian history and how they influence the modern Saudi discourse on lineages and origins. I examine here two sets of texts, one a trove of historical documents from the central

Arabian town of al-Ghāṭ, the other al-Jāsir's volume on the Bāhila tribe. I begin by demonstrating how the marital patterns found in the al-Ghāṭ documents preserve knowledge of premodern social hierarchies, and how this knowledge is challenged or obscured by today's genealogical claimants. Examining premodern Arabian marital patterns through the al-Ghāṭ documents helps cast the modern lineage claims of Saudis in sharper focus, and illuminates aspects of the kingdom's genealogical culture that would otherwise remain implicit.

Any effort to treat kinship practices such as marriage as an expression of the implicit dynamics of a particular society must take into account the lengthy history of this endeavor in Western scholarship. Marital practices have been used to assert some grandiose claims about the trajectory of human civilization; Goody, for example, located the origins of modern capitalism in the marital politics of Henry VIII's court.[4] In the first half of the twentieth century, the anthropological study of kinship practices was the single most essential method for investigating the nature of non-Western societies. Developments in the natural sciences that encouraged the discovery of fundamental laws in the physical world had a profound influence on anthropologists, who sought to uncover comparable laws in the social life of humankind. Yet anthropologists could never achieve consensus on the animating principles of these laws of kinship.[5] The axioms that were thought to govern kinship behaviors were subsequently reformulated as tendencies and preferences, a concession that allowed for greater flexibility in the way ethnography and theory might interact. Kinship practices in the Middle East, for example, came to be seen as but one expression of the great diversity of modes of social organization in the world, and the region's principal combinatory tendency, tribal endogamy, just one dimension of the complex fabric of Middle Eastern societies.

GENEALOGY AND TOWNSHIP SOLIDARITY

Scholars have long considered tribal endogamy to be one of the key animating principles of Middle Eastern social life.[6] Western travelers and anthropologists who interacted with Arabia's bedouin populations observed among them a strong preference for tribal endogamy, and specifically, paternal cousin marriage or its variants.[7] Central Arabia's sedentary populations were likewise perceived to be constituted on the basis of a principle of family or tribal endogamy. Al-Juhany held that "the marital relationship of an individual . . . was decisively determined by his tribal affiliation."[8] Yet what did this mean in practice? What bearing did tribal affiliation have on the marriage patterns of central Arabian sedentary communities, and by what measure were the communities in question constituted? The recent publication of two thousand local documents from the central Arabian town of al-Ghāṭ sheds important new light on the social life and marital patterns of the sedentary populations of premodern central Arabia, and the role of genealogical affiliation in the town's life, past and present. The documents reveal a strong tendency on the part of the town's inhabitants to marry across tribal lineages, a fact that testifies to the influence of patterns of cohabitation on the formation of communal solidarities, above and beyond the role of lineal descent.

Al-Ghāṭ is an oasis town in central Arabia located approximately 250 kilometers northwest of Riyadh. First settled in the last quarter of the seventeenth century,[9] al-Ghāṭ was the traditional seat of the Sudayrīs of the Dawāsir tribe, the second or third most prominent Najdi family in modern times after the Āl Saʿūd, with whom the Sudayrīs have been allied and intermarried for generations. Al-Ghāṭ's most famous inhabitant was undoubtedly Sāra bint Aḥmad al-Sudayrī (d. 1908). After the death of her first husband, Sāra married and bore children with ʿAbd al-Raḥmān b. Fayṣal, one of whom was ʿAbd al-ʿAzīz Ibn Saʿūd, founder of the modern Saudi state.[10] Writing at the beginning of the twentieth century, the British official J. G. Lorimer described al-Ghāṭ as a village of 170 houses.[11] Like the inhabitants of many central Arabian towns before the oil age, those of al-Ghāṭ were a mixture of descendants of various Arabian tribes.[12] Al-Ghāṭ was also home to a population of non-tribal and lower status tribal inhabitants,[13] who tended to marry amongst themselves, and whose story, like that of the lineage seekers recounted earlier, is a key dimension of this chapter.

The al-Ghāṭ documents, which span from the eighteenth century through 1950 and deal mostly with matters of inheritance or sale of family date palm plots, are helpful for establishing a baseline picture of marriage patterns in premodern central Arabia. Of 225 marital pairings identified in the documents, 80 (36 percent) involved descendants of the same tribe.[14] Of these 80 tribally endogamous marriages, 31 occurred within the same family.[15] While kin endogamy clearly exerted its pull on the inhabitants of al-Ghāṭ, it is the statistical prevalence of out-marriage that marks the sedentary experience as distinctive, as it underscores the importance of relations across lineages, and the intimate forms of knowledge about one's neighbors on which these relations were built. Village residents of unblemished tribal descent were considered viable marriage partners, whatever their specific patriline. Those of non-tribal or low-status tribal origin were excluded from this larger pool, and so were compelled to marry within their own smaller circles. It is in these cross-cut patterns of endogamy and exogamy that the social hierarchies of the town emerge most clearly.

In the marriage patterns of the ruling al-Sudayrī family, a high rate of tribal endogamy prevailed. Of 27 marriages in which at least one partner was identified as al-Sudayrī, 16 involved families from the same tribe (Dawāsir), while 11 of these 27 included two al-Sudayrī partners. The prevalence of al-Sudayrī family and tribal endogamy can be interpreted as a political strategy designed to broaden the ruling house's legitimacy within the larger patriline.[16] For the Sudayrīs, endogamy was a prerogative of rule that was exercised freely.

At the opposite end of the social spectrum were the non-tribal inhabitants of al-Ghāṭ. Non-tribals married exclusively into other non-tribal families, yet their marital exclusivity was of a different kind than that of the Sudayrī elite.[17] For non-tribals, who worked often as craftsmen or handymen in central Arabia's villages and towns, endogamy was not a choice, but simply the cost of doing business. One interpretation of the data from al-Ghāṭ suggests that approximately 14 of the 225 documented marriages involved non-tribal families, though Lorimer counted a higher proportion of non-tribal residents ("Bani Khadhīr") in the village's population. Judging by the diversity of their surname pairings, non-tribal families were never in short supply in al-Ghāṭ.

Among the non-ruling, tribal-origin families of al-Ghāṭ, who accounted for the vast majority of documented marriages, social pairing advanced along less predictable lines. A small number of established families such as the Āl Fawzān of the Banī Tamīm tribe, for example, tended to marry within their own family. Most al-Ghāṭ families, such as the Āl ʿAlī of the Subayʿ tribe, intermarried with a host of different families from different tribes, and almost never with the same family twice. Despite the sense advanced by Ḥamad al-Jāsir and other Saudi scholars that Najdi settlers and nomads enjoyed a broad commonality of tribal-genealogical outlook,[18] the marital practices of central Arabia's sedentary populations were materially distinct from those of the surrounding bedouin communities. Rather than a tribally endogamous oasis of sedentarized bedouin, then, al-Ghāṭ is best thought of as a town of date farmers of diverse lineages whose common economic lot and sustained cohabitation helped naturalize the process of marital exchange between them. If a tendency toward tribal and family endogamy existed in al-Ghāṭ's history, this tendency was often overwhelmed by the exigencies of central Arabian settled life, which demanded a flexible attitude toward one's solidarities.

A measure of this township solidarity can be observed in the frequency of marriage and remarriage across lineages in al-Ghāṭ. Female remarriage in particular was a frequent occurrence. Fāṭima bint ʿAbdallāh b. Dāghir, for example, was married to three different men over the course of her lifetime, each from a different tribal background.[19] A number of other al-Ghāṭ women were also married several times during their lifetime, most often following the deaths of their first or second husbands. Such practices contributed to the often wide disparities in the ages of husbands and wives, a phenomenon that persists to a certain extent in the modern kingdom, especially in rural areas. The frequency of female remarriage across lineages in the al-Ghāṭ documents is evidence as well of a societal priority to ensure the extension of the social safety net to widows, and would seem to override the kinship priority of retaining a woman's share of her inheritance within the agnatic line.[20]

The notion of township solidarity emerges most clearly when we compare the al-Ghāṭ records with findings from a comparable source, an early twentieth-century marital register from the western Arabian port city of Jeddah. The marital register of Shaykh Ṣāliḥ Qandīl contains entries for at least 127 marriages contracted among Jeddah's inhabitants between 1930 and 1950.[21] The register is a cornucopia of diverse names and national origins, reflecting the ethnic diversity of Jeddah's historical inhabitants. Though larger than al-Ghāṭ, Jeddah was no doubt still a smallish community during this period, as evidenced by the fact that the witnesses to several marriages are the grooms in others. Significantly, whereas 13.5 percent of marriages contracted in al-Ghāṭ during this same period (1930–50) were endogamous within a given family, only 4.7 percent of the marriages in the Jeddah register were thus.[22] The inhabitants of Jeddah, even more than those of al-Ghāṭ, practiced a sort of urban or township endogamy.[23] On the one hand, these comparative measures lend weight to the perception that the population centers of central Arabia were more insular and homogeneous than the coastal townships of the Hijaz. On the other, they reveal a common tendency within these two ecologically and sociologically distinct township populations to favor marriage with unrelated neighbors over members of one's own descent line.

The rich and detailed al-Ghāṭ documents are notable as much for what they confirm about historical patterns of endogamy in Middle Eastern societies, as for the license they provide to contemplate kinship and genealogy independent of an endogamy preference, particularly in sedentary contexts. Patrilateral parallel cousin marriage, that ubiquitous trope in the literature on Middle Eastern societies,[24] was not a prevalent feature of the kinship patterns in al-Ghāṭ. By statistical measure, marriages in al-Ghāṭ were more coincidental pairings than affirmations of lineal solidarity.

CULTIVATING THE FAMILY TREE

The marital history of one tribal-origin al-Ghāṭ family stands in conspicuous defiance of the above-described order. Between 1837 and 1950, the Āl Sulaymān family is recorded to have contracted nine marriages in the town of al-Ghāṭ.[25] In each of these cases, the Āl Sulaymān married members of their own family. The Āl Sulaymān were thought to descend from the ʿAwāzim, a tribe that is ascribed less than prestigious origins in central Arabian historical and popular perception.[26] Unlike al-Ghāṭ's other tribal-origin families, it seems, the Āl Sulaymān were stuck in an endogamous trap, unable to marry up or out of their social circumstances. During his fieldwork among the Āl Murra bedouin of the Empty Quarter, Donald Cole observed that three of the Āl Murra's branches, comprising less than a tenth of its population, were excluded from the pool of prospective marital exchanges with the tribe's majority branches, as they were thought to descend from the union between a tribal male and a woman of slave status.[27] It was likely some such reputational hazard that compelled the Āl Sulaymān to practice a form of family endogamy unusual within their surrounding community. The marital patterns of the Āl Sulaymān family provide uncommon historical evidence for the ubiquitous yet empirically elusive sense of social hierarchy that pervades the modern Saudi imagination. In the ordinary muddle of the al-Ghāṭ documents, that pattern is at least clear.

The earliest reference to the Āl Sulaymān family in the al-Ghāṭ documents dates from 1837, in which year Aḥmad b. Sulaymān sold a tamarisk tree inherited from his father to a fellow town resident. In 1850, Aḥmad's brother Ḥusayn b. Sulaymān issued a last testament apportioning his date palms among his wife, parents, and other members of his family, while reserving a sizeable plot for the provisioning of hospitality to future guests and passing indigents. The final mention of the family dates from May 1950, in a document that deals again with the distribution of an inheritance. The tribal affiliation of the Āl Sulaymān, like that of every other inhabitant of al-Ghāṭ, was never documented on paper. It was a matter of oral record, an inheritance passed from generation to generation, like so many date palms and tamarisk trees. Now, with the dispersion of kin groups throughout the new Saudi Arabia, the need many Saudis feel to construct an organic and pristine vision of the lives of their ancestors has bumped up against some of the uncomfortable truths about the position of those ancestors within the premodern social fabric. Thus begins the process of lineal reinvention, concerning which the Āl Sulaymān provide only the example of the day. In recent years, members of the Āl Sulaymān family have launched a multi-pronged campaign—waged mostly on the Internet—to dissociate themselves from an ʿAwāzim connection and affirm a different lineage, a Prophetic lineage. On the family's website, Ḥusayn b. Sulaymān has thus become al-Sharīf Ḥusayn b. Sulaymān, and his brother Aḥmad has been affixed as a central node in the family tree that traces the Āl Sulaymān's roots back to the grandson of the Prophet Muḥammad, Ḥasan b. ʿAlī b. Abī Ṭālib.

The Āl Sulaymān family tree is the crowning statement of this new genealogical turn, a colorful announcement of the family's liberation from the small-town constraints of old. The tree is planted two dimensionally in the foreground of a photograph from the Ghāṭ region. Date palms grow in the background. Unlike most other central Arabian family trees, which authorize themselves by invoking Quranic verse 49:13 (". . . we have made you peoples and tribes so that you may come to know one another . . ."), the Āl Sulaymān tree is prefaced by a different verse (33:33: ". . . God wishes only to remove uncleanliness from you, O people of the family [of the Prophet], and purify you completely . . ."), a choice typical of Saudi Ashrāf genealogies. Sulaymān, father of the Aḥmad referenced in the 1837 document, is situated seven places up from the tree's base, his progeny amassed above him in the branches and leaves. At the base of the trunk sits another Sulaymān, the family's *jadd al-jāmiʿ* ("the unifying ancestor"), the ancestor around whom the lineage is ontologically formed.

For the key turn in the narrative, the arboreal imagery is left behind, and the tree's creator shifts to bold-faced, annotated prose. At the bottom of the diagram, listed horizontally across the page, are the names of the 23 ancestors that link this original Sulaymān to the Prophet's son-in-law ʿAlī (through Ḥasan). To the left side of the tree are the signatures and seals of four purported Ashrāf authorities, who vouch for the veracity of the tree's genealogical claims. For all of its aesthetic appeal, the Sulaymān tree, like thousands of others of its kind created in Saudi Arabia over the past thirty or so years, is no more than an exercise in speculative reasoning, an effort to shape new social realities against a bleak historiographical landscape. The Āl Sulaymān tree was created in response to a problem, namely, the family's dissatisfaction with the inherited understanding of its lineal origins. The al-Ghāṭ documents preserved the family's marital history, which expressed in latent form a social problem that had remained local and implicit until the moment of their aggregation and publication. The transmission of such implicit understandings into the modern period reinforces one of the secondary contentions of this book, that Saudi attachment to caste-like social hierarchies reflects a degree of continuity with the Arabian past, and is not purely an invention of the Saudi oil age.

The appearance of the Āl Sulaymān website and the publication of the Āl Sulaymān family tree injured the feelings of at least one local family who, not coincidentally, also claimed Ashrāf descent. Ashrāf lineages are relatively uncommon in Najd. While Prophetic genealogies are those most glorified in Islam, for both religious and political reasons they carry less prestige in central Arabia than in the Hijaz. In religious terms, Wahhabism has always been strongly suspicious of any personifications of divinity, and the veneration of Prophetic (Ashrāf) lineages that was practiced historically in the Hijaz (as in many other Islamic societies) is seen by strict Wahhabis as an extension of this slippage into heterodoxy. In political terms, the dominant rivals of the Āl Saʿūd in the early twentieth century, the Hashemite rulers of western Arabia, claimed a Prophetic lineage, and their displacement meant also the downgrading of the ideology that legitimated their rule in Najdi popular consciousness. Despite these considerations, assertions of Ashrāf lineages have become an increasingly common vehicle for Najdi *ḥaḍar* reputational rehabilitation, not least because such assertions are more difficult to confirm or deny than claims of attachment to more familiar Najdi lineages.

In May 2013, a member of an aggrieved al-Ghāṭ family created an anonymous blog dedicated solely to refuting the Āl Sulaymān's claims to Ashrāf status and restoring the family's ʿAwāzim association as a matter of public record. The blogger provided no explanation for his action beyond a desire to clarify the local record, but his family's own assertion of Ashrāf origins suggests an anxiety about the veracity of its own genealogical claims, and the effect that the aggressive mythologizing of historical neighbors might have on them. The story of the Āl Sulaymān thus initiates us into the blood sport that is the kingdom's modern genealogical culture. Second, it highlights the significance of marital patterns as corollaries to the unspoken norms that govern the kingdom's kinship politics. Lastly, the Āl Sulaymān story demonstrates some important lessons about the symbolic interaction of blood and soil in the production of modern Saudi genealogies.

More so than the dissolution of the kinship unit, it is the breakdown of the territorial unit and the trust that came from knowing one's neighbors and their lineal origins that explains why marriage has been foisted front and center into the kingdom's modern genealogical struggles. We have moved from the Arabia of Cole in which a bedouin from the Āl Murra might encounter a herder in the desert and by inquiring about his lineage come to know "almost everything about him."[28] With the game of obscuring and reinventing lineages in the modern urban Saudi context, there is often very little one can learn from an assertion of lineal affiliation.

For Ḥamad al-Jāsir, who stood at the epicenter of this new turn—as its Prime Mover, some would say—the game of obscuring lineages complicated the objective of his genealogical project, which, though proceeding by the flawed means of taxonomical ordering, aimed to restore a lost sense of solidarity to modern Arabian society. In the absence of credible documentary sources, achieving this aim meant bringing to bear scholarly methods drawn less from the historical tradition in which al-Jāsir was immersed and more from the anthropological study of kinship relations, and specifically, marital patterns. Turning marital patterns into a tool of lineal authentication was a way to resolve the problem that arose from the dispersion of formerly rural populations throughout the kingdom. With this dispersion, local knowledge concerning the marriageability of one's historical neighbors had become obscured, and new anxieties set in respecting the genealogical provenance of one's colleagues and cohabitants.[29]

For petitioners requesting mention in his genealogical volumes, al-Jāsir would press them to provide detailed information about their families' marital patterns as a condition for acceptance.[30] In the scholar's view, marital patterns were the unblemished substrate of a modern genealogical discourse that had been hopelessly polluted by fictions and fabrications. They were the key, not only for unlocking the true identities of individual families claiming tribal origins, but also for recasting the dominant narrative about entire tribes. Though intended to restore a sense of symbolic order to his society, al-Jāsir's genealogical project was also a rehabilitative one. This dimension was seen in the scholar's efforts, discussed in the previous chapter, to prove the authentic tribal origins of central Arabia's putatively non-tribal populations. It could be found as well in his frequent defense of tribes whose reputations had been historically maligned. To take an example, al-Jāsir was a sympathetic advocate for the Āl Sulaymān family's tribe, ʿAwāzim, defending its Arabian roots against the insinuations of skeptics and doubters.[31] Al-Jāsir's most sustained defense of a historically maligned tribe was his 1990 volume *Bāhila: al-Qabīla al-Muftarā ʿAlayhā* (*Bāhila: The Slandered Tribe*), and the most compelling evidence he would muster in its defense was the tribe's marital patterns. The scholar's 726-page polemic against the disparagers of the Bāhila tribe is fascinating as well for what it reveals about the interplay between religion and other facets of culture in the modern kingdom.

BĀHILA: THE SLANDERED TRIBE

As a genealogist, Ḥamad al-Jāsir had a reputation for being "encyclopedic" (*mawsūʿī*). Unlike that of the generation of micro-historians and genealogists that succeeded him, al-Jāsir's focus was the broader tribal history of Arabia, in which the histories of individual tribes were merely exemplifications of a larger phenomenon. Why then did the scholar devote years of time and attention to a monograph about a single, reasonably obscure Saudi tribe? Three answers present themselves. First, *Bāhila* was in all likelihood a commissioned project. In a letter, al-Jāsir alluded to the fact that he had written *Bāhila* "by request" (*ḥasab al-ṭalab*), one likely originating with prominent Saudi Bāhilīs whose power base was the governorship of the town of al-Dirʿiyya.[32] Second, al-Jāsir's father's second wife was of Bāhila origin, and his half-brothers were therefore part Bāhilī.[33] As relevant as they may be to the factual reconstruction of *Bāhila*'s history, these financial and personal incentives fail to explain very much about the content, method, and approach behind the book, nor do they explain why al-Jāsir's introduction of marital patterns as a tool of lineal authentication was so novel and interesting a turn in modern Saudi genealogical and religious discourse. To get at these more salient concerns, some background about the book *Bāhila* is in order.

As al-Jāsir explained, his interest in the Bāhila story was aroused when he observed one of his daughters reading a book by the Syrian religious scholar ʿAlī al-Ṭanṭāwī titled *Rijāl min al-Tārīkh* (*Great Men in History*).[34] Al-Ṭanṭāwī's volume of popular Islamic history, first published in 1958 and in numerous subsequent editions, featured biographical sketches of important historical personalities from the Islamic world, including the early Muslim commander Qutayba b. Muslim (d. 715), who is credited with conquering large sections of Central Asia for Islam. Wringing out as much dramatic contrast as he could muster, al-Ṭanṭāwī described Qutayba b. Muslim's famously problematic lineage: "[Qutayba b. Muslim] was a man whose lineage failed to elevate him, as he was from the basest of the Arab tribes, and the lowliest in status, from a tribe whose sons were ashamed to belong to it, one that served as the proverbial example of baseness, a tribe upon whose mention the status of [all other] Arabs was elevated—Bāhila."[35] Al-Ṭanṭāwī's description of the Bāhila lineage reflected the dominant perception of the Bāhila tribe in Arab history, one that clung to the central Arabian descendants of the tribe into the twentieth century, or was discovered anew in the age of mass literacy.[36] Al-Jāsir himself described how as a child in his hometown of al-Burūd, he and his friends would taunt a local Bāhilī shaykh with a popular line of invective poetry, which called attention to the stain of association with the tribe, even in the most sanctified of places:

> If you were in heaven and your neighbor
> was a Bāhilī
>
> then get out of heaven and seek
> refuge (*izban*) in hell![37]

Mustering a wide range of historical and literary sources, al-Jāsir would devote the succeeding 700 pages of his volume to refuting al-Ṭanṭāwī's premise and the cultural detritus upon which it had been built.

Al-Jāsir's thesis was simple: the Bāhila tribe was a victim of the Shuʿūbiyya, a largely Persian-influenced socio-political movement in early Islam that denied the privileged position of Arabs within the faith.[38] The nobility of the Bāhila tribe would have gone unquestioned, its contributions to Islamic civilization undisputed, had it not been for the Shuʿūbiyya and its medieval Muslim partisans, who, beginning in the ʿAbbāsid era (eighth to thirteenth centuries), came to exercise a strong influence on the tenor of Islamic historiography, and whose anti-Arab biases color Muslim attitudes toward Arabs and Arab lineages to the present day.[39] ʿAlī al-Ṭanṭāwī, like many other learned scholars before him, was an unwitting dupe to this controversy, and was guilty of nothing more than the faithful transmission of a misbegotten piece of Islamic heritage.

To make his case, al-Jāsir and his assistants scoured the canonical history books to compile a biographical dictionary of famous Bawāhil (sing. Bāhilī), whose achievements in letters, politics, and jurisprudence were then juxtaposed alongside those of contemporary members of the lineage, including, for example, the governor and deputy governor of al-Dirʿiyya.[40] Pride of place was reserved for the two most famous Bawāhil, however, Qutayba b. Muslim and the philologist al-Aṣmaʿī (d. 828). It is revealing of the scholar's intellectual sympathies that the entry for al-Aṣmaʿī, at twenty-four pages, is twice the length of that for Qutayba b. Muslim.

No more comprehensive rebuttal of al-Ṭanṭāwī's assertion about the Bāhila tribe could have been mustered.[41] Yet a larger question remains: why did a thirty-year-old book of popular history so stir the ire of an elderly central Arabian historian and his patrons? The answer to this question requires a digression into a field largely unexplored in this book, namely, the modern religious culture of Saudi Arabia, and its influence on public life in the kingdom. ʿAlī al-Ṭanṭāwī, the object of al-Jāsir's opprobrium in *Bāhila*, was an important symbol of this new religious culture. A Damascus-born religious scholar, he rose to a prominent position in the Syrian judiciary before being purged in the Baʿthist revolution of 1963.[42] Exiled from his homeland, al-Ṭanṭāwī, like many other Islamist intellectuals, took up residence in Saudi Arabia (Mecca and later Jeddah) and became one of the most influential religious personalities in the kingdom.

A comparative glance at the biographies of al-Ṭanṭāwī and al-Jāsir reveals how much the two elderly luminaries had in common. They were born roughly a year apart at the beginning of the twentieth century, and died within a year of one another, both having lived past ninety. They were among the first members of their respective societies to receive educations in both traditional Islamic settings (Quranic schools and study circles) and Western-influenced (*niẓāmī*) schools,[43] and both applied their educations as teachers, columnists, and shariah judges.[44] As outspoken activists, both al-Jāsir and al-Ṭanṭāwī ran into trouble with their governments, and both experienced the pain of exile, though for al-Ṭanṭāwī, this pain was permanent. These similarities, however, masked profound differences in their orientation toward the Islamic scholarly tradition, a fact that would emerge clearly in *Bāhila*.

There is some disagreement in the scholarly literature concerning ʿAlī al-Ṭanṭāwī's intellectual orientation. He is described alternatively as a Salafist,[45] a member of the Muslim Brotherhood,[46] and a literary figure.[47] In the context of late twentieth-century Saudi Arabia, however, ʿAlī al-Ṭanṭāwī is best thought of as a pioneering televangelist, a grandfatherly religious scholar with a Levantine accent whose popular moralizing was a fixture of Saudi television and radio programming for over three decades, particularly during Ramaḍān.[48] Al-Ṭānṭāwī was the original "satellite scholar,"[49] a mass media representative of the new wave of religiosity that had set upon the kingdom in the last quarter of the century, the Ṣaḥwa (Awakening). Ḥamad al-Jāsir's relationship to this new wave is significant for explaining the nature of his challenge to al-Ṭanṭāwī, and the motivation behind it.

The Ṣaḥwa was a religious and political movement that emerged in Saudi Arabia in the last quarter of the twentieth century and achieved prominence during the mobilization of domestic Saudi opposition to the 1991 Gulf War. The Ṣaḥwa represented the marriage between the kingdom's developmentalist policies on the one hand and its promotion of Wahhabism as a political ideology on the other. A core component of Saudi Arabia's development strategy in the second half of the twentieth century was the creation of a wide network of educational institutions through which to socialize its citizenry. A central feature of these institutions, whether those designated for general education or those dedicated to training religious functionaries, was an emphasis on religious instruction in the core tenets of Wahhabi Islam.[50] ʿAlī al-Ṭanṭāwī's first job in Saudi Arabia was as a teacher in the system of religious schools established by Muḥammad b. Ibrāhīm Āl al-Shaykh. It was out of these state institutions that the first generation of mass-literate Saudis emerged, and through whom the diverse expressions of the Ṣaḥwa movement would be realized.[51] Of the many ideological dispensations to emerge from the Ṣaḥwa, the lineages of which have been ably unraveled by Stéphane Lacroix, the Salafi movement stands out for its prominence within the Saudi scene.

As Bernard Haykel explains, Salafism is a particular orientation toward Islamic religious authority that is characterized by an emphasis on the creedal tenets of Sunni Islam, particularly the doctrine of God's unicity (*tawḥīd*); a rejection of the *madhhab* (legal school) tradition of Islamic jurisprudence in favor of direct engagement with Islamic proof texts (Quran and Sunna); and an active suspicion of rival movements within the faith, especially Sufism and Shiism.[52] Classical Wahhabism upheld two of these three positions,[53] and its worldwide propagation by the modern Saudi state ensured a widely influential place for a Saudi-inflected Salafism in modern Islamic thought. "The Salafi imagination reconstructs the early Muslims' sartorial, linguistic, cultural and ethical habits and insists on being exactly like them."[54] Though sartorially ʿAlī al-Ṭanṭāwī may have looked the part of a Salafi on television, and though his late career credentials may have been grudgingly acknowledged by the influential Salafi scholar Nāṣir al-Dīn al-Albānī,[55] as a fellow polymath, al-Ṭanṭāwī's Salafi religiosity was less doctrinaire and textualist than the variant that had come to predominate in Saudi Arabia during the final decades of al-Jāsir's life.[56]

Al-Jāsir's relationship to the kingdom's dominant religious tradition, Wahhabism, was complex. On the one hand, he idealized Muḥammad b. ʿAbd al-Wahhāb as a sort of founding father of the Arabian politico-religious renaissance. Yet while publicly al-Jāsir remained a dutiful proponent of Saudi

Salafism, and was not wont to see a great distinction between the national and religious facets of the kingdom's identity, the scholar complained privately of the influence of the Ṣaḥwa movement in the education process, in its turning out an excessive number of religious functionaries, for example.[57] While critics were often quick to harp on his crypto-secular habits, al-Jāsir seemed satisfied by the fact that his body rhythms were synchronized to the Islamic prayer calendar, and would mock younger scholars who considered that a morning appointment at the Shaykh's home meant nine in the morning, when it really meant five or six.[58] In one sense, modern Salafism was a continuation of Muḥammad b. ʿAbd al-Wahhāb and his Wahhabi movement's effort to denude Arabia of its cultural specificity, by imposing the semblance of another culture, that of the Prophet Muḥammad and his times. Such a turn was distasteful to a historian such as al-Jāsir, whose sympathies for the heritage of his locale were on display at almost every stage of his life. Rather than an endorsement of this delocalizing turn, then, al-Jāsir's consistent praise of Muḥammad b. ʿAbd al-Wahhāb's legacy is better viewed as a form of pride in the accomplishments of an Arabian native son. It was this central Arabian nativism that would greatly color al-Jāsir's critique of al-Ṭanṭāwī.

Al-Jāsir's polemic against ʿAlī al-Ṭanṭāwī was his first public challenge to a religious scholar since the 1950s. When he had last confronted the sanctified position of the central Arabian religious establishment, he was shunted from public life and nearly executed. Yet it was not for doctrinal reasons that al-Jāsir went after al-Ṭanṭāwī. As influential a figure as he was in matters of popular religious interpretation, al-Ṭanṭāwī was a foreigner in Saudi Arabia, and therefore low-hanging fruit. Even more significant was the fact that ʿAlī al-Ṭanṭāwī had trampled through the domain of Arabian genealogies, territory to which Ḥamad al-Jāsir held near-exclusive claim. To find his interests in genealogy appropriated by a prominent foreign-born purveyor of Ṣaḥwī religious discourse seemed a revelatory moment for al-Jāsir. Now a senior and respected figure, long released from dependency on Muḥammad b. Ibrāhīm (d. 1969) and the Wahhabi religious establishment, al-Jāsir could appropriate Ṣaḥwī discourse and turn it on its head to advance his own arguments about what was truly right and wrong, ethical and unethical, in an Arabian context. The big-tent religiosity of al-Ṭanṭāwī and the Saudi Ṣaḥwī scholars who came under his influence would not be achieved at the expense of the good name of central Arabia's tribes.[59]

Since it was a polemic against an eminent religious authority, al-Jāsir crafted *Bāhila* with pious care, and with a keen sense for the necessary decorum. At the outset of the volume, the scholar could be seen clearing a wide berth for his subsequent assault. "As the most exalted sayer [i.e., God] said: 'Verily, the most noble among you is the most God-fearing.'"[60] Here, in this excerpt from Quran 49:13 embedded in *Bāhila*'s first paragraph, was al-Jāsir's assertion of the privileging of the community of believers over peoples and tribes in God's final reckoning. As a quasi-colophonic device it was a marked departure from the emphasis of his earlier genealogical volumes, and was an affirmation that al-Jāsir would proceed in the remainder of the volume to stand on its head.

To refute al-Ṭanṭāwī's assertions and the authority on which they were based, al-Jāsir adopted methods drawn from Salafi religious discourse, co-opting basic Salafi tenets for a distinctly un-Salafi historicism. Thus, al-Ṭanṭāwī's rote transmission of inherited attitudes toward the Bāhila tribe amounted to *taqlīd*, technically an Islamic legal practice that involved emulating the opinions of juristic forebears, though here used by al-Jāsir in the more popular pejorative sense of blind imitation.[61] "My love and respect for this exalted imam would not possess me to accept everything he said on its own terms, without my being convinced of its soundness."[62] Building on this critique, and as a way of further emphasizing al-Ṭanṭāwī's non-Arabian provenance, al-Jāsir singled out his adherence to certain misguided precepts of the Ḥanafī legal school, Ḥanbalism being the dominant school in Saudi Arabia, and the school of Muḥammad b. ʿAbd al-Wahhāb. Specifically, al-Jāsir accused al-Ṭanṭāwī of being unduly influenced by a tendency within the late Ḥanafī legal literature on lineal compatibility in marriage (*kafāʾa fī l-nasab*) to make explicit reference to the base status of Bāhila as evidence for the legitimacy of marital hierarchies among the Arabs.[63]

The principle of lineal compatibility in marriage was a central feature of Islamic jurisprudence from its inception. This principle affirmed the validity of marital status hierarchies in Arab societies, and thus provided legal justification for diverse forms of marital endogamy.[64] In central Arabia's settled communities, lineal compatibility in marriage was a principle validated by generations of Islamic judges.[65] Yet underlying the legal discourse on *kafāʾa* was always a visceral sense of the compelling force of social practice, *ʿurf*, the apprehension of which, al-Jāsir argued, had escaped al-Ṭanṭāwī and other critics of Bāhila.[66] While in private al-Jāsir criticized Najdi religious scholars for their surrender to the popular will on matters of lineal compatibility,[67] in *Bāhila* he redirected his angst toward a scholarly migrant who gave this will insufficient credence.

As al-Jāsir reasoned, Bāhila's unjustified insertion into the Islamic legal record as a proverbial example of lineal incompatibility was belied by the historical and contemporary evidence of the tribe's marital patterns in Arabia. These patterns revealed that

> . . . the Bāhila tribe had lived in its lands on the Najdi plateau, among its sisters, who formed with it links of lineage and adjacent residency, from the earliest times to the present. It lived a life of harmony, coop-

> eration, and familial closeness in every respect. Never did there occur any estrangement that set the tribe apart from others, and never was the tribe known for any moral turpitude that would have caused any sort of boycott of the tribe throughout these centuries. There is no better evidence for the ignorance of those who wish to create a gulf between Bāhila and her sister Arab tribes than their lack of awareness about this tribe's deep and firmly rooted ties to every Arab tribe, ties that remain strong and continuous. These ties would be known by those who lived among the tribe in its homeland in the heart of the Peninsula of the Arabs (*jazīrat al-ʿarab*). As for those who describe [Bāhila] when they are as far away from it as can be, or those who grab after what has been written about it without verifying its truthfulness, it is inappropriate for them to lead others astray, to describe the tribe with qualities of which it is innocent, and so do it injustice. . . .[68]

For al-Jāsir, the ultimate refutation of the injustice visited upon Bāhila was to be found with resort to a form of recondite knowledge inaccessible to others, the tribe's marital patterns. Beginning with Bāhila's ties to ancient tribes, al-Jāsir turned to its marital relations with modern Arabian families and tribes: "Bāhila, like its sister tribes . . . continues to preserve its social position among the tribes. Just as it had strengthened its connections to the ancient tribes such as Quraysh, Tamīm, and others, it continued its strong and lasting ties with every modern tribe, without exception."[69] In minute detail, al-Jāsir then proceeded to adduce Bāhila's ties of marriage to the families and tribes of Saudi Arabia, including his own. Exposing the personal details of Saudi family life was an unprecedented turn in the history of letters in the kingdom, but a necessary one if the scholar's ends were to be resolutely achieved. The marriage patterns of the Bāhila families reflected the inner logic of Arabian society, against which centuries of invective poetry, jurisprudential reasoning, and popular conjecture would be compelled to retreat.[70]

It is unclear what if anything al-Ṭanṭāwī had to say about this lengthy polemic directed against him. His own views on the transience and insignificance of kinship ties and the impossibility of solace outside of God's embrace, captured in a lecture he presented on his Ramaḍān program, *ʿAlā Māʾidat al-Ifṭār* (*At the Fast-Breaking Table*), suggest that al-Jāsir's erudite challenge rang hollow and unanswered.[71] Yet the dispute over the historical reputation of the Bāhila tribe illustrates how purveyors of Arabia's modern genealogical discourse, with al-Jāsir at their helm, used local knowledge, such as that of marital patterns, to counteract universalizing tendencies of the sort promoted by al-Ṭanṭāwī. In the case of *Bāhila*, it was not so much the dispersion of kin groups by the forces of the national market that had obscured this local knowledge, as the expanding reign of a media-driven, delocalized religious culture, the Ṣaḥwa, which sought to blur the distinctions that gave meaning to the intellectual life and personal identity of Ḥamad al-Jāsir and so many other Saudis. With *Bāhila*, marital patterns were presented by al-Jāsir as a solution to a genealogical problem that had accompanied the Bāhila tribe throughout its long history. Ethnographic facts of this kind were central to al-Jāsir's conception of an authentic Arabian ethics, one grounded in lineal rootedness in the Najdi locale, and oriented toward a conference of cohabitants ("peoples and tribes") in the final reckoning.

AN ABSENT PRESENCE: WOMEN AND GENEALOGY

One aspect of al-Jāsir's description of the modern marriage patterns of the Bāhila tribe appears curious. Documenting a marriage between two families in his hometown of al-Burūd, the scholar wrote: "ʿAbdallāh b. ʿAbd al-Karīm Āl Nāhiḍ married the daughter of Fahd b. Rāshid al-Bāhilī."[72] Though the groom's name was mentioned, the name of the bride was censored. This practice was not unique to al-Jāsir, and reflected the emergence of a new sense of decorum in Saudi letters, in which women's names would be obscured from public life like their physical persons, through restrictions on dress, mobility, employment, and other aspects of life in modern Saudi Arabia. The novelty of this exclusion of women's names from the genealogical register is emphasized when one compares al-Jāsir's approach to that of Ibn ʿĪsā, whom al-Jāsir respected as one of the foremost historians and genealogists of premodern central Arabia. In an undated pre-1925 text listing the members of his lineage, Ibn ʿĪsā included the names of family matriarchs alongside those of patriarchs.[73] Unconcerned with attaching his kinship group to a mythical ancient ancestor in the way of modern genealogists, Ibn ʿĪṣā's document epitomized the localized nature of the premodern Arabian genealogical imagination, one in which women could be viewed as relatively equal progenitors in the life of the kinship group, and gender roles had yet to be defined in modern ideological terms by the political and religious institutions of the Saudi state.[74] In a contemporaneous rendering of Ibn ʿĪsā's lineage as a family tree, however, the names of family matriarchs were excluded.[75] At this higher level of abstraction, the Arabian genealogical imagination could not abide a bifurcated narrative of origination.[76]

As noted, al-Jāsir's censoring of women's names from the genealogical register was not unique to the scholar. The withholding of women's names was a common practice in the kingdom's emergent print culture, and was a symbolic reflection of the glorification and protection of women's private honor by male guardians, and their simultaneous exclusion from the Saudi public sphere. This "veiling" of women's names pointed to a number of changes in modern Saudi life: the emergence of a new print culture in which

Figure 4.1. Āl ʿĪsā family tree (undated). Courtesy of the King Abdulaziz Foundation for Research and Archives.

the private lives of Saudis could be exposed to public scrutiny, as they were in *Bāhila*, and the semantic measures taken to circumvent such outcomes; the dispersion of kinship groups and the weakening of the bonds of trust among the members of Saudi society, now living as mutually unfamiliar cohabitants in the kingdom's new urban centers;[77] and the emergence of the Ṣaḥwa movement and its influence on Saudi public life, which culminated in an effort to create a segregated space in which women would experience a gender-specific, state-authorized Saudi modernity. Taken together, these developments positioned women, especially young marriageable women, as a central battleground in the kinship politics of the modern kingdom. One story in particular, a family reunification narrative recounted by a witness to the events, is illustrative of how women have become instrumentalized in the kingdom's genealogical politics.

The ʿAdwān were a family of several hundred members from the northern Arabian town of Dūmat al-Jandal. They were known historically in their hometown as carpenters and rifle makers, *ṣunnāʿ*, or artisans of non-tribal descent. Two decades ago, a member of the family produced a genealogical tree affirming the family's descent from the Ḥarb tribe of Medina. As with the Āl Sulaymān family, the creation of the ʿAdwān family tree was a manifestation of a growing desire to escape the stigma of their known origins and attach their lineages to a prominent Arabian tribe. The population of Dūmat al-Jandal, an ancient town in the Jawf region, was a mixture of tribal and non-tribal inhabitants. Members of the ʿAdwān, though well-off financially, were sometimes made the subject of ridicule by tribal inhabitants of the town, who considered them modern interlopers without any true standing in the region. The competition for tribal prestige in the town was compounded by a scramble for government jobs, in which members of tribal lineages were known to extend the hand of patronage to fellow kinsmen, while non-tribals, having fewer such connections in that town, were restricted from such avenues of advancement.

Assured of their lineal provenance, and with arboreal evidence in hand, members of the ʿAdwān contacted leaders of the Zughaybāt, a branch of the Ḥarb tribe in Medina. Far from rejecting their entreaty, the Zughaybāt shaykhs agreed to provide an official testimonial affirming the ʿAdwān's belonging to their lineage. Despite the lineal poverty of the ʿAdwān, its members were comparatively well-off, and the Zughaybāt could benefit materially from their new (or renewed) association with the family. In addition, the Zughaybāt shaykhs viewed the incorporation of far-flung elements of their lineage into the tribe as a way of enhancing their national prestige and reach. It didn't hurt that the ʿAdwān were the right shade of brown—non-tribal, yet not too dark to suggest African descent, which, as will be shown in the next chapter, connoted slave or migrant origin.

The Zughaybāt leaders made their approval of the incorporation of the ʿAdwān contingent on one condition—that the ʿAdwān desist from marrying their daughters to non-tribal families. In response to this proposal, the head of the ʿAdwān family invited the patriarchs of the various al-ʿAdwān branches to a meeting at his home in Dūmat al-Jandal, where he presented the Zughaybāt leaders' testimonial to the group and described the condition for its execution. All were in agreement regarding the condition of incorporation, except one member, ʿAbdallāh al-ʿAdwān. ʿAbdallāh al-ʿAdwān was a progressive man, who had no interest in the family's play for tribal recognition, or at least none that involved such intrusive conditions. While the rest of the family implemented the Zughaybāt shaykhs' condition, marrying off some of their daughters within the Zughaybāt tribe to strengthen mutual ties between them, ʿAbdallāh refused to play along. After the divorce of one of his daughters, ʿAbdallāh al-ʿAdwān arranged for her remarriage to a non-tribal man, in violation of the family's agreement. As a result, ʿAbdallāh was shunned by the rest of his family, who refused to marry his daughters or marry their daughters to his sons. He had been shorn of family in a society that cherished kinship, for the simple reason that he had refused to go along with a ruse.

The condition imposed by the Zughaybāt shaykhs on the ʿAdwān created some unexpected problems for the family. The ʿAdwān had a large number of daughters of marrying age. Yet they were limited by the terms of their agreement to seeking suitors from tribal families. At the same time, the tribal families in the Dūmat al-Jandal region were unmoved by the ʿAdwān's newfound assertions of tribal origin, and so refused to marry into the family. The ʿAdwān had created a bind for themselves with their genealogical aspirations, which resulted in an increase in spinsterhood within the family. One member of the family decreed a solution to this problem: "we will marry our daughters off internally, within the family."

Thus by contingent and roundabout means, the ʿAdwān family was returned, at least in principle, to a pattern of strict, endogamous marriage. Like the Āl Sulaymān family of al-Ghāt, the ʿAdwān sought to escape the confines of their small-town reputations with recourse to broader and more resonant identity claims. To achieve their new lineal position, the ʿAdwān redirected the marital choices of their daughters, until these choices ran dry. The discovery of tribal identities is thus revealed to have real consequences for the lives of Saudi women, such as the ʿAdwān daughters, who, even if they might benefit materially and symbolically from the laundering of their identities, seem not to have been consulted in their family's decision, and yet were forced to absorb its consequences.

The modern genealogical discourse of Saudi Arabia is driven almost entirely by men. Why is this so? One might think of genealogy as a domain of privilege for men, even more explicitly so than the strongly patriarchal Saudi religious domain. Whereas Islam works in part against male privilege, or possesses normative checks on such privilege,[78] genealogy, through the principle of patrilineage, enshrines this privilege as its animating virtue. As the Saudi state assumes guardianship over the progress of women in society, increasingly removing them from the authority of male guardians, male privilege appears to slip further away. The glorification of patrilineal roots and family trees conveys the sense that this slippage can be arrested.[79]

For their count, Saudi women have less incentive to reinforce the ideology of patrilineage that lies at the heart of modern affirmations of tribal identity. By their nature, such affirmations marginalize the importance of matrilineages to the legitimation of social position, and thus diminish the feminine subject.[80] One manifestation of this phenomenon is the stigma attached to surnames associated with women. Today, Saudi men believed to descend from a feminine eponym will often work hard to rewrite the narratives of their own origins, whitewashing this perception by shaping their patrilineage along more palatable gender lines.[81]

Though the breathless inquiries of Ḥamad al-Jāsir's female phone petitioners would appear to reinforce or perpetuate this patrilineal discourse, their inquiries were just as likely of a pragmatic bent, a nod to social conventions or the expectations of their families, both mothers and fathers. While tribal origin is a necessary criterion for desirability as a marriage partner, it is not a sufficient one, and the invention of tribal roots can be a forgivable offense when other qualities prove attractive. In matters of marriage, tribal identity is often no more than a box to be checked, an acquiescence to social norms that helps avoid unwanted attention. At the opposite extreme, the absence of a correct lineage can lead to the forced breakup of marriages by aggrieved agnates, as in the well-publicized recent court case of Fāṭima al-ʿAzzāz and Manṣūr al-Taymānī,[82] and as transpired a century earlier in Ḥamad al-Jāsir's own family. The Ashrāf grandmother of al-Jāsir's wife was herself victimized by a rude form of Arabian marital politics, when her marriage to a non-Ashrāf Najdi male was forcibly nullified by the ruler of Mecca,[83] and she was compelled to return to the guardianship of her father in Mecca, leaving her young daughter (Ḥamad al-Jāsir's mother-in-law) behind to be raised by her former in-laws.

While the dispersion of kinship groups may be a driving force behind the desire to authenticate the tribal lineages of prospective marriage partners and others, it is the continued concentration of these groups in the kingdom's small towns and cities and their interaction with bedouin-origin populations that has propelled their own claims to pure tribal origins, and often in the face of deep skepticism toward such claims. In the following chapter, we look closely at the history of one such community, and the racial stigmas that linger in the background of its genealogical assertions.

CHAPTER FIVE

Parallel Migrations, Divergent Destinations

Mushaylih al-Blūwwī: Who is Ḥamad al-Jāsir?
Mālik Āl Ḥasan: The Scholar. The Scholar of genealogy and history.

As the *al-ʿArab* letters make apparent, the modern genealogical culture of Saudi Arabia is principally about the reclamation of widely recognized tribal identities from the loose grip of history. Those without prominent tribal or family names aspire to universal recognition of their origins; so, obscure toponymic and family or clan surnames are discarded, and prominent and well-known tribal names (e.g., Dawsarī, Qaḥṭānī, Ḥarbī) are embraced in pursuit of conformity and prestige. This chapter plots two such reclamations, and the various obstacles that litter the path to universal recognition of pure tribal origins for Saudis of sedentary background. Inspiring these acts of reclamation are two stories of migration from a common point of origin, the villages and grazing lands south of Medina. It was from Medina's outskirts that the Shubūl, Ḥamad al-Jāsir's ancestral clan, were believed to have migrated east to Najd in the early part of the eighteenth century, and, several centuries earlier, one Ḥasan al-Nuʿaymī was thought to have departed for the northwest Arabian oasis town of al-ʿUlā, where his descendants now live.[1] The parallel migration narratives that frame this chapter are rooted principally in the collective memories of these two kin groups. These groups share little in common apart from their putative Medinan origins, their claims to descent from the same mythic tribal forefather, Ḥarb, and their sometimes quixotic attachment to a murky genealogical paper trail. Both face the challenge of authenticating their belonging in the Kingdom of Saudi Arabia, where the anonymity of the tribal name or affiliation—that comforting obscurity derived from attachment to a like-named multitude—is the surest defense against stigmatization.

Through the efforts of their respective genealogists, the Shubūl and the people of al-ʿUlā were able to achieve a measure of recognition in the modern genealogical culture of the kingdom. Ḥamad al-Jāsir's prominent status within central Arabian society and his expertise in genealogy reinforced the authority of his assertions about his own lineal identity, and contributed to his embrace by Ḥarb historians and biographers as an iconic member of the tribe.[2] By contrast, the people of al-ʿUlā have had to deal with a legacy of skepticism concerning their origins, a skepticism rooted in questions of perceived racial or ethnic difference and the often unacknowledged stain of slave origins.[3] This skepticism is compounded by the integration of their far-flung western Arabian oasis into central Arabia's kingdom, where narratives of lineal exclusivity have become measures of authentic national belonging. The intermingling of bedouin-origin and sedentary Saudis in towns such as al-ʿUlā has cast this skepticism in relief, and compelled the historical inhabitants of the town to intensify their assertions of tribal authenticity, to mixed results. In plotting the parallel narratives of the tribal origins of the people of al-ʿUlā and those of Ḥamad al-Jāsir's hometown, al-Burūd, this chapter calls attention to the role played by perceptions of racial difference in Saudi narratives of tribal authenticity. Further, by focusing on the histories of two parallel though disparate claimants to lineal origination within the Ḥarb tribe, I hope to demonstrate the multiple levels of signification—local and national, oral and textual—at which tribal identities have been asserted and contested in modern Saudi Arabia.

AL-ʿULĀ: A SINGULAR OASIS

Al-ʿUlā is an oasis town in the northwest of Saudi Arabia. It is situated in Wādī al-Qurā, "The Valley of the Towns," an important battleground during the early Islamic conquests, and one of the most fertile valleys in northern Arabia. Because of its abundant fresh water springs, fed by an underground aquifer, Wādī al-Qurā was for centuries an important caravan station for merchants, pilgrims, and bedouin, traders and raiders alike. The valley was also home to a sedentary population, who cultivated date palms and exchanged goods with visitors transiting to or from the holy cities of Mecca and Medina, the latter of which sits approximately 220 miles south of the valley. Al-ʿUlā was the largest settlement in Wādī al-Qurā, which extends approximately 30 miles from its northern reaches near al-Ḥijr, site of the famous Nabatean ruins of Madā'in Ṣāliḥ, to the village of Mughayra in the south. Like most settlements in premodern Arabia, al-ʿUlā was a town built largely of mud-brick and surrounded by a protective wall. It was situated at one of the

Figure 5.1. Al-ʿUlā's date palm plantations, with a woman in a wheat field in the foreground (1910). Courtesy of the Ècole Biblique et Archéologique Française de Jerusalem.

narrowest points of Wādī al-Qurā, on an oblong plateau that juts out of the sheer rock face along the valley's western edge, a location chosen to protect against flash floods and bedouin raids.[4]

Charles Doughty, who visited al-ʿUlā in 1876, estimated 1,300 inhabitants of the town, a number reaffirmed by the French archaeologists Antonin Jaussen and Raphaël Savignac, who visited the area in 1909.[5] It was only in the 1960s that the population began to expand beyond the traditional confines of the old town, when the infrastructure of modern living was introduced—asphalt roads, electricity, concrete buildings—and when the character of al-ʿUlā was permanently refashioned. Today, al-ʿUlā Province, encompassing the town, surrounding villages, and bedouin settlements (*hujar*), is home to more than 100,000 people. To picture al-ʿUlā before this transformation is to envision an oasis at the center of an arid region of more than 100,000 square miles populated mostly by nomadic bedouin. To the north were the Fuqarā branch of the ʿAnaza confederation, whose grazing lands extended north from al-Ḥijr, forming part of a band of ʿAnaza branches that stretched from al-ʿUlā to the Syrian steppe. To the west and south were bedouin of the Balī tribe,[6] whose leader Ibn Rifāda revolted unsuccessfully against Saudi authority in the early part of the twentieth century.[7] By the 1960s, these bedouin groups had been settled in *hujar* communities attached administratively to the town center.

"Civilization imposed itself on the bedouin," Shaykh Fahd b. Sulṭān of the Fuqarā said with a hint of a smile, as we reclined in the massive, semi-permanent tent erected next to his home in the *hijra* of ʿUdhayb, ten minutes north of al-ʿUlā. Just outside of the tent was a decorative fountain, newly installed and gushing water, of a size often seen in a public square. The town of al-ʿUlā is striking for the number of public fountains to be found in its streets and squares; al-ʿUlā's fountains seem to outnumber those of central Riyadh, a city possibly one hundred times its size. Some residents of al-ʿUlā consider these decorative public fountains to be a waste of precious fresh water. Yet the symbolism of the public fountain is apparent, as it transposes into the modern public space al-ʿUlā's historical identity as an oasis with abundant subterranean springs.

Beyond its centrality to the caravan routes, Wādī al-Qurā's capacity to produce agricultural surpluses made it a center of trade in western Arabia second only to Medina. The range of currencies and denominations that circulated in al-ʿUlā before the introduction of the Saudi riyal—dirhams, majīdīs, riyal Faransī (after Franz Joseph I), qurūsh—mirrors the diversity of ancient epigraphy etched on the rock formations that encircle the town—Dedanite, Lihyanite, Nabatean Aramaic, Hebrew, and Arabic. Al-ʿUlā's distinctive identity is marked further by the dating conventions that were particular to the town and surrounding bedouin regions. For the people of al-ʿUlā, as for those of Tabūk to its north and the ʿAnaza bedouin situated in between them, the first calendar month of the year was known as ʿAshūr,[8] while the third through sixth months were known as "the four twins" (*arbaʿ al-tawʾam*), a shorthand reference to two pairs of like-named months in the Islamic calendar.[9]

In the eyes of Western travelers, the people of al-ʿUlā were distinguished by their piety, at least in comparison with other northwest Arabian oases.[10] When the Ottoman authorities, who ruled western Arabia for most of the four centuries prior to World War One, decided to build a rail station in al-ʿUlā in the first decade of the twentieth century, its residents rose in protest, disturbed by the prospect of having to mingle with non-believers.[11] With its proximity to Madāʾin Ṣāliḥ, one of the kingdom's two UNESCO World Heritage Sites, and with the influx of foreign laborers to Saudi Arabia's cities and small towns in the oil age, non-Muslims are increasingly integrated into the fabric of the town's economy, whether in the guise of Western tourists or Asian laborers. Yet the austerity of the Wahhabi age has not skipped over al-ʿUlā, and in some ways has seemed to reinforce some of the town's traditional conservative tendencies. An example is the issue of music. Like many devout Saudis, most people in al-ʿUlā tend to frown on the performance of

Figure 5.2. Jaussen and Savignac's guide Quftān al-Faqīr (1910). Courtesy of the Ècole Biblique et Archéologique Française de Jerusalem.

music for entertainment purposes. Accordingly, there are no longer any music stores in al-ʿUlā. The last such store was shuttered in 2011 when its disapproving landlord refused to renew the shopkeeper's lease.

Despite a deeply ingrained tradition of textual religiosity in the town, magical thinking still persists in the al-ʿUlā region. One particularly fantastical tale is captured in a volume by a local historian, concerning a Wādī al-Qurā villager by the name of Mufḍī. Mufḍī, who was thought to be alive at the time of the writing of the account (1996), owned a small farm. Because his personal well was dry, he was forced to draw water from a nearby bedouin settlement. On his way home from collecting water, he found a group of thirsty camels at the threshold of his small farm. Over the protests of his own family, Mufḍī allowed the camels to drink from the water he had collected. The next day, Mufḍī awoke to find his personal well filled with fresh water, a reward from God for his kindness to the camels.[12]

Miraculous events, textual piety, and reverence for the camel are joined yet tighter in the story for which the al-ʿUlā region is best known—the Quranic tale of the destruction of Thamūd. Thamūd, a pre-Islamic, proto-monotheistic Arabian people referenced in Muslim scripture, were gifted a miraculous, giant she-camel by God through the mediation of his prophet Ṣāliḥ. At first appreciative of the miracle performed for them, the people grew to resent the she-camel's drain on their water resources. Defying Ṣāliḥ's orders, members of Thamūd killed the camel, and the Thamūdic people were punished by God with destruction as a consequence.[13] The Nabatean ruins of Madā'in Ṣāliḥ are commonly held to be the site where the people of Thamūd received their divine retribution. The legacy of Thamūd lingers in the untoward reputation al-ʿUlā retains within the Saudi popular imagination. Influenced by scholarly admonitions elaborated from Traditions of the Prophet,[14] Saudis generally avoid visiting the al-ʿUlā region if they can, considering it to harbor the Wahhabi equivalent of bad vibes. For the inhabitants of al-ʿUlā, this attitude is somewhat puzzling. A teacher from the town elaborated on this sentiment: "I feel that sometimes people from elsewhere in the kingdom try to bury this place, make it seem as if it didn't exist. Many people think that it is wrong to eat here, to drink here, to visit here. This is ridiculous—where do they want us to go? We live here."[15]

If al-ʿUlā was kept at arm's length in the Saudi religious imagination, its inhabitants' sense of having been neglected or forgotten extends to other facets of their collective memory. For most of the twentieth century, al-ʿUlā was literally the end of the road. From its origins as a way station for pilgrim caravans and traders, al-ʿUlā saw its function eclipsed in the 1950s by Taymāʾ, the oasis town to its northeast through which the main highway in the region, the Tabūk-Medina road, was built, bypassing Wādī al-Qurā. Working as well against the town was the fact that the area surrounding al-ʿUlā was the traditional territory of the Balī tribe, whose early revolt against Saudi authority seems to have been a factor in the underdevelopment of the region.[16] When Ḥamad al-Jāsir visited northwest Arabia in the late 1960s to gather materials for a contribution to the geographical dictionary he was then compiling, al-ʿUlā was not on his itinerary. To stop there would have involved a lengthy detour off the main highway, which wound from Tabūk to Medina east of al-ʿUlā through Taymāʾ and Khaybar.

BEDOUIN AND TOWN DWELLERS IN WĀDĪ AL-QURĀ

Before their state-managed sedentarization in the twentieth century, the bedouin of northwest Arabia exercised a measure of control over the region's oases. In Wādī al-Qurā, the Balī and ʿAnaza tribes competed over the extraction of the *khuwwā* (brotherhood) tax from the settled communities.[17] Effectively a protection payment meant to immunize the oases against bedouin predation, *khuwwā* symbolized the absence of central government in northwest Arabia, and the dependency of settlers on bedouin good will for security on the roads leading to and from their oases.[18] The bedouin of the al-ʿUlā region were settled in *hujar* communities at a comparatively late date, during the reign of King Fayṣal (1964–75).[19] Some, such as the Fuqarā, traditional hegemons over Taymāʾ, and to a lesser extent al-ʿUlā, were relocated from their tribal lands in the area of Madāʾin Ṣāliḥ and settled in an adjacent *hijra*, ʿUdhayb, in 1980. Their uprooting was prompted by pressure from religious clergy, who disapproved of the Fuqarā's presence on the site of Thamūd's believed retribution, and so forced the Saudi government's hand.[20] To this day, only a negligible percentage of the Fuqarā live in al-ʿUlā proper. Despite the increasing dependency of bedouin-origin Saudis on the jobs and services of urban centers such as al-ʿUlā, the Fuqarā continue to keep a symbolic distance from the town.[21] By contrast, Balī, the largest bedouin tribe in the Wādī al-Qurā region, is more integrated into al-ʿUlā town life, and several members of the tribe have occupied high positions in local government.[22]

Education is what attracted the bedouin to sedentary life, a longtime al-ʿUlā teacher named Khālid explained to me one evening in his home. Beginning in the 1960s, the Saudi government established primary schools in a number of the new *hujar* communities surrounding al-ʿUlā. State-sponsored primary education was one of the few elements of modernity that intersected with bedouin life during the transition to sedentary living. Wādī al-Qurā bedouin would sometimes be found camping outside of a school building erected in their territories, only to disappear into the desert when the term was over. For secondary education, however, the bedouin had to come to al-ʿUlā. It was for high schools, jobs, and hospitals, then, that bedouin-origin Saudis began migrating en masse to urbanizing areas such as al-ʿUlā in the

Figure 5.3. Al-ʿUlā today. Courtesy of author.

latter part of the twentieth century.[23] Today, members of Balī and other bedouin tribes comprise a sizeable proportion of the inhabitants of the town of al-ʿUlā. Yet bedouinism as a distinctive mode of social and political organization is no more, and the integration of bedouin-origin and settled al-ʿUlā residents advances through mass education, public sector employment, and intermarriage.

As Saudi scholar ʿAbdallāh al-Ghadhdhāmī has argued, one of the unforeseen consequences of the integration of bedouin-origin and sedentary-origin Saudis in the public school system has been the reinscribing of tribal identities in the consciousness of children. Bedouin-origin youth, who are socialized in a genealogically conscious environment, bring to school a value system that ascribes high worth to eminent (tribal) genealogies. The process of genealogical classification and distinction introduced by bedouin youth into urban schools, he argues, influences children of sedentary background to inquire with their parents about their tribal origins. From this is born the elaborate enterprise of tracing out and documenting tribal roots in books and family trees, as the kingdom's modern genealogical culture moves from Saudi schools to homes. The effort by non-tribal urban families to identify their tribal lineages, Ghadhdhāmī concludes, certifies and sanctifies the importance of tribal identity, while discrediting the legitimacy of urban-based social identity.[24]

The rude culture of genealogical contest described by al-Ghadhdhāmī had become a steady feature of the school system in al-ʿUlā, Khālid, the teacher, observed:

> When students come from outside to the schools inside the town here, of course . . . there is the stirring up of tribalism. . . . My son . . . or one of our relative's sons, or a neighbor, all of them will tell you that [bedouin] students come from outside . . . and say 'we are [such-and-such tribe] . . . what is your tribe (*ish qabīlatak int*)? . . . from what tribe do you descend'?

It was this tribal stirring that had compelled the sedentary-origin inhabitants of al-ʿUlā to affirm their tribal roots and defend the legitimacy of their presence there, Khālid explained:

> Before the arrival of students from outside of al-ʿUlā, [the heightened concern over genealogies] was perhaps limited, or may not have existed at all. But when they came, there was a stirring up of this issue. This influenced the people of al-ʿUlā to go back to the old documents. The people of al-ʿUlā, the majority of them descend from the Ḥarb [tribe], in Madīna al-Munawwara, on the outskirts of Madīna. Perhaps you have heard about Ḥarb?[25]

Ḥarb, Ḥamad al-Jāsir's tribe, was also the tribal affiliation claimed by many of the historical inhabitants of al-ʿUlā. In recent decades the people of al-ʿUlā have gone rummaging through their papers, searching for documents that affirm their authentic attachment to Ḥarb and other bedouin tribes. Why was this the case? In the observations of Khālid and ʿAbdallāh al-Ghadhdhāmī, we have already identified one possible answer to this question. The next section of this chapter will be devoted to explaining why genealogies matter to the modern-day inhabitants of al-ʿUlā.

THE GENEALOGICAL POLITICS OF AL-ʿULĀ

As I sat in the *majlis* of Khālid's home, his fifteen-year-old son Muḥammad moved quietly in and out of the room. Wearing a T-shirt and sweatpants, Khālid's son was indistinguishable from an American teenager. Muḥammad brought the third plate of hot food out from the kitchen to present to his father's guest, and then took a seat on my left, listening quietly to our discussion of the influence of bedouin-origin Saudis on the culture of al-ʿUlā. Turning to Muḥammad, a prospective eyewitness to the question of tribalism in the school system, I asked him if he felt this influence in his own school. Muḥammad responded that there was no difference between bedouin and *ḥaḍar*. His reply seemed to echo countless hours of lessons imparted in Saudi schools and mosques, lessons that declaimed the government's successful integration of these once sociologically distinct populations. I was unsatisfied with his reply, but refrained from pressing him further. Khālid's dissatisfaction could not be contained, however, and he began peppering his son with questions: "OK, but what do you say when a child of bedouin background comes up and says to you, 'Who are your people? Where do you come from? We are such and such, from such and such place. You don't have any origin'. What do you say to them? How do you respond?" Though Khālid had earlier insisted that it was the youth of al-ʿUlā who were more injured by the tribal stirring, it was apparent from his reaction that this was not entirely the case.

In al-ʿUlā, it is common to find bedouin-origin Saudis studying or working alongside descendants of the town's original inhabitants, ʿAlāwna, as they were known historically.[26] Particularly bright, intrepid, or fortunate young men find opportunity to resettle in big cities such as Riyadh or Jeddah, but the ever-replenishing ranks of al-ʿUlā youth, bedouin-origin and settled, seem unaffected by their departures. It was during my first visit to the town, as a tourist in March 2011, that I caught a flavor of al-ʿUlā's genealogical culture, of the silent competition between Saudis of bedouin and sedentary origin for pride of place in that regional center. Mushayliḥ al-Blūwwī, a twenty-four year old security guard for the local antiquities museum, provided me with some information about local genealogies. Mushayliḥ was of bedouin origin on his father's side, and his understanding of the sociology of Wādī al-Qurā was undoubtedly influenced by this fact: "In al-ʿUlā there are Juhanī, Blūwwī, and ʿAnazī [i.e., descendants of three bedouin tribes]. The original inhabitants of al-ʿUlā are called ʿAlāwna. They are tribal, but in the last two years, they've begun switching their tribal affiliation. The reason for this, I feel, is that no one outside al-ʿUlā knows their tribe." Mushayliḥ noted that the tribe with which the ʿAlāwna most commonly sought affiliation was Ḥarb.[27] That many of the ʿAlāwna affiliated with Ḥarb was a well-established fact. When Doughty visited al-ʿUlā in 1876, he met with the town's leader, Dāhir, who "boasted himself a sheykh of ancestry in the lineage of Harb."[28] As Mushayliḥ would demonstrate, and Doughty well before him, skepticism of ʿAlāwna claims to Ḥarb origins was almost as old as these claims themselves.

Later that day, a guide employed by the museum, Mālik Āl Ḥasan, joined us for a conversation. Mālik, around thirty years old, was a descendant of the town's original inhabitants, had good knowledge of its history, and was pleased to share what he knew of town genealogies. As the discussion continued, Mushaylih invoked the story he had mentioned earlier, about residents of the town switching their tribal affiliation to Ḥarb, to demonstrate the fluid process of combination and bifurcation that underpinned the Arabian tribal system. Mushayliḥ's example touched a nerve with Mālik, however, as Mālik's family claimed Ḥarb ancestry.

> MUSHAYLIḤ: The Ḥurūb [sing. Ḥarb], you see . . . the system of the Ḥurūb, anyone comes and changes their affiliation and joins them, easily, very easily.
>
> MĀLIK [interrupting]: Umm, no.
>
> MUSHAYLIḤ: Like, you have the Slifa branch (*fakhdh*), many people joined it, wallāh.
>
> MĀLIK: They joined, but of course, they have origins within it, it isn't that [they are inventing the relationship]. . . .[29]

Mālik quietly bristled at Mushayliḥ's suggestion that the ʿAlāwna who had joined Ḥarb had somehow done something deceitful. Mālik belonged to the Slifa, and his uncle, Ḥākim Āl Ḥasan, was an important genealogist in al-ʿUlā, who had spent many of his free hours compiling evidence of the family's lineal affiliation with Ḥarb. From Mālik's vantage point, little distinguished his family's reaffirmation of belonging to Ḥarb from the multitude of authentic tribal and family reunifications transpiring across the kingdom. Mushayliḥ's casual slight against Mālik's origins was driven, half-innocently, by an abundance of self-assuredness, namely, a confidence that his own local tribal leader, the shaykh of Balī, upheld a more rigorous standard for the entry of putative blood members into the tribe. It was true that Mushayliḥ's mother was from the ʿAlāwna, giving him one foot in the world whose lineal authenticity he seemed to doubt; but, in Arabian social affairs, patrilineage made the man, and Mushayliḥ's conception was no doubt colored by this fact.

Visiting Malīk's uncle, the genealogist Ḥākim Āl Ḥasan, I was shown evidence of the extended family's reconnection to its Ḥarb root. In March of 1993, Ḥākim and his cousins from three other al-ʿUlā clans gathered in the town to certify the reattachment of the four kin groups to their parent clan. In attendance were their invited guests, shaykhs of the Slifa from Medina and Riyadh, along with the latters' retinues. The minutes of the meeting discussed the points of agreement among the parties to the gathering, most significantly, mutual affirmation of the authentic linkage of the al-ʿUlā branches with their Ḥarb *fakhdh*, or subtribe, with allusions to some of the reciprocal rights and obligations associated with this newly (re)constituted circle of relations.[30] That a meeting between bedouin-origin and settled-origin Saudis was taking place could be discerned easily by the names of those in attendance—the rough-hewn bedouin names of the Slifa (Mifliḥ, Duḥayyān, ʿAshwā) contrasted starkly with the scriptural names of their ʿAlāwna counterparts (ʿĪsā, Muḥammad, Mūsā). With this document, and a more authoritative version of it filed with the al-ʿUlā court, Mālik's uncle possessed proof that his extended family belonged lineally to the Ḥarb tribe. If that was the case, then why were Mushayliḥ and so many other Saudis dismissive of Mālik's and other al-ʿUlā residents' claims to Ḥarb origins?

NAMES, TRIBES, AND RACE

Invited one evening to a gathering in al-ʿUlā in December 2011, I was brought by a friend, ʿAwda, to meet the members of his social circle. I entered his *shabba*, or rest house,[31] to find thirteen dark-skinned men in their late thirties or early forties, reclining against cushions along the walls and conversing quietly with one another. A giant flat-screen television was showing footage of protests in Bahrain, but all eyes were on the out-of-town guest. Taking a seat after greeting the group, one of its members took advantage of a pause in the ensuing discussion to ask if I had noticed anything in particular about the men, anything they had in common. When I hesitated, they began to laugh. A voice rose above the others, half in jest: "we all come from the same ancestor!" Two of the men I had greeted left for prayer shortly after. When they returned, I rose unaware to greet them again. "But you had already greeted us before!" they ribbed me. "We all look the same to him!"

Fourteen clans comprise the ʿAlāwna, as they were known to the outside world, and as they sometimes referred to themselves in documents.[32] The Alsatian traveler Charles Huber, who visited al-ʿUlā in November of 1880, described its inhabitants as being "all negroes to varying degrees," its population resembling "a mélange of negroes and Jews," in the parlance of nineteenth-century European racial thought.[33] Huber's assessment was echoed in the accounts of Doughty, Jaussen and Savignac, and other Western visitors to the region. The ʿAlāwna, whose racial origins were perceived by Western travelers and bedouin alike to be different from those of the surrounding bedouin communities,[34] maintained their own sedentary culture centered on the cultivation of the date palm. Their history, as an elderly imam with deep roots in the town informed me, was a history of "*fallāḥīn*," peasant cultivators, who sang praise songs to their date trees as they ascended their trunks during pollination and harvest times. The ʿAlāwna recorded their *qawāʿid* (sing. *qāʿida*), or customary laws, in detailed documents, the tradition of literacy, however rudimentary in its premodern expression, being a point of pride among the town's historical inhabitants.

The economy of the town revolved around its many natural springs, such as ʿAyn Tidʿil. The leaders of the fourteen clans would gather daily in their respective *qāhāwī*, or council rooms,[35] to discuss the latest news concerning the springs. If Tidʿil required maintenance, they would issue the call—"Tidʿil needs your help"—and the people would converge on the spring, dredging out its mud-plugged channels that distributed water to scores of small family plots, or shoring up its walls. It was in this same way that new homes in the old town were built, and old ones reinforced, without a penny exchanged. When money did change hands, it was most often for the leasing of a share of the water supply, in units called *wajba*s, *sūd*s, or *waraqa*s. After the many varieties of dates cultivated in al-ʿUlā, these units of water formed the principal commodity of the town. The nostalgia of town elders, whose documents and recollections are aggregated above, stopped short of a desire to revisit in full pre-1970s al-ʿUlā, when the town was without electricity and many other modern conveniences. Yet in their words there was an unmistakable longing for the easy social solidarity of an earlier age, a wistfulness that was no doubt compounded by a new reality, that the collective noun ʿAlāwna, the toponymic that encapsulated their historical identity, had become a bad word.

Two episodes clued me in to this semantic shift. Touring the old town with Mushaylih̤ al-Blūwwī, the museum security guard, Mushaylih̤ referred me to Ḥasan, a driver who would be arriving shortly after. Ḥasan was ʿAlāwna, I was told, but I shouldn't say this to his face, as he might be offended. Ḥasan, it became apparent shortly after, was a dark-skinned man in his thirties. That the term ʿAlāwna could carry multiple connotations was reinforced one evening in December 2011, during a conversation at the *shabba* of a Ḥarb shaykh in a southerly neighborhood of al-ʿUlā. ʿAwda, the engineer who had been taking me to visit various personalities and places in the town, was of Ḥarb descent, but of a different branch than Mālik and Ḥākim's family. ʿAwda drove us to the home of the shaykh of his clan, Shaykh Aḥmad. Having been nominated by his clan and appointed by the Saudi government only a few years earlier, Shaykh Aḥmad was in the process of constructing an enormous *majlis* on the grounds of his home, and before answering questions was eager to give his guest a tour.

Back in the *shabba*, as the fire crackled, the conversation took a turn and I became silent. ʿAwda had invoked the term ʿAlāwna with reference to the historical inhabitants of al-ʿUlā, when Shaykh Aḥmad interrupted him. Don't use that word, the young shaykh chastised him. The term is derogatory, and means that the people of al-ʿUlā have no lineage. It is far better to represent oneself according to one's tribal origins, he suggested, giving the example of his own name, Aḥmad b. Ṣāliḥ al-Fakhrī al-Ḥarbī. ʿAwda, with his easygoing, confident demeanor, saw no problem with the term ʿAlāwna, even taking pride in its connotation, as representing a group identity distinct from that of the bedouin latecomers to the town, with whom ʿAwda felt no common cause. These claims to Ḥarb origins were at the very least unproveable, and at most doubtful, he reckoned, and so the people of al-ʿUlā should be satisfied with the name by which they had always been known. A third voice rose in Shaykh Aḥmad's favor: why was it that a person of Balī bedouin origin who was a resident of al-ʿUlā could go around and be known legitimately by the last name (*nisba*) Blūwwī, he asked, but the ʿAlāwna were not free to do the same with their own name? Shaykh Aḥmad cut the conversation short. Affiliating lineally with a place simply does not work, he stated with finality, if no great authority. The only way to represent oneself was with reference to one's family or tribal background. If the people of al-ʿUlā used tribal names, then the difficulty they faced in authenticating their tribal lineages would disappear, he concluded.[36]

AN OPEN SECRET

It was becoming apparent that a certain connection existed between naming practices, race, and tribal origins. In the new Saudi Arabia, the toponymic *nisba* (i.e., surname) ʿAlāwī, like those derived from the names of other northwestern Arabian oases, Taymānī or Khaybarī, connoted blackness, which in turn connoted non-tribal status. For those inhabitants of al-ʿUlā concerned with legitimating their genealogical position in the kingdom, ridding themselves of the ʿAlāwna label was a first step in establishing a basis of commonality with the kingdom's dominant status group, sedentary Saudis of recognizable tribal origin. Mushayliḥ al-Blūwwī, whose skepticism of ʿAlāwna origination claims was tempered by his status as an al-ʿUlā insider, gave subtle expression to this logic. When I broached the subject of ʿAlāwna genealogies with a prominent doctor of Ḥarb origin in Riyadh, the subtext of Mushayliḥ's attitude became clearer:

> DOCTOR: . . . When you go to the city of al-ʿUlā itself, the city itself . . . they are black. The people of al-ʿUlā, the original inhabitants. The Faqīr [i.e., the Fuqarā bedouin, who live north of al-ʿUlā] . . . they are different than the people of the city.
>
> NS: But many of them [i.e., the people of al-ʿUlā] belong to Ḥarb.
>
> DOCTOR: No, no. Don't believe them. You should know that [this notion of] their belonging to Ḥarb is not correct [laughing]. Perhaps *mawālī*, meaning, slaves *(ʿabīd)* of Ḥarb. I know that the blacks of al-ʿUlā claim belonging to Ḥarb, but it isn't correct. Don't believe them . . . Khaybar, Khaybar is also black. And they [claim to] belong [chuckling]. This is a tough issue. . . . Among the Arabs, in the

> past, the dark-skinned, the Africans, were *mawālī*, slaves, and they affiliated lineally with the tribe. They were called *muwallad*. Meaning, a black person who was born in the tribe, and lived with them, his father having been a slave.[37]

Though slavery in Saudi Arabia was outlawed in 1962,[38] its legacy remains a raw and open wound that has gone largely unacknowledged in Saudi historiography. The silence surrounding the history of slavery belies an important fact, that for hundreds if not thousands of years, slavery was a central facet of the social, economic, and political life of the Arabian Peninsula, and western Arabia in particular. The right to own slaves was enshrined in Islamic law, and this right was exercised freely in the Hijaz by the Ottoman and Arab elite, urban notables and bedouin leaders alike. The modern history of slavery in Arabia begins with the nineteenth-century Ottoman campaign to repulse the expansionary Wahhabi movement, which had dislodged the Ottomans from the holy cities of Mecca and Medina in 1806. Between 1823 and 1840, thousands of Sudanese slave soldiers—whole brigades of Muhammad Ali's modern, all-slave army—were deployed to the Hijaz to consolidate the 1818 victory of Ottoman forces over their Wahhabi challengers at the empire's frontier.[39] Under the command of Ottoman officers, these slave brigades were sent to bolster the thin ranks of Ottoman army regulars who had been tasked with preventing a Saudi resurgence in central Arabia.[40] Though Muhammad Ali's campaign temporarily restored Ottoman authority in Arabia, Britain's rising influence in the Middle East would soon force a reconsideration of Ottoman policy toward slavery.

In March 1857, in the face of mounting pressure from British lawmakers, the Ottoman Sultan Abdülmecid I issued an order prohibiting the African slave trade in all Ottoman territories.[41] Owing to "well-known circumstances of delicacy," however, the Hijaz was exempted from this order.[42] At the symbolic level, this delicacy reflected an Ottoman desire to preserve the legitimacy of the Porte's custodianship over Islam's two holy places, for which reason western Arabia was granted a near-blanket release from the modernizing legal and institutional reforms of the Tanzimat. At the material level, the delicacy in question concerned the fierce resistance of local Hijazi authorities to the curtailment of the lucrative trade in human chattel, which contributed to their enrichment and the general satisfaction of their important elite constituents. Yet slavery in the Hijaz was not confined to the elite. "All Hijaz families except the poorest have household slaves, most of whom are of Sudanese or West African origin," a British agent in Jeddah wrote the High Commissioner for Egypt in 1925.[43] According to various testimonials, including a Saudi government statistical assessment, between 1934 and 1952, the number of slaves in the kingdom doubled to 70,000, with upper-limit estimates approaching several hundred thousand.[44] Despite Ottoman, British, and Saudi legal and policing measures, slavery was a ubiquitous facet of life in western Arabia well into the twentieth century.

British archival records demonstrate that members of Ḥarb and other bedouin tribes owned slaves. These would be purchased in Jeddah or surrounding ports and employed in cultivation or pearl diving.[45] Most slaves were children aged six to eighteen who were brought over from the East African coast, while others were captured in Arabia. One bedouin informant from Wādī Fāṭima, in which Ḥarb and several other tribes were concentrated, explained in 1933 that in former times, bedouin used to descend on caravans of West African pilgrims, capturing and enslaving as many as one hundred at a time.[46] In Khurayba, just northeast of al-ʿUlā, bedouin reportedly captured and enslaved a group of British Nigerian pilgrims.[47]

Among the runaway slaves who appeared at the door of the British Consulate in Jeddah in 1883 were Ambarek and his son Berki. Ambarek, originally from the Zanzibar coast, had worked for nine years for Atiah Fallah of the Zubayd tribe (a subbranch of Ḥarb), and before that for Atiah's cousin Salih, who was forced to transfer ownership of Ambarek to Atiah in relief of a debt. While in Atiah's household, Atiah's mother had arranged for Ambarek's marriage to a slave woman named Hadeyah. At the consulate, Ambarek showed the consular officers a certificate of manumission for Hadeyah and her children. His own certificate had been seized by his master, he claimed.[48] There were several methods by which a slave might be manumitted under Islamic law, for example, upon the death of his or her master (in the absence of inheritors), or through agreement with his or her master. The offspring of a slave owner and his female slave was also born free. In each of these cases, an official document attesting to the manumission would have to be issued. The document required witness signatures (Hadeyah's certificate was unsigned), and a copy would have to be registered with the court and preserved by the judge.[49]

Though failing to realize it at the time, my first encounter with these manumission documents or their likes was at the home of Ḥākim Āl Ḥasan, the elderly genealogist from al-ʿUlā. Ḥākim, whose appearance betrayed a strong suggestion of non-Arabian origins, was flipping through binders full of documents, demonstrating for his guest the antiquity and breadth of his collection. With Ḥākim afterwards engrossed in a volume on early Islamic history, his son ʿAbdallāh, around forty-five years old, pulled me aside and offered his perspective on his father's documents and how they related to the lineal aspirations of certain individuals in the town of al-ʿUlā:

> In society, you have your rank . . . so you are proud to say, I am from such-and-such tribe. . . . [Yet] some of the official documents in our

> possession . . . [indicate that] these statements are completely incorrect. The documents indicate that you do not possess the affiliation which you claim with respect to your loftiness and greatness in relation to society. In plain Arabic, the documents refer to the former slave status (*ʿubūdiyya*) of some of them. If this came out, it would cause a stir among the people.
>
> You might be someone who has a noble lineage, and because you have this, they will not ask [about your background], they will come to you and marry with you. Why? Because of your claim that you are such-and-such person from such-and-such tribe, from this and from that, whereas in reality, here there are documents, that were composed a long time ago, that testify to the opposite.[50]

In light of the modern history of slavery in the Hijaz, it was not surprising to learn that some of the people of al-ʿUlā were believed within the community to descend from emancipated slaves.[51] Whether descendants of illicit unions between slave owners and female servants, or those born of the lawful marriage of these parties (as was known also to occur),[52] the lineages of these *muwalladūn* were undoubtedly an important factor in the genealogical politics of al-ʿUlā and other Arabian communities like it.

Engseng Ho described the genealogical challenges of another group of Arabian *muwalladūn*, the mixed origin descendants of the Ḥaḍramī Indian Ocean diaspora. Unlike the ʿAlāwna, whose family histories acknowledged no external point of origination, the Ḥaḍramī *muwalladūn* were usually Indonesian-born returnees to Yemen—in Ḥaḍramawt, but not of it. Their liminality was distinct from that of the ʿAlāwna, whose genealogical inquiries were usually stripped clean of the creole religiosity of the Ḥaḍramī migrants, and whose historical memories fused lineage and locale somewhat more seamlessly, even if the same compulsion to establish an authentic position in Arabia's distant past seemed to trail them.[53]

Georg August Wallin, the ethnic-Swede Finnish traveler who visited northwest Arabia in the 1840s and was the first European to write about al-ʿUlā, described it as a town of three hundred families, "including a great many Mutawallidīn."[54] An 1869 letter by German naturalist George Wilhelm Schimper to the British Foreign Office described a "mud village" near Mecca inhabited by "freed negro slaves," who lodged and fed slaves newly arrived from across the Red Sea, likely before their transport to market.[55] These assessments are echoed in the observations of other Western travelers, and in the impressions of the professor of Ḥarb origin in Riyadh. Yet as the comments by Ḥākim's son made apparent, the people of al-ʿUlā, and other Hijazi oases like it, rejected a connection to this difficult history, and instead differentiated their status internally among themselves, as descendants of tribes or descendants of slaves. It was this internal differentiation that formed an important part of their strategy for affirming correct tribal origins.

The nostalgia of al-ʿUlā elders for a bygone social solidarity tended to gloss over the internal distinctions that operated within the town. While the shaykhs of al-ʿUlā's fourteen clans may have gathered in their *qahāwī* (meeting rooms) for socializing and administration, the common folk, the majority of the town, congregated in the streets, in the town's markets.[56] Huber, whose somewhat dubious pronouncements on race and intermarriage in al-ʿUlā were questioned by his own editor, noted however the presence of a fair-skinned aristocracy in al-ʿUlā that was differentiated from other segments of the town population.[57] One childhood resident of al-ʿUlā described this system of internal differentiation as it related to marriage: "Even the ʿAlāwna, they had a hierarchy, a hierarchy for the elite, and for the common people, the *ʿabīd*. The former would not marry the latter."[58]

The equating of the common people with *ʿabīd* (slaves) underscored the sense that an internal differentiation based on degrees of former bondedness or liberty existed historically in al-ʿUlā. The relationship between internal differentiation and lineal authenticity was most apparent in an exchange between two al-ʿUlā residents introduced earlier, Mālik Āl Ḥasan and Mushayliḥ al-Blūwwī. When Mushayliḥ spoke critically of the way by which al-ʿUlā families moved easily to affiliate with prominent tribes, Mālik invoked the notion of internal differentiation in his own tribal branch, the Slifa, to counter him: "Among [the Slifa] are pure (*aṣīl*), original Slifa. But, it has subbranches, and maybe one of [these subbranches] has five families. Three of [these families] are original, while two families joined from outside. But when they affiliate [with Ḥarb], they affiliate as a collective. *There* is the problem."[59]

In justifying his tribal subbranch's affiliation with Ḥarb, Mālik drew attention away from his own family's origins, laying blame for any skepticism about their claims on the presence of allied outsider (i.e., non-consanguineous) families within the subbranch. In the modern genealogical politics of the Gulf region, it is time and again the perceived dilution of the tribe's authentic lineal identity by allied, non-blood members that rears its head as a source of controversy.

A NAJDI VIEW OF THE HIJAZI OASES

While the inhabitants of al-ʿUlā might have distinguished internally between their free or slave origins, it was apparent that Najdis and other tribal-origin Saudis did not often recognize these distinctions. Both Mushayliḥ al-Blūwwī and the professor of Ḥarb origin in Riyadh affirmed this fact. Further evidence for it emerges in the letters of Ḥamad al-Jāsir. Al-Jāsir was dubious of the tribal origins of many of the inhabitants of al-ʿUlā, and left discussion of this subject unelaborated in his writings,[60] to the dissatisfaction of some in the town. Like Saudis elsewhere throughout the kingdom, ʿAlāwna interested in genealogical matters viewed Ḥamad al-Jāsir as an important authority, and would solicit his judgment on questions pertaining to their origins. In reply to one such query, al-Jāsir professed his skepticism about the lineages of the town's inhabitants: ". . . all of what is said [in al-ʿUlā about the lineages of its inhabitants], I do not feel to be founded on a sound basis."[61] When a cousin of Khālid, the al-ʿUlā teacher, wrote al-Jāsir asking if the scholar might authenticate certain documents attesting to the family's belonging to a branch of the Ḥarb tribe,[62] al-Jāsir refused his petition, writing: "as for the photocopied documents . . . I didn't find within them anything that might be beneficial or reassuring. . . ."[63]

The racial subtext to al-Jāsir's responses emerges in another of the scholar's works, the volume he prepared on northwest Arabia for his geographical dictionary, the *Muʿjam al-Jughrāfī*. Writing of the history of bedouin-sedentary relations in Khaybar, an oasis in western Arabia that was historically similar in many respects to al-ʿUlā, al-Jāsir described a town of sedentary agriculturalists subject to powerful bedouin overlords, who owned Khaybar's many date palm plantations and, unfit for the malarial climate, engaged *mawālī*, slaves of African origin, to work the land on their behalf.[64] Al-Jāsir then stated: "It is the strangest thing that black people are not affected by malarial fevers. For this reason, many of the people who work in agriculture in the parts of the Arabian Peninsula in which swamps are plentiful, all [*sic*] of them are black, and they are not affected by the malarial fevers. They possess perhaps a natural immunity. . . ."[65]

Al-Jāsir's pseudoscientific observations on race and its connection to bedouin-sedentary power dynamics in Khaybar's history met with a fierce response from one of the town's native sons. In a letter to al-Jāsir, a Khaybar-born petitioner attacked the scholar for a series of offending statements centered on al-Jāsir's denial of Arab tribal lineages to the people of Khaybar. The Khaybar letter is significant for this chapter, as, among other qualities, it demonstrates further the strategy of internal differentiation that Hijazi oasis dwellers often invoke and outsiders typically ignore. For this reason, it is quoted extensively below:

> Dear teacher of ours . . . with respect to the inhabitants of this town, your description of them could not be further from the true nature of their current and past situation. Dear teacher of ours, if you had studied deeply the condition of the inhabitants of Khaybar from the ancient past to the present, you would have found a great disparity between what you described and the reality of the inhabitants of Khaybar. We wonder, does what you write have a source, and we ask, where did you

> find this information about the original lineages from which they descend? They have remained silent throughout this lengthy period of time, and refrained from responding to your publications and those of others, publications that led to the creation of many problems and conflicts between the inhabitants of this town and others. . . . It should be known that the residents of this province who affiliate lineally as al-Khaybarī have a lineage and a deep-rooted provenance, which is undoubtedly proven by evidence preserved by the leaders and shaykhs of every tribe [in Khaybar]. Likewise, we do not deny to you that there are a small number of *mawālī* in this province, who are known as such by the people and the shaykhs of this province. . . . We are your sons, O dear father of ours, and we covet from you a reconsideration of the *nasab* of the people of this town. You have from us our complete respect and gratitude, appreciation, and affection.[66]

It is the interpretation of history and historical memory that determines who is up and who is down on the genealogical scale. Naturally, behind the capacity to produce authoritative interpretations is the power to project a dominant narrative into the far-flung corners of the kingdom. By marking former slave status as exceptional, al-Jāsir's Khaybar petitioner preserved the possibility that the majority of Khaybar's historical inhabitants possessed authentic tribal origins. As in al-ʿUlā, unloading the problem of suspect lineages onto others permitted the affirmation of genealogical truth claims about one's kin that could be recognized at the local level. Yet at the national level, on the stage where Ḥamad al-Jāsir's genealogical project was played, broader recognition of the genealogical claims of the inhabitants of the oases of northwest Arabia was checked by a skepticism rooted in questions of race and regional origin. This skepticism was rendered more potent by the sparse documentary record of Arabian history, which made the existence of authoritative documents affirming the lineal origins of specific families both highly prized and highly contested.

DOCUMENTING TRIBAL ORIGINS IN AL-ʿULĀ

During my first visit to al-ʿUlā, Mālik Āl Ḥasan had described to me his uncle Ḥākim's collection of genealogical documents, and their importance for proving the lineal attachment of the family to Ḥarb. Ḥākim had a reputation in the town for keeping his documents close to his chest,[67] for reasons to which his son had perhaps alluded. Ḥākim was not solely a document collector, though. When a member of his extended clan or affiliated kin group required evidence of his belonging to Ḥākim's tribal branch, and therefore to Ḥarb, Ḥākim would draw up a letter attesting to this fact. In genealogical matters, Ḥākim was the family's archivist, scribe, and notary public. Yet despite the antiquity of some of the documents in his possession, few had any credible bearing on his family's claims to Ḥarb tribal origin. According to the historian of al-ʿUlā ʿAbdallāh Naṣīf, when a newcomer would arrive in the town and express a desire to settle among its population, a detailed record of his arrival would be prepared. Known as a *qāʿidat al-ansāb* (customary record of lineages), the document would list the person's name, lineage, and place of origin, and would be preserved for posterity.[68]

Ḥākim explained that his ancestor Ḥasan al-Nuʿaymī had arrived in al-ʿUlā from the southern outskirts of Medina in the year 1397/8. Al-Nuʿaymī had four sons, each of whom would become the progenitor of a contemporary al-ʿUlā clan. When I asked Ḥākim if among the antique documents in his possession the family had preserved its *qāʿidat al-ansāb*, he replied:

> It was lost. My brother Dāwūd used to work in Tabūk. He took it with him to make a copy so that it wouldn't deteriorate. It was very old. Very, very old, from [1397]. Then, he had an accident in the Nahḍa section of Tabūk, and when the accident happened, he came here. . . . He stayed with us around a month here . . . and when we went to his house, it had been broken into, and the *qāʾida* had been removed from it.[69]

Later, while photographing the documents in Ḥākim's binders, the elderly genealogist pressed me for his attention. "Photograph this one," he said, holding a document out in front of him. The document Ḥākim was suggesting I copy seemed upon scrutiny to be an outlier within his collection of old papers. It looked to be written on papyrus, in the thin, uniform strokes of a ball-point pen. "Photograph this one," he repeated. "This is a *qāʿida* from the *qawāʿid* of the people of al-ʿUlā," the document read, "which they have passed down as an inheritance, fathers from grandfathers. Every ancestor records what he knows so that his children are not forgotten, or his grandchildren or ancestors, and so that his children might know their kin and the tribe (*ʿashīra*) from which they broke off, and so that they might know about their possessions."

While Ḥākim's document bore the air of antiquity, the purposeful, self-conscious tone of its opening lines, detached from the rude functionality of premodern Arabian genealogical documentation, marked it as a counterfeit. The text, which attested to the migration of Ḥākim's ancestor from the western outskirts of Medina to al-ʿUlā in the year 1397/8, indicated that the document was a copy made in 1527/8 of an original dated 1430/1. Arabic papyri disappear after the second half of the eleventh century,[70] while the ball-point pen appears only in the twentieth. Much else about the document was suspect, as two historians in Riyadh would later confirm. Was this *qāʿida*, which Ḥākim was quite pleased to have reproduced and perhaps authenticated in the tangle of a Western scholarly monograph, an attempt to compensate for the loss, under vague and mysterious circumstances, of the original *qāʿida* attesting to his family's origins? Or had the sheer will to believe in the family's tribal origin narrative somehow spirited this vaguely antique-looking document into his possession, no questions asked? Perhaps none of this mattered. With the Slifa reunification described above, Ḥākim and his family had secured their desired recognition as an authentic part of the Ḥarb tribe twenty years earlier, and Ḥākim's authority as a genealogist had been magnified accordingly. Why would it matter then that the historical paper trail, littered with lost or fabricated documents, was hardly supportive of Ḥākim and his family's claims?

The act of naming, Claude Lévi-Strauss once argued, is no more than a means of classifying and ordering.[71] If that is the case, if identities in Saudi Arabia remain structured, in a sense, by ascriptive kinship affiliations, then the process of renaming, in which Ḥākim and his kin group were engaged, is one of reordering or reclassifying, an attempt to shuffle the deck and emerge with a new and winning hand. In the modern genealogical culture of Saudi Arabia, this reshuffling can be an elaborate process, performed with the complicity of the receiving tribal branch (e.g., the Slifa). Other times it can be as simple as picking up a book of Arabian genealogies and choosing a credible entry point into the stream of a particular tribal history, as has been known to occur among many families in the kingdom. Most often, the effort to reconstitute lineal origins advances simultaneously on multiple fronts, historical and contemporary, oral and textual. In so doing, it parallels the broader desire by Saudis of all backgrounds to diminish the span of the rupture in Arabian history and restore a sense of continuity with a viscerally compelling, imagined past.

For Ḥākim and his kin group, shedding the pejorative ʿAlāwna label in favor of Ḥarb tribal distinction was the first step in achieving conformity with the dominant social model of the kingdom, in which the tribal name and the justification to claim it have become markers of authentic belonging. As Gabriele vom Bruck and Barbara Bodenhorn explain: "It is their detachability that renders names a powerful political tool for establishing or erasing formal identity, and gives them commodity-like value."[72] Yet in Saudi Arabia, the power to attach or withhold a name is not wielded equally by everyone. For example, Ḥamad al-Jāsir's authority as a genealogist resonated far beyond that of Ḥākim Āl Ḥasan's, who was largely unknown outside of his hometown. Al-Jāsir's proximity to the dominant Najdi culture, his capacity to synthesize historical evidence, and his overall reputation made the scholar's genealogical pronouncements stick where others couldn't seem to. Yet even al-Jāsir, today a celebrated icon of modern Ḥarb identity,[73] struggled to retrieve his kin group's name from the oral historical record and attach it unequivocally to its Ḥarb beginnings. Like Ḥākim Āl Ḥasan, al-Jāsir looked for more definitive proof of his origins in the spotty textual record, an effort that produced for him mixed results.

ḤARB AND AL-BURŪD

Most Saudi historians locate the origins of the Ḥarb tribe in ancient north Yemen, from where it migrated northwest in the early Islamic period, settling in the area between Mecca and Medina.[74] By the early nineteenth century, Ḥarb was considered one of the most powerful tribal confederations in Arabia, "the masters of Hedjaz," in Burckhardt's words.[75] Like many large Arabian tribes, Ḥarb tribesmen were spread out across diverse ecological zones, from the Hijaz mountains, to the plains surrounding Medina on three sides, to the sea.[76] As such, Ḥarbīs were fishermen, farmers, nomads, and traders.[77] Ḥarb bedouin depended for subsistence on the protection taxes they extracted from pilgrims passing to and from the holy cities, or on indirect taxes received as subsidies from the Ottoman-Hijazi government to refrain from such predations. When these subsidies were withheld for economic or political reasons, Ḥarb bedouin took their grievances directly to the roads, in a habitual pattern of conflict and competition with the centralized authorities of the Hijaz's town centers.

If the security environment of the Hijaz was at the mercy of its hinterland bedouin, the urban centers of the region exercised their own effect on the surrounding nomadic populations. Banī ʿAlī, the branch of the Ḥarb tribe from which Ḥamad al-Jāsir originated, was described by Burckhardt in 1814–15 as being "of the Persian creed, and followers of Aly."[78] The assertion that the Banī ʿAlī of the early nineteenth century adhered to the Shia sect of Islam, though uniformly ignored by historians of the Ḥarb tribe, stands to reason in light of the sectarian history of the Hijaz.[79] For much of the second millennium CE, the nominal rulers of Medina were the wealthy and influential Ḥusaynid Ashrāf. During the period of Faṭimid rule over the Hijaz (tenth to twelfth centuries), the Ḥusaynids professed a Zaydī Shia orientation, and were believed to have maintained pro-Shia sympathies for centuries after. When the Ḥusaynids were displaced by an Ottoman decree in the late seventeenth century, they moved their primary residence to al-ʿAwālī,[80] a southern suburb of Medina in which the Banī ʿAlī branch of Ḥarb was situated.[81] Other Ḥarb villagers were thought to have converted to the dominant Twelver or Imami stream of Shiism as late as the nineteenth century. Contemporary Wahhabi accusations that elements of Ḥarb profess Shiism are the spillover from a centuries-old Sunni orthodox polemic against Shia influence in the holy cities. For our purposes, they are emblematic of the controversies that litter the path for Saudis seeking to reattach themselves to prominent tribes and shake off the less salutary aspects (by Saudi-Wahhabi terms) of these tribes' historical reputations and sectarian affiliations.

Along with these lingering rumors about its sectarian orientation, Ḥarb had also to overcome its difficult position in Arabian historiography, as a prominent tribe that at times resisted the Wahhabi advance into the Hijaz. While the Furūm shaykhs of Banī ʿAlī supported Ibn Saʿūd during the decisive period of conflict with the Ikhwān rebels in early 1929,[82] the Banī ʿAlī had been aligned just a few years earlier with the Hijaz's Hashemite rulers, and had switched sides only when Saudi victory in the Hijaz was assured.[83] Like other Ḥarb historians, al-Jāsir played his part in reinterpreting Ḥarb's historical loyalties, even if his primary interests in the tribe's history were more intimate and personal. The twentieth-century Saudi conquest of the Hijaz, al-Jāsir argued in an essay on the tribe, was enabled by Ḥarb's unwavering loyalty, which was foreshadowed by the oath of allegiance Medina's Ḥarb rulers swore to Muḥammad b. Saʿūd after the first Saudi conquest of Medina in 1806.[84] Though the reality of Ḥarb's loyalties at the time of the latter-day Saudi conquest was demonstrably more complex, the clarity of al-Jāsir's themes resonated well for Ḥarb historians and admirers.[85]

There is little dispute that branches of the Banī ʿAlī migrated from the vicinity of Medina to the Sirr region of western Najd sometime after the early eighteenth century.[86] Writing around 1917, Harry St. John Bridger Philby documented the presence of Ḥarb sections in Najd on the border of Qaṣīm, south of Jabal Shammar, including the Banī ʿAlī.[87] The Furūm, shaykhs of Banī ʿAlī, were settled by the state in the *hijra* of Qubā, east of the city of Burayda.[88] In al-Burūd, Ḥamad al-Jāsir's birthplace, common wisdom held that the founding families of the village, among whom were the Āl Jāsir, descended from the Shubūl, a sub-clan of the Banī ʿAlī. Al-Jāsir's final book, *Baldat al-Burūd: Mawqiʿan, wa-Tārīkhan, wa-Sukkānan* (*The Village of al-Burūd: Its Geography, History, and Inhabitants*), was the scholar's effort to prove the connection between his immediate kin group, the Shubūl, and the chain of ancestors that led back to Ḥarb through the Banī ʿAlī.

Gathering his waning energy for one final inquiry, al-Jāsir drew upon the oral narrations of al-Burūd elders, indirect documentary evidence, and the power of inference to chart an elaborate theory explaining the Shubūl's connection to the Banī ʿAlī, and how this connection had become obscured in the fog of time. When the Shubūl departed Medina, he argued, they were embedded as allies of another tribe, the Āl Ḥusayn (Ḥusaynids), who were themselves embedded in the Ẓafīr, a major tribal confederation from eastern Hijaz that migrated to central Arabia between the seventeenth and eighteenth centuries.[89] These multiple layers of obscuring helped wash away the traces of the Shubūl's authentic attachment to Ḥarb, an attachment that al-Jāsir sought to restore for posterity. The passage of time struck the final blow to this sinuous chain of ancestry. When the Shubūl families multiplied over the centuries, they began to affiliate with their near ancestors, losing onomastic attachment to the root clan and its *nisba*, al-Shiblī.[90]

Such concern over the dissolution of top-level tribal identity through the severance of linkages between root and branch had been articulated by al-Jāsir disciple and Ḥarb historian ʿĀtiq al-Bilādī as early as 1978: "the day will come when the people will speak about this tribe [i.e., Ḥarb] the way they speak today about Banī Asad, or Taghlib, or Ghaṭfān [i.e., ancient Arabian tribes that had disappeared]."[91] *Al-Burūd* was al-Jāsir's effort to arrest this dissolution, to document, like so many of his petitioners, the connection between the tribal root, Ḥarb, and his own subbranch, the Shubūl; to prove, through an array of evidence, the people of al-Burūd's conformity to the dominant social pattern of the kingdom, the tribal pattern; and, in so doing, to demonstrate what distinguished them as a group from every other town in the kingdom. In an era in which other elements of modern identity were, in the scholar's view, mere replications of a drab sameness, possessing a lineage—any lineage—was a marker of distinction.[92] Whether bitten by the genealogical bug he helped to gestate, stung by some of the criticisms of his own lineage, or simply resolved to make one final, definitive statement about the primacy of local knowledge, *al-Burūd* found al-Jāsir wading into the murky waters of his own lineal origins, equipped with only a spare documentary record and a confidence in the genealogical common wisdom that he had otherwise come to discount or disparage. *Al-Burūd* is a detailed work of historical inquiry. And yet, al-Jāsir's elaborate effort within it to demonstrate the credibility of the Shubūl's genealogical claims situates the volume squarely as a product of the emergent genealogical culture of the kingdom.

AL-JĀSIR'S ORIGIN NARRATIVE

Historic al-Burūd is today a heap of crumbling, mud-brick ruins just down the road from the *hijra* of Sājir, birthplace of Juhaymān al-ʿUtaybī and the largest population center in al-Sirr.[93] In Ḥamad al-Jāsir's youth, al-Burūd was a village of several hundred inhabitants occupying one of the few cultivable patches of land in the area. The village was flanked on either side by long strips of desert or otherwise arid terrain extending south from the great Nafūd and inhabited by bedouin of the ʿUtayba and Muṭayr tribes. Like the ʿAlāwna of al-ʿUlā, al-Burūd's residents were *fallāḥīn*, peasant farmers who cultivated date palms under sometimes onerous debt burdens. More so than al-ʿUlā, which was sheltered by its topography and relative population density, al-Burūd was vulnerable to the surrounding bedouin, to whom it paid the *khuwwā* protection tax.[94]

Al-Burūd was distinguished in the annals of Saudi history for a battle that transpired there in the late eighteenth century, a period of reciprocal violence between the Ashrāf and the Saudis, respective rulers of western and central Arabia. Ibn Ghannām, the earliest significant chronicler of Saudi history, recounted two successive assaults on the town by Ashrāf forces, in which twenty al-Burūd residents beat back a diverse host of bedouin auxiliaries.[95] While Ibn Ghannām lauded the residents of al-Burūd for their loyal defense of the Saudi-Wahhabi cause against Ashrāf incursions, his successor Ibn Bishr added a further identifying detail. Al-Burūd's defenders numbered thirty, he wrote, and, apart from the proprietors of the town's fortress, the Āl Bassām and their kin, they were of Hutaym and ʿAwāzim tribal roots.[96] Hutaym was the name of a historically low status tribe from northwest Arabia, while ʿAwāzim, as noted in the previous chapter, was a similarly reputed tribe from the Peninsula's northeast.[97] These heroic defenders of al-Burūd were undifferentiated peasants, who had found their way to the town from far-flung and indistinct corners, Ibn Bishr seemed almost to be suggesting.

No direct evidence exists for the settling of the Shubūl in al-Burūd. Historians of Ḥarb believe that the Banī ʿAlī migration to the Sirr region of Najd took place in 1699/1700 following a dispute between the tribe and the Ottoman authorities in Medina.[98] The people of al-Burūd believe that their ancestors settled in the town shortly after this migration.[99] Since the battle for al-Burūd took place in 1790/1,[100] Ibn Bishr's account would appear to challenge the oral narrative of the lineal origins of the town's inhabitants, the narrative espoused by Ḥamad al-Jāsir and elaborated on by his disciples ʿĀtiq al-Bilādī and Fāyiz al-Badrānī. Refuting Ibn Bishr would thus be essential for advancing an alternative narrative of origins. "How much of what Ibn Bishr and other historians before and after him have to say is merely mistakes and fictions!" Ḥamad al-Jāsir exclaimed in a footnote to his study.[101] Echoing the many letters from his readers anxious to prove their genealogical origins, al-Jāsir took aim at Ibn Bishr's description of the lineal origins of the people of his hometown:

> On account of the ignorance of the history of these lands, its inhabitants were known, among the masses, by the name of Hutaym. This is a name given by the Arabs of recent times to those who are ignorant of their origins. But God forbid that they should be described by any disparaging adjective that devalues their capacities, as they are Arab Muslims, characterized by all of the qualities of masculine courage and nobility and gallantry . . . and they descend in their origins from pure

> Arab roots, possessing noble lineage. And yet, ignorance inflicted itself upon them, without their having a hand in it. In this, they are like many other tribes who became weak after being strong, and became ignorant of the origins of their lineages, and became despised on account of their weakness.[102]

What time had undone, patient scholarship, carefully culled oral narrations, and knowledge of the tendencies of Arabian history might correct. Reinforcing his refutation of Ibn Bishr's pronouncement is the clear sense that in advocating for a people wrongly labeled Hutaym, al-Jāsir was defending an outside group from disparagement, one that unequivocally excluded him and his kin.

Inquiring with the patriarch of the Āl Nāhiḍ, the traditional rulers of al-Burūd, al-Jāsir was told that the founding families of the town, the Āl Jāsir included, were all kin to the Āl Bassām, who had migrated from Medina along with al-Jāsir's ancestors, and who were listed by Ibn Bishr as the owners of the fortress being defended during that eighteenth-century battle.[103] Equipped with this oral narration from a local authority, al-Jāsir was able to weld his origin narrative to the documentary evidence in a plausible fashion, and thereby immunize his lineage from the perception of a Hutaym connection. Reliant solely on oral evidence for his claim, what strength there was in al-Jāsir's argument derived from his personal charisma and reputation, which eclipsed that of long-dead historians such as Ibn Bishr, and which enabled him to present his own origin narrative as part of a broader set of authoritative genealogical and historical assertions that comprised his oeuvre. What is more, by refuting the Hutaym connection and emphasizing the heroic role played by the Banī ʿAlī in defending a Najdi town against the invading Ashrāf, al-Jāsir was able to integrate his kin group as righteous protagonists in the pre-Saudi history of central Arabia. The scholar's Ḥarb origin narrative demonstrates further the power of the Arabian oral tradition to endure when aligned favorably with the historiography of the Saudi state.

When al-Jāsir's parochial views on race and language are interwoven with his egalitarian vision of central Arabian tribal genealogies, however, the implicit violence of his taxonomical authority becomes evident. When soliciting inputs for his study of al-Burūd and the wider al-Sirr region, al-Jāsir found himself answering preemptively to the charge that his interest in genealogies had turned him into a divisive public figure. Writing a non-tribal or low status family for information about a historical well in al-Sirr, al-Jāsir downplayed the genealogical angle of his study, stating: "I am not interested in the origins of lineages, because I believe that all of the inhabitants of Najd possess Arab lineages . . . for this reason, I don't use in my book repugnant terms like *khaḍīrī* or *Hutaymī* or others, as these things are not permitted to be spoken, because the Prophet . . . obligated the Muslim to call his brother by the name most beloved to him."[104] This and other such disclaimers seemed a response to a concern felt by al-Jāsir that his reputation had perhaps been damaged, and that he had come to be known primarily as a genealogist who classified people into categories of lineal purity or impurity. In *al-Burūd*, al-Jāsir attributed the origins of the above-mentioned family to the Banū Rashīd,[105] a more polite term for Hutaym.[106] Parrying with subtle decorum the twin challenges of his changed reputation and of Ibn Bishr's antique claims, al-Jāsir could thus be seen practicing his own version of the internal differentiation that was so prevalent a part of the genealogical discourse observed in al-ʿUlā.[107]

Like Ḥākim Āl Ḥasan, the genealogist in al-ʿUlā whose kin group sought recognition from the historical leaders of the Ḥarb subtribe to which they claimed belonging, Ḥamad al-Jāsir petitioned the leaders of his own Ḥarb subtribe, the Banī ʿAlī, for affirmation of his genealogical claims. In a letter to the scholar, Shaykh Nāyif b. ʿAbd al-Muḥsin al-Firm documented for al-Jāsir what the latter already knew, that the Shubūl were one of the hundreds of clans and sub-clans that could legitimately claim descent from Banī ʿAlī.[108] Al-Jāsir was even able to corroborate the details of this affiliation through the oral testimonial of an al-Burūd elder who had no relation to the Banī ʿAlī tribal leader, he explained.[109] Despite the agreement between these contemporary testimonies, al-Jāsir knew they would not suffice as historical evidence for his arguments. Oral narratives had been devalued in the modern age, victims of the traffic in lineages and the fabrication of poetical glories. Further evidence, contemporaneous textual evidence, would be required for al-Jāsir's Ḥarb origin narrative to pass muster in his own eyes.

GENEALOGY AND SLAVERY REVISITED

It was the good fortune of the Ḥarb tribe to be situated close to the holy cities of Mecca and Medina for much of its history. Unlike most other prominent Arabian tribes, Ḥarb's frequent interaction with Ottoman, Hijazi, and British authorities landed its name and the names of its subtribes and prominent leaders in the bureaucratic registers of these cities' administrators over the centuries. Reviewing documents preserved in the Islamic court of Medina, Ḥarb historian Fāyiz al-Badrānī identified the names of hundreds of previously unknown Ḥarb notables, some of whose *nisbas* appeared to demonstrate connections to Ḥamad al-Jāsir's ancestry. For al-Jāsir, al-Badrānī's findings constituted the most direct documentary evidence linking the Shubūl to Medina.[110] Specifically, al-Badrānī found two documents from 1553 and 1559, in the name of one Shaykh ʿAbd al-Razzāq b. ʿAbdallāh al-Shiblī. The first concerned the sale of a house in Medina, while the second the sale of an African slave in the city. Al-Jāsir was enthusiastic about al-Badrānī's findings and their implications for his own personal history. "It seems to me that this man had a high social position, as he was given the honorific (*laqab*) shaykh, and this is an honorific that is not usually given in that time, except to a scholar, or the shaykh of a tribe. Likewise, his owning of a home and of a slave in an age in which few people owned such things apart from those of status, makes clear that he possessed wealth and social rank."[111]

Ultimately, al-Jāsir found that the traffic in slaves by his putative ancestor was one of the few evidentiary bases upon which his claim to Ḥarb origins could be affirmed. One can only speculate about the fate of the slave noted in the transaction, whose emancipated descendants might have found their way to one or another of the oases of northwest Arabia, melting anonymously into the population until the age of documentation and mass-circulated print forced a reckoning with their family histories. This much is certain, however—while Ḥamad al-Jāsir would call attention to the documentary record of slavery in Arabia to help affirm his tribal origins, the people of al-ʿUlā, engaged in this same process of affirmation, try mightily to suppress the memory of such documents and their associated histories.

For the ʿAlāwna, such memories bubble to the surface on occasion, and in a manner unencumbered by the pretense of internal differentiation that appears so central a strategy of Arabia's genealogical culture. Defending the native legitimacy and foresight of his cohabitants, one town resident sounded an unusual echo of the tribal and Najdi narrative of the oasis community's origins: "we don't [explain our sedentary origins by saying] that we were [formerly] in servitude (*mawāliyya*) but rather, that we possessed the intelligence (*ʿaqliyya*) that helped us to distinguish the fact that security is to be found in settled life (*istiqrār*), economic prosperity in settled life."[112] Echoes of this alternative narrative can be heard as well in the words of the old imam mentioned earlier, for whom the people of al-ʿUlā were nothing more complicated than *fallāḥīn*, cultivators who worked their plantations without concern for bedouin-derived notions of prestige. Both admissions suggest a less convoluted history for the people of al-ʿUlā, one in which the descendants of African migrants and emancipated slaves became subject-citizens of the Saudi kingdom, and were then compelled to invest their lives with meaning according to its sometimes confusing and inconsistent standards. As will be demonstrated in the concluding chapter, this confusion and inconsistency in the definition of civic virtue derives from the duality at the heart of the Saudi state, which over the course of the twentieth century has worked at cross-purposes with itself to produce Saudis who are at once modern citizens and genealogically differentiated tribesmen.

CHAPTER SIX

Toward a Genealogical Rule of Governance

The Manasir, when questioned as to their loyalty, often replied that they were independent.[1]

—*Martin Buckmaster*

Tribal belonging is a central facet of modern Saudi identity. The lineage seekers of the *al-ʿArab* correspondence, the Āl Sulaymān family of al-Ghāṭ, and the people of al-ʿUlā proved themselves willing to go to elaborate lengths to demonstrate their authentic descent from one of a number of historically recognized Arabian tribes or lineages. These aspirations reflect the continuing salience of traditional Arabian hierarchies and symbols of prestige in the modern kingdom. Asserting a lengthy genealogy through a historically recognized Arabian tribe connects Saudis to their history in a way that feels meaningful to them, and grounds them in a sense of continuity with the past that is difficult to locate along the strip malls and endless highways of the modern kingdom.

Genealogical consciousness is one of the few vestigial legacies of Arabia's nomadic past. It has survived sedentarization and the erosion of kinship ties brought about through religious conditioning to occupy a central place in the modern Saudi imagination. Yet the centrality of tribal markers of identity in modern Saudi Arabia cannot be explained fully in relation to Arabian tradition, nor is the modern genealogical culture of Saudi Arabia solely an organic outgrowth of this tradition. The Saudi state was deeply influential in generating the acute genealogical consciousness that is today resonant throughout the kingdom. It is the interaction of two distinct concepts of genealogy, one a historically rooted artifact of Arabia's past, the other an invented tradition fashioned by the modern Saudi state, that frames the discussion in this concluding chapter.

The modern compulsion to claim tribal belonging, this concluding chapter argues, cannot be understood without reference to a set of institutional policies and techniques adopted by the modern Saudi state over the course of the twentieth century. Viewed as a whole, these policies and techniques combine to produce a genealogical rule of governance that underpins political practice in the kingdom. This chapter traces the origins and multiplex contours of this genealogical rule, and the various streams of modern Saudi political history that combine to produce it. From the kingdom's founding until the early 1950s, I show how a weak state grafted itself onto the preexisting social structures of town and nomadic life, intervening to shape identities where its powers would allow. In the Buraymī dispute of the 1950s, I identify a transitional moment in the kingdom's politics, when British and American experts systematized local genealogical knowledge to assert territorial claims on behalf of their Gulf sovereign clients. It was only in the 1960s that the genealogical rule I identify began to assume its modern form. I describe the Saudi state's efforts, from that decade through today, to standardize citizen identities according to genealogical criteria, to promote lineal authentication as a core political function, and to privilege kinship as a dominant symbol of Āl Saʿūd rule. In this political order, genealogy has become a pervasive aspect of modern Saudi life.

Readers may notice the waning position of Ḥamad al-Jāsir in this concluding narrative. Al-Jāsir, who loomed so large in the development of modern Saudi culture and historiography, was throughout his life a prisoner of numerous constraints, none more potent than the centralizing Saudi state. In 1994, after the Saudi government announced that it was slashing its budget by 20 percent following an oil price collapse, al-Jāsir received word that the governorate of ʿAsīr province would be cancelling its subscription to *al-ʿArab* magazine. ʿAsīr province was administered at the time by Khālid al-Fayṣal, a son of the late King Fayṣal, who was the scholar's patron and protector in the trying days of the late 1950s. Al-Jāsir maneuvered quickly to staunch the bleeding: "*Al-ʿArab Magazine* is a generous hand from the martyred King Fayṣal . . . and is a legacy from among his eternal legacies," he wrote to one of the governor's deputies. "No person looking at the legacy of this man would be pleased unless they saw it continuing. . . ."[2] Al-Jāsir's deft rhetoric, seen here working to bind the reputations of an Āl Saʿūd monarch and son to that of his own intellectual offspring, defined him as a scholar and a man. So too did the dynamic of dependency found in this letter, which characterized al-Jāsir's economic life as it did so many other Saudis'. Yet the vast majority of the state's petitioners did not have direct access to kings and senior princes. Their relationship with the centralizing state was more formal and impersonal, and was subject to vicissitudes that could not be settled via private letter or courtly appeal.

The Saudi state has until now been a background player in this study. The modern history of Saudi Arabia is too often recounted from the institutional heights, with little attention given to the social life of the kingdom's populations and the forms of agency they are given to exercise within the confines of politics and social circumstance. Whereas the diverse contours of Arabian genealogical circumstance have been addressed in previous chapters (in discussions of historical contingency, endogamous marriage, and slavery/manumission, for example), in this concluding chapter I outline the political straits into which the Saudi "genealogical imagination" has been set adrift.[3]

One additional note is required before proceeding. The twentieth-century history of Saudi Arabia is often recounted as two unequal acts separated by a long intermission. Most volumes on the early history of the modern Saudi state conclude in the early 1930s, when the Hijaz was definitively subdued by the Saudis, the Ikhwān threat averted, and the Kingdom of Saudi Arabia declared.[4] The story then resumes in the postwar period, with the emergence of the oil industry and the institutions of the modern Saudi state,[5] developments preserved in Western and Saudi records. Historical accounts that deal with the intervening two decades are scarce, and those that exist tend to utilize few original documents. Madawi al-Rasheed summarizes the common view of this period: "In the 1930s and 1940s the state had no archives or documents."[6] This chapter, which draws upon scores of unexamined administrative documents preserved in the Institute of Public Administration (IPA) archive in Riyadh, will undermine the latter claim. The IPA documents render the Saudi state visible during this otherwise opaque and understudied time period, for which we are otherwise left essentially to rely on the memoirs of various courtiers. More importantly, these documents provide a view into how the emergent Saudi state, though weak and inconsistent in its operations, commenced the process of shaping the political identities of its citizens, and how it promoted conformity within a tribal-genealogical mold.

THE *TĀBIʿIYYA* AND THE CONSTRUCTION OF A POLITY

When Ibn Saʿūd announced the formation of the Kingdom of Saudi Arabia in September 1932, the last major internal challenge to his rule had been suppressed,[7] and the Saudi state could begin shifting its energies from territorial expansion to peacetime consolidation and governance. The capital of this new state was Mecca, and its center of gravity was the urbanizing Hijaz. A conservative and insular Najdi-Wahhabi order had imposed itself on a heterogeneous, Ottoman-Sharifian rump state, a bifurcation that would resolve itself only decades later, when the Saudis shifted their capital to Riyadh. This duality was complicated by a still more significant distinction. The Saudi conquerors had inherited a population with two broadly distinct sociological profiles: one town-based, commerce-oriented, and ethnically diverse; the other rural, pastoralist, and tribal. Governing these two populations would require distinctive tools and approaches.

In rural areas of the Hijaz, where state authority was weak, and devolution of power to tribal leaders was a necessity, the tribe or kinship group remained the primary unit through which the Saudi state conceived of and interacted with its population. Recognizing the authority of tribal leaders at the local level, making them responsible for policing their own populations, was the path of least resistance for the religiously inspired Saudi government, "the surest and most convenient (*aqrab*) means for preventing corruption and striking the hands of corrupters," in the Quranic register of a 1938 government document.[8] As the decades progressed, this tribal system of accountability was to be maintained in a modified form, one that agreed with the aspirations of a centralizing state for subordination to its will, both in letter and spirit.

In 1935, the Majlis al-Shūrā heard a complaint from Muḥammad b. Ṣāliḥ al-Qārizī, shaykh of the Fuqahāʾ tribe in the kingdom's southwest. The Fuqahāʾ wished to detach themselves administratively from the Līth province and join with the Zahrān tribe, for reasons that most likely had to do with taxation. Ibn Saʿūd rejected al-Qārizī's request. "His majesty the king's desire that the Fuqahāʾ be a part of Līth was [earlier] decreed . . . and the king's will must be obeyed."[9] In 1938, members of the Banī al-Muntashir tribe, also of the kingdom's southwest, approached their former leader, Jārī b. Barakāt, and swore allegiance to him in place of their current leader, Saʿd b. Ḍayfallāh, who by all appearances had been assigned to them by the Saudi government. Considering this exercise of political autonomy to be a reflection of "factionalism and opposition" to its will, the government reversed the move, fining and imprisoning the conspirators.[10] Of the many ways in which tribal prerogatives were to be usurped within the new Saudi order, the imposing of limits on genealogical combination and bifurcation was perhaps the most profound. Ibn Saʿūd's decision to restrict these southern tribes' genealogical (and political) mobility was equivalent to gumming up the system by which tribal identities had been generated over centuries. It eliminated one of the traditional mechanisms by which Arabian tribes were constituted or reconstituted in times of need. In the predominantly rural and bedouin polity inherited by Ibn Saʿūd, the capacity for tribal subgroups to change their lineal affiliations or leadership structures ran counter to the need to fix the identities of the kingdom's subjects in a single place, a prerequisite for their efficient management and control.

A 1938 directive further illustrates the changing nature of the new political order, and foreshadows the way the modern Saudi state would reinscribe preestablished kinship notions in its own image. In reaction to incidents of theft against pilgrims en route to Medina, the Saudi-appointed governor of the administrative center of al-Bāḥa province, in the kingdom's southwest, reached an agreement with the tribal leaders of the surrounding villages over procedures for isolating and punishing criminal offenders. The points of this agreement were sent to the new Saudi capital of Mecca for review, where members of the king's advisory council (Majlis al-Shūrā) set to work amending them,[11] they explained, to bring them into conformity with Islamic law. The original agreement specified that the villages would elect "four trustworthy persons, who would be responsible before [the head of the tribe]" for settling any and all criminal activities occurring in their villages. The Majlis al-Shūrā revised the document to read that the four trustworthy persons were to be "delegated jointly with the head of the tribe" (*yukallafūn bi-l-taḍāmun maʿa raʾīs al-qabīla*) to investigate all such criminal violations.[12] Under the new Saudi writ, Ibn Saʿūd and his deputies alone had the power to delegate and enforce authority. The council's amendment was a reminder that in the view of this state, the tribal shaykh and those who answered to him were to be classed functionally on an equally subordinate plane.

Whereas in rural areas Ibn Saʿūd's government worked through tribal networks to assert its authority, in the principal towns of the Hijaz the Saudis inherited a basic administrative apparatus from the Ottoman-Sharifian administration. This apparatus, though insulated from many of the modernizing Tanzimat reforms by the special circumstances of Hijazi life, nevertheless bore some of the trappings of modern statehood: telegraphs, post offices, hospitals, and schools.[13] James Scott has drawn attention to another important dimension of modern state practice, namely, the techniques used by states to identify, order, and sort their populations, exemplified in the use of standardized surnames and identity cards. Building on Ottoman precedent, in 1926 the Saudi government issued its first Nationality Regulations, which instructed Hijaz residents to acquire Saudi identification papers, called *tābiʿiyya*.[14] The term *tābiʿiyya* derived from the Ottoman administrative lexicon of the nineteenth century. A *tābiʿ* was one who "followed" the ruler, or, an Ottoman subject, the word being a translation of the French word *sujet*.[15] The notion of *tābiʿiyya* was thus suitable for both an Ottoman monarchical order and its Arabian inheritor state.

Tābiʿiyya or nationality papers were issued first to employees of the government, many of whom had worked previously for the Ottoman or Hashemite administrations.[16] The *tābiʿiyya*'s chief purpose at the time was to help the Saudi government distinguish its population from the subjects of foreign governments residing in the Hijaz. Secondarily, its purpose was to compel former Ottoman and Hashemite subjects out of the grey area of statelessness and into the embrace of the Saudi state. The *tābiʿiyya* had little to do with modern notions of citizenship rights and responsibilities, though it did help determine the taxes one was committed to paying and those from which one was exempted.[17]

In its first few decades, the Saudi state adopted an expansive notion of citizenship. Writing in 1934, the Qāḍī of Medina indicated that in practice it was his rule to consider everyone present in the Hijaz from the date of the *tābiʿiyya* decree, including bedouin and former Ottoman subjects, to be Saudis.[18] The criteria for inclusion in the new Saudi polity were expansive and loose, as the government sought to augment its subject population and so bolster its legitimacy and tax base. Yet embedded within this flexible legal framework, adopted no doubt to harmonize with the realities of an ethnically diverse Hijazi town population, was a genealogical conception of citizenship that rested on intuitive knowledge and informality, one that seemed directed in part toward the opaque structures of bedouin life. For example, one clause in the 1933 citizenship law maintained that "anyone born of two parents who are known by lineage to follow the Saudi Arabian government yet do not possess *tābiʿiyya* papers are considered citizens of the Kingdom of Saudi Arabia."[19]

From an early stage, bedouin were largely exempted from the requirement to carry identifying documents.[20] Though the spirit of the 1926 *tābiʿiyya* decree intended that all citizens be placed on an equal footing,[21] in practice the *tābiʿiyya* was very much an urban calling card, with little rural utility. In the *bādiya* or tribal hinterland, the word of the tribal shaykh still reigned as the most effective form of identification.[22] Low rates of literacy helped preserve the oral cultural authority of the rural tribal leader, who was expected to act as the eyes and ears of the government in regions beyond its ken. The authenticating function of the tribal leader was the crucial avenue by which the bulk of the Saudi population was made legible to the state.

The early introduction of identity papers in settled areas suggests that the institutions of the Saudi government were taking shape from an earlier period than has previously been considered. Yet it would take several decades before the *tābiʿiyya* became standardized across the kingdom, decades in which the quantity of identification regimes proliferated. At one point, bedouin were issued their own identification papers distinct from those of the population centers,[23] though when or why this policy was initiated remains unclear. To take another example, identification papers issued in al-Aḥsāʾ in 1941 and signed by the governor of that province, Saʿūd b. ʿAbdallāh al-Jilūwwī, possessed a format distinct from that of Hijazi documents.[24] Unlike the latter, the al-Aḥsāʾ papers asked for their bearer's sectarian identity, a fact that demonstrated the Wahhabi government's acute interest in sectioning off its Shia population, which was concentrated in the oil-rich eastern part of the kingdom.

These nonstandard identity papers from the kingdom's two flanks had one important feature in common, however: both asked for the bearer's proper name, the name of the bearer's father, and the bearer's *laqab* or *shuhra*, the name by which they were known publicly outside of their kin group. The bearer's maximal tribal affiliation, his connection to the tribe's root, was not considered necessary information; administrators saw little need for the lengthy composite names by which Saudis are known today. Saudi identification papers of the early 1940s used relatively narrow genealogical parameters for defining personal identity, reflecting their function as access points to sedentary populations whose genealogical imaginations were, like those of the Saudi state at the time, rather ordinary and limited.

By most measures of modern state capacity—education, healthcare, finance—the institutional footprint of the Saudi government remained largely absent from central Arabia until the 1950s. This institutional void extended to the provisioning of identification papers. A 1947 decree urging Saudi citizens to acquire *tābiʿiyya* papers, for example, was applicable to the Hijaz alone, with Najd exempted.[25] When such papers were introduced to central Arabia, they struck a nerve with many Najdis, who saw in them a plot to circumscribe their identities as a prelude to military conscription. To register new cardholders, officials from the Saudi statistics bureau would accompany police officers on periodic market raids, where citizens could be seen climbing over walls to escape the demographers' notice.[26]

Well into the twentieth century, the Saudi state's interaction with its central Arabian population continued to be mediated by bedouin shaykhs and oasis town leaders. Najd's prolonged immunity from the instruments of the modern Saudi state can be explained by its remoteness from the kingdom's administrative center of gravity (Hijaz), and by the deep-rooted suspicions of Wahhabi ʿulamāʾ toward modern techniques of governance. One might recall here Ḥamad al-Jāsir's youthful byline in the Hijazi press, "A bedouin of the Najd, al-Jāsir." Bedouinism was in that instance an imprecise shorthand for the exoticism and remoteness of Najd, whose full integration into the modern kingdom would depend on an ordering and sorting of its populations—both bedouin and sedentary—that in 1947 was still beyond the capacity or interest of the state. Ironically, at this mid-point of the twentieth century, it was at the edge of the Rubʿ al-Khālī (The Empty Quarter), in the oases of Līwā and Buraymī at the kingdom's distant southeastern frontiers, that the most comprehensive and systematic program to comprehend the identities and affiliations of the bedouin tribes would commence, and at the hands not of Saudi, but of Western experts.

BURAYMĪ AND THE TRANSITION TO MODERN GOVERNANCE

If in the urban Hijazi centers of the 1930s and 1940s, the Saudi government was busy recruiting citizens and sorting them via diverse identifying techniques, on the kingdom's southeastern frontiers a different sort of contest for loyalties was transpiring. The discovery of large deposits of oil near the eastern Saudi Arabian village of Dammam in 1938 set off a race to affirm sovereign jurisdiction over adjacent territories, in what are today the Gulf states of Qatar, the United Arab Emirates, and Oman. While Saudi Arabia's northern borders had been determined in negotiations with the British following the Kuwait Conference of 1923–4, and parts of its southern boundary with Yemen had been settled de facto following the 1934 Saudi-Yemeni War, the kingdom's southeastern boundaries remained fully contested into the 1970s. The discovery of oil in Arabia injected a new urgency into jurisdictional claims, as the Saudis, emboldened by their victories and alliance with the United States, sought to further assert their domination over the Arabian Peninsula by expanding their reach to encompass the oases of Līwā and Buraymī, where oil deposits were thought to exist. Opposing them were the rulers of Abu Dhabi and Oman and their principal backer, Great Britain. In confronting Saudi claims, the British government aimed to secure sizeable hinterlands for its coastal clients who ruled the statelets lining the Persian Gulf coast, protect the crumbling monopolies of its Iraq Petroleum Company, and guard the frontiers of its Aden Protectorate against incursions by Saudi-American oil prospecting teams.[27]

These disputes over territories and boundaries played out in an Arabia in which dominion over persons ranked before territory as the operative criterion of traditional sovereignty,[28] one in which power inhered in the allegiances and fealties of nomadic tribes and settlers, and the perceived genealogical linkages that bound the one to the other.[29] With the Buraymī dispute, that traditional criterion of Arabian sovereignty, tribal allegiance, was introduced into a novel landscape, one being refashioned by the forces of Western commercial and political influence, and the introduction of the territorial nation-state. British government officials and researchers from the Arabian American Oil Company (Aramco) were centrally involved in the effort to defend the claims of their respective Arabian allies to the oases of Līwā and Buraymī. In the protracted dispute over these oases, whose substance was captured in dueling reports issued between 1950 and 1953 by Aramco and the British government respectively, Western experts used traditional measures of Arabian authority to assert novel forms of dominion based on territorial demarcation. In so doing, they ushered in a new way of doing politics in the Arab Gulf, one in which systematized genealogical knowledge could be used to influence and shape the practice of governance.

Ironically, in advancing what were quite obviously territorial claims over the Buraymī and Līwā regions, Ibn Saʿūd and his advisers were reluctant to acknowledge the Westphalian terms of their end game.[30] Instead, the Saudis insisted on making the tribal affiliations and loyalties of the inhabitants of Līwā and Buraymī the main object of contention, forcing a reluctant Britain and its clients to respond in those same "uncertain and changing" terms.[31] For Aramco's researchers and their rivals in the British government, inquiring into the genealogical picture in the two contested oases was therefore central to how territory could be won for local rulers in the new Arabia.[32] By affirming the centrality of traditional Arabian governing structures, boundary negotiations could proceed according to Westphalian norms (where citizenship and loyalty were linked to territory) without acknowledging them as such. Once the boundaries of the state were fixed, the Saudi government would adopt the measures developed by these Western experts and expand them within the framework of ordering and sorting its population. From the vantage point of world history, the Buraymī dispute reveals a clash between two twentieth-century great powers, one waxing, the other waning, each championing the claims of their local clients for their own commercial and political interests, and mustering genealogical knowledge in support of their rival contentions.

FIXING BURAYMĪ

Through mid-century, Saudi ministers remained deeply reliant on Aramco's Arabian Research Division for information about eastern Arabian geography, prospective border demarcations, and tribal demographic and migration patterns.[33] In subsequent decades, men like Ḥamad al-Jāsir would replace the Research Division as local sources of knowledge about the kingdom. In the late 1940s, however, it was Aramco's research arm under the leadership of the Arabist George Rentz that was tasked by the Saudi government with mapping the demography of eastern Arabia, in anticipation of the Saudis' refashioned claims to the region.[34] The outcome was *The Eastern Reaches of al-Hasa Province*, Aramco's detailed ethnographic study of the lineages and habitation patterns of the tribal populations of eastern Arabia, based on the reports of a range of local informants, both Aramco employees and others.

The Saudis claimed the allegiances of five predominantly nomadic tribes inhabiting the southern and eastern rim of their acknowledged domains: Banī Hājir, ʿAwāmir, Āl Murra, Dawāsir, and Manāṣīr.[35] Of these, only the Manāṣīr tribe had a notable presence in the disputed oasis of Līwā,[36] and to a lesser extent Buraymī. Beside the Manāṣīr of Līwā lived branches of the Banī Yās tribe and their affiliates, whose center of gravity was the British protectorate of Abu Dhabi, which was ruled by a branch of the Banī Yās, the Āl Bū Falāḥ.[37] For Aramco's researchers, advancing Saudi claims to Līwā and Buraymī meant first minimizing the Banī Yās presence in the oases and the Banī Yās tribe's historical connections to them. The Aramco reports are filled with subtle disparagement of the Banī Yās, who are described repeatedly as transient "seafarers" with no permanent foothold in the oases, "more of a maritime race" than the solid Manāṣīr bedouin.[38] The loyalties of the majority of the "authentic" inhabitants of Līwā oasis and surrounding areas (i.e., the Manāṣīr) were firmly with Ibn Saʿūd, the researchers argued.[39]

By what criteria did Aramco's researchers measure such authenticity? Part of their effort to define this quality involved positioning the Banī Yās inhabitants of the coastal hinterlands as sociologically the wrong kind of transients.[40] The disparagement of the Banī Yās "seafarers" was not purely commercial in its motivation, though. It reflected as well the influence of bedouin-derived notions of lineal purity and prestige (*aṣāla*) that Aramco's researchers had absorbed from their Najdi sponsors. These notions found expression elsewhere in the report, in the authors' general infatuation with the bedouin tribes of eastern Arabia. Not merely introducing American-style ethnic segregation into the Arabian mix, as Vitalis has argued,[41] Aramco was here effecting a converse process of exchange, transmitting Arabian ethnic categories through its corporate reporting instruments.

Whereas Aramco researchers focused their attention on the inland migrations of predominantly bedouin tribes, such as the Manāṣīr, the protagonists in the story told by various British officials in the field were the Banī Yās, whose regular traffic between shore and inland oases demonstrated their deep and authentic attachments to the Gulf coastal hinterlands.[42] Against Aramco notions of Manāṣīr permanence and authenticity, British field investigators who surveyed the same populations viewed transience as the universal norm in the contested oasis of Līwā, wherein both Banī Yās and Manāṣīr (though particularly the former) migrated seasonally from the date palm plantations and grazing lands of the hinterlands to the coastal regions in pursuit of pearling and other commercial activities.

If Aramco was to be the Saudi government's eyes and ears in Līwā and Buraymī, the British government played the company's opposite on behalf of its own client, Shaykh Shakhbūt of Abu Dhabi. Like the American oilmen with their Saudi sponsors,[43] British investigators involved in the dispute were surprised by the Abu Dhabi shaykh's lack of knowledge about the contested oases. The famously insular Shakhbūt's vague ideas about the borders of his realm were attributed in part to the fact that "he was not personally familiar with the southern and western reaches of what is claimed to be his territory."[44] While demonstrating the sometimes paper-thin legitimacy of the colonial enterprise, the parallel circumstances in which the two opposing parties found themselves with respect to knowledge about the contested oases was significant in another important way: both Aramco and British researchers used their opposing clients' lack of knowledge about their so-called subjects to underscore the illegitimacy of their respective claims. It was for these Western agents to fill in the informational gaps through systematic surveying of the populations of the oases, the results of which would be captured in two major internal reports. At the heart of these rival assertions of expertise was a genealogical conception of ultimate truth. Genealogy was the source code of the Buraymī dispute, the material out of which would be constructed the tribal edifice and through it the map of local allegiances that would be crucial for winning new territories and their subterranean bounty.

There was substantial disagreement between British and Aramco officials over the demographic picture in Līwā oasis. As noted, the question before the Aramco and British researchers, which was supposed to determine sovereignty over Līwā, concerned the relative size of the Banī Yās and Manāṣīr populations in the oasis and the loyalties of its Manāṣīr inhabitants. In order to assess these loyalties, the Banī Yās and Manāṣīr would have to be properly counted and sorted. This proved to be a hopeless exercise, in which the British and the Americans could find no common empirical ground. Aramco's George Rentz counted approximately 83 Līwā villages belonging to the Manāṣīr, and 42 to the Banī Yās.[45] The British, operating perhaps under the influence of the unilineal descent models of kinship that were in anthropological vogue at that time, rejected Aramco characterizations of Manāsīr permanence and Banī Yās transience,[46] preferring a tally of oasis kinship units and their loyalties as their chosen method. By these measures, the British surveyor Buckmaster found that 535 families in Līwā (mostly Banī Yās) supported Abu Dhabi, while 269 families supported the Saudis.[47] On the question of ownership over Līwā, Buckmaster was unequivocal: "The unanimous opinion of all questioned was that Līwā belongs, and always has belonged within living memory, to the Āl Bū Falāḥ. . . ."[48]

A similar circumstance applied in Buraymī, the territorial heart of the dispute, and a region over which the Saudis and the Āl Bū Falāḥ rulers of Abu Dhabi had been fighting since the early nineteenth century. As with Līwā, the British government viewed Buraymī as the territory of Banī Yās and its affiliates.[49] From the Saudi vantage point, recorded dutifully by Aramco's researchers, the rulers of Abu Dhabi, though increasingly influential in the hinterland, were truly only rulers of a coastal town, whose writ failed to extend far beyond the coast. The Saudis, by contrast, ruled via a *daʿwa* or religious mission that was historically hegemonic throughout much of Arabia, including Buraymī.[50] In 1952, as tensions between Abu Dhabi and Riyadh increased, the Saudis dispatched Turkī b. ʿUṭayshān with a group of fifty soldiers to assume control over the Buraymī town of Ḥamāsa and rally the local tribes to the Saudi-Wahhabi banner.[51] To justify their intervention, the Saudis claimed that they were simply acceding to the wishes of the tribal shaykhs of Buraymī, who had implored them repeatedly to establish a presence in the oasis.[52] Several of the leaders in question belonged to tribes that possessed historical affinities with the Wahhabis, and those affinities were being rekindled via generous cash payments from the Saudi government.[53]

To advance their rival claims, Aramco researchers and British officials introduced assorted arguments relating to the historical legitimacy, numerical preponderance, and genealogical affiliation of Buraymī's tribes. Though Banī Yās had in recent decades grown ascendant in the Buraymī oasis, Aramco's researchers observed, the tribe of Nuʿaym, to which two of the three pro-Saudi shaykhs in the oasis belonged,[54] were considered Buraymī's original owners.[55] More significantly, though Banī Yās controlled six of the oasis's nine settlements, its numerical preponderance was illusory, as three of those settlements were in the hands of Banī Yās's Ẓawāhir allies, whose genealogical affiliation with Banī Yās, the Aramco authors noted repeatedly, was suspect.[56] Aramco's efforts to bend Buraymī's genealogical picture in the Saudis' favor is exemplified most vividly in a map prepared by the company detailing the dominant tribal groups of the oasis and surrounding areas. In the company's visual rendering of Buraymī, the pro-Saudi Nuʿaym are, despite their acknowledged numerical and political disadvantage, the only tribe represented.[57]

After negotiations over the disputed territory broke down in 1955, a British-backed force invaded Buraymī and expelled the Saudi troops and their local supporters.[58] In a 1956 document submitted to the U.N. arbitration committee for Buraymī, the government of Saudi Arabia included images of what it described as the three "principal Shaykhs of Buraimi." These were the three pro-Saudi local tribal leaders who had made common cause with Ibn ʿUṭayshān and had been expelled from their home villages during the subsequent fighting.[59] As might be anticipated, Britain's reading of the demographic scene in Buraymī and thus the leadership picture diverged widely from the Aramco-Saudi assessments. From the British vantage point, Buraymī comprised ten villages, of which seven were controlled by the Bānī Yās or their historical allies from the Ẓawāhir tribe, totaling approximately 860 households, whereas the three pro-Saudi shaykhs controlled three villages, comprising only 530 households.[60] The Saudi claim that the three pro-Saudi shaykhs were the "principal Shaykhs of Buraimi" was thus not a received fact, but the very subject of contention.

Though Britain won Buraymī and Līwā for its client state, it was fighting a losing battle for broader influence in the region against the United States and its Saudi ally. In 1955, Prime Minister Anthony Eden declared with respect to Buraymī that his government was willing to "uphold a line which is more favourable to Saudi Arabia," giving public recognition to Britain's diminishing sway in the Middle East.[61] The epigraph for the 1953 report sum-

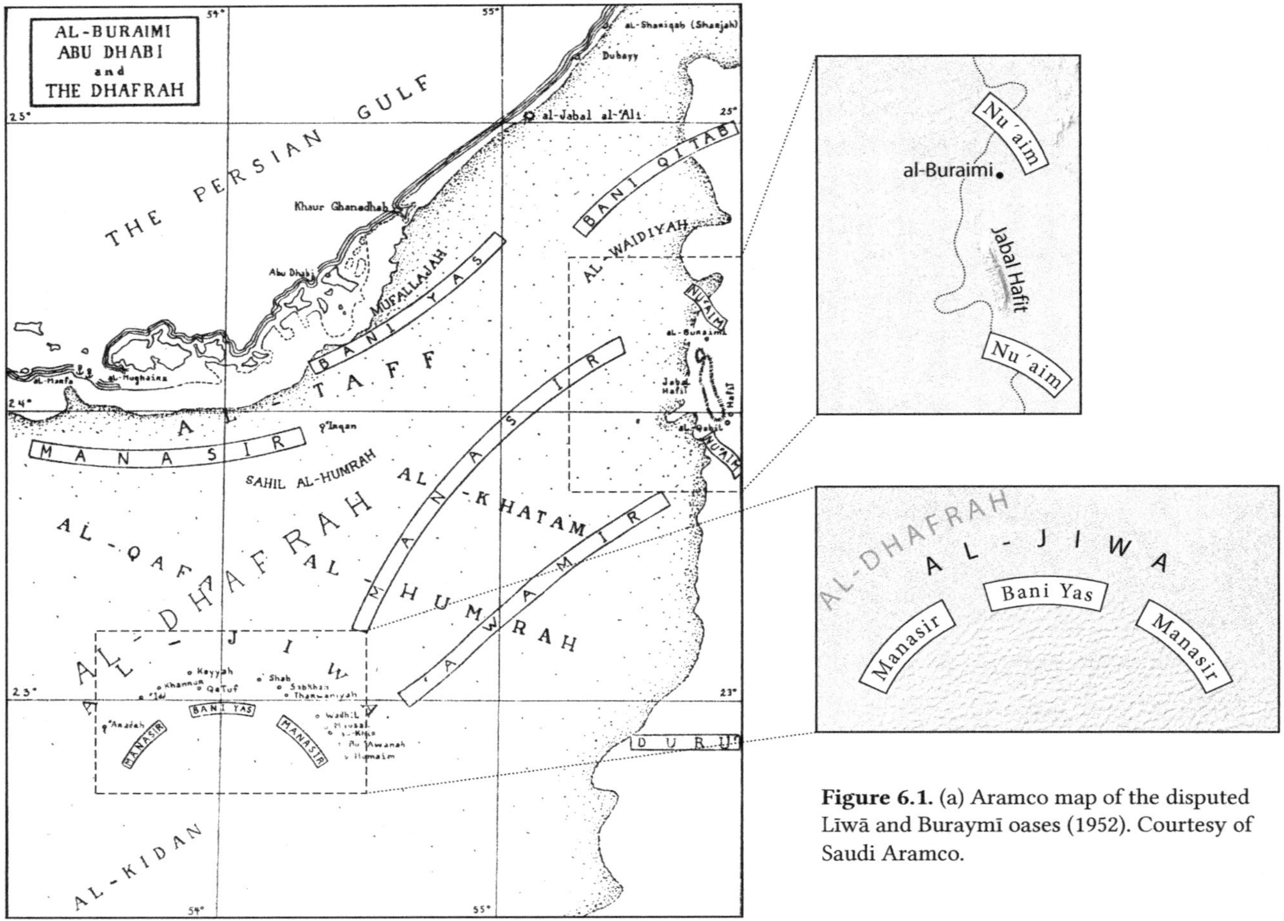

Figure 6.1. (a) Aramco map of the disputed Līwā and Buraymī oases (1952). Courtesy of Saudi Aramco.

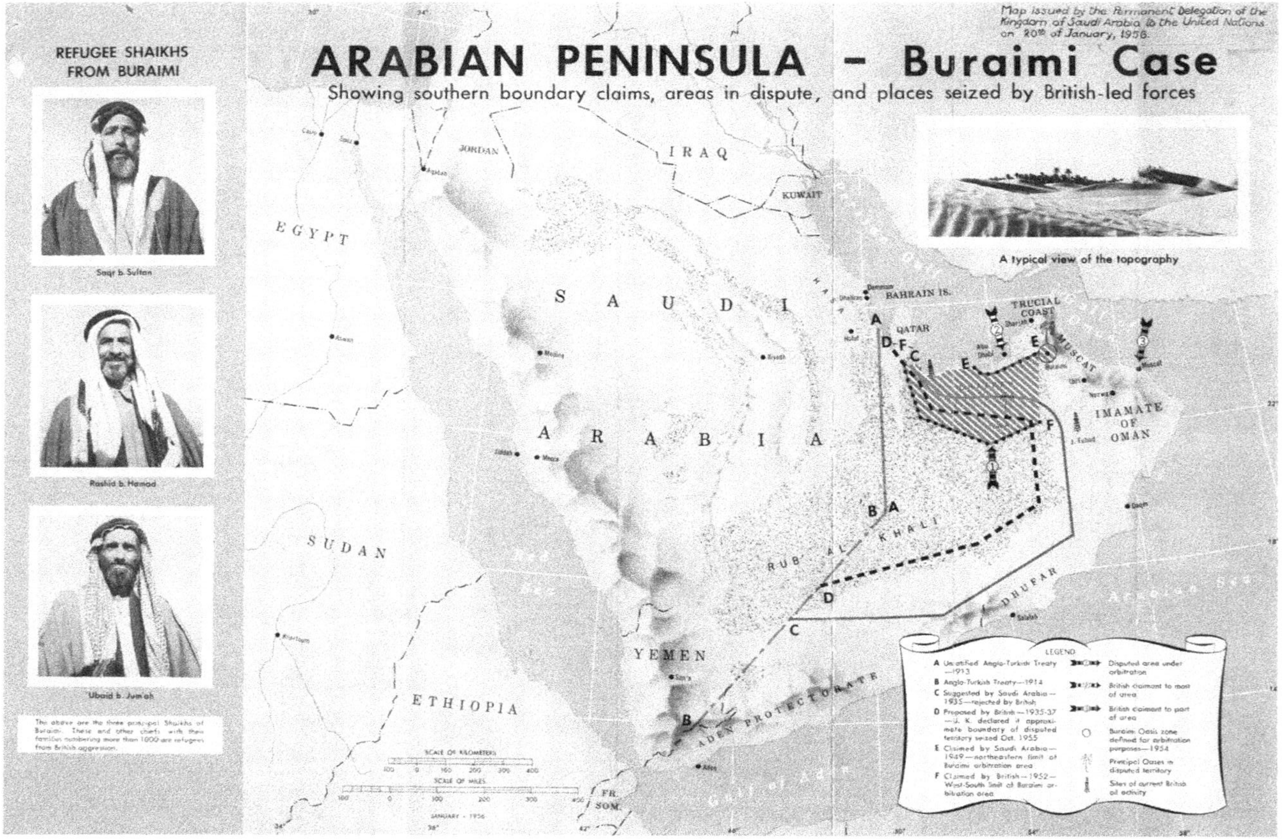

Figure 6.1. (b) Saudi government map and description of Buraymī dispute (1956). The first sentence in the caption below the left column reads: "Above are the three principal Shaikhs of Buraimi." Courtesy of Saudi Mission to the UN.

marizing the British government's involvement in the Buraymī dispute to that point included quotations from two famous British observers of the Gulf, J. G. Lorimer and Wilfred Thesiger:

> The position of an Arab Shaikh was not that of an absolute or arbitrary monarch; he ruled by influence over subjects who voluntarily accepted his dominion and his subjects and subordinate allies possessed a large degree of local freedom and even rights that he could not with safety invade. (Lorimer. I.P. 1063)

> Everywhere in Northern Oman jealous and often hostile shaikhs rely upon uncertain support of the bedu to maintain their position. . . . None of these shaikhs is prepared to acknowledge a paramount power nor is any of them able to enforce his authority over the Bedu: indeed none of them would venture to try lest by doing so he should alienate their support in time of need. (Thesiger. *Geographical Journal*, Volume CXVI. Page 139)

For official audiences more accustomed to Western notions of territorial sovereignty, the quotations capture a sense of the limited power and authority of the Arab tribal shaykh.[62] One is tempted as well to read these allusions as an indirect plea for recognition of Great Britain's new, more limited role in Arabia, cloaked in the ethnographic description of a subject people.

BURAYMĪ'S LEGACY

Thus by foreign scribes enacting a local writ, a genealogical rule of governance was inaugurated in modern Saudi Arabia. The Buraymī dispute represents the discovery of the tribe by the classificatory instruments of the modern state,[63] and so foreshadows how an expanding Saudi government would interact with its own bedouin and sedentary populations in the second half of the twentieth century. The techniques of commercial-colonial ethnography employed by Aramco's researchers and their British official counterparts would be picked up and implemented by the Saudi government, no longer for the purposes of boundary determination, but in the more mundane pursuit of law and order. At a time when Ḥamad al-Jāsir's interactions with Western Orientalists was inspiring his emergent interest in Arabian genealogies, the Saudi state was embarking on its own program of ethnographic collection and identification, one introduced first by Western experts in Buraymī.[64]

At this still early period in Saudi state formation, the instruments used by Aramco and the British government for genealogical tracking were relatively primitive in nature. This fact is reflected in the level of generality at which affiliations were documented in Aramco and British records, that is, at a level no more granular than the tribal subbranch.[65] Outside of identifying and cultivating specific tribal leaders, notions of personal identity remained subordinated to the collectivized conceptions promoted by both local governments and their foreign sponsors. These simplifications suited a state that was still probing the limits of its own frontiers, and still contending with the legacy of bedouin oral culture and social structures. They also suited foreign observers who lacked intimacy with the subjects of their research and were heavily reliant on local informants. In subsequent decades, the Saudis would enhance the sophistication of their documentary techniques by introducing more robust and intrusive measures of genealogical affiliation. At mid-century, in the remote outposts of Līwā and Buraymī, they would have to make do with the usefully imprecise assessments of their American commercial agents.

GENEALOGY SURVIVES THE TRIBE

Historians of twentieth-century Saudi Arabia tend to locate the beginnings of the kingdom's modern development in the Saudi succession crisis of 1958–64, when, with a coalition of royal and clerical supporters, Ibn Saʿūd's son Fayṣal overtook his increasingly unpopular brother Saʿūd for leadership of the state. One of Fayṣal's first acts after being confirmed king in 1964 was to issue his "Ten Point Program," which outlined the economic and social policies the Saudi government would undertake to shore up domestic support and counter pro-Nasserist pressures. Notable among the Program's provisions was its articulation of a vision in which the preservation of Saudi values and traditions would occupy a key place in the development process. In her recent study of this development process, Sarah Yizraeli adopts this notion of cultural preservation as an analytical touchstone, considering that the Saudi state implemented the promise outlined in the Program to preserve both the tribal and religious structures and the value systems of its society. Yet the notion that a society whose material life has undergone a radical transformation can somehow remain immune from change or be preserved in a sort of pickled state defies reasonable expectation. Over the course of the twentieth century, Saudi tribal and kinship networks underwent profound changes that transformed the modern tribe until it bore little resemblance to that of the early period of state formation. The deterritorialization of kinship networks through urban migration and labor market integration gave rise to new forms of tribalism, embodied most clearly in the kingdom's modern genealogical culture, in which the idea of tribal communion replaced its physical and political reality. Crucial to the development of this culture was a genealogical rule of governance, defined here as the sum total of the Saudi state's policies for identifying, managing, and projecting ideological power toward its population of subject-citizens.

Among its many significant reforms, which included the outlawing of slavery, the Ten Point Program inaugurated a vast social welfare system designed to undercut the populist pro-Nasser movements that had been coalescing inside the kingdom since the 1950s. Influenced as well by a growing intimacy with the U.S. government and its anti-Soviet foreign policy, the kingdom positioned itself as a regional bulwark of liberal economic principles. King Fayṣal again set the tone, affirming in 1965 Saudi Arabia's commitment to a free enterprise system.[66] Steffen Hertog has complicated this liberal utopian view of mid-century Saudi state formation by showing how the kingdom's political system emerged as an inelegant jumble of institutions layered thinly over circles of patronage, each tied to key members of the ruling family. Hertog's description of Saudi ministries as isolated fiefdoms is useful here, as it allows us to think of Saudi Arabia not as a monolithic authoritarian state, but as a fragmented regime whose institutions worked at cross purposes with one another in shaping the aspirations and attitudes of its citizens. The rhetoric of meritocratic advancement and self-improvement touted by the Saudi government from the 1960s forward, though often directed at international markets and outside centers of political influence, found internal expression in the state's more visible sectors, for example, those charged with managing public education and economic development.[67] Cold War-era declarations of economic philosophy by Saudi policy makers emphasized the virtues of "individual effort and achievement" and asserted "a basic respect for the self-improving efforts of the individual."[68] Concurrently, successive generations of Saudi intellectuals, from ʿAbd al-Quddūs al-Anṣārī (d. 1983) and Ḥamad al-Jāsir (d. 2000) to Ghāzī al-Quṣaybī (d. 2010), trumpeted the rewards of modern education and meritocratic advancement.

And yet, despite its prominence in the discourse of officials and public intellectuals, the rhetoric of the invisible hand was just one of several competing propositions influencing the state's ideological orientation. At the same time as it was inviting its citizens to compete equitably for the rewards of academic excellence or business acumen, the Saudi government was ordering and sorting them according to largely immutable genealogical criteria. Unburdened by the need to conform to international rhetorical norms, the institutions responsible for ordering, sorting, and controlling the population, particularly the Ministry of Interior, cultivated a countervailing ethic, a tribal-genealogical ethic, by which its citizens would come to be defined. Just as exogenous forces such as the Cold War influenced the Saudi state's conception of its political imperatives, so too would the introduction of Western techniques of identification influence the meaning and shape of the tribe and kin group in the modern kingdom.

There is no doubt that Saudi tribes *qua* tribes were major losers in the development process, during which a distributive (as opposed to extractive), Western-backed security state appropriated the core functions of the traditional tribal group: the provisioning of economic goods and physical security. As will be demonstrated below, however, the narrative of tribal decline recited almost uniformly by scholars fails to consider the extent to which the essential organizing principle of the tribe, the genealogical principle, came to pervade the social, ideological, and political life of the modern kingdom.[69] It is where this genealogical rule of governance combines with a deep-seated Arabian kinship consciousness that the story of modern Saudi Arabia truly begins.

RECONSTITUTING THE TRIBE IN THE OIL AGE

Despite the ambitious development agenda announced in the Ten Point Program, the Saudi state remained ill-equipped to manage the demands of its burgeoning populations, particularly the bedouin-origin migrants who began crowding into Riyadh's new neighborhoods in the 1960s.[70] As Pascal Menoret explains:

> Most migrants came from small towns, villages and nomadic encampments, and had no economic or cultural capital. . . . Desperate for work, they found employment at the royal palace, the national oil company Petromin and the new ministries, around which slums soon sprouted. Migrants would be hired as construction workers, guards, and soldiers or as bus, taxi and truck drivers. Some more fortunate became gamekeepers (*khwi*) for the royal family. They tended to live alone and send remittances to their families back home, waiting for a good opportunity to bring them to Riyadh. . . . Described as unruly, unpredictable and volatile by Saudi technocrats and experts, slum dwellers were seen as a threat to the established way of life of the sedentary population.[71]

Though Ibn Saʿūd's forcible sedentarization of Arabia's bedouin in *hujar* communities has been mythologized by scholars as the key turn in Arabian history,[72] it was the silent and voluntary migration of hundreds of thousands of bedouin to the outskirts of cities and towns in the second half of the twentieth century that constituted the more radical change. As an indicator of the challenge this internal migration posed for the state, in 1961 the Ministry of Finance ordered that its agencies refrain from disbursing social welfare payments to bedouin families of more than five persons.[73] This indirect effort at population control was one of a number of measures the Saudi state adopted to reshape its bedouin populations and help manage bedouin dependency on its emergent welfare programs.

The urban migration of the bedouin signaled the beginning of the end of tribal cohabitation, and thus the weakening of traditional kinship ties built around the coterminous foundations of blood (real or imagined) and soil. The revision of conventions governing bedouin property ownership contributed further to this reconstitution of tribal identities. From 1925, when the Saudi government began its de facto land appropriations by withdrawing recognition of bedouin claims to tribal grazing lands (*dīras*),[74] to 1968, when the state introduced a program to redistribute agricultural plots to bedouin entrepreneurs, bedouin land had concluded a radical transition from collective to state to individual property.

The wholesale displacement of traditional modes of bedouin life was mirrored in the restructuring of kinship networks around the Saudi court. "Access to the expanding court," Hertog writes, "offered great opportunities of social and economic mobility."[75] Among those in search of such opportunities were the recently displaced leaders of Arabia's prominent tribes. Writing in 1955, Aramco's resident anthropologist Federico Vidal commented on this phenomenon: "Arab Bedouin chiefs are now being slowly converted from tribal leaders into royal courtiers. The prestige that was correlated with being independent overlords is being replaced by the prestige of being in attendance, by cash subsidies, official positions, etc., while the royal family can keep their activities under control. Many of the Bedouin chieftains have for these reasons moved to the al-Riyadh district."[76]

Bedouin saw recognition of claims to leadership of their tribal section as a sure route to subsidization by the government. The prospective rewards of the titular honorific *shaykh* induced many to announce themselves as tribal leaders in the 1960s.[77] These tribal leaders were typically excluded from formal administrative roles in major population centers,[78] though they were counted on for mediating local disputes, as well as for the important function of lineal authentication, discussed in detail below. In these capacities they were made answerable to the kingdom's regional governors, who reported to the Minister of Interior.[79] From the apex of authority in traditional Arabian society, the tribal leader had descended to occupy the lowest rungs of the new bureaucratic hierarchy.

In earlier decades, when the Saudi government was still reliant on tax payments from local leaders for much of its revenue, it allowed tribal shaykhs to withhold a fixed portion of the annual *zakāt* payments collected from their kinsmen for their own use.[80] By the 1960s, the Interior Ministry was dispensing regular stipends to these same leaders in exchange for no more than tacit acquiescence to their diminished autonomy.[81] The distributive economy had its rewards, and its humiliations. Yet the state was sensitive to maintaining the appearance of dignifying tribal leaders, as it remained wary of threats emanating from disaffected tribes.[82] Thus the modern Saudi culture of praise, and the celebration of lineal prestige that forms a core dimension of it, was promoted in part as a strategy of governance, designed to limit feelings of alienation by subordinated tribes.

TRIBAL IDENTITY AND THE FOUR-PART NAME

As noted earlier, an important extension of the process of fixing tribal identities was the introduction of standardized identification papers. In the state's early incarnation as an extractive body, the registration of personal and tribal names served principally for the benefit of Ibn Saʿūd's tax collectors, and so was resisted in many quarters. Yet as its extractive profile faded and a new distributive model of economic life took hold in the kingdom, the possession of identifying documents and standardized personal names became a *sine qua non* for the receipt of state subsidies and employment. With such new incentives in play, citizen opposition to the *tābiʿiyya* diminished. Scott has argued that in most cases, naming and identification practices were closely tied to efforts by the state "to put its fiscal system on a sounder and more lucrative footing."[83] Yet the kingdom's push to standardize identification practices, and thereby refine "the quality of information" available to it, emerged only in the 1960s,[84] when Saudi Arabia began moving away from a traditional extractive model and toward a distributive one. The need to better comprehend the population seemed to have more to do with the permanent potential for antagonism in the state's relationship with its subject-citizens, or the anxiety that the formerly nomadic tribes were perpetually lying in wait for the regime's demise.

In 1954, the Saudi government issued its first citizenship regulations since the declaration of the Kingdom of Saudi Arabia some thirty years earlier.[85] Largely a restatement of the 1926 Nationality Regulations, their impact would not be felt immediately. As part of his broader effort to standardize the state's still largely informal governing structures, in 1961 Prince Fayṣal issued a decree through his Council of Ministers that sought to unify the kingdom's disparate identification regimes and require all Saudis to carry the new standard issue *tābiʿiyya*.[86] Notably, the decree mandated the seizure and destruction of all bedouin identification cards, and the issuing of a uniform *tābiʿiyya* to bedouin-origin as well as sedentary-origin Saudis. These normalizing measures underscore the piecemeal nature of statecraft in that period, where a monochrome nationality might be bestowed by decree yet remain unrecognized both to subject and ruler for almost a decade. Still, in this effort to standardize the methods by which its sociologically diffuse populations might be identified, one can observe the increasing ambition and reach of the Saudi state. Such regulations foreshadowed an emerging tension facing state officials, namely, whether they would seek to mold a newly forming polity into a uniformly conditioned population of individualized Saudi citizens, or a loyal yet haphazard assortment of kinship collectives. While its administrative structures grew in sophistication, the state's continuing ambivalence toward the question of how to shape Saudi citizen identity helped breathe new life into tribal and kinship structures.

While postcolonial governments in Morocco and Sudan were formally abolishing tribes as administrative units,[87] the Saudi state was repurposing the tribe and tribal identity as a tool of modern governance. At the same time as revolutionary Arab republics like Egypt were removing the vestiges of genealogical and spiritual privilege through such measures as eliminating the position of the *naqīb al-ashrāf*,[88] Saudi Arabia was enshrining lineal status as an essential criterion for citizenship. Whatever one is to make of the broader import and resonance of the progressive Saudi movements that emerged in the 1950s to challenge the emergent order, and of Ḥamad al-Jāsir's own struggles within them, these movements at the very least pointed to the possibility of an alternative conception of citizenship, one which the Saudi ruling family rejected emphatically as unsuitable for the political ecology of Arabia and, more significantly, for its continued dominion. Yet the rejection of a disruptive program of social engineering of the kind favored by rival revolutionary Arab states did not entail the embrace of a crisp alternative.

At the bureaucratic level, a growing concern within the government was the infrequent use of surnames by Saudis and the consequent incapacity to differentiate among citizens with common names.[89] In 1969, the deputy director of the General Auditing Bureau authored a memorandum to the director of the Employees Bureau complaining about a confusing list of state religious functionaries that had crossed his desk. "The presence of [two- and three-part names] . . . makes a precise review difficult. . . . For this reason, we have recommended that three-part names have the tribal or popular name added to them, so as to limit the confusion. . . . We hope . . . that you will write out complete names . . . for all ministries and governmental interests."[90] The elaboration of the Saudi name into a "complete" four-part structure encompassing a first name, father's name, grandfather's name, and tribal name, was an important development that would have implications for the kingdom's modern genealogical culture.[91]

The success of a state's disciplinary power, Michel Foucault once argued, derives from its use of techniques of "hierarchical observation," which are perfected in the architecture of modern military camps, hospitals, asylums, schools, and other such institutions.[92] In twentieth-century Saudi Arabia, a country whose hegemonic center had barely emerged from a lengthy period of relative isolation from the broader Muslim, let alone non-Muslim world, the crowning technique of hierarchical observation was not one of the many modern edifices devised by foreign experts and built for the new state, but the four-part name, through which a nascent society might be instantaneously penetrated and interrogated. The four-part name lent dimensionality to what was previously a rather fuzzy concept of citizen personhood. By drawing on an idiom of governance that had tremendous resonance in Arabian historical memory, the state could ease citizen immersion into new economic, social, and political modes of life, while at the same time slowing or arresting the prospects of revolutionary ferment. For tribal genealogies to be useful to the Saudi government, however, they would first have to be stabilized and removed from the domain of oral culture. As Saad Sowayan explained:

> The tribe now is not the tribe it used to be. Now, it has been frozen . . . like a still picture. . . . When the country was united under King ʿAbd al-ʿAzīz, the existing situation at that moment was frozen, so the dynamics of tribal membership have been disrupted, and whoever is ʿUtaybī or Ḥarbī will remain forever ʿUtaybī and Ḥarbī. . . .[93]

The many tribal and family reunification narratives discussed in earlier chapters can be read in part as evidence of tacit resistance to the state's new taxonomical authority.

Sedentary-origin Saudis of a certain age recall the moment when a maximal tribal identity was first imposed on them:

> The first time I got a *tābiʿiyya*, more than forty years ago . . . there was someone there at the passport office, in Riyadh, he said to me: "Brother, what tribe are you from?" I said: "Brother, I am from such-and-such tribe, but I don't want it mentioned in my *tābiʿiyya* name or my i.d. My name is my family name." He stood and said: "no, you must mention your tribal name."[94]

As a childhood resident of al-ʿUlā recounted with respect to the town's long-settled families, "when the state . . . imposed the requirement that you include the tribal name . . . [the al-ʿUlā] families renounced their family names."[95] For Saudis, particularly those of sedentary origin, the four-part name created the grounds for a fixation on tribal belonging, as it placed the individual's tribe at the foreground of their public identity, and invented a new inadequacy for those whose popular name (*al-shuhra*) could not be linked credibly to a prominent tribe. Some sedentary-origin Saudis blamed Ḥamad al-Jāsir for creating this new, fine-grain taxonomy:

> . . . In Riyadh there are more than 800,000 people from the southern regions . . . they come here and live, all of them in this region. . . . The new generation doesn't know whether this one is Qaḥṭānī or this one Shahrānī or Ghāmidī or such. So they came, and they got to know each other, and they married one another, and they had no problem. But after [Ḥamad al-Jāsir] there appeared this sense of, "no, I need to verify what kind of Qaḥṭānī this one is. Is he a Qaḥṭānī [of high status] or not?"[96]

Yet the four-part name was a state initiative that predated Ḥamad al-Jāsir's genealogical project, and can therefore be said to have potentially influenced the scholar's own approach to or interest in modern Arabian genealogical classification.

For bedouin-origin Saudis, the introduction of standardized names and identification cards was part of a broader process of atomizing traditional tribal structures and recombining them in ways favorable to effective governance. Rather than seeking exclusively to undermine the internal cohesion of Saudi tribes, as al-Rasheed has argued,[97] the Saudi state promoted specific *forms* of tribal cohesion that facilitated the management of its populations at the local and national level. On the one hand, the state continued to recognize the juridical validity of the small kinship collective (*khamsa*) for the purposes of low-level conflict management and mediation.[98] On the other, it promoted identification with top-level tribal names through its documentation policies. The molding of these two distinct forms of tribal cohesion helps explain the fixation by many Saudis, both sedentary- and bedouin-origin, on the lacunae of the intermediate linkages that are missing from their lineage chains.[99] The bifurcated nature of tribal histories noted by Alois Musil, Madawi al-Rasheed, and the historian Lucette Valensi was thus in the twentieth century not merely a function of the sociology of tribal memory, but of how state policies promoted certain kinds of tribal conceptions, from the small-scale and intimate to the grandiose and mythic.[100]

LINEAL AUTHENTICATION BECOMES THE STATE

On March 15, 1981, in a decree that would mark the end of an era, King Khālid declared that no new *hujar* communities were to be founded for newly sedentarizing bedouin.[101] By compulsion or volition, the bedouin had been fixed in place in the kingdom's villages, towns, and cities, and the state could now turn its efforts to furthering their integration into its governing structures. In response to the dual challenge of integrating and policing its bedouin populations, the Saudi government invented new functions and roles for them. This effort to rationalize its administrative systems, however, led to a paradoxical outcome, as the state would move to institutionalize the informality that had for long characterized its interaction with its bedouin populations.

In 1964, the Ministry of Interior initiated a formal effort to recruit bedouin experts into its service. These were to be "trusted bedouin men, who are acquainted with and possess wide knowledge about the tribes and the villages, and their problems and conditions, who will be quasi-employees of the ministry with partial salaries."[102] In 1978 and again in 1981, it would look to have these experts' titles exempted from standard civil service regulations and competitive examinations.[103] The Ministry argued its case as follows: "these positions require individuals who possess specific personal qualities such as complete familiarity with bedouin customs and traditions and knowledge of bedouin leaders, as well as common sense (*rajāḥat al-ʿaql*) and good behavior. These are qualities that cannot be measured by the standards of [civil service] competition."[104] The emergence of these bedouin experts and their exemption from the rules applicable within the more transparent part of the Saudi administrative structure revealed how the loose formality of state-bedouin relations might persist into the Saudi bureaucratic age.[105] The Ministry of Interior's bedouin experts were to have one foot in the modern bureaucracy, and one foot in a realm of informality that bore only a passing resemblance to the political structures of Arabia's past.

The recruitment of bedouin experts by the Ministry of Interior was a minor episode in the broader transformation of political authority in the Arabian Peninsula. As the state began to draw in and formalize its relations with its citizen kinship collectives, new forms of political authority were invented out of the husks of older ones. In the early days of the modern kingdom, the authenticating function of the tribal leader was the vehicle by which the bulk of the population could be accessed. It was the tribal leader who verified the identities of his branch members for the central government, and served as the state's primary conduit for policing local behavior. This authenticating function was an important source of authority for tribal leaders, who continued to perform this role after the waning of their formal political power.

By the 1980s, however, the tribal leader had been joined by competitors: genealogical verification committees, scholar-experts such as Ḥamad al-Jāsir, but also new figures on the scene, *muʿarrifūn*, quasi-official bedouin authenticators who served the state as lineal notaries public. In a distributive state governed by a genealogical principle, lineal authentication became the core function of substate political agents. Authenticators would come to play important roles in the new Saudi economy, from the validation of citizenship claims, to the distribution of state subsidies, to the facilitation of foreign labor import schemes—they could even influence the composition of the royal family itself. In a state characterized by a deep concentration of power and a weakness of comprehensive vision, authentication was one of the few political functions that demanded delegation to semi-autonomous agents. The four-part name may have pointed the way to a particular person, but the state required local experts to get to his or her door.

Of the emergent crop of lineal authenticators in the new Saudi Arabia, the figure of the *muʿarrif* stands out as the most intriguing.[106] The *muʿarrif* was to be a local bedouin community leader or rural notable who was employed by the Ministry of Interior in a quasi-official fashion to serve as the Ministry's eyes and ears within his kin group. The *muʿarrif* might double as a tribe's shaykh or leader, but was more often his less prominent competitor, assigned to serve as the state's window into a tribal subbranch, and often in circumvention of the overall shaykh's authority.[107] Though not without precedent in the Islamic tradition,[108] the *muʿarrif*'s function, *taʿrīf*, or identification, was a quintessentially modern one, a symbol of the formalization of tribe-state relations on a corporatist basis.[109]

The invention of the *muʿarrif* testified to two countervailing processes: the deterritorialization of the tribe, and the spatial fixing of its members in a new place. The decline of tribal cohabitation produced the need for the *muʿarrif*; by virtue of the former, the kin group was decoupled from its identifying anchor, its *dīra* or traditional home territory, and its members were distributed through the cash economy into the impersonal urban spaces of the modern kingdom. The appointment of *muʿarrifūn* in bedouin micro-communities signified further the inadequacy of the traditional tribal shaykh, whose kin group had been dispersed beyond his authority, if not beyond his ken. As with most political functions in the kingdom, the *muʿarrif* evolved from an informal role to a more formal one. In earlier decades, the state made sure to lavish attention not only on a tribal branch's shaykh, but also its most prominent notables (*ʿurafāʾ*).[110] By the 1990s, these *ʿurafāʾ*, literally "those in the know," had shed their passive function to become *muʿarrifūn*, those who identify or make known for the state. The move from passive to active roles paralleled the diffusion of authentication as a core political function for substate actors in the modern kingdom.

The *muʿarrif* began to emerge in or around the early 1990s. A memorandum from the governor of Riyadh Province, Prince Salmān b. ʿAbd al-ʿAzīz, called attention to the *muʿarrif*'s centrality to the new Saudi economy:

> ... Saudi nationals have come to recruitment offices with testimonials and statements of identification (*taʿrīf*) issued by certain *muʿarrifīn* ... in support of citizen requests to recruit [foreign laborers], or affirming the existence of a farm whose owner could not obtain a [legal proof of ownership] ... so as to be able to recruit for it.... In some of these

> cases, these testimonials and statements that came to them were false, and were given out of courtesy for the person making the request, or may have been prepared by the sons of the *muʿarrifīn* without their knowledge. These testimonials and statements are important, and are relied upon for granting [foreign] workers to citizens and plantation owners. Some testimonials have been issued attesting to the presence of grazing animals or of a farm where in reality no grazing animals or farm existed in the possession of the person making the request. The result of this is that [the recipient] would end up acquiring workers . . . without having the need for them. This leads to the exploitation of laborers for purposes other than those for which they were recruited.[111]

Their ability to lubricate labor importation schemes on behalf of members of their lineage reflected the power of authenticators in the new Saudi economy, and the importance of *taʿrīf*. The dubious practices about which Riyadh governor Prince Salmān warned in his memorandum were themselves widespread among members of the royal family at the time. Entrepreneurial princes were given license to import large numbers of foreign laborers and release them to find work in the informal economy, in exchange for a regular fee paid to their royal sponsor. A U.S. government assessment speculated that these royal labor import schemes were responsible for the fifty percent increase in the number of foreign workers arriving in Saudi Arabia in the first half of the 1990s, a number totaling 6.5 million in 1996.[112]

As with its bedouin experts, the Ministry of Interior sought to recruit its *muʿarrifūn* from the education sector. For one thing, bedouin-origin Saudis who worked in the security services were excluded from holding positions of leadership in their tribes, a policy that underscored the perceived incommensurability of tribal and state authority. For another, the Ministry of Interior favored bedouin authenticators from this sector because they were seen as crucial channels to the world of literacy and documentary authority through which the Saudi state sought to represent itself before its citizenry. As a Ministry document noted, such *muʿarrifūn* "are educated, and it is expected that they would be a source of trust in society. Likewise, they are more capable than others of comprehending instructions and implementing what is requested of them. Government agencies possess confidence in their authentication of the documents of their [kin] groups more than that of others who cannot read or write."[113] The document's reference to the nonliterate status of other potential claimants to the title *muʿarrif* was a clear allusion to traditional tribal leaders and the increasingly discredited oral authority they embodied. The connection between literacy, genealogy, and new techniques of control was thus affirmed in the person of the *muʿarrif*. Yet the *muʿarrif* was only one of a number of authenticating agents to emerge in Saudi Arabia in the final decades of the twentieth century. Appearing as well were genealogical authentication committees like the Special Committee for the Authentication and Documentation of the Lineages of the Ashrāf in the Kingdom of Saudi Arabia.[114] To understand its significance, some brief background on the modern political history of western Arabia is here useful.

After wresting the Hijaz from its Ashrāf rulers in 1926, one of Ibn Saʿūd's primary concerns over the next decade was to limit their lingering influence in the region.[115] An illuminating 1937 letter to Ibn Saʿūd from his son and deputy Fayṣal addressing the question of whether to restore the authority of a local leader in the Jāzān region is illustrative of the conquerors' apprehensions:

> The man you mentioned is from the Ashrāf. As you know, in times past, the people used to think highly of them and rely on them. There is no doubt, however, that after the annexing of the Jāzān province to your majesty, the coercive weight of the Ashrāf was lifted, and the people began to understand the truth about them. So if, for example, this person were to be granted some authority, then that would open the door for all of the Ashrāf present there to agitate for the restoration of their authority. . . .[116]

In a region in which the Ashrāf had exercised some version of rule for over a millennium, the nascent Saudi government's capacity to definitively stamp out their influence was limited. Working through loyalist Ashrāf who had remained in the Hijaz, Ibn Saʿūd appointed Sharīf Hazzāʿ al-ʿAbdalī as district governor (Qāʾimmaqām) of Mecca,[117] and charged him with keeping the peace among the tribes of the region.[118] This title was bequeathed in 1966 to Sharīf Hazzāʿ's son Shākir b. Hazzāʿ al-ʿAbdalī, who held it until 1991, when the post of Qāʾimmaqām, an administrative relic of the Ottoman era, was eliminated. Shorn of titular authority, Ashrāf leaders approached the Interior Ministry about forming a new, formal entity around which to constitute their collective identities, and through which disputes over the distribution of the Hijazi Ashrāf's lucrative pious endowments (*awqāf*) might be adjudicated. The religious and financial privileges associated with belonging to the Ashrāf made claims to such belonging a sometimes hotly contested matter.[119] The entity that ostensibly replaced the Qāʾimmaqām was the Special Committee for the Authentication and Documentation of the Lineages of the Ashrāf in the Kingdom of Saudi Arabia, a quasi-official body supervised by the Interior Ministry.[120] It is of a piece with our story here that the vestigial political association permitted to the modern-day Ashrāf is a genealogical one, whose function is lineal authentication.

Lineal authentication became a core political function not only at the once-dominant margins, but at the highest reaches of the Saudi state. Exemplifying this turn is the Ministry of Finance's Office of Disbursements and Stipends.[121] Founded around mid-century by Ibn Saʿūd, when it was known as the Riyadh Finance Office, the Office of Disbursements and Stipends is responsible for distributing often lavish subsidies to the descendants of ʿAbd al-ʿAzīz Ibn Saʿūd, as well as associated noble families such as the Āl al-Shaykh.[122] Inclusion in the ranks of known descendants of the kingdom's founder means a lifetime of prosperity and privilege. It was likely on account of such possibilities that in 1996, Riyadh province governor Prince Salmān b. ʿAbd al-ʿAzīz solicited Ḥamad al-Jāsir's advice about a curiously long lost Āl Saʿūd returnee from Qatar who was claiming lineal belonging to the royal family.

When the genealogical knowledge of the state reached its limits, expert authenticators such as Ḥamad al-Jāsir were consulted to fill in the gaps. Al-Jāsir listed the reasons for his skepticism about such a claim: nowhere was the existence of the Āl Saʿūd branch in question documented by Najdi historians; what's more, if it were truly Āl Saʿūd, then the branch would be known by someone within the family. With typically biting subtlety, al-Jāsir concluded: "Therefore, we reject the lineal affiliation of the above-mentioned to the esteemed [Āl Saʿūd] family, except by way of clientage, historical aid in arms, or affection (*maḥabba*)."[123] Asked in 1998 by the Saudi Arabian National Guard (SANG) to provide comments on a map of the traditional distribution of the kingdom's tribes, al-Jāsir dotted his copy with red marker corrections before rejecting it as "imprecise and unreliable."[124] As a traditional scholar with one foot in the world of tribal arcana and the other in the emergent Saudi public sphere, al-Jāsir was able to move fluidly between the tribal state and the state of experts. More than a reflection of its incomplete maturation, however, the state's continuing need for traditional forms of expertise reflected its deliberate efforts to reify genealogical identity as a tool of governance and population management.

Like a *muʿarrif*, al-Jāsir was at times solicited by petitioners to certify their claims to Saudi citizenship. Though Saudi nationality could be "bought for a few riyal" in the kingdom's first few decades,[125] citizenship and its attendant privileges became a more exclusive acquisition in the oil age. Legal reforms in the late 1970s made tribal leaders in rural areas and community leaders in town districts formally responsible for validating citizenship requests by non-Saudi petitioners.[126] It was on such basis that Ḥamad al-Jāsir was contacted in 1993 by a man who had been living in Saudi Arabia for eleven years, but who claimed descent from a tribe with roots in the kingdom's northwestern border region. His inquiry seemed part of a broader pattern emergent in Saudi Arabia since the 1960s, in which bedouin-origin inhabitants of Saudi Arabia's poorer neighbors invoked their genealogical ties to the kingdom to justify requests for Saudi citizenship or residency.[127] The author, a teacher in the Najdi town of Ḍrumā', had noticed a recent newspaper article by al-Jāsir discussing his tribal branch, and wrote to the scholar to solicit assistance with his petition for Saudi citizenship:

> Everything . . . you have mentioned [in your article] proves and affirms that my tribal branch is a branch of Saudi origin. Because of my desire to approach relevant agencies to request a Saudi *tābiʿiyya*, I have the utmost hope from your greatness that you will help me . . . by providing me . . . with a written letter that verifies the correctness of my branch's belonging to this country that is so dear to my heart and soul. . . . This is the hope of a son from his father.[128]

As the privileges of Saudi citizenship or residency became increasingly coveted, the lineage considerations implicit in the state's early conception of what it meant to be Saudi grew entangled with the emerging discourse on tribal authenticity, of which Ḥamad al-Jāsir was both facilitator and promoter. Though he may have resisted drawing together these threads in his own mind, al-Jāsir's role as a scholarly authenticator placed him at the center of the kingdom's genealogical politics.

The multiple levels at which lineal authentication as a technique of governance is practiced in modern Saudi Arabia—individual, associational, institutional—demonstrates the extent to which genealogy and politics are interwoven in the kingdom. From Ḥākim Āl Ḥasan, lineal authenticator for his ʿAlāwna kin, to King Salmān b. ʿAbd al-ʿAzīz, unofficial genealogist of his own family, the Āl Saʿūd, Saudi Arabia is well supplied with genealogical border guards policing the traffic into and out of their kinship collectives. And yet, despite the pervasiveness of this genealogical rule, politics in Saudi Arabia is most often cast as a contest between pro-Western modernizers and religious conservatives, or between competing factions of religious extremists.[129] Expanding the conceptual terrain of Saudi politics to encompass the genealogical casts critical light on the Saudi regime's techniques of legitimation, as it does on important aspects of its political practice.

THE KINSHIP IDEOLOGY OF THE ĀL SAʿŪD

In the view of Michael Herb, a key dimension of the resiliency of Gulf oil monarchies is the practice of family rule. Instead of concentrating power in the hands of a single monarch, the ruling families of the Gulf distribute authority through their members and branches.[130] In Saudi Arabia, though the king may be first among equals, it is the institution of the royal family that stands above the state and its organs as the ultimate guarantor of personal safety, prosperity, and Islamic devotion. The reproduction of the notion of family rule at the symbolic level calls perpetual attention to the kinship dynamics that underpin the kingdom's governance, and contributes to the creation of what al-Rasheed has called an "ancestor cult" of the kingdom's founder, ʿAbd al-ʿAzīz Ibn Saʿūd,[131] and of the Āl Saʿūd genealogy more generally. The symbolic manifestation of family rule is a kinship ideology whose centerpiece is permanent dominion over the Saudi state by the descendants of ʿAbd al-ʿAzīz b. Saʿūd through the paternal line.

Through its kinship ideology, the royal family works to constitute itself as the ideal type of sovereign, one that governs by consensus and reflects the true composition and aspirations of its genealogically invested populace. The kinship ideology of the Saudi ruling family is especially robust, as it is underpinned by abundant instruments of both coercion and persuasion. Yet as a building block for a national project, the Āl Saʿūd kinship ideology is also untenable—one cannot *be* Āl Saʿūd, in the way one can be Finnish or American; one can only aspire to be *like* the Āl Saʿūd, that is, to celebrate one's own ancestry as a royal family in miniature. The most successful such imitators are those whose illustrious ancestors are known to have kept close quarters with historical scions of the Āl Saʿūd dating back to the eighteenth century. Prominent beneficiaries of such associations today are the descendants of Muḥammad b. ʿAbd al-Wahhāb, the Āl al-Shaykh, as well as relatives by marriage, such as the Sudayrīs. In the letters of Ḥamad al-Jāsir, one can observe efforts by lineage seekers to fuse their personal and genealogical stories to watershed moments in Saudi history, in the hopes of capturing some of the royal family's surplus charisma or favor.[132] And yet, while popular imitations of this kinship ideology are most often used to express fealty to the state, they can also be wielded in opposition to it. In the controversy surrounding the genealogy of the Āl Saʿūd, for example, one finds an important window into the nature of political contestation in modern Saudi Arabia.

As rulers of a religiously conservative and genealogically invested state—a state of their making—the Āl Saʿūd are required to legitimate their origins on both tribal and religious grounds. The lines between these twin pillars of legitimation are often blurred, however. One of the most virulent challenges to Āl Saʿūd rule appeared in 1979, when Juhaymān al-ʿUtaybī and his band of followers seized control of the Great Mosque of Mecca, denounced the royal family, and declared the arrival of the Muslim Messiah, or Mahdī. The influence of Juhaymān al-ʿUtaybī's failed millenarian coup was so great that educated Saudis age forty and over will often periodize their lives in terms of pre- and post-Juhaymān eras. In the months before the attack, when Juhaymān and his band were feeling pressed to justify the radical political and theological views announced in their early propaganda pamphlets, they responded by sharpening their paper barrage against the Āl Saʿūd.

In one pamphlet from this second series,[133] Juhaymān listed the qualities that made the Āl Saʿūd unfit for rule. The first quality to be mentioned was their genealogical deficiency—the Āl Saʿūd did not descend from the tribe of Quraysh, the Prophet Muḥammad's tribe. According to Sunni law, the Muslim community's leader, or imam, should descend from the tribe of Quraysh. The popular historian of the kingdom, Robert Lacey, dismissed Juhaymān's genealogical critique as "a pointless exercise" because the Āl Saʿūd derived their legitimacy from other sources, and never claimed to be descendants of the Prophet.[134] Yet Lacey himself may have missed the point, namely, that in a state governed by a genealogical principle, Juhaymān's critique of the Āl Saʿūd's genealogy was in fact the central critique. For an avowed Muslim pietist, Juhaymān had a curious infatuation with his own tribe, ʿUtayba, and a disdain for non-tribal sedentary-origin Saudis that suggested a deep preoccupation with questions of lineal prestige.[135] What's more, Juhaymān's adherence to Sunni orthodoxy on this genealogical point seemed out of place, as there was little else orthodox about his overall program.[136] Shorn of its theological adornments, Juhaymān's critique seems both modern and familiar—a denial of genealogical legitimacy of the sort encountered in the letters of Ḥamad al-Jāsir, in a country being organized according to a genealogical principle. More than a pietistic challenger to the religiously wayward Āl Saʿūd, Juhaymān was a bedouin-origin Saudi calling the ruling family out on their genealogical state. Juhaymān's invoking of the Quraysh condition was a rejoinder to the Āl Saʿūd's kinship ideology, a handing back, in polemical fashion, of its genealogical rule of governance.

If the Āl Saʿūd were not Quraysh, then what were they exactly? Like so much else about the modern genealogical culture of Saudi Arabia, the answer to this question has defied stabilization and consensus. Herb comments on the lack of ambiguity in the chains of descent of Arabian ruling families.[137] With respect to the Āl Saʿūd, however, he is incorrect. As noted previously, the origin of the Āl Saʿūd has long been contested; Madawi al-Rasheed has gone so far as to develop a theory of state formation in Saudi Arabia around the Āl Saʿūd's lack of an established tribal provenance.[138] As noted in an earlier chapter, two dominant interpretations of Āl Saʿūd origins have survived into the modern age, one linking the royal family to the bedouin ʿAnaza confederation, the other to the sedentary Banī Ḥanīfa tribe. Over the past thirty-five years, the Saudi royal family has invested a significant amount of effort in influencing the Saudi popular imagination on this question, actively steering public opinion away from the ʿAnaza association and toward the Banī Ḥanīfa lineage. The shift from ʿAnaza to Banī Ḥanīfa origins reflects important changes in the bases of legitimacy for Saudi rule, whose implications, both symbolic and material, are explored below.

In 1972, the government of Saudi Arabia established the King Abdulaziz Foundation for Research and Archives (Dārat al-Malik ʿAbd al-ʿAzīz), known informally as the Dāra. The Dāra's purpose was to serve as a repository for historical documents, material artifacts, and oral traditions concerning the royal family, which were to be gathered, preserved, and utilized in the creation of an official historiography for the Saudi state. One of the Dāra's early publications was a 1979 critical edition of a nineteenth-century genealogical work on central Arabia's historical rulers, titled *Muthīr al-Wajd fī Ansāb Mulūk Najd* (*The Exciter of Ardor Concerning the Lineages of the Rulers of Central Arabia*).[139] In the introduction to the volume, its Egyptian editor ʿAbd al-Wāḥid Muḥammad Rāghib weighed in on the question of Āl Saʿūd origins. After calling attention to the tortured history of the debate over the question, Rāghib concluded that the founding ancestor of the royal family, Māniʿ al-Muraydī, most likely descended from the ʿAnaza tribe.[140] ʿAnaza, whose many branches stretch across western Saudi Arabia to Syria and Iraq, is one of the largest tribes in the Arabian Peninsula. The early twentieth-century ʿAnaza leader Nūrī al-Shaʿlān was considered by T. E. Lawrence to be the fourth-most powerful chieftain in Arabia.[141] As the historian Munīr al-ʿAjlānī noted presciently, ʿAnaza had grown so large over the past several centuries that "an ʿAnaza affiliation [was] more like a national or political identity than a lineal or blood connection."[142] Genealogist Ḥamad al-Ḥuqayl's panegyrics for his ʿAnaza tribe would underscore the perception of its continued prestige and formidableness in the Saudi imagination.[143]

It seemed precisely for these reasons that the Āl Saʿūd, who had spent generations subjugating the bedouin and forcibly dissociating them from their fractious substate political identities, thought it so important to disavow their imagined toehold in a specific aspect of that bedouin past. When the state was still reliant on the bedouin Ikhwān to conquer and subdue territories, it could motivate and inspire its cadres through appeals to a shared bedouin heritage.[144] Once the Āl Saʿūd had consolidated their hold and shifted from direct to indirect forms of coercion, they required a form of genealogical legitimation that, in the manner of the Hashemite monarchy of Jordan, permitted a perch above the fray. Banī Ḥanīfa, a long-settled tribe with very little visceral presence in the modern kingdom, was an origin that suited this requirement.

Perhaps more significantly, the transition to a Banī Ḥanīfa consensus reflected the Saudi state's imposition of a new method of reckoning authoritative knowledge, a bureaucratic, documentary method, one that brooked no ambiguity and so could not abide multiple origin narratives and the oral cultural wellspring from which they derived. With Ḥamad al-Jāsir's 1980 *Jamhara* entry for the Āl Saʿūd (the lengthiest in the volume), the two divergent origin narratives of the royal family could still coexist in amicable disagreement. Al-Jāsir found merit in both Āl Saʿūd narratives, though, in an odd turn for a genealogical index, he concluded his entry by changing the subject, asking rhetorically, "what benefit are ancient lineages without noble actions?"[145]

In 1999, as a contribution to the one hundredth anniversary celebration of the establishment of the modern kingdom of Saudi Arabia,[146] the Dāra reissued *Muthīr al-Wajd* with a new critical introduction by the well-known Saudi genealogist and al-Jāsir disciple, Abū ʿAbd al-Raḥmān b. ʿAqīl al-Ẓāhirī. By commissioning a practiced polemicist, Ibn ʿAqīl, for the job, the Dāra was in effect launching a frontal assault on the position it had endorsed two decades earlier concerning the Āl Saʿūd's origins. Ibn ʿAqīl claimed that the ʿAnaza connection was a centuries-old rumor that had been kept alive by Saudi leaders and others at various turns for political advantage. "The proliferation of statements [about the Āl Saʿūd's lineage] does not entail a proliferation of realities. Rather, there is only one reality," Ibn ʿAqīl stated forcefully—"that the Āl Saʿūd are from Banī Ḥanīfa."[147] Ibn ʿAqīl's ardent promotion of the Banī Ḥanīfa origin narrative revealed a state laboring to produce definition out of ambiguity, ideology out of genealogy.

The crowning turn in the state's lineage-seeking project appeared in 2012, with the Dāra's publication of the volume *Nasab Āl Saʿūd* by Fāyiz al-Badrānī and Rāshid al-ʿAsākir. To prove definitively the falseness of the ʿAnaza claim and the accuracy of the Banī Ḥanīfa affiliation, the volume's authors moved exhaustively through every shred of documentary evidence relating to the Āl Saʿūd's origins. *Nasab Āl Saʿūd* and its Banī Ḥanīfa agenda was the brainchild of then Prince Salmān b. ʿAbd al-ʿAzīz, whose many roles included directing the Dāra.[148] In a 2008 letter to a television station included with the volume, Prince Salmān echoed another common refrain in the Banī Ḥanīfa-ʿAnaza debate, the notion that on account of the historical intermingling of Arabia's tribes, he felt himself personally to be of joint Banī Ḥanīfa-ʿAnaza origin. Arguments by Saudi scholars and intellectuals that seek to reconcile the Āl Saʿūd's Banī Ḥanīfa and ʿAnaza origins through emphasis on the shared ancestry of their eponymous forebears are particularly specious, as they deflect attention toward the distant past and away from the deeply political and ideological motivations behind the royal family's genealogical pivot. There is some irony in the fact that, by virtue of the genealogically ordered society that Prince Salmān and his kin helped engender, ordinary Saudis cannot afford the luxury of two patrilineages, or the social complications and stigmas that such claims might entail.

Despite Prince Salmān (now King Salmān) and the Dāra's ample efforts, Saudis of ʿAnaza origin have yet to relinquish their claims of lineal attachment to the royal family.[149] Such is the nature of genealogical politics in a fragmented state, which, in seeking to script its own history, remains captive to the oral cultural backdrop from which it has only recently emerged. One is tempted to read into the politics of the Āl Saʿūd origin narrative a lingering tension in the kingdom's definition of itself, between a state that, in sociological terms, is the perfection of settled town life, whose very success is a definitive statement about the place of bedouinness in the modern world, and one that, for reasons to be discussed below, has been compelled to embrace the very same ethos of bedouinness it has otherwise sought to eradicate.

THE BARGAIN WITH THE BEDOUIN

Shifting from symbolic to tactical terrain, one finds corollaries to the Āl Saʿūd's genealogical pivot in its political practice. The Saudi regime's effort to distance itself genealogically from a now dormant though potentially adversarial substate collective is mirrored in the pattern of distribution of high-level government jobs. Bedouin-origin Saudis are almost never represented in the Saudi cabinet, for example,[150] with the royal family favoring cabinets comprised of members of the Āl Saʿūd and Āl al-Shaykh, and reinforced with technocrats from sedentary, often Hijazi, backgrounds. The regime's wariness about privileging a particular bedouin tribe ensures that none are represented at the highest reaches of the state.

Bedouin-origin Saudis are represented most prominently in the lower and middle ranks of the security services, particularly the National Guard. As Herb notes, Gulf oil monarchies depend for their continued survival on alignment with their marginalized bedouin populations,[151] who populate the ranks of their security services and constitute a loyal and readily mobilized collective. This bargain with the bedouin is predicated on a particular system of governance, one that elevates the genealogical principle as the basis for collective identity to the exclusion of more impersonal measures. The example of the Saudi Arabian National Guard is instructive. The National Guard was formed in 1955 out of the remnants of the Ikhwān movement.[152] Initially a vehicle for co-opting the ruling family's tribal opposition, this elite force evolved into a de facto Praetorian Guard whose purpose was to protect the throne and, more precisely, its late occupant, King ʿAbdallāh b. ʿAbd al-ʿAzīz, its commander from 1963 to 2010.[153] It was the National Guard—not the army—that was deployed to quell labor unrest in the Eastern Province in the 1950s, to suppress demonstrations in the kingdom's cities during the 1967 war, and to confront Shiite protestors in al-Aḥsāʾ during the upheavals of 1979.[154]

Today, bedouin-origin high school graduates in Saudi *hujar* communities will more often than not aspire to enter the ranks of the Guard and the kingdom's other security services.[155] As former Guard officer Muḥammad Ṣunaytān has argued, employment in the security sector has become a kind of inheritance across generations of bedouin-origin Saudis, less on account of their martial aptitude or taste for military glory, and more for lack of viable alternatives.[156] In its public discourse, represented, for example, in its magazine *al-Ḥaras al-Waṭanī*, the National Guard promotes an ethic of national unity, fealty to the royal family, and military expertise. Yet more than a national institution, the National Guard is also a mechanism for managing the kingdom's kinship collectives, and is invested with the same genealogical ethic that animates much of the kingdom's political practice.

The political dynamics of the Guard are revealing of how genealogy informs the institutional politics of the kingdom's security services. The Guard is a largely tribal force in that its membership is recruited almost entirely from the population of bedouin-origin Saudis. Command of its brigades, each comprising approximately twenty thousand guardsmen,[157] is set aside largely for members of prominent Saudi bedouin tribes. For example, two brigade commands are known to be reserved for the prominent ʿUtayba tribe, whose traditional territories span across Hijaz and Najd, and whose former leader Sulṭān b. Bijād was one of the two prime movers of the Ikhwān rebellion.[158] In September 2005, shortly after King ʿAbdallāh ascended the throne, ʿUtayba's two brigade leaders placed full-page advertisements on behalf of their units in *al-Ḥaras al-Waṭanī*, pledging renewed loyalty to their commander-turned-king.[159] Such affirmations demonstrate the harmonious fusion of tribal and national sentiments at the official level, below which a more complicated and opaque informality continues to predominate.

By law, Saudis who hold military rank are prohibited from occupying formal positions of authority in their tribe.[160] In practice, however, National Guard brigade and battalion commanders will often treat their bases as hospitality tents for visitors from their tribe, who travel long distances to call on their influential kinsmen for favors. The choice of brigade leaders has as much to do with an individual's influence within their tribe as it does their professional achievement and promise.[161] The rank and file members of a brigade, by contrast, are drawn from a variety of bedouin tribes,[162] though their distribution is determined by an unofficial quota system that seeks to both limit the concentration of a particular tribe in a given brigade,[163] and ensure that the allocation of positions in the Guard accords with informal historical agreements between the ruling family and the tribes that predominate within SANG. Through the National Guard, Saudi bedouin tribes are rewarded for their loyalty as tribes and at the same time constrained from exhibiting such loyalties as tribal collectives. It is in part through the culture and practices of security services such as the National Guard that the modern tribal ethic is reinforced in Saudi public life.

The modern state, as Scott has argued, endeavors to create populations "with precisely those standardized characteristics that will be easiest to monitor, count, assess and manage."[164] As a state newly emergent from a predominantly bedouin ecology, and as a patrimony disinclined toward power-sharing, Saudi Arabia chose to make tribal genealogy one of these standardized characteristics. This was a comfortable turn for both the state and its subject-citizens, as it allowed the new solidarities of an emergent Saudi national culture to resonate with the distinctive ring of older and more familiar ones. The state's ambivalence toward the project of fashioning a homogenous populace of a kind that might eventually demand political rights curtailed the atomization of Saudi society and breathed new life into tribal and kinship structures. The means chosen by the state to subordinate its former rivals in the bedouin tribes contributed to the adoption of a genealogical rule of governance across the breadth of Saudi society, encompassing bedouin and sedentary, tribal and non-tribal alike. This genealogical rule was among the most subtle of the regime's instruments of coercion, and as such, its influence was seen most in the social and cultural arena, where it helped transmute historically intimate and localized concerns about the nature of one's kin relations into a lexicon for aggressive hierarchical ordering of the modern social sphere.

Reading the modern Saudi *ḥaḍar* quest for lineal affirmation in terms of the techniques and practices of the Saudi state, what emerges most distinctively is that state's complex and calculated relationship with its bedouin populations. By instrumentalizing the bedouin populations of the kingdom through recruitment into the security services and promoting their tribal ethos as a local cultural correlate to religious conservatism, the Saudi regime amplified the resonance of the tribal-genealogical ethic in civic life. It was in part through this bargain with the bedouin that the culture of the tribal periphery achieved unanticipated influence in the urban spaces of the modern kingdom. Said plainly, bedouin-origin Saudis were enlisted to police the population, in exchange for which their culture was glorified by the state as the true essence of Arabian life. Ḥamad al-Jāsir's nostalgia for an irretrievable past in which central Arabian bedouin and settlers lived homogenously and unpolluted by the outside world transferred this sentiment into the sphere of literacy and respectability. Yet as a non-royal *ḥaḍarī*, al-Jāsir had no place within this bargain, except as a spectator. It was through this bargain and its diverse institutional and cultural manifestations that the genealogical ethic was amplified, and came to be infused into aspects of life in the kingdom that would otherwise have fallen beyond the appeal of a purely familial or historical fascination with kinship. Finally, it is perhaps on account of this bargain that sedentary-origin Saudis of uncertain or undistinguished tribal provenance have grown out of place in their own country and have felt compelled to correct their lineages, by hook or by crook.

Conclusion

In his celebrated study of nationalism and identity formation, Benedict Anderson identified what he took to be an important feature of the passage to modernity, namely, the disappearance in modern literature of "those prefatory genealogies, often ascending to the origin of man, which are so characteristic a feature of ancient chronicles, legends, and holy books."[1] It is interesting to inquire, therefore, why such representations are so prevalent in a country partially created and largely sustained by the powers of the modern world economy and political order. The notion that a genealogical rule of governance pervades Saudi Arabia would require less elaboration if it were not for the potency of Wahhabism as an ideology of Saudi statehood, or as international shorthand for an unnervingly literalist Islam. While the kingdom's religious culture is more rich and complex than its critics might allow, there is a poverty of conception that results from the equating of Saudi Arabia exclusively with this religious culture—in the pressure to link Arabian scholarly themes to a post-9/11 international security narrative; in the privileging of those religious movements that are most engaged in removing culture from Islamic discourse, or delocalizing Islamic belief and practice.

By one measure, the modern genealogical culture of Saudi Arabia is a direct consequence of the rise of Salafi religiosity in the kingdom. A faith increasingly denuded of its localizing elements demands some sort of response from within the resonant discourse of its stripped-down locale. The genealogical imaginarium, through its intense focus on shared historical and social experiences, commands the space previously occupied by folk religious conceptions and practices, before the austerity of Saudi urban life and piety-driven economic development constricted the breathing space of Arabian cultural particularities. When every pious utterance contains within it the seed of potential rebellion against or hollow fealty toward the state, religion as an autonomous facet of culture is emptied of its broader vitality. Stepping into the breach, with the collusion of the Saudi state, has been the modern genealogical culture of the kingdom, rich as it is in resonant symbols of a once-vital, autonomous past.

Wahhabism is so insistent a religious movement precisely because of the inherently destabilizing nature of the tribal ethos it has sought perpetually to obliterate. Though politicized, the tribe cannot be fully subverted in the manner of the Wahhabi religious establishment, which can at most serve as a complement to the state's aggression, but can never subjugate it. Because of the potential incommensurability of tribal and state power, the tribe has remained partially beyond the range of the state, rendering tribal discourse one of the few autonomous symbolic spaces for Saudis in the kingdom. Eluding the state's efforts at complete encapsulation, the acute genealogical consciousness of modern Saudi society is thus a form of bedouin tribal vengeance against modernity.

In light of the modern Saudi state's substantial powers of coercion, however, conceiving of tribal and state authority as dueling equals takes us only so far. The romance of camel nomadic autonomy, central to the nostalgic ideal of bedouinism that pervades many aspects of Saudi popular culture, stands in stark contrast to the almost complete *dependence* of the Saudi population on state largesse. The reach for bedouin lineages is in part a way of asserting symbolic independence from this state of being. Others have channeled the yearning for independence into more disturbing romances, the romance of al-Qaeda, for instance. ʿAbd al-ʿAzīz al-Muqrin, a founding leader of al-Qaeda in the Arabian Peninsula, whose family shares an ancestor with the Āl Saʿūd, attacked the economic foundations of the Saudi state in an interview for the militant publication, *Ṣawt al-Jihād*:

> Recently, people have begun to imagine that making a living can only be accomplished by securing a government job. This is a vulgar notion that the apostate traitorous rulers have planted in people's heads. They also planted in their minds the notion that you will not be able to eat or drink until they control you and you become their employee. Praise God, after economic difficulties beset them, the people have begun returning to commerce and depending on themselves."[2]

The state's paternalism had stifled personal autonomy and the martial spirit, al-Muqrin complained. While these two qualities might be thought to harmonize with the bedouin ethos, al-Qaeda's appeal to the tribes as collectives was for the most part paper-thin. A headline splashed across the front cover of a *Ṣawt al-Jihād* edition illustrates this point quite literally. The headline appeared to announce a feature story inside: "The ʿUtayba Tribe Celebrates one of its Sons as a Martyr."[3] This was a crude form of false advertising, however, as inside the magazine's pages, no such celebration was described.

The tribes of Saudi Arabia had greater concerns after September 11, when thousands of innocent Shihrīs, Ghāmidīs, and Ḥazmīs came to be scrutinized at foreign airports and borders, suspected of close kin relations with the fifteen Saudi hijackers.[4] The state's naming practices thus induced a novel form of collective tribal guilt that it was unprepared or unwilling to remedy.

Just as the economic paternalism of the Saudi state has influenced the discourse and strategies of al-Qaeda, the kingdom's economic model has also played an important role in shaping its modern genealogical culture. The competition to secure from the state the indirect spoils of oil wealth demands a symbolic corollary, and finds one in the jockeying for lineal position that is characteristic of the kingdom's genealogical fixation. This competition has been exacerbated over the past half-century by the new demographic realities of the Gulf region. The presence of millions of migrant laborers now working in the region has not gone unnoticed in the symbolic vocabularies of the Gulf states. Though subordinated from the onset by the *kafāla* system of temporary labor sponsorship, foreign migrant laborers are an acute reminder of the transformation of the Gulf region in the modern age, their presence helping to coax out a nostalgia for things lost. Waḥīd Ragab, an Egyptian who worked as Ḥamad al-Jāsir's private secretary for the scholar's final two decades and performed much of the scribal grunt work behind al-Jāsir's genealogical correspondence,[5] is in certain ways a paramount reflection of this new turn. His story reminds us how even something as manifestly Arabian as the unfolding of al-Jāsir's philosophy of local knowledge was, at its defining moment, filtered through non-local hands.

The tribe has added resonance today because it permits the articulation of the new class hierarchy between citizens and migrant laborers in comfortable and familiar terms. In Saudi Arabia, this hierarchy begins at the airport, with sometimes separate lines for laborers and white-collar business travelers, and persists throughout most aspects of society and the economy. The distributive model of the Saudi economy undoubtedly plays a role in the perpetuation of the kingdom's genealogical culture as well. The dogma of tribal inclusion and exclusion can be seen as the symbolic language of the Saudi rentier state, a language borrowed from its mechanisms, in which proximity to well-positioned families helps determine one's economic prospects. Through subsidies, grants, or informal rewards, every Saudi is theoretically entitled to a share of national income. In such a situation, the affirmation or denial of lineage claims is analogous to the acceptance or rejection of claims to these economic goods.

Though Saudis will most often deny it, the assertion of lineage claims is undoubtedly influenced by the enormous demographic transformations that have visited the Gulf region over the past half-century. While the connection between these phenomena is somewhat obscured by the still-preponderant position of Saudi nationals within the kingdom's resident population, it finds explicit expression in the emergent genealogical culture of the United Arab Emirates, whose citizens comprise a small minority of the country's residents. In the foreword to a 2007, state-sponsored genealogical volume on the lineages of the Banī Yās by the Emirati folklorist Ḥamād al-Khāṭirī,[6] the late Emirati intellectual Muḥammad b. Khalīfa b. Ḥāḍir described the book's purpose in revealing terms:

> The objective of this valuable study is to define the national identity of the United Arab Emirates. . . . National identity can only be defined through uncovering the pure Arab origin to which the Emirati people belong. [From this pure original state], waves of every ethnicity and color poured onto the Arab Gulf shores until, amidst [these] foreign migrants (*al-wāfidīn*), the pure Arabs became like an island in a human sea encompassing almost every nation of mankind, overflowing onto the purities of this island (*al-jazīra*) from every direction,[7] while its people search for a guardian (*ʿāṣim*) who might defend them from this deluge.[8]

Ḥamad al-Jāsir was central Arabia's guardian of heritage and lineage, with all of the double-edged meaning invested in that phrase. Even before his death, however, al-Jāsir had ceded his post to a host of micro-genealogists, who, responding to his call, began documenting the histories and lineages of their own tribes and families, to similarly controversial effect. The signature quality of Ḥamad al-Jāsir' genealogical project, particularly its initial manifestation of the 1970s and early 1980s, was that it preceded the wholesale politicization of the oral tradition, and the tying in of economic incentives to historical and lineage claims. Al-Jāsir's project allows a view into a time before genealogical claims were hardened into ideological ones, when the Āl Saʿūd could plausibly maintain two lineal origin narratives, or when a hitchhiker could be considered an authoritative source of local knowledge. Though the autonomy of Ḥamad al-Jāsir and his genealogist disciples was diminished by the Saudi state's steadily expanding interest in lineages, the attachment to the Arabian past that drove his project was real and visceral, and not purely an ideological fetish encouraged or manufactured by that state. One may wish to dismiss the kingdom's modern genealogical culture as so much historical arcana, its purveyors frozen in the last gasps of a false consciousness that will soon give way to the sobering reality of modern Saudi life. Yet it is my hope that this book will lead us to reconsider what we know about Saudi Arabia, and what it is possible to know about Arabian history against the oral cultural backdrop of its recounting.

Notes

INTRODUCTION

1. J. Horace Round, *Peerage and Pedigree: Studies in Peerage Law and Family History* (London: James Nisbet & Co., 1910), xiii.
2. "Our Vision," Kingdom of Saudi Arabia, Ministry of Foreign Affairs, www.mofa.gov.sa/sites/mofaen/aboutMinistry/Pages/MinistryVision.aspx.
3. ". . . once a matter of vital importance in the Arabian scheme [i.e., genealogies] . . . there are few members of the great families today, including the Saʿuds, who concern themselves with such trifles in the busy go-getting of the modern world." Remarks of this sort by earlier observers of Saudi Arabia's modern history should thus not be construed as terminal. H. St. J. B. Philby, *The Land of Midian* (London: Ernest Benn Limited, 1957), 45.
4. R. Bayly Winder, *Saudi Arabia in the Nineteenth Century* (London: Macmillan, 1965), 18–19.
5. Toby C. Jones, "State of Nature: The Politics of Water in the Making of Saudi Arabia," in *Water on Sand: Environmental Histories of the Middle East and North Africa*, ed. Alan Mikhail (Oxford: Oxford University Press, 2012), 239–40.
6. Madawi al-Rasheed, *Politics in an Arabian Oasis* (London: I. B. Tauris, 1991); *Tribes and State Formation in the Middle East*, ed. Phillip S. Khoury and Joseph Kostiner (Berkeley: University of California Press, 1990); David Sneath, *The Headless State: Aristocratic Orders, Kinship Society, and Misrepresentations of Nomadic Inner Asia* (New York: Columbia University Press, 2007).
7. al-Rasheed, *Politics in an Arabian Oasis*, 17–19; Dale F. Eickelman, *The Middle East and Central Asia: An Anthropological Approach* (Upper Saddle River: Prentice Hall, 1998), 124; Lois Beck, "Tribes and the State in Nineteenth- and Twentieth-Century Iran," in *Tribes and State Formation in the Middle East*, 187–90.
8. Engseng Ho, "Names Beyond Nations: The Making of Local Cosmopolitans," *Études rurales* 3, no. 163/4 (2002): 215–231.
9. Eickelman, *Middle East and Central Asia*, 141.

10. In this book, I have borrowed the term *inqiṭāʿ* (rupture) from informal Saudi discourse and formalized it as a concept that denotes not only the rupture in historical time separating the Islamic past from the Saudi present, but also the problematic and contested space that exists between the oral and textual fields of Arabia's history. For a discussion of rupture in a related context, see Muhammad Qasim Zaman, *The Ulama in Contemporary Islam: Custodians of Change* (Princeton: Princeton University Press, 2002), 7–10.
11. Benedict Anderson, *Imagined Communities* (London: Verso, 2006), 9–36.
12. Saad Abdallah Sowayan, *al-Ṣaḥrāʾ al-ʿArabiyya: Thaqāfatuhā wa-Shiʿruhā ʿabra al-ʿUṣūr* (Beirut: al-Markaz al-Thaqāfī al-ʿArabī, 2010). For orality as a paradigm of historical and anthropological interpretation in other contexts, see *Literacy in Traditional Societies*, ed. Jack Goody (Cambridge: Cambridge University Press, 1968); Jack Goody, *The Interface between the Written and the Oral* (Cambridge: Cambridge University Press, 1987); Jack Goody, *The Power of the Written Tradition* (Washington: Smithsonian Institution Press, 2000); Eric Havelock, *Preface to Plato* (Cambridge: Harvard University Press, 1963); Walter Ong, *Orality and Literacy: The Technologizing of the Word* (London: Methuen, 1982); Andrew Shryock, *Nationalism and the Genealogical Imagination: Oral History and Textual Authority in Tribal Jordan* (Berkeley: University of California Press, 1997); Paul Dresch, *Tribes, Government, and History in Yemen* (Oxford: Oxford University Press, 1989).
13. For the utility of this paradigm, see Sowayan, *al-Ṣaḥrāʾ al-ʿArabiyya*, 13–46, 227–320. For a critique, see Joseph Massad, "Reviving the Discredited," review of *Nationalism and the Genealogical Imagination: Oral History and Textual Authority in Tribal Jordan* by Andrew Shryock, *Journal of Palestine Studies* 27, no. 1 (1997): 103–6.
14. An exception would be the kingdom's southwest (ʿAsīr), where settled, agricultural communities predominated. Ḥamad al-Jāsir, *Fī Sarāt Ghāmid wa-Zahrān: Nuṣūs, Mushāhadāt, Inṭibāʿāt* (Riyadh: Dār al-Yamāma li-l-Baḥth wa-l-Tarjama wa-l-Nashr, 1971), 9.
15. ʿAbdallāh b. ʿAbd al-Raḥmān Āl Bassām, *ʿUlamāʾ Najd khilāl Thamāniyat Qurūn*, vol. 1 (Riyadh: Dār al-ʿĀṣima li-l-Nashr wa-l-Tawzīʿ, 1998), 11–12; Uwaidah M. al-Juhany, *Najd Before the Salafi Reform Movement: Social Political and Religious Conditions During the Three Centuries Preceding the Rise of the Saudi State* (Reading: Ithaca Press, 2002), 4–5; Michael Cook, "The Historians of Pre-Wahhabi Najd," *Studia Islamica* no. 76 (1992): 163–76.
16. Rosalind Thomas, *Literacy and Orality in Ancient Greece* (Cambridge: Cambridge University Press, 1992), 15–28; *Orality and Literacy: Reflections across Disciplines*, ed. Keith Thor Carlson, Kristina Fagan et al. (Toronto: University of Toronto Press, 2011), 3–18. For a critique of Goody from an Arabian vantage point, see Brinkley Messick, "Legal Documents and the Concept of 'Restricted Literacy' in a Traditional Society," *International Journal of the Sociology of Language* no. 42 (1983): 41–52. See as well Brinkley Messick, *The*

Calligraphic State: Textual Domination and History in a Muslim Society (Berkeley: University of California, 1993).

17. Messick, *Calligraphic State*, 15–36; similarly, until the second half of the twentieth century, literacy in the Ibāḍī heartland of Oman was restricted to a handful of religious scholars, who often came from prominent tribal lineages. Dale F. Eickelman, "Traditional Islamic Learning and Ideas of the Person in the Twentieth Century," in *Middle Eastern Lives: The Practice of Biography and Self-Narrative*, ed. Martin Kramer (Syracuse: Syracuse University Press, 1991), 50–52.
18. Messick, *Calligraphic State*, 18.
19. Ruth Pike, *Linajudos and Conversos in Seville: Greed and Prejudice in Sixteenth- and Seventeenth-Century Spain* (New York: Peter Lang, 2000). I thank James Boyden for this reference.
20. Martha Mundy, *Domestic Government: Kinship, Community and Polity in Northern Yemen* (London: I. B. Tauris, 1995), 39–40. In Oman and Morocco as well, such elaborations were not expected of those in whom social prestige did not already inhere. Eickleman, *Middle East and Central Asia*, 171.
21. The literature on this subject is vast. See W.H.R. Rivers, "The Genealogical Method of Anthropological Inquiry," *Sociological Review* 3 (1910): 1–12; *African Political Systems*, ed. Meyer Fortes and E. E. Evans-Pritchard (London: Oxford University Press, 1940); E. E. Evans-Pritchard, *The Nuer: A Description of the Modes of Livelihood and Political Institutions of a Nilotic People* (Oxford: The Clarendon Press, 1947); Claude Lévi-Strauss, *The Elementary Structures of Kinship* (Boston: Beacon Press, 1969); as well as subsequent critiques by Schneider, Bourdieu, Kuper, Holy, and others referenced throughout this volume.
22. Adam Kuper, *The Invention of Primitive Society: Transformations of an Illusion* (London: Routledge, 1988).
23. Melbourne Tapper, "Blood/Kinship, Governmentality, and Cultures of Order in Colonial Africa," in *Relative Values: Reconfiguring Kinship Studies*, ed. Sarah Franklin and Susan McKinnon (Durham: Duke University Press, 2001), 329–55; J. Teresa Holmes, "When Blood Matters: Making Kinship in Colonial Kenya," in *Kinship and Beyond: The Genealogical Model Reconsidered*, ed. Sandra Bamford and James Leach (Oxford: Berghahn Books, 2009), 50–83.
24. David Schneider, *A Critique of the Study of Kinship* (Ann Arbor: University of Michigan, 1984).
25. Massad, "Reviving the Discredited"; Messick, "Legal Documents and the Concept of 'Restricted Literacy.'"
26. Ceren Belge, "State Building and the Limits of Legibility: Kinship Networks and Kurdish Resistance in Turkey," *International Journal of Middle East Studies* 43, no. 1 (2011): 95–114.
27. Nicholas B. Dirks, *Castes of Mind: Colonialism and the Making of Modern India* (Princeton: Princeton University Press, 2001); James C. Scott, *Seeing Like a State: How Certain Schemes to Improve the Human Condition Have Failed* (New

Haven: Yale University Press, 1998). For an interesting counterpoint to the above, see Sneath, *Headless State.*

28. Department of State cable, January 14, 1954. *Confidential U.S. State Department Central Files. Saudi Arabia. Internal and Foreign Affairs, 1950–1954* (Frederick: University Publications of America, 1985).
29. "Saudi King Returns Home to Reshaped Mideast," *Agence France-Presse*, February 23, 2011.
30. David Gullette, *The Genealogical Construction of the Kyrgyz Republic: Kinship, State and Tribalism* (Folkestone: Global Oriental, 2010), 129–32.
31. Rāshid b. Ḥumayd is a pseudonym I have created to conceal the identity of the person in question. Other details about his life and those associated with him have been modified as well.
32. The story of interest to me is primarily a Saudi one; al-Jāsir's voluminous exchange of letters with non-Saudi Arabs, non-Arab Muslims, and Westerners is therefore beyond the scope of this study.
33. Hundreds of letters exist from the period prior to al-Jāsir's thirteen-year residency in Lebanon (1962–1975), many of which inform the biographical sketch of al-Jāsir's life in the first chapter.
34. One exception must be noted. Several incoming letters to the scholar are both undated and uncataloged. In such cases, I felt the need to include the real names of their authors.

CHAPTER ONE. ḤAMAD AL-JĀSIR: A LIFE IN CONTEXT

1. *Ḥamad al-Jāsir fī l-Ṣuḥuf al-Saʿūdiyya: Kashshāf bi-mā Nushira Lahu wa-ʿAnhu* (Riyadh: Markaz Ḥamad al-Jāsir al-Thaqāfī, 2007), 168–204; *Ḥamad al-Jāsir fī ʿUyūn al-Ākharīn* (Riyadh: Markaz Ḥamad al-Jāsir al-Thaqāfī, 2003); Maʿan al-Jāsir, "Shukr wa-ʿIrfān," *al-ʿArab* 36, no. 3/4 (2000/2001): 97–98. The Saudi government hired a private plane to have his body flown back to the kingdom from Boston along with his immediate family.
2. See Jörg Determann's study, *Historiography in Saudi Arabia: Globalization and the State in the Middle East* (London: I. B. Tauris, 2014).
3. Madawi al-Rasheed, *A History of Saudi Arabia* (Cambridge: Cambridge University Press, 2002), 49.
4. al-Juhany, *Salafi Reform Movement*; Cook, "Historians of Pre-Wahhabi Najd."
5. Sowayan, *al-Ṣaḥrāʾ al-ʿArabiyya*, 14.
6. ʿAbd al-ʿAzīz al-ʿAbdallāh al-Tuwayjirī, "Ḥamad al-Jāsir Ab Rūḥī li-l-Ajyāl," *ʿUkāẓ*, March 7, 1988.
7. Goody, *Literacy in Traditional Societies*, 1–26; for literacy in the Arabian context, see Guido Steinberg, "Ecology, Knowledge, and Trade in Central Arabia (Najd) during the Nineteenth and Early Twentieth Centuries," in *Counter-Narratives: History, Contemporary Society, and Politics in Saudi Arabia and Yemen*, ed. Madawi al-Rasheed and Robert Vitalis (New York: Palgrave Macmillan, 2004), 77–102.

8. Muḥammad b. ʿAbd al-Raḥmān Āl Ismāʿīl, *al-Shaykh Muḥammad b. Ibrāhīm Āl al-Shaykh wa-Atharu Madrasatihi fī l-Nahḍa al-ʿIlmiyya wa-l-Adabiyya* (Beirut: Dar al-Bashāʾir al-Islāmiyya, 1999), 98–102.
9. By contrast, a recent biography of al-Jāsir pietizes the scholar's life and downplays his deep frustration with the central Arabian religious establishment. ʿAbdallāh b. ʿAbd al-Raḥīm ʿUsaylān, *Ḥamad al-Jāsir wa-Juhūduhu al-ʿIlmiyya* (Medina: Nādī al-Madīna al-Munawwara al-Adabī, 2010), 50.
10. Isaiah Berlin, *Liberty* (Oxford: Oxford University Press, 2002), 186.
11. Ḥamad al-Jāsir, "Wa-li-Liḥya Manāfiʿ," *al-Masāʾiyya*, August 23, 1983, 16.
12. Al-Jāsir corresponded with Maudoodi, who described his time spent with the scholar in Riyadh as "among the happiest days of my life." Abul ʿAla Maudoodi to Ḥamad al-Jāsir, February 6, 1960, Maktabat al-ʿArab, Riyadh.
13. (3/25)—Outgoing, June 15, 1995, Maktabat al-ʿArab, Riyadh. Al-Jāsir was born in the nearby hamlet of Sharqa and raised in al-Burūd. His precise date of birth, like those of others of his generation, seems a matter of disagreement. The editor of his memoirs, ʿAbd al-Raḥmān al-Shubaylī, assigns to it 1909. Ḥamad al-Jāsir, *Min Sawāniḥ al-Dhikrayāt* (Riyadh: Dār al-Yamāma li-l-Baḥth wa-l-Tarjama wa-l-Nashr, 2006), 15.
14. P. Marcel Kurpershoek, *Oral Poetry and Narratives from Central Arabia, Volume II: The Story of a Desert Knight* (Leiden: Brill, 1995), 507.
15. Ḥamad al-Jāsir, *Jamharat Ansāb al-Usar al-Mutaḥaḍḍira fī Najd*, vol. 1 (Riyadh: Dār al-Yamāma, 2001 [1981]), 89, 128.
16. Ḥamad al-Jāsir, *Baldat al-Burūd: Mawqiʿan, wa-Tārīkhan, wa-Sukkānan* (Riyadh: Majalat al-ʿArab, 2000), 26–27.
17. Unlike al-Jāsir's father, his maternal grandfather ʿAlī had basic command of reading and writing, and was the scholar's first teacher. (277)—Outgoing, October 13, 1998, Maktabat al-ʿArab, Riyadh.
18. al-Jāsir, *Sawāniḥ*, 115. The state of education in Najd at the time was such that the village school in al-Burūd where al-Jāsir taught was furnished only with sand, which the students had to transport themselves from outside of the village.
19. ʿUsaylān, *Ḥamad al-Jāsir wa-Juhūduhu*, 50.
20. In 1921/22, the Wahhabi scholar Sulaymān b. Saḥmān (d. 1930) noted the presence of approximately one hundred students training under the senior scholars in Riyadh. Sulaymān b. Saḥmān, *Irshād al-Ṭālib ilā Ahamm al-Maṭālib* (Cairo: Maṭbaʿat al-Manār, 1926/7), 76.
21. Like many other prominent Najdi ʿulamāʾ, ʿAbd al-Raḥmān b. ʿAbd al-Laṭīf was blind. For the link between blindness and literate knowledge, see Steinberg, "Ecology, Knowledge, and Trade in Central Arabia," 86–87; H. St. J. B. Philby, *The Heart of Arabia: A Record of Travel and Exploration*, vol. 1 (London: Constable, 1922), 138–39.
22. For historical context on the politics of sedentarization, see Joseph Kostiner, *The Making of Saudi Arabia, 1916–1936: From Chieftancy to Monarchical State* (New York: Oxford University Press, 1993), 76–77.

23. Philby described the work of these missionary scholars and their young apprentices. Below the ranks of the senior scholars and *muṭawwaʿūn* was "a body of *Talamidh* or candidates for orders, who, under the guidance of the *Mutawwa*'s aspire one day to be enrolled among them, and so to take an active share in God's handiwork among men." Philby, *Heart of Arabia*, vol. 1, 297–98.
24. Al-Jāsir also worked at one point as a scribe for Ikhwān rebel leader Mājid b. Khuthayla. (469)—Outgoing, January 17, 2000, Maktabat al-ʿArab, Riyadh.
25. al-Jāsir, *Sawāniḥ*, 249–54.
26. Among the policies enacted by Ibn Saʿūd in October 1929 in response to the Ikhwān rebels was one in which "every *hijra* which succumbed to corruption will be evacuated . . . its inhabitants . . . distributed among the tribes . . . ," John S. Habib, *Ibn Saʿud's Warriors of Islam: The Ikhwan of Najd and their Role in the Creation of the Saʿudi Kingdom, 1910–1930* (Brill: Leiden, 1978), 146.
27. ʿAbd al-Raḥmān al-Shubaylī, *al-Shaykh Ḥamad al-Jāsir fī Ḥiwār Tilfizyūnī Tawthīqī* (Riyadh: ʿAbd al-Raḥmān al-Shubaylī, 2003), 29.
28. al-Shubaylī, *al-Shaykh Ḥamad al-Jāsir fī Ḥiwār*, 29.
29. Yaḥyā b. Junayd, *Ḥamad al-Jāsir: Dirāsa li-Ḥayātihi Maʿa Bibliyūjrāfiyya Shāmila li-Aʿmālihi al-Manshūra* (Riyadh: Maṭābiʿ al-Farazdaq al-Tijāriyya, 1995), 121.
30. al-Jāsir, *Sawāniḥ*, 309–23.
31. ʿAbd al-ʿAzīz b. Ṣāliḥ b. Salama, *Ḥamad al-Jāsir wa-Maṣīrat al-Ṣiḥāfa wa-l-Ṭibāʿa wa-l-Nashr fī Madīnat al-Riyāḍ* (Riyadh: ʿAbd al-ʿAzīz b. Salama, 2002), 21.
32. Ibid., 342–43.
33. For example, Abū Qubays was the site where the Black Stone that rests inside the Kaʿba (or cube) was thought to have landed. See Francis E. Peters, *Mecca: A Literary History of the Muslim Holy Land* (Princeton: Princeton University Press, 1994), 264.
34. C. Snouck Hurgronje, *Mekka in the Latter Part of the 19th Century* (Leiden: Brill, 2006), 12.
35. (No number)—June 5, 1930, Institute of Public Administration (IPA) Archive, Riyadh; al-Jāsir, *Sawāniḥ*, 329.
36. The people of Jeddah, for example, believe that Eve is buried in their city, about which al-Jāsir remarked: "You might find in some of the works of the more recent scholars of Mecca and Jeddah those whose sympathies lead them to affect the attribution of Eve to the city of Jeddah, but this is nothing but superstition as far as I'm concerned." Al-Jāsir maintained this view despite his sustained defense of the historicity of other ancient personalities such as ʿAdnān and Qaḥṭān, the mythic progenitors of the Arab people. (Catalog Number Missing)—Outgoing, May 21, 1998, Maktabat al-ʿArab, Riyadh; Ḥamad al-Jāsir, "Bayn ʿIlmī al-Tārīkh wa-l-Āthār (Part 2)," *ʿUkāẓ*, October 18, 1999, 20.
37. Snouck, *Mekka*, 50.

38. Sufism was a conception of Islam opposed by the Wahhabi movement's founder, Muḥammad b. ʿAbd al-Wahhāb. Wahhabism insisted on the unmediated relationship between a believer and God, and was established to root out heterodox central Arabian religious practices that elsewhere might have been described as Sufi. For more on the suppression of Sufism in the Hijaz at the time, see William Ochsenwald, "Islam and Loyalty in the Saudi Hijaz, 1926–1939," *Die Welt des Islams* 47, no. 1 (2007): 22.
39. Late in life, for example, he expressed disapproval of Arab scholars who chose to edit Sufi manuscripts. Ḥāsin al-Bunyān, "Ḥamad al-Jāsir Yatahim al-Nāshirīn bi-l-Irtizāq wa-l-Tazwīr: al-Mustashriqūn Akthar Ḥirṣan ʿAlā al-Thaqāfa min al-Muhaqqaqīn al-Jāhilīn," *al-Sharq al-Awsaṭ*, November 23, 1995, 27.
40. ʿUsaylān, *Ḥamad al-Jāsir wa-Juhūduhu*, 57.
41. Khayr al-Dīn al-Ziriklī, *al-Wajīz fī Sīrat al-Malik ʿAbd al-ʿAzīz* (Beirut: Dār al-ʿIlm li-l-Malāyīn, 1971), 156–57.
42. Kostiner, *Making of Saudi Arabia*, 158–60.
43. On the incorporation of the Hijaz into the Saudi kingdom, see Ochsenwald, "Islam and Loyalty."
44. This involved, for example, diminishing the practical application of Shāfiʿī and Ḥanafī law in the Hijaz, the latter of which was the official legal school of the formerly sovereign Ottoman Empire. ʿUsaylān, *Ḥamad al-Jāsir wa-Juhūduhu*, 74.
45. Ibid.
46. Salama, *Maṣīrat al-Ṣiḥāfa*, 21.
47. al-Jāsir, *Sawāniḥ*, 605.
48. Ibid., 624–25; al-Shubaylī, *al-Shaykh Ḥamad al-Jāsir fī Ḥiwār*, 48.
49. al-Jāsir, *Sawāniḥ*, 622.
50. ʿUsaylān, *Ḥamad al-Jāsir wa-Juhūduhu*, 63. While public education was not yet established in the kingdom, a few private schools whose curriculums included some nontraditional subjects had existed since the late Ottoman period, the most famous being the al-Fallāḥ school in Jeddah. See William Ochsenwald, "Arab Nationalism in the Hijaz," in *The Origins of Arab Nationalism*, ed. Rashid Khalidi, Lisa Anderson et al. (New York: Columbia University Press, 1991), 198.
51. (11291)—September 16, 1945, IPA Archive, Riyadh.
52. Robert Vitalis, *America's Kingdom: Myth-Making on the Saudi Oil Frontier* (Stanford: Stanford University Press, 2007), 113.
53. al-Jāsir, *Sawāniḥ*, 737–54.
54. Statistics vary substantially from source to source. Heyward G. Hill, "Latest Official List of Schools in Saudi Arabia," *Confidential U.S. State Department Central Files. Saudi Arabia. Internal Affairs and Foreign Affairs, 1950–54* (Frederick: University Publications of America, 1985); Muḥammad b. ʿAbdallāh b. Sulaymān al-Salmān, *al-Taʿlīm fī Najd fī ʿAhd al-Malik ʿAbd al-ʿAzīz* (Burayda: Nādī al-Qaṣīm al-Adabī bi-Burayda, 1999).

55. al-Jāsir, *Sawāniḥ*, 685–86.
56. Ibid., 667.
57. al-Jāsir, *Sawāniḥ*, 936. Al-Jāsir explained that Crown Prince Saʿūd expressed to him his "strong desire to establish the various elements that would distinguish Riyadh's position as the center of the country in all aspects of life."
58. (Uncataloged)—Outgoing, April 29, 1959, Maktabat al-ʿArab, Riyadh; Interview with Ḥamad al-Jāsir, "Qiṣṣatī Maʿa al-Maṭbūʿāt wa-Inshāʾ Jarīdat al-Riyāḍ (Part 5 of 9)," *al-Sharq al-Awsaṭ*, October 14, 1991, 7.
59. In 1954, Najd's only high school was in its first year, and its public library was only a few months old. Salama, *Maṣīrat al-Ṣiḥāfa*, 156.
60. Ibid., 171.
61. Ibid., 155.
62. A similar column appeared in Issue 11, in which al-Jāsir corrected mistakes in E. Lévi-Provençal's edition of *Nasab Quraysh*. Ḥamad al-Jāsir, "Kitāb 'Nasab Quraysh'," *al-Yamāma* 1, no. 11 (1954): 11–14.
63. Author interview, January 2011, Riyadh.
64. Salama, *Maṣīrat al-Ṣiḥāfa*, 173.
65. al-Jāsir, *Sawāniḥ*, 924.
66. Ḥamad al-Jāsir, "Hāʾūlāʾ al-Kuttāb al-Muḍallilūn," *al-Yāmama*, May 3, 1959, 1–2.
67. For more on al-Juhaymān, see Toby Craig Jones, *Desert Kingdom: How Oil and Water Forged Modern Saudi Arabia* (Cambridge: Harvard University Press, 2011), 149–50.
68. While agreeing on the death sentence, they could not reach consensus over whether he was to be killed as a Muslim who had committed a Quranically proscribed (*ḥadd*) offense or as an unbeliever (*kāfir*). Al-Jāsir later denied that he had been referring to religious scholars in particular, but his choice of words in the article suggests otherwise. (Khāṣ)—Outgoing, January 26, 1989, Maktabat al-ʿArab, Riyadh.
69. (2/98)—Outgoing, July 20, 1995, Maktabat al-ʿArab, Riyadh.
70. al-Rasheed, *History of Saudi Arabia*, 116.
71. An unsigned letter of complaint from Prince Ṭalāl to King Saʿūd found lying loose in al-Jāsir's library provides a tantalizing suggestion of the scholar's intimacy with the principal internal opposition figure of his age. Could al-Jāsir have served as Ṭalāl's scribe?
72. (Uncataloged)—Outgoing, February 20, 1954, Maktabat al-ʿArab, Riyadh.
73. (Uncataloged)—Incoming, August 17, 1960, Maktabat al-ʿArab, Riyadh. Al-ʿAwwāmī was from a family of Shia notables in al-Qaṭīf.
74. ʿAbdallāh Nūr, "Kayfa Rafaʿat al-Raqāba al-Ḥukūmiyya min al-Ṣuḥuf al-Saʿūdiyya," *al-Masāʾiyya*, October 23, 1983, 16.
75. (Uncataloged)—Outgoing, October 31, 1960, Maktabat al-ʿArab, Riyadh.
76. (Uncataloged)—Incoming, October 24, 1960, Maktabat al-ʿArab, Riyadh.
77. The inter-dynastic squabbles of this era are captured succinctly by Herb. Michael Herb, *All in the Family: Absolutism, Revolution, and Democracy in Middle*

Eastern Monarchies (Albany: State University of New York Press, 1999), 91–104.

78. Author interview, January 2012, Riyadh.
79. This was a prescient move, as al-Jāsir's nonroyal allies in the Free Princes Movement paid materially for their mistaken wager. Author interview, January 2012, Riyadh.
80. For Nasser's involvement in the Yemen Civil War of 1962, see Paul Dresch, *A Modern History of Yemen* (Cambridge: Cambridge University Press, 2000), 102.
81. ʿUsaylān, *Ḥamad al-Jāsir wa-Juhūduhu*, 87.
82. al-Jāsir, *Sawāniḥ*, 963–64.
83. Permission to first launch *al-Riyāḍ* as a weekly in 1957 was granted on the condition that the paper "avoid involvement in politics or journalistic wrangling." (Uncataloged)—Incoming, June 29, 1957, Maktabat al-ʿArab, Riyadh.
84. See Ḥamad al-Jāsir, "Ḥadīth Ṣarīḥ Maʿa Ḥamad al-Jāsir," *ʿUkāẓ*, June 22, 1966, 7.
85. al-Jāsir, *Sawāniḥ*, 785.
86. While in the publishing hub of Beirut, al-Jāsir also became an important liaison for other Saudi authors, who benefited from the scholar's networks there.
87. Contrast al-Juhany's far less expansive delineation of the ancient boundaries of al-Yamāma, also derived by inference from the reports of the early Arab geographers. al-Juhany, *Salafi Reform Movement*, 170–71, n. 1.
88. ". . . the sun of the city of Ḥajr began to set slowly from the middle of the [ninth] century." Al-Jāsir relates that the Ukhayḍirīyūn, who ruled al-Yamāma from approximately 867 to 1075, were followers of the Zaydī branch of Shia Islam, a dynasty of which ruled northern Yemen until the mid-twentieth century. Ḥamad al-Jāsir, *Madīnat al-Riyāḍ ʿabra Aṭwār al-Tārīkh* (Riyadh: Dār al-Yamāma li-l-Baḥth wa-l-Tarjama wa-l-Nashr, 1966), 69.
89. Ibid., 135.
90. Interview with Ḥamad al-Jāsir, "Lastu Mutaʿaṣṣiban li-l-ʿArab bal li-Risālat al-Islām (Part 1 of 9)," *al-Sharq al-Awsaṭ*, September 30, 1991, 9; Nāṣir al-Dīn al-Asad, "Ḥamad al-Jāsir wa-Abū ʿAlī al-Hajarī fī 'al-Taʿlīqāt wa-l-Nawādir'," in *al-Sijill al-ʿIlmī li-Nadwat al-Shaykh Ḥamad al-Jāsir wa-Juhūduhu al-ʿIlmiyya* (Riyadh: Kulliyyat al-Ādāb [King Saud University], 2003), 1–14.
91. Ḥamad al-Jāsir, "Allāh Qawwā al-ʿArab bi-l-Islām (Part 3 of 9)," *al-Sharq al-Awsaṭ*, October 7, 1991, 7.
92. Shryock, *Genealogical Imagination*.
93. al-Shubaylī, *al-Shaykh Ḥamad al-Jāsir fī Ḥiwār*, 20.
94. This legacy of antagonism has deep roots in Islamic societies, and is epitomized in the fourteenth-century North African scholar Ibn Khaldūn's famous study *The Muqaddimah*. Ibn Khaldūn, *The Muqaddimah: An Introduction to History* (Princeton: Princeton University Press, 1967).
95. These percentages derive from data presented by Fu'ād Ḥamza in his 1933 volume *Qalb Jazīrat al-ʿArab*. Scrutinizing population ratios in this way is important because it helps establish the bedouin/oral cultural backdrop of

modern Saudi history. Sarah Yizraeli has drawn attention to the inaccuracy of Saudi population counts conducted in the middle decades of the twentieth century, particularly to the tendency to inflate the proportion of bedouin in the population. Yizraeli's study is concerned with the period after 1960, and so does not consider the influence of the sedentarization policies of the early state period on bedouin population figures. While certainty on the matter will remain elusive, what is important to consider is that from the time of Muḥammad b. ʿAbd al-Wahhāb until at least the middle decades of the twentieth century, the sedentary populations of central Arabia believed themselves to be substantially outnumbered by the surrounding nomadic communities. Fuʾād Ḥamza, *Qalb Jazīrat al-ʿArab* (Cairo: al-Maṭbaʿa al-Salafiyya, 1933), 77–78; Sarah Yizraeli, *Politics and Society in Saudi Arabia: The Crucial Years of Development, 1960–1982* (New York: Columbia University Press, 2012), 172–75.

96. Ḥamad al-Jāsir, "al-Bādiya: ʿIrḍ wa-Amal," *al-Yamāma* 1, no. 12 (1954): 7.
97. Author interview, March 2011, Riyadh.
98. Abdulaziz H. Al Fahad, "The ʿImama vs. the ʿIqal: Hadari-Bedouin Conflict and the Formation of the Saudi State," in *Counter-Narratives*, 36.
99. Juhaymān b. Sayf al-ʿUtaybī, *al-Fitan wa-Akhbār al-Mahdī wa-Nuzūl ʿĪsā ʿAlayhi al-Salām wa-Ashrāṭ al-Sāʿa*, 15, www.tawhed.ws/r?i=jsgm8fzr.
100. Ibid., 11.
101. Juhaymān b. Sayf al-ʿUtaybī, *al-Bayān wa-l-Tafṣīl fī Maʿrifat al-Dalīl*, 15–18, www.tawhed.ws/dl?i=5iicoqrb.
102. For the various ways in which Juhaymān's movement has been interpreted, and the privileging of the religious discourse, see Thomas Hegghammer and Stéphane Lacroix, "Rejectionist Islamism in Saudi Arabia: The story of Juhayman al-ʿUtaybi Revisited," *International Journal of Middle East Studies* 39, no. 1 (2007): 103–22.
103. al-Jāsir, *Sawāniḥ*, 31. Alternatively, he considered them essentially disciplined groups from which certain stray characters emerged to scheme for opportunities to raid and create commotion, but whose actions could not be attributed to the tribes themselves.
104. Ibid., 223.
105. Ibid., 67, 126.
106. Ibid., 65.
107. Ibn Khaldūn, *Muqaddimah*, 94.
108. Ḥamad al-Jāsir, "al-ʿArīn: Bilād Qaḥṭān Māḍin wa-Ḥaḍāratin," *al-Riyāḍ*, August 2, 1998, 12.
109. Ḥamad al-Jāsir, "al-Bādiya: Aṣl al-ʿArab," *al-Nadwa*, December 4, 1986, 7.
110. Hādī ʿAlī Abū ʿĀmariyya, "Hal al-Jāsir Yuʾkhadh min Qawlihi wa-Yuradd?" *al-Sharq al-Awsaṭ*, April 17, 1998, 8; author interview, April 2011, Riyadh.
111. P. Marcel Kurpershoek, *Oral Poetry and Narratives from Central Arabia, Volume IV: A Saudi Tribal History: Honour and Faith in the Traditions of the Dawāsir* (Leiden: Brill, 2002), 7.

112. B. Lewin, "al-Aṣmaʿī," *Encyclopaedia of Islam, Second Edition,* ed. P. Bearman, Th. Bianquis et al. (Brill Online, 2013).
113. al-Shubaylī, *al-Shaykh Ḥamad al-Jāsir fī Ḥiwār,* 21.
114. This followed appointments in 1951 and 1954 as a corresponding member of the academies of Syria and Iraq, respectively. Al-Jabūrī argues that these appointments came unsolicited, though less charitable views about the Saudi government's role in the scholar's appointments have been expressed to this author in interviews. A. D. Yaḥyā al-Jabūrī, *Maʿa al-Makhṭūṭāt al-ʿArabiyya: Dhikrayāt wa-Asfār wa-Ṣilāt bi-Muḥibbī al-Turāth* (Amman: Dār al-Majdalāwī, 2012), 91–92.
115. Nāṣir al-Dīn al-Asad, "al-ʿAllāma al-Shaykh Ḥamad al-Jāsir: al-Nassāba, al-Jughrāfī, al-Lughawī," in *Ḥamad al-Jāsir: ʿAllāmat al-Jazīra al-ʿArabiyya* (Beirut: Maṭbaʿat ʿAlī Mūsā, 2002), 90–98.
116. Ḥamad al-Jāsir, "al-Jusūr lā l-Kabārī," *al-Masāʾiyya,* August 14, 1983, 16; (2/67)—Outgoing, January 12, 1995, Maktabat al-ʿArab, Riyadh.
117. Ḥamad al-Jāsir, "al-Shiʿr al-Shaʿbī Aṣbaḥa Wasīlatan li-l-Irtizāq" *ʿUkāẓ,* May 5, 1992.
118. (2/67)—Outgoing, January 12, 1995, Maktabat al-ʿArab, Riyadh; ʿUsaylān, *Ḥamad al-Jāsir wa-Juhūduhu,* 238.
119. Ḥamad al-Jāsir, "Lā Budd min al-ʿAwda ilā Manābiʿ Dīninā al-Ṣaḥīḥa," *al-Yawm,* August 13, 1996, 13.
120. Ḥamad al-Jāsir, "Ayyām wa-Layālī: Ḥawl al-Shiʿr al-ʿĀmmī," *ʿUkāẓ,* May 24, 1989, 8.
121. al-Jāsir, "Allāh Qawwā al-ʿArab."
122. Long-established overland pilgrimage routes stretched from Iran through Najd to the holy cities of Mecca and Medina. In addition, the Yemeni geographer al-Hamdāni (d. 945), whom al-Jāsir respected as the primary ancient authority on Arabian history, documented the existence of a Zoroastrian community in Najd, whose fire temples lay in ruins at the time of his visit. Patricia Crone, *Meccan Trade and the Rise of Islam* (Princeton: Princeton University Press, 1987), 46–47.
123. For evidence that supports al-Jāsir's claim at the regional level (i.e., Shammar tribal dialects), see Saad A. Sowayan, *The Arabian Oral Historical Narrative: an Ethnographic and Linguistic Analysis* (Wiesbaden: Otto Harrassowitz, 1992), 59. Generalizing this uniformity and stability across the whole of central Arabian geography and history would seem unsustainable on its face, however.
124. For broader echoes of this sentiment, see Kurpershoek, *A Saudi Tribal History,* 21–22.
125. Patrick Geary, *The Myth of Nations: The Medieval Origins of Europe* (Princeton: Princeton University Press, 2002), 33.
126. Al-Jāsir's negative attitude toward this vernacular art form can be viewed as a response to the proliferation of collections and recordings of *nabaṭī* poetry in the 1970s. Sowayan, *al-Ṣaḥrāʾ al-ʿArabiyya,* 277.
127. Specifically, al-Jāsir asserted that the establishment of the radio program

"Bedouin Corner" on Riyadh radio caused popular poetry to be contaminated by "fabrication, exaggeration, and deficiency." al-Jāsir, "al-Shiʿr al-Shaʿbī," *ʿUkāẓ*; Ḥamad al-Jāsir, "al-Qaṣīda al-Shaʿbiyya Maṣdar Muhim li-Dirāsat al-Lahajāt," *al-Yawm*, June 19, 1998, 10.

128. al-Jāsir, "al-Qaṣīda," *al-Yawm*.
129. al-Jāsir, "Allāh Qawwā al-ʿArab."
130. (2/1942)—Outgoing, November 16, 1994, Maktabat al-ʿArab, Riyadh.
131. Ḥamad al-Jāsir, "Ghalaṭ . . . Ghalaṭ! Yā Ustādh," *al-Masāʾiyya*, September 26, 1983, 16.
132. al-Jāsir, "Lastu Mutaʿaṣṣiban li-l-ʿArab."
133. Kamal Salibi relied heavily on al-Jāsir's compendium for his volume *The Bible Came from Arabia*, which argued that the events of the Old Testament took place in southwestern Arabia as opposed to ancient Palestine. Al-Jāsir rejected Salibi's findings. Kamal Salibi, *The Bible Came from Arabia* (London: Jonathan Cape, 1985); Ḥamad al-Jāsir, "Dr. Kamāl al-Ṣalībī ʿAbatha bi-l-Dīn wa-l-Tārīkh (Part 2)," *al-Sharq al-Awsaṭ*, October 3, 1991, 7.
134. ʿUsaylān, *Ḥamad al-Jāsir wa-Juhūduhu*, 114.
135. al-Jāsir, "Lastu Mutaʿaṣṣiban li-l-ʿArab."
136. Muḥammad al-ʿUbūdī, "al-Shaykh Ḥamad al-Jāsir wa-Juhūduhu al-Jughrāfiyya," in *al-Sijill al-ʿIlmī*, 65–81.
137. Ḥamad al-Jāsir, *al-Muʿjam al-Jughrāfī li-l-Bilād al-ʿArabiyya al-Saʿūdiyya: al-Minṭaqa al-Sharqiyya (Baḥrayn Qadīman)*" (Riyadh: Dār al-Yamāma li-l-Baḥth wa-l-Tarjama wa-l-Nashr, 1979), 4.
138. See, for example, Hawting's repudiation of al-Jāsir's method for identifying the ancient port of al-Shuʿayba. G. R. Hawting, "The Origin of Jeddah and the Problem of al-Shuʿayba," *Arabica* 31, no. 3 (1984): 324–25.
139. Quoted in Fāyiz al-Badrānī, *Ẓāhirat al-Taʾlīf fī l-Qabāʾil wa-l-Ansāb: al-Asbāb wa-l-Ḍawābiṭ al-Maṭlūba* (Riyadh: Fāyiz al-Ḥarbī, 2006), 48.
140. Similarly, his 1959 visit to an Arabian horse farm while touring the United States inspired a volume he prepared late in life on the lineages of Arabian horses. (Khāṣ)—Outgoing, April 17, 1994, Maktabat al-ʿArab, Riyadh.
141. Author interview, January 2012, Riyadh; Ḥamad al-Jāsir, "ʿIlāqatī bi-l-Mustashriqīn Badaʾat min Kutub al-Ansāb," *al-Sharq al-Awsaṭ*, February 3, 1998, 20. About Lévi-Provençal, Werner Caskel, and Levi Della Vida's Jewish heritage, al-Jāsir remarked: "the believer is asked to acquire wisdom wherever he finds it, as that is his object."
142. al-Jāsir, "Kitāb 'Nasab Quraysh'," 11; Ḥamad al-Jāsir, "Ansāb al-Qabāʾil: Dirāsatuhā wa-Nashr Uṣūlihā," *al-ʿArab* 5, no. 9 (1969): 11.
143. Fāyiz al-Badrānī, *Ẓāhirat al-Taʾlīf*, 45.
144. (Uncataloged)—Incoming, January 9, 1993, Maktabat al-ʿArab, Riyadh; (2/898)—Outgoing, August 28, 1996, Maktabat al-ʿArab, Riyadh.
145. Ḥamad al-Jāsir, "ʿIlm al-Dharra wa-Bulūgh al-Qamar!" *al-ʿArab* 1, no. 1 (1966): 2–3.
146. Sayyid Qutb, *Milestones* (Indianapolis: American Trust Publications, 1990),

79–90; Syed Abul ʿAla Maudoodi, *The Islamic Movement: Dynamics of Values, Power and Change* (London: The Islamic Foundation, 1984), 25–28; most striking for our purposes is this passage from Ayatollah Khomeini's *Islamic Government* (1970): "We must now take into consideration . . . the dazzling effect that the material progress of the imperialist countries has had on some members of our society. . . . When the moon landings took place, for instance, they concluded that Muslims should jettison their laws! . . . Let them go all the way to Mars or beyond the Milky Way; they will still be deprived of true happiness, moral virtue, and spiritual advancement and be unable to solve their own social problems. For the solution of social problems and the relief of human misery require foundations in faith and morals; merely acquiring material power and wealth, conquering nature and space, have no effect in this regard. They must be supplemented by, and balanced with, the faith, conviction, and the morality of Islam in order truly to serve humanity instead of endangering it. This conviction, this morality, these laws that are needed, *we* already possess. So as soon as someone goes somewhere or invents something, we should not hurry to abandon our religion and its laws, which regulate the life of man and provide for his well-being in this world and the hereafter." Ruhollah Khomeini, *Islam and Revolution*, trans. Hamid Algar (Berkeley: Mizan Press, 1981), 35–36.

CHAPTER TWO. THE DARK MATTER OF TRIBAL BELONGING

1. *al-wajh al-zlāba*, i.e., the poet's father or grandfather.
2. Excerpted from a *nabaṭī* poem by Saʿd b. Nāṣir al-Musāʿad, better know as Muṭawwaʿ Nafī. ʿAbd al-Raḥmān b. ʿAbd al-ʿAzīz al-Mānīʿ, *Muqtaṭafāt min al-Qiṣaṣ wa-l-Nawādir wa-l-Amthāl wa-l-Ashʿār al-Najdiyya* (Riyadh: ʿAbd al-Raḥmān b. ʿAbd al-ʿAzīz al-Mānīʿ, 2004), 208.
3. Ibrāhīm b. Ṣāliḥ b. ʿĪsā, *Tārīkh Baʿḍ al-Ḥawādith al-Wāqiʿa fī Najd* (Riyadh: Dārat al-Malik ʿAbd al-ʿAzīz, 1999), 67.
4. John Lewis Burckhardt, *Notes on the Bedouins and Wahábys*, vol. 1 (London: H. Colburn and R. Bentley, 1831), 250.
5. Burckhardt did not visit central Arabia, but instead relied on the reporting of local informants.
6. As late as 1978, almost 80 percent of the Saudi population was illiterate. Abubaker Aḥmed Bagader, "Literacy and Social Change: The Case of Saudi Arabia" (PhD diss., University of Wisconsin, 1978), 3.
7. For more on the restricted nature of literacy in premodern central Arabia, see Steinberg, "Ecology, Knowledge, and Trade," 88–89.
8. Addressing an ally in the town of Tharmadāʾ, Muḥammad b. ʿAbd al-Wahhāb attacked an anti-Wahhabi tract that had been delivered there by an individual "who recited it among you, and debated our group (*jamāʿatinā*) on its basis." Muḥammad b. ʿAbd al-Wahhāb, *Muʾallafāt al-Shaykh al-Imām Muḥammad b. ʿAbd al-Wahhāb*, vol. 5 (Riyadh: Jāmiʾat al-Imām Muḥammad b. Saʿūd, 1981),

20; Commins notes the recitational feel of Ibn ʿAbd al-Wahhāb's well-known book of creed, *Kitāb al-Tawḥīd*. David Dean Commins, *The Wahhabi Mission and Saudi Arabia* (New York: I. B. Tauris, 2006), 13.

9. Aḥmad b. ʿAlī al-Qabbānī, *Naqd Qawāʿid al-Ḍalāl wa-Rafḍ ʿAqāʾid al-Ḍullāl*, ms. Princeton, Yahuda 2636.
10. Burckhardt, *Notes*, vol. 1, 75.
11. Alois Musil, *The Manners and Customs of the Rwala Bedouins* (New York: American Geographical Society, 1928), 309.
12. Philby, *Heart of Arabia*, vol. 1, 160.
13. Burckhardt, *Notes*, vol. 1, 96.
14. Ibn ʿAbd al-Wahhāb, *Muʾallafāt al-Shaykh*, vol. 5, 323.
15. ʿUthmān b. Bishr, *ʿUnwān al-Majd fī Tārīkh Najd*, vol. 1 (Riyadh: Dārat al-Malik ʿAbd al-ʿAzīz, 1982), 29.
16. These qualities are even more pronounced in the earliest major work of Najdi history, *Tārīkh Najd*, by the early supporter of Muḥammad b. ʿAbd al-Wahhāb, Ḥusayn b. Ghannām (d. 1810). Ibn Bishr modeled his history after that of Ibn Ghannām. Being largely a history of the Wahhabi movement, Ibn Ghannām's *Tārīkh* is not especially concerned with documenting lineages (the first true genealogist among the Najdi chroniclers was Ibn ʿĪsā). In the histories of both Ibn Ghannām and Ibn Bishr, one is more likely to find information about the tribal genealogies of the leaders of bedouin tribes than about the sedentary populations of central Arabia, which are the primary concern of this book. A notable exception is the lineage of Muḥammad b. ʿAbd al-Wahhāb himself, which Ibn Ghannām traces back to the sedentary Najdi tribe of Banī Tamīm. Ḥusayn b. Ghannām, *Tārīkh Najd* (Beirut: Dār al-Shurūq, 1985), 81. For a discussion of Ibn ʿAbd al-Wahhāb's lineage that resonates with the kingdom's modern discourse of genealogical affirmation and denial, see Muḥammad b. ʿAbd al-Wahhāb, *Masāʾil allatī Khālafa fīhā Rasūl Allāh Ahl al-Jāhiliyya*, ed. Yūsuf b. Muḥammad al-Saʿīd, vol. 1 (Saudi Arabia: Dār al-Muʾayyad, 1996), 662–71.
17. al-Juhany, *Salafi Reform Movement*.
18. Michael Cook, "The Historians of Pre-Wahhabi Najd"; "The Expansion of the First Saudi State: The Case of Washm," in *The Islamic World From Classical to Modern Times: Essays in Honor of Bernard Lewis*, ed. C. E. Bosworth, Charles Issawi et al. (Princeton: The Darwin Press, 1989), 661–99.
19. M. J. Crawford, "Civil War, Foreign Intervention, and the Question of Political Legitimacy: A Nineteenth-Century Saʿudi Qadi's Dilemma," *International Journal of Middle East Studies* 14, no. 3 (1982): 227–48.
20. Fahad, "The ʿImama vs. the ʿIqal."
21. Dale F. Eickelman and James Piscatori, *Muslim Politics* (Princeton: Princeton University Press, 1996), 37–45; Jonathan Berkey, "Madrasas Medieval and Modern: Politics, Education, and the Problem of Muslim Identity," in *Schooling Islam*, ed. Robert W. Hefner and Muhammad Qasim Zaman (Princeton: Princeton University Press, 2007), 40–60.

22. James Fox, "Sister's Child as Plant: Metaphors in an Idiom of Consanguinity," in *Rethinking Kinship and Marriage*, ed. Rodney Needham (London: Tavistock, 1971), 219–52.
23. In the context of his research among the Kabyle communities of Algeria, Bourdieu discussed how the contrasting perceptions of male and female members of a kinship unit can influence the determination of the boundaries of that unit. Pierre Bourdieu, *Outline of a Theory of Practice* (Cambridge: Cambridge University Press, 1995), 41–43. In the Saudi culture of genealogical documentation I am investigating, the genealogical imagination of women is most often obscured from public scrutiny. For a discussion of this point, see chapter four.
24. Musil, *Manners and Customs*, 137; Sowayan, *al-Ṣaḥrāʾ al-ʿArabiyya*, 516–19.
25. Musil, *Manners and Customs*, 46–50, 491–503. Conversely, if no suitable marriage partners could be found within the expected degrees of consanguinity, the activated range of agnates might be wider than that found in a case of collective liability (e.g., to include the descendants of the great-grandfather's brother). Ibid., 137.
26. Ibrāhīm b. Ṣāliḥ b. ʿĪsā, *ʿIqd al-Durar fīmā Waqaʿa fī Najd min al-Ḥawādith fī Ākhir al-Qarn al-Thālith ʿAshar wa-Awwal al-Rābiʿ ʿAshar* (Riyadh: Dārat al-Malik ʿAbd al-ʿAzīz, 1999), 29.
27. Ibn ʿĪsā, *ʿIqd al-Durar*, 89–90.
28. al-Juhany remarks on the prevalence of internecine fighting among the Wuhaba of Ushayqir, which drove many to settle elsewhere. al-Juhany, *Salafi Reform Movement*, 115.
29. "*al-ʿĀʾidhī nasaban, al-Ḥanbalī madhhaban, al-Najdī baladan.*" Ibn ʿĪsā, *ʿIqd al-Durar*, 55.
30. ʿAbd al-Raḥmān b. Ḥamad b. Zayd al-Mughīrī, *al-Muntakhab fī Dhikr Nasab Qabāʾil al-ʿArab* (Damascus: al-Maktab al-Islāmī, 1966), 3.
31. Musil, *Manners and Customs*, 51.
32. Ibid., 426.
33. Ibn ʿAbd al-Wahhāb, *Muʾallafāt al-Shaykh*, vol. 5, 75, 240. Idrīs and his sons are also mentioned.
34. Ḥamad al-Ḥuqayl, *Kanz al-Ansāb wa-Majmaʿ al-Ādāb* (Ḥamad al-Ḥuqayl, 1967), 6.
35. William G. Palgrave, *Personal Narrative of a Year's Journey through Central and Eastern Arabia (1862–63)* (London: Macmillan and Co., 1869), 23.
36. Ibn Bishr explains that he reversed the chronology of his accounting because Wahhabi history was a part of Islamic history, whereas what preceded the Wahhabi *daʿwa* or mission was not. Ibn Bishr, *Sawābiq*, 168–69.
37. al-Dirʿiyya is likely a diminutive of al-Durūʿ.
38. Ibn Bishr, *ʿUnwān al-Majd*, vol. 2, 12–16. Ibn Bishr relied for this genealogy on Ibn Manṣūr (d. 1865). Ibn Manṣūr appears to have relied on oral sources, as he remarked: "*hādhā alladhī yuqāl al-yawm*" ("this is what is said today [i.e., about the lineage of the Āl Saʿūd]"); al-Juhany, *Salafi Reform Movement*,

6; Ḥamad b. Muḥammad b. Laʿbūn, *Tārīkh Ḥamad b. Muḥammad b. Laʿbūn al-Wāʾilī al-Ḥanbalī al-Najdī* (Ṭāʾif: Maktabat al-Maʿārif, 1988), 38. Ibn Laʿbūn's reference to the lineage of the Āl Saʿūd is grounded similarly in a sense of what was commonly understood through oral transmission ("*alladhī istafāḍ* [*sic*] *fī* . . .").

39. al-Juhany, *Salafi Reform Movement*, 76–81.
40. al-Jāsir, *Madīnat al-Riyāḍ*, 96–99.
41. Ibn Bishr accords this development to 1682, a date difficult to reconcile with al-Jāsir's chronology of Dahhām's wars with the Āl Saʿūd. Ibn Bishr, *Sawābiq*, 101.
42. Ibid.
43. To the author's knowledge, this is the only instance (and a relatively late one) in which the category of non-tribal is acknowledged explicitly in the Najdi chronicles. Ibn ʿĪsā, *Tārīkh Baʿḍ al-Ḥawādith*, 121.
44. Dirks, *Castes of Mind*, 46.
45. Edward W. Lane, *An Account of the Manners and Customs of the Modern Egyptians* (Cairo: American University in Cairo Press, 2003); Daniel Varisco, *Reading Orientalism: Said and the Unsaid* (Seattle: University of Washington Press, 2007), 33–36.
46. For example, Burckhardt, whose travels in the Middle East preceded those of Lane by several decades, included in his study of Arabia chapters on "Warfare and Predatory Excursion" and "Blood-Revenge," concerns central to societies with substantial bedouin populations.
47. Carsten Niebuhr, *Travels through Arabia and Other Countries in the East*, vol. 1 (Reading: Garnet, 1994), 2; S. D. Goitein conveyed the same impression in relation to the Yemenite Jews of the early twentieth century. See Mark Wagner, *Like Joseph in Beauty: Yemeni-Vernacular Poetry and Arab-Jewish Symbiosis* (Leiden: Brill, 2009), 5–6.
48. Dirks, *Castes of Mind*, 21–28.
49. Theodore Procházka Sr., "Alois Musil and Prince Nūrī b. Shaʿlān," *Proceedings of the Fifteenth Seminar for Arabian Studies* 12 (1982): 61.
50. Musil, *Manners and Customs*, 136. Bracketed terms are modified from Musil's Arabic transliterations to reflect modern conventions.
51. Georg August Wallin, *Travels in Arabia (1845 and 1848)* (Cambridge: Oleander Press, 1979), 125. "The rule of sanctuary for fugitives was strictly upheld in Arabia in the past both in town and desert . . . ," Hafiz Wahba, *Arabian Days* (London: A. Barker, 1864), 69–70.
52. Niebuhr, *Travels through Arabia*, vol. 2, 210–11.
53. Lane defined the word *khuḍra*, from which the expression noted by Palgrave likely derived, as follows: "(Ṣ, K) in men [and in other things] *a tawny, or brownish, colour* syn. *sumra*: (Ṣ) [and *a blackish hue:* and *a blackish hue inclining to green:*] and *blackness*: (TA) [and *intense blackness* . . .]." Edward W. Lane, *An Arabic-English Lexicon* (London: Williams and Norgate, 1863–93), 755. The

abbreviations in Lane's entry (e.g., Ṣ) refer to the classical Arabic dictionaries out of which he built his *Lexicon*.

54. Ḥamad al-Jāsir, "Ḥawla Uṣūl al-Qabā'il al-ʿArabiyya al-Ḥadītha (Part 8)," *al-Ḥaras al-Waṭanī*, May 1984.
55. (2/1293)—Outgoing, December 13, 1993, Maktabat al-ʿArab, Riyadh.
56. Bernard Lewis, *Race and Slavery in the Middle East* (Oxford: Oxford University Press, 1990), 19, 100–102.
57. Palgrave, *Journey*, vol. 2 (London: Macmillan and Co., 1866), 391.
58. Musil, *Manners and Customs*, 278.
59. Philby, who more than others had internalized the rhetoric of tribal nobility associated with the Saudi court, disparaged the "Bani Khadir" as being "of ultimate servile extraction, the droppings as it were of migrating hordes." Philby, *Heart*, vol. 1, 113.
60. Palgrave considered the "Benoo-Khoḍeyr" to be a new element in Najdi society ("Thus in central Nejed society presents a new element pervading it from its highest to its lowest grades.") This sense of newness may have been influenced by his Arabian informants and their sense of the alienness or foreignness of these communities, of their being extrinsic to the dominant kinship structures. Palgrave, *Journey*, vol. 2, 458–59.
61. Palgrave noted that the relatively light skin of the "Solibahs" confirms "the northerly origin of these wanderers. . . ." Palgrave, *Journey*, vol. 1, 203; Philby, *Heart of Arabia*, vol. 1, 267–68.
62. Ibn ʿĪsā, *ʿIqd al-Durar*, 18.
63. Niebuhr, *Travels through Arabia*, vol. 2, 203–4.
64. Ibid., 204.
65. Musil, *Manners and Customs*, 48.
66. Ibid., 56–57. Numerous bedouin tribes are named for female ancestors, a point discussed further in chapter four.
67. al-Rasheed, *Politics in an Arabian Oasis*, 10; Lucette Valensi, *Tunisian Peasants in the Eighteenth and Nineteenth Centuries* (Cambridge: Cambridge University Press, 1985), 20–25.
68. Philby, *Heart*, vol. 1, 160.
69. Musil, *Manners and Customs*, 48.
70. Ibid., 46.
71. Ibid., 47.
72. For examples of bedouin-sedentary relations from the North and West African contexts, see Ibn Khaldūn, *Muqaddimah*, 91–122; Aḥmad al-Bakkā'ī b. Muḥammad b. al-Mukhtār al-Kuntī, *Rawḍat al-Ḥamā'il li-l-Khayyār wa-Shafrat al-Ṣawārim ʿalā al-Ashrār*, ms. Timbuktu, L'Organisation non gouvernementale pour la sauvegarde et la valorisation des manuscrits pour la défense de la culture Islamique (ONG SAVAMA-DCI); ʿAbd al-Qādir al-Jazā'irī, *A Poem Concerning Nomads and Townsfolk*, ms. Timbuktu (ONG SAVAMA-DCI).
73. Sowayan, *al-Ṣaḥrā' al-ʿArabiyya*; Fahad, "The ʿImama vs. the ʿIqal."

74. al-Juhany, *Salafi Reform Movement*, 76. See also al-Rasheed, *Politics in an Arabian Oasis*, 87.
75. Alois Musil, *Northern Negd: A Topographical Itinerary* (New York: AMS Press, 1978), 182.
76. These are the names of three settlements in eastern Saudi Arabia. The bride-to-be belongs to the ʿAjmān, a bedouin tribe that inhabited the region.
77. *Mā lī bi-Dārīn wa-lā bi-l-Gaṭīfi* *wa-lā bi-dhā l-Ḥillā wa-lā man dahalhā*
Shaffī ʿalā wuḍḥin ḥbālih tihīfi *asbag min illī ʿalligū fī digalhā*
Wa-lagṭ al-zbaydī min trābin naẓīfi *fī gafratin yaʿjibak rīḥat nafalhā*

Sowayan, *al-Ṣaḥrāʿ al-ʿArabiyya*, 348. I am indebted to ʿAbd al-Raḥmān al-Shuqayr for his help interpreting and translating this and other poems in this chapter.
78. The origins of this trope go back at least to the Umayyad era and the marriage of the caliph Muʿāwiyya to a bedouin woman, Maysūn, immortalized in a poem attributed to Maysūn, which begins:
A tent through which the winds whip is more beloved to me than a lofty castle
La-baytun takhfiqu l-aryāḥu fīhi *aḥabbu ilayā min qaṣrin munīfi*

Ghāzī Ṭulaymāt and ʿIrfān al-Ashqar, *al-Shuʿarāʾ fī l-ʿAṣr al-Umawī* (Damascus: Dār al-Fikr, 2009), 801.
79. *W-ushīb ʿaynī min guʿūdī bi-garya* *wa-min baygarānin ribṭhā fī ḥulūghā*
Hannī bināt al-badw yarʿana bi-gafra *rīḥ al-khuzāmā wa-l-nafal fī ghabūghā*

Ibid. For camel's night milk (*ghabūg*), see Kurpershoek, *Oral Poetry and Narratives, Volume II*, 420.
80. Ibn Bishr, *ʿUnwān al-Majd*, vol. 1, 140–1; Ibn ʿĪsā, *Tārīkh Baʿḍ al-Ḥawādith*, 95–96; Ibn ʿĪsā, *al-ʿIqd al-Durar*, 31–32.
81. Ibn Laʿbūn, *Tārīkh Ibn Laʿbūn*, 5. This practice is still maintained today.
82. This would suggest a seventeenth-century dating of the episode, as the Āl Mughīra bedouin were active in Najd in the seventeenth century, and disappeared from the Najdi sources in the eighteenth century, having been eclipsed by the ʿAnaza and other tribes. See al-Juhany, *Salafi Reform Movement*, 64–65, 71.
83. Ibn Laʿbūn, *Tārīkh Ibn Laʿbūn*, 94.
84. Ibn Laʿbūn's understanding is mirrored in an interpretation advanced recently by Sowayan. Sowayan, *al-Ṣaḥrāʾ al-ʿArabiyya*, 345–72.
85. Ibn Laʿbūn, *Tārīkh Ibn Laʿbūn*, 109. Ibn Bishr comments that Ibn Laʿbūn's son, the well-regarded poet Muḥammad b. Ḥamad b. Laʿbūn (d. 1831/2), conveyed a flawed conception of the Wahhabi creed in his work, but was believed to have composed a penitent poem prior to his death. Ibn Bishr, *ʿUnwān al-Majd*, vol. 2, 84. For more on anti-Wahhabi sentiments and exile, see Steinberg, "Ecology, Knowledge, and Trade," 84.
86. Ibn Bishr, *ʿUnwān al-Majd*, vol. 2, 17.

87. Ibn Bishr remarks that prior to the Wahhabi mission, when a town dweller was ill, he would be brought for treatment to a bedouin medicine man, who would prescribe non-canonical or heretical sacrifices as a remedy. Ibn Bishr, *ʿUnwān al-Majd*, vol. 1, 34.
88. Ibn ʿAbd al-Wahhāb, *Muʾallafāt al-Shaykh*, vol. 5, 235.
89. Ibid., 25.
90. Lane, *Lexicon*, 528.
91. Fahad, "The ʿImama vs. the ʿIqal," 45.
92. al-Rasheed, *Politics in an Arabian Oasis*, 122.
93. Fahad, "The ʿImama vs. the ʿIqal," 51.
94. Sulaymān b. Saḥmān, *Minhāj Ahl al-Ḥaqq wa-l-Aṭbāʿ fī Mukhālafat Ahl al-Jahl wa-l-Ibtidāʿ* (Cairo: Maṭbaʿat al-Manār, 1926/7), 61. Ibn Saḥmān makes this point more explicitly in response to a legal question concerning whether a bedouin who has settled and is a Muslim can bequeath his possessions to a relative who has yet to settle. Ibid., 65.
95. Ibid., p. 66. For more on this question, see Habib, *Ibn Saʿud's Warriors*, 80–82.
96. See note 36 in this chapter.
97. Anderson calls this pre-objectified state an "unselfconscious coherence." Anderson, *Imagined Communities*, 16.
98. Eickelman and Piscatori, *Muslim Politics*, 37–38.
99. Ṣalāḥ b. Ibrāhīm al-Zāmil, *al-Muʾarrikh wa-l-Nassāba Ḥamad b. Ibrāhīm al-Ḥuqayl: Shaykh al-Udabāʾ wa-Adīb al-Shuyūkh* (Riyadh: al-Dār al-Waṭaniyya al-Saʿūdiyya, 2006), 11–12.
100. Determann, *Historiography in Saudi Arabia*, 139–66.
101. al-Ḥuqayl, *Kanz al-Ansāb*, 40–41.
102. Ibid., 28.
103. Ibid., 53.
104. Like al-Ḥuqayl, al-Mughīrī's father was a merchant, whose home was a magnet for bedouin traders and pilgrims passing to and from Mecca. Āl Bassām, *ʿUlamāʾ Najd*, vol. 3, 32.
105. Khalīl b. Aybak al-Ṣafadī, *Kitāb al-Wāfī bi-l-Wafayāt*, vol. 6, part 27 (Beirut: al-Nasharāt al-Islāmiyya, 1997), 362, cited in Zoltán Szombathy, *The Roots of Arabic Genealogy: A Study in Historical Anthropology* (Piliscsaba: The Avicenna Institute of Middle Eastern Studies, 2003), 41.
106. By contrast, Ibn Laʿbūn and Ibn Bishr seem less concerned with justifying their interest in genealogy, sufficing with an oblique reference to a Prophetic Tradition that encourages believers to know their kin, and making no mention of Quranic evidence. Ibn Laʿbūn, *Tārīkh Ibn Laʿbūn*, 5; Ibn Bishr, *ʿUnwān al-Majd*, vol. 2, 11. Genealogists of the classical period of Islamic scholarship, however, frequently resort to Quranic evidence, particularly verse 49:13.
107. al-Mughīrī, *al-Muntakhab*, 3.
108. al-Ḥuqayl, *Kanz al-Ansāb*, 178.
109. Ibid., 179.

110. al-Ḥuqayl, *Kanz al-Ansāb*, 45. Emphasis added.
111. This sense of dispersion is captured by al-Rasheed in an interview with a retired bedouin employee of Aramco. Madawi al-Rasheed, *History of Saudi Arabia*, 97.
112. (253)—Incoming, October 5, 1998, Maktabat al-ʿArab, Riyadh.
113. Ibn Bishr, *ʿUnwān al-Majd*, 23. The tribal origin of the Murada seems a secondary matter for Ibn Bishr. It is the family genealogy that is paramount, and the fact that its origins can be traced back to a founding ancestor, the one who established the family's presence in al-Dirʿiyya.
114. Ibn Laʿbūn, *Tārīkh Ibn Laʿbūn*, 38.
115. al-Juhany, *Salafi Reform Movement*, 62–64.
116. Burckhardt, *Notes on the Bedouins*, vol. 2, 98; al-Ḥuqayl, *Kanz al-Ansāb*, 40. As noted above, al-Ḥuqayl agreed with Burckhardt's assessment: "Among the most important settled ʿAnaza families are the Āl Saʿūd, the greatest personalities of the Arabian Peninsula. Almost all Arab and English authors agree on this *nasab*." Significantly, Ibn Saʿūd's Arab advisors, who would have had intimate knowledge of the family's perception of its own lineage, concurred with al-Ḥuqayl. Wahba, *Arabian Days*, 101.
117. For a related phenomenon, see al-Juhany, *Salafi Reform Movement*, 108.

CHAPTER THREE. THE ORACLE OF AL-WURŪD: ḤAMAD AL-JĀSIR'S GENEALOGICAL CORRESPONDENCE

1. *Man yuridi l-taḥqīqa fī nisbatin* *aʿyat ʿalā l-awwali wa-l-ākhiri*
   aw mawḍiʿin fī sababin ḥāʾirin *ʿan madraji l-wāridi wa-l-ṣādiri*
   aqul lahu daʿ ʿanka mā kaththarū *wa-ltamisi l-amra ladā l-Jāsiri*
   talqa l-ladhī kunta tarā mithlahū *ʿilman mina l-mundarisi l-dāthiri*

   (Uncataloged)—Incoming, January 9, 1993, Maktabat al-ʿArab, Riyadh.
2. Interview with May Ḥamad al-Jaser, January 2012, Riyadh.
3. (2/1808)—Outgoing, September 16, 1994, Maktabat al-ʿArab, Riyadh.
4. The letters are a microcosm in that their authors exhibit diversity of age, economic status, education level, and geographical location within the kingdom. By one important measure of social background, however, they are not diverse: bedouin-origin Saudis rarely wrote Ḥamad al-Jāsir with genealogical queries.
5. (Uncataloged)—Incoming, March 26, 1999, Maktabat al-ʿArab, Riyadh; (Uncataloged)—Outgoing August, 29, 1996, Maktabat al-ʿArab, Riyadh.
6. (2/1966)—Incoming, November 28, 1994, Maktabat al-ʿArab, Riyadh.
7. (Uncataloged)—Incoming, May 11, 1993, Maktabat al-ʿArab, Riyadh.
8. (2/1344)—Incoming, January 24, 1994, Maktabat al-ʿArab, Riyadh; (Uncataloged)—Incoming September 27, 1996, Maktabat al-ʿArab, Riyadh.
9. (Uncataloged)—Incoming, November 9, 1995, Maktabat al-ʿArab, Riyadh.
10. (2/103)—Incoming, January 30, 1995, Maktabat al-ʿArab, Riyadh.

11. (Uncataloged)—Incoming email, October 2005, Ḥamad al-Jāsir Cultural Center, Riyadh.
12. As al-Jāsir informed the author of one such rejected submission: "one of the editors [of *al-ʿArab*] tried to patch it up, but the holes were too big for the cobbler!" (2/1751)—Outgoing, August 15, 1994, Maktabat al-ʿArab, Riyadh.
13. (574)—Incoming, February 19, 2000, Maktabat al-ʿArab, Riyadh.
14. (21)—Incoming, November 1, 1998, Maktabat al-ʿArab, Riyadh.
15. Dale F. Eickelman, "Communication and Control in the Middle East: Publication and its Discontents," in *New Media in the Muslim World: The Emerging Public Sphere*, ed. Dale F. Eickelman and John W. Anderson (Bloomington: Indiana University Press, 2003), 29–40.
16. (2/1534)—Outgoing, April 24, 1994, Maktabat al-ʿArab, Riyadh; (2/1798)—Outgoing, September 11, 1994, Maktabat al-ʿArab, Riyadh.
17. (2/564)—Outgoing, March 11, 1996, Maktabat al-ʿArab, Riyadh. By this criterion, and despite his sympathies for the bedouin, al-Jāsir showed himself to be in line with earlier Najdi historians, including Ibn ʿĪsā and Ibn Ghannām, for whom the bedouin and their genealogies were largely prehistoric, or outside of history.
18. In this paragraph, I combine selections from a number of different letters to al-Jāsir.
19. (2/1945)—Incoming, November 16, 1994, Maktabat al-ʿArab, Riyadh.
20. (2/396)—Incoming, March 10, 1997, Maktabat al-ʿArab, Riyadh.
21. (2/889)—Incoming, August 27, 1996; (2/396)—Incoming, March 10, 1997, Maktabat al-ʿArab, Riyadh.
22. (94)—Incoming, September 5, 1999, Maktabat al-ʿArab, Riyadh.
23. (219)—Incoming, September 15, 1998, Maktabat al-ʿArab, Riyadh.
24. (94)—Incoming, September 5, 1999, Maktabat al-ʿArab, Riyadh.
25. (2/176)—Incoming, October 9, 1995, Maktabat al-ʿArab, Riyadh.
26. (2/1309)—Incoming December 20, 1993, Maktabat al-ʿArab, Riyadh.
27. (2/1966)—Incoming November 28, 1994; (2/1763)—Incoming, August 24, 1994, Maktabat al-ʿArab, Riyadh.
28. (2/1737)—Incoming, August 9, 1994, Maktabat al-ʿArab, Riyadh.
29. (2/1309)—Incoming, December 20, 1993, Maktabat al-ʿArab, Riyadh.
30. (2/396)—Incoming, March 10, 1997, Riyadh.
31. Engseng Ho, *The Graves of Tarim: Genealogy and Mobility across the Indian Ocean* (Berkeley: University of California Press, 2006).
32. (2/1730)—Incoming, August 8, 1994; (2/396)—Incoming, March 10, 1997, Maktabat al-ʿArab, Riyadh.
33. (2/1737)—Incoming, August 9, 1994, Maktabat al-ʿArab, Riyadh.
34. (2/1122)—Incoming, October 5, 1993, Maktabat al-ʿArab, Riyadh.
35. (703)—Incoming, March 5, 1998, Maktabat al-ʿArab, Riyadh.
36. (2/291)—Incoming, November 28, 1995; (2/678)—Incoming, February 1, 1993, Maktabat al-ʿArab, Riyadh.
37. al-Rasheed, *Politics in an Arabian Oasis*, 184–200; Steven Caton, *"Peaks of*

Yemen I Summon": Poetry as Cultural Practice in a North Yemeni Tribe (Berkeley: University of California Press, 1990), 5; Mai Yamani, *The Hijaz and the Quest for an Arabian Identity* (London: I. B. Tauris, 2004), 25–26.

38. (2/176)—Incoming and Outgoing, October 9, 1995, Maktabat al-ʿArab, Riyadh.
39. (2/449)—Incoming, April 6, 1997, Maktabat al-ʿArab, Riyadh. His study was motivated by a letter of reply al-Jāsir sent to the economist in 1989—a copy of which was enclosed with the newer letter—encouraging him to investigate his origins.
40. *al-kunya allatī lāzamatnā*, with the connotation of something unwanted hanging around, it appears.
41. Contrast this stigma with social attitudes in a country such as Iran, for example, where toponymics do not have the same negative connotation. Conversely, the stigma seems there to concern those who betray evidence of tribal origins. See Soheila Shahshahani, "The Tribal Schools of Iran: Sedentarisation through Education," in *Contemporary Society, Tribal Studies Volume Five: The Concept of Tribal Society* (New Delhi: Concept Publishing, 2002), 316–17; Susan Bayly, *Caste, Society and Politics in India from the Eighteenth Century to the Modern Age* (Cambridge: Cambridge University Press, 1999), 29. The 'tribals' of India are ascribed a similarly low status.
42. For a parallel view from the Yemeni highlands, see Caton, "*Peaks of Yemen*," 36.
43. Snouck, *Mekka in the Latter Part of the 19th Century*, 8.
44. Ibid., 7.
45. (2/349)—Incoming and Outgoing, April, 23, 1995, Maktabat al-ʿArab, Riyadh.
46. For a similar discussion, see (2/906)—Outgoing, September 3, 1996, Maktabat al-ʿArab, Riyadh.
47. (2/291)—Incoming, November 28, 1995, Maktabat al-ʿArab, Riyadh.
48. On this point, see ʿAbdallāh Āl Bassām's entry for the prominent nineteenth-century scholar Ḥamad al-ʿAtīq (d. 1884) in his biographical dictionary, *ʿUlamāʾ Najd khilāl Thamāniyat Qurūn*. The biography commences with a reference to the family's geographical (as opposed to tribal) origins, a format that is often an indicator of non-tribal status. Āl Bassām, *ʿUlamāʾ Najd*, vol. 2, 84; Ibn ʿĪsā, *ʿIqd al-Durar*, 109. Ibn ʿĪsā's mention of the death of the family patriarch is also notable for its lack of any genealogical details about the scholar.
49. (779)—Outgoing, April 13, 1998, Maktabat al-ʿArab, Riyadh.
50. Ḥamad here refers to Ḥamad al-ʿAtīq. Āl Bassām, *ʿUlamāʾ Najd*, 84–95.
51. (224)—Outgoing, September 20, 1998, Maktabat al-ʿArab, Riyadh.
52. (Uncataloged)—Incoming, August 13, 1997, Maktabat al-ʿArab, Riyadh.
53. (2/1172)—Incoming, October 17, 1993, Maktabat al-ʿArab, Riyadh.
54. (359)—Incoming, February 25, 1999, Maktabat al-ʿArab, Riyadh.
55. By contingency is meant here a historical interpretative device for engaging with a deeply opaque Arabian past. For the application of a similar notion of

contingency to natural history, see Stephen J. Gould, *Wonderful Life: The Burgess Shale and the Nature of History* (New York: W. W. Norton, 1989).

56. Under the heading "How lineages become confused," Ibn Khaldūn wrote: "It is clear that a person of a certain descent may become attached to people of another descent, either because he feels well-disposed toward them, or because there exists an alliance or client(-master) relationship, or yet because he had to flee from his own people by reason of some crime he committed. . . . In the course of time, the original descent is almost forgotten. . . . Family lines in this manner continually changed from one tribal group to another . . . ," Ibn Khaldūn, *Muqaddimah*, 100. For the broader context of this passage, see 98–107.
57. (673)—Outgoing, March 16, 1973, Maktabat al-ʿArab, Riyadh.
58. (2/449)—Outgoing, April 6, 1997, Maktabat al-ʿArab, Riyadh.
59. al-Jāsir, *Jamharat Ansāb*, First Ed. (1981), vol. 1, 6.
60. (2/1706)—Outgoing, July 21, 1994, Maktabat al-ʿArab, Riyadh.
61. (2/103)—Incoming, January 30, 1995, Maktabat al-ʿArab, Riyadh; interviews with Saudi genealogists, February–March 2011, Riyadh and Jeddah; Ḥamād b. ʿAbdallāh al-Khāṭirī, *Awthaq al-Maʿāyīr fī Nasab Banī Yās wa-l-Manāṣīr* (Abu Dhabi: Center for Research and Documentation, 2007). This notion of blood kinship can be observed as well in the publications of genealogists in other Gulf countries.
62. Ḥamad al-Jāsir, *Muʿjam Qabāʾil al-Mamlaka al-ʿArabiyya al-Saʿūdiyya* (Riyadh: Dār al-Yamāma li-l-Baḥth wa-l-Tarjama wa-l-Nashr, 1980), 4.
63. (2/98)—Incoming and Outgoing, January 26, 1995, Maktabat al-ʿArab, Riyadh.
64. Schneider, *Critique of the Study of Kinship*, 35; Ladislav Holy, *Anthropological Perspectives on Kinship* (Ann Arbor: Pluto Press, 1996), 37.
65. al-Jāsir, *Jamharat Ansāb*, First Ed. (1981), vol. 1, 3.
66. Ibid., 5.
67. (Uncataloged)—Incoming, Undated (c. April 1994), Maktabat al-ʿArab, Riyadh.
68. (2/109)—Incoming, February 3, 1995, Maktabat al-ʿArab, Riyadh.
69. (224)—Incoming, September 20, 1998, Maktabat al-ʿArab, Riyadh.
70. Al-Jāsir titled his aborted volume *Naẓarāt fī Ikhtilāṭ al-Ansāb wa-Tadākhkhuluhā* ("Reflections on the Intermingling and Interpenetration of Lineages"). ʿĀʾidh al-Raddādī, *ʿInāyat al-Shaykh Ḥamad al-Jāsir bi-l-Ansāb* (Riyadh: ʿĀʾidh al-Raddādī, 2003), 32; al-Jāsir, *Sawāniḥ*, 696.
71. (224)—Outgoing, September 20, 1998, Maktabat al-ʿArab, Riyadh; interview with Ḥamad al-Jāsir, "Siyāj al-Umma al-Qawwī Lughatuhā (Part 4 of 9)," *al-Sharq al-Awsaṭ*, October 10, 1991, 7.
72. Kuper, *Invention of Primitive Society*, 4–5.
73. *al-ʿArab* 10, no. 9/10 (1976).
74. The advertisement occupied the bottom half of the back cover, with the announcement of the release of al-Jāsir's geographical dictionary above it. The

geographical and genealogical volumes seemed here conceived as two parts of a single larger study.

75. Interview with Rāshid b. Ḥumayd, January 2012, Riyadh.
76. Ḥamad al-Jāsir, "Qabīlat ʿUtayba: Aṣluhā wa-Furūʿuhā," *al-ʿArab* 3, no. 9 (1969): 26.
77. Author interview, January 2012, Riyadh.
78. One genealogist interviewed by the author recounted a disagreement over tribal affiliation between a father and son that spilled over into litigation. Author interview, January 2011, Riyadh.
79. For a discussion of this point, see Muḥammad b. Ṣunaytān, *al-Saʿūdiyya: al-Siyāsī wa-l-Qabīla* (Beirut: Arab Network for Research and Publishing, 2008), 77.
80. One unfortunate consequence of my method here is that I am unable to provide citations to Mr. Ḥumayd's publications.
81. Interview with Rāshid b. Ḥumayd, January 2012, Riyadh.
82. I thank Bernard Haykel for this insight.
83. (2/1322)—Incoming, January 2, 1994, Maktabat al-ʿArab, Riyadh.
84. Interview with Rāshid b. Ḥumayd, January 8, 2012, Riyadh.
85. (2/1277)—Incoming, December 3, 1993, Maktabat al-ʿArab, Riyadh.
86. (2/1277)—Outgoing, December 3, 1993, Maktabat al-ʿArab, Riyadh.
87. Al-Jāsir would himself acknowledge this discrediting, remarking late in life that his genealogical works were "no more than a record of that which is commonly known (*mutaʿāraf*) among the tribes, that is, they aren't deep studies." (105)—Outgoing, June 19, 1997, Maktabat al-ʿArab, Riyadh.
88. (357)—Outgoing, December 11, 1999, Maktabat al-ʿArab, Riyadh.
89. (2/193)—Incoming, January 27, 1997, Maktabat al-ʿArab, Riyadh.
90. (2/656)—Incoming, January 17, 1993, Maktabat al-ʿArab, Riyadh.
91. Robert Hoyland, review of *Muhammad and the Believers: At the Origins of Islam* by Fred M. Donner, *International Journal of Middle East Studies* 44, no. 3 (2012): 573–6.
92. Caton's observation vis-à-vis late twentieth-century Yemen, that "technology and modern economics have not inhibited the oral tradition," is useful here. Caton, *"Peaks of Yemen"*, 62.
93. "Most of the events of the past ages of our people [*ummatinā*, i.e., Saudi Arabia] were not recorded, among which are those that are still being transmitted orally," al-Jāsir wrote a prominent tribal historian. (2/78)—Outgoing, January 18, 1995, Maktabat al-ʿArab, Riyadh.
94. ʿAbdallāh b. Khamīs (d. 2011) was a prolific Najdi historian, writer, and genealogist who is often thought of alongside al-Jāsir as one of the early intellectuals of modern Najd. Ibn Khamīs composed one of the volumes of al-Jāsir's geographical dictionary.
95. Saʿd b. Junaydil (d. 2006) was an influential historian of Arabia and a contributor to al-Jāsir's *Muʿjam al-Jūghrāfī*.
96. Interview with Rāshid b. Ḥumayd, January 2012, Riyadh.

97. Shryock, *Nationalism and the Genealogical Imagination*; Goody, *Power of the Written Tradition*, 13.
98. Sowayan, *al-Ṣaḥrāʾ al-ʿArabiyya*, 34.
99. (319)—Incoming, November 6, 1997; (2/1228)—Incoming, November 8, 1993; (91)—Incoming, May 29, 1998, Maktabat al-ʿArab, Riyadh.
100. Ironically, those confused petitioners whose knowledge did not extend beyond their fourth ancestor presented what was probably a more honest accounting of their ancestry than those whose inquiries came prefaced with lineage chains of fourteen generations and assurances of pure tribal origins. An exception might be the Descendants of the Prophet (*Ashrāf*), for whom the preservation of lineal connections to the Prophet Muḥammad is central to their religious position and group identity, even if Saudi Ashrāf genealogies are today highly contested.
101. For example, (2/87)—Outgoing, January 19, 1995; (2/449)—Outgoing, April 6, 1997; (61)—Incoming, May 18, 1998; (115)—Incoming, December 21, 1998, Maktabat al-ʿArab, Riyadh.
102. (2/449)—Outgoing, April 6, 1997, Maktabat al-ʿArab, Riyadh.
103. (2/1798)—Outgoing, September 11, 1994, Maktabat al-ʿArab, Riyadh; (2/1967) November 29, 1994, Maktabat al-ʿArab, Riyadh.
104. Interview with Emirati historian, September 2010, ʿAjmān, United Arab Emirates; interview with Emirati historian, September 2010, al-ʿAyn, United Arab Emirates; author interview, December 2011, Riyadh.
105. See, for example, *Wathāʾiq min al-Ghāṭ*, ed. Fāyiz b. Mūsā al-Badrānī (Riyadh: ʿAbd al-Raḥmān al-Sudayrī Charitable Foundation, 2010).
106. I.e., with two consecutive consonants.
107. Interview with ʿAbd al-Raḥmān al-Shuqayr, November 2011, Riyadh.
108. (Uncataloged)—Incoming, October 29, 1995, Maktabat al-ʿArab, Riyadh.
109. al-Jāsir, *Jamharat Ansāb*, First Ed. (1981), vol. 2, 983.
110. al-Jāsir, *Jamharat Ansāb*, Third Ed. (2001), vol. 2, 918.
111. Muḥammad al-ʿUbūdī, *Muʿjam Usar Burayda* (Riyadh: al-Thulūthiyya Press, 2010).
112. Interviews with al-Jāsir associates, March 2011, Riyadh; interview with al-ʿUbūdī associate, February, 2011, Riyadh; interview with Saudi author, January 2011, Riyadh.
113. Shuʿayb b. ʿAbd al-Ḥamīd al-Dawsarī, *Imtāʿ al-Sāmir bi-Takmilat Mutʿat al-Nāẓir* (Riyadh: King Abdulaziz Foundation, 1998). Al-Jāsir utilized *Imtāʿ al-Sāmir* as a source for the second edition of his *Jamhara* (1988).
114. (2/180)—Outgoing, October 9, 1995, Maktabat al-ʿArab, Riyadh.
115. The Majlis al-Shūrā is a council of unelected expert appointees charged with debating important political, economic, and social issues and providing policy recommendations to the king.
116. Emphasis added.
117. (401)—Incoming, March 18, 1999, Maktabat al-ʿArab, Riyadh.
118. "Paper truths" is a phrase coined by the anthropologist Emma Tarlo to refer

to a set of local administrative documents she encountered in New Delhi, which concealed behind their euphemistic formalism a dynamic and sometimes unsettling story of social and political contestation. Emma Tarlo, *Unsettling Memories: Narratives of the Emergency in Delhi* (Berkeley: University of California Press, 2003), 62–93.

119. Interview with Rāshid b. Ḥumayd, January 2012, Riyadh.
120. (2/1322)—Incoming, January 2, 1994, Maktabat al-ʿArab, Riyadh.
121. Note that Rāshid refers to this person as *the* leader of the tribe.
122. The text of this testimonial, taken here from *al-ʿArab* and modified to preserve anonymity, bears quoting: "The [Āl Ḥumayd] family belongs to the ʿAjmān tribe. They are a settled family who have no branches outside of the kingdom. They are known to us beyond a doubt, and they possess Saudi citizenship papers. They desire that the name of their tribe 'al-ʿAjmī' be added to their official documents after their family name Āl Ḥumayd, in order to preserve their lineage and on account of their pride in their tribal affiliation. Because of our complete confidence in the aforementioned information, we have no objection to this, and they had been granted this authentication (*taʿrīf*) on the basis of their request." For more on the practice of lineal authentication, see chapter six.
123. al-Badrānī, *Ẓāhirat al-Taʾlīf*, 55.
124. (673)—Outgoing, March 16, 1973, Maktabat al-ʿArab, Riyadh.
125. (Uncataloged)—Incoming, February 23, 1993, Maktabat al-ʿArab, Riyadh. This letter is one of several in which sons are seen attempting to burnish their fathers' legacies by convincing al-Jāsir to modify their families' genealogical entries in his volumes. Other examples are: (2/1811)—Incoming, August 18, 1994; (2/1802)—Incoming, September 11, 1994, Maktabat al-ʿArab, Riyadh.
126. Ḥamad al-Jāsir, *Bāhila: al-Qabīla al-Muftarā ʿAlayhā* (Riyadh: Dar al-Yamāma, 1990).
127. (6/310)—Incoming, February 17, 1993, Maktabat al-ʿArab, Riyadh; author interview, March 2011, Riyadh. This amounted to several thousand copies; (2/1534)—Incoming, April 24, 1994, Maktabat al-ʿArab, Riyadh. To be sure, the businessman's attitude was only one of many reactions to the book by members of the tribe. For example, a Kuwaiti man who claimed affiliation with Bāhila wrote al-Jāsir complaining that his family's name was absent from the volume. He noted pointedly that members of his family interpreted this omission as a diminution of the family's standing.
128. (Uncataloged)—Incoming, February 23, 1993, Maktabat al-ʿArab, Riyadh.
129. (2/714)—Incoming, February 18, 1993, Maktabat al-ʿArab, Riyadh.
130. For more on these tropes, see Sowayan, *al-Ṣaḥrāʾ al-ʿArabiyya*, 403–32.
131. Ḥamad al-Jāsir, "Min Aʿyān al-Usra al-Nafīsiyya (Āl Nafīsa)," *al-Riyāḍ*, March 26, 1997, 16. As al-Jāsir explained, unfearing of lambs (*al-ṭulay*) refers to those who put sticks in the mouths of small lambs to prohibit them from nursing so that they might appropriate their mother's milk.

132. Nazih Ayubi, *Overstating the Arab State: Politics and Society in the Middle East* (London: I. B. Tauris, 1995), 124–25.
133. Salama, *Maṣīrat al-Ṣiḥāfa*, 171; Jones, *Desert Kingdom*, 148–50.
134. Marwan Kraidy, "Saudi Arabia, Lebanon and the Changing Arab Information Order," *International Journal of Communication* 1 (2007): 145.
135. (Uncataloged)—Incoming, November 9, 1995, Maktabat al-ʿArab, Riyadh.
136. (490)—Outgoing, April 17, 1999, Maktabat al-ʿArab, Riyadh.
137. Author interview, January 2012, Riyadh.
138. (2/210)—Outgoing, October 20, 1995, Maktabat al-ʿArab, Riyadh.
139. (2/3)—Outgoing, June 4, 1995, Maktabat al-ʿArab, Riyadh.
140. (448)—Outgoing, April 6, 1999, Maktabat al-ʿArab, Riyadh.
141. (624)—Outgoing, June 2, 1999, Maktabat al-ʿArab, Riyadh.
142. (436)—Outgoing, April 12, 1972, Maktabat al-ʿArab, Riyadh.
143. For more on the notion of names as commodities, see *The Anthropology of Names and Naming*, ed. Gabriele vom Bruck and Barbara Bodenhorn (Cambridge: Cambridge University Press, 2006), 1–5.
144. For a similar formulation, see (Uncataloged)—Incoming, September 15, 1995, Maktabat al-ʿArab, Riyadh.
145. (2/1344)—Incoming and Outgoing, January 24, 1994, Maktabat al-ʿArab, Riyadh.
146. Though perhaps a coincidence, it is interesting that, when counting up from the government liaison, the claim of affiliation is made at the level of the sixth ancestor. Below this is the *khamsa*, a genealogical unit that possesses a certain juridical validity in Saudi Arabia, in that the obligation to contribute to the blood payment in the event of a murder or accidental killing falls upon members of this unit. Sowayan has argued that it is above the *khamsa*, at a level of generality where the specific genealogies are more opaque, that an outside branch has a better chance of merging into the larger tribe and eventually forging some sort of genealogical relationship with it. Sowayan, *al-Ṣaḥrāʾ al-ʿArabiyya*, 553.
147. A legal *Ṣakk* is "a signed and sealed record of a judge's decision." C. E. Bosworth, "Ṣakk," *Encyclopaedia of Islam, Second Edition*, ed. P. Bearman, Th. Bianquis et al. (Brill Online, 2013).
148. *Ṣukūk* of a historical nature that testified to certain facts about a family's history were considered important forms of evidence by al-Jāsir's petitioners. For examples, see (2/449)—Incoming, April 6, 1997; (703)—Incoming, March 5, 1998, Maktabat al-ʿArab, Riyadh.
149. (490)—Outgoing, April 17, 1999, Maktabat al-ʿArab, Riyadh.
150. (Uncataloged)—Incoming, November 9, 1995, Maktabat al-ʿArab, Riyadh.
151. (624)—Outgoing, June 9, 1999, Maktabat al-ʿArab, Riyadh.
152. Eviatar Zerubavel, *Ancestors and Relatives: Genealogy, Identity, and Community* (New York: Oxford University Press, 2012).
153. Several such narratives involve families from outside of Saudi Arabia claiming close lineal connection with Saudi citizens, thereby invoking an important

corollary to lineal prestige, the privilege of Saudi citizenship. (2/1363)—Incoming, February 11, 1994; (Uncataloged)—Incoming, Undated (c. January 1995), Ibrāhīm b. Muḥammad b. Saʿd al-Musayḥil to al-Jāsir, Maktabat al-ʿArab, Riyadh; (Uncataloged)—Incoming email, Undated (post-2000) Sālim b. Bashīr b. Sālim b. ʿAbdallāh Āl ʿĀshiq to al-Jāsir, Ḥamad al-Jāsir Cultural Center, Riyadh.

154. On the morning of September 30, 1975, al-Jāsir's first-born son Muḥammad was killed when his Malév Hungarian Airlines flight from Budapest crashed near the Beirut shore. While the cause of the crash has never been definitively established, one hypothesis, that the plane was shot down by an Israeli rocket because it was believed to be carrying arms for the Palestinian Liberation Organization, has come to be favored by members of the al-Jāsir family.
155. al-Shubaylī, *al-Shaykh Ḥamad al-Jāsir fī Ḥiwār*, 55.
156. "Taʿallamū min ansābikum mā taṣilūna bihi arḥāmakum . . . ," Aḥmad b. Ḥanbal, *Musnad al-Imām Aḥmad b. Ḥanbal*, ed. Samīr Ṭāhā al-Majzūb, vol. 2 (Beirut: al-Maktab al-Islāmī, 1993), 492–93.
157. This marriage of genealogy, personal history, and fidelity to the Saudi regime is echoed in another letter, in which the author describes for al-Jāsir the origins of his family name and the reason behind its odd construction (Āl Muqayyrin). The author attributes the origin of his family name to a grief-stricken utterance by the founder of the Saudi dynasty, Muḥammad b. Saʿūd (d. 1765). The author's ancestor, he explains, was a warrior who fought on the Saudi side. When Muḥammad b. Saʿūd learned that the warrior, whose name was Muqrin, had been killed in battle, he expressed his remorse by invoking Muqrin's name in the diminutive form (Muqayyrin), a marker of affection that stuck indelibly. (10)—Incoming, June 17, 1997; see also (43)—Incoming, June 30, 1999; (534)—Incoming, May 3, 1999, Maktabat al-ʿArab, Riyadh.
158. (2/978)—Incoming, October 21, 1996, Maktabat al-ʿArab, Riyadh.

CHAPTER FOUR. MARRIAGE AND LINEAL AUTHENTICATION

1. Interview with May Ḥamad al-Jaser, January 2012, Riyadh. In numerous letters to his lineage-seeking petitioners, al-Jāsir would profess this same polite form of ignorance.
2. For further context, observe the case of Khālid al-Jiraysī and his controversial volume, *al-ʿAṣabiyya al-Qabaliyya min al-Manẓūr al-Islāmī* (*Tribal Chauvinism from an Islamic Perspective*) (Riyadh: al-Jiraysī Foundation, 2007). Al-Jiraysī's volume is discussed in Nadav Samin, "*Kafāʾa fī l-Nasab* in Saudi Arabia: Islamic Law, Tribal Custom, and Social Change," *Journal of Arabian Studies* 2, no. 2 (2012): 109–26.
3. For some examples of marital inquiries in the *al-ʿArab* letters, see (Uncataloged)—Incoming, May 11, 1993; (Catalog Number Missing)—Khālid ʿAbd al-Raḥmān al-ʿArīdī to Ḥamad al-Jāsir, Undated (c. 1999), Maktabat al-ʿArab,

Riyadh. Some of al-Jāsir's petitioners were explicitly concerned with knowing the social category to which they belonged, i.e., tribal (*qabīlī*) or non-tribal (*khaḍīrī*): (2/1966)—Incoming, November 28, 1994; (2/889)—Incoming, August 27, 1996, Maktabat al-ʿArab, Riyadh.

4. Jack Goody, *The Development of the Family and Marriage in Europe* (Cambridge: Cambridge University Press, 1983), 157–82.
5. In the case of the Middle East, the preference for marriage within the patrilineal descent group proved difficult for anthropologists to assimiliate into the two traditionally dominant theories of kinship, descent theory and alliance theory. Holy, *Anthropological Perspectives*, 137; Bourdieu, *Outline of a Theory*, 31; Donald Cole, *Nomads of the Nomads: The Al Murrah Bedouin of the Empty Quarter* (Lancaster: AHM publishing, 1975), 8.
6. Mounira M. Charrad, *States and Women's Rights: The Making of Postcolonial Tunisia, Algeria, and Morocco* (Berkeley: University of California Press, 2001), 51–83.
7. Musil, *Manners and Customs*, 137; Antonin Jaussen and Raphaël Savignac, *Mission archéologique en Arabie*, supplement to vol. 2 (Paris: E. Leroux, 1909), 2, 23; Cole, *Nomads*, 71; Sowayan, *al-Ṣaḥrāʾ al-ʿArabiyya*, 514.
8. al-Juhany, *Salafi Reform Movement*, 95.
9. Ibid., 86.
10. *Wathāʾiq min al-Ghāṭ*, 1015.
11. Lorimer claimed that more than two-thirds of al-Ghāṭ's inhabitants belonged to the Dawāsir tribe. This is likely an exaggeration, however, as less than one-third of all marriages recorded in the al-Ghāṭ documents involved a Dawāsir partner. J. G. Lorimer, *Gazetteer of the Persian Gulf, Oman, and Central Arabia*, vol. 2 (Calcutta: Superintendent Government Printing, 1915), 1638.
12. E.g., Dawāsir, Banī Tamīm, Subayʿ, ʿAnaza, Shammar, Ẓafīr, Banī Khālid, and ʿAwāzim.
13. Lorimer estimated that 12 percent of the village's population were "Bani Khadhīr." Lorimer, *Gazetteer of the Persian Gulf*, vol. 2, 1638.
14. Notably, these proportions agree with Monira Charrad's findings from her meta-analysis of studies of marriage patterns across the Middle East. Charrad, *States and Women's Rights*, 61.
15. By "same family" is meant a husband and wife who possess the same surname or clan name (typically the name of a common ancestor from the not-so-remote past, e.g., Āl ʿAwād). This is a fairly strict definition of family endogamy, and one that, given the historically small size of the town's population, suggests a reasonably close degree of consanguinity. If the definition of "same family" is expanded to encompass the descendants of a common ancestor who belong to the same tribal branch but do not share a surname or clan name, then the number of family endogamous marriages in the al-Ghāṭ records increases.
16. Notably, tribal endogamy among the Sudayrīs appears to have increased with the passage of time. Of eleven marriages contracted by members of the family

with spouses from outside of their tribe, eight date from prior to 1880. Al-Rasheed has argued that during the early stages of the consolidation of their leadership, the Rashidi rulers of Ḥāʾil preferred exogamous marriage, as a means of cementing alliances with recently subdued or potentially rival factions and clans. Whether such marital strategies applied as much to regional governors, such as the Sudayrīs, as they did to autonomous emirate rulers is an open question, but one that would have bearing on the nature of political authority in premodern Arabia. Al-Rasheed, *Politics in an Arabian Oasis*, 194–98. The number of exogamous marriages in her sample is quite small (four out of a total of twenty-eight marriages).

17. While it is exceedingly difficult to make definitive claims about the tribal or non-tribal status of individuals referenced in the al-Ghāṭ documents, this status can be discerned in part from glosses by the document project's compiler and editor, Fāyiz al-Badrānī.
18. al-Juhany, *Salafi Reform Movement*, 95.
19. *Wathāʾiq min al-Ghāṭ*, 1130, 1792, 2107.
20. Polygamy was not uncommon in al-Ghāṭ, yet seems to have been concentrated within a specific segment of the population. Twenty of 195 al-Ghāṭ men mentioned in the documents accounted for up to forty-seven instances of polygamous marriage (assuming that none of these were remarriages), with the remaining 178 marriages being monogamous.
21. "Afrāḥ Jidda fī Thamānīn ʿĀman," *Majallat Jidda*, 18–41 (March 2009–February 2011).
22. Three of these six endogamous marriages involved the wealthy and influential Jamjūm merchant family.
23. According to Altorki, an important consideration for a bride's family was a groom's descent, by which was meant his membership in one of the "known old recognized families" of Jeddah. Soraya Altorki, *Women in Saudi Arabia: Ideology and Behavior among the Elite* (New York: Columbia University Press, 1986), 131.
24. Burckhardt, *Notes*, vol. 1, 112–13; Musil, *Manners and Customs*, 137; ed. P. Bonte and E. Conte, *al-Ansâb: La quête des origines. Anthropologie historique de la société tribale Arabe* (Paris: Fondation de la Maison des Sciences de l'Homme, 1991), 29; Holy, *Anthropological Perspectives*, 137; Sowayan, *al-Ṣaḥrāʾ al-ʿArabiyya*, 516–19.
25. Āl Sulaymān is a pseudonym for the family in question.
26. Musil, *Manners and Customs*, 136; Fahad, "The ʿImama vs. the ʿIqal," 60, n. 21; Lorimer, *Gazetteer of the Persian* Gulf, vol. 2, 188. Lorimer records the presence of ʿAwāzim in al-Ghāṭ.
27. Cole, *Nomads*, 88.
28. Cole, *Nomads*, 84.
29. For a vivid example, see (Uncataloged)—Incoming, May 11, 1993, Maktabat al-ʿArab, Riyadh.
30. (382)—Outgoing, March 10, 1999; (2/1534)—Outgoing, April 24, 1994, Makta-

bat al-ʿArab, Riyadh. For examples unrelated to his books, see (2/310)—Outgoing, October 24, 1985; (2/1718)—Incoming, August 4, 1994, Maktabat al-ʿArab, Riyadh.

31. ʿAbd al-Raḥmān b. ʿAbd al-Karīm al-ʿUbayyid, *Qabīlat al-ʿAwāzim: Dirāsa ʿan Aṣlihā wa-Mujtamaʿihā wa-Diyārihā* (Kuwait: Maktabat al-Ādāb, 1971), 11–17; (2/1966)—Incoming and Outgoing, November 28, 1994; (2/204)—Outgoing, October 19, 1995, Maktabat al-ʿArab, Riyadh.
32. (Uncataloged)—Outgoing, April 3, 1996, Maktabat al-ʿArab, Riyadh; Ḥamad al-Jāsir, *Bāhila*, 90–98. Both al-Dirʿiyya's governor Muḥammad b. ʿAbd al-Raḥmān al-Bāhilī (d. 2005) and its deputy governor ʿAbd al-Raḥmān b. Ṣāliḥ Āl ʿAbd al-Laṭīf were from the Bāhila tribe.
33. ʿUsaylān, *Ḥamad al-Jāsir wa-Juhūduhu*, 17. Perhaps coincidentally, one of these siblings, al-Jāsir's half-brother ʿAlī, passed away in July of 1988, two years before the publication of *Bāhila*.
34. al-Jāsir, *Bāhila*, 20.
35. ʿAlī al-Ṭanṭāwī, *Rijāl min al-Tārīkh* (Damascus: Muʾassasat al-Salām li-l-Ṭibāʿa wa-l-Nashr, 1958), 80.
36. Coincidentally, the modern-day Bāhila tribe of central Arabia is commonly believed to originate in al-Ghāṭ. See al-Jāsir, *Bāhila*, 87.
37. Ibid., 24–5; for the vernacular root *zbn*, see Kurpershoek, *Oral Poetry, Volume II*, 374.
38. S. Enderwitz, "al-Shuʿūbiyya," *Encyclopaedia of Islam, Second Edition*, ed. P. Bearman, Th. Bianquis et al. (Brill Online, 2013); for an influential statement on this controversy, see Roy P. Mottahedeh, "The Shuʿūbīyah Controversy and the Social History of Early Islamic Iran," *International Journal of Middle East Studies* 7, no. 2 (1976): 161–82.
39. The twelfth-century genealogist Ibn al-Samʿānī wrote of Bāhila: "the bedouin used to scorn lineal affiliation with Bāhila, as if the tribe had no honor in their estimation." *Kitāb al-Ansāb*, vol. 1 (Beirut: Dār Iḥyāʾ al-Turāth al-ʿArabī, 1999), 191.
40. The family of the latter receives particularly laudatory treatment in the volume. al-Jāsir, *Bāhila*, 95–98.
41. The book includes a section devoted to anti-Bāhila invective poetry, with generous examples compiled by al-Jāsir from the Arabic literary canon. It is partly for this reason that *Bāhila* was considered by many members of the tribe to be a "bibliography of insults," and thus to have achieved the opposite of its intended effect. Author interview, November 2011, Riyadh.
42. "Scholar of Renown Sheikh Ali al-Tantawi," *Arab News*, June 18, 2001, www.arabnews.com/node/212775.
43. Like al-Jāsir, the young ʿAlī al-Ṭanṭāwī met with the dean of Cairo University's Faculty of Literature, Ṭāhā Ḥusayn, in hopes of being admitted there. Unfortunately for al-Ṭānṭāwī, his maternal uncle was the noted Islamic author and Ḥusayn detractor Muḥibb al-Dīn al-Khaṭīb; for this reason, al-Ṭanṭāwī believed, he was denied admission. Rāʾid al-Samhūrī, *ʿAli al-Ṭanṭāwī*

wa-Ārāʾuhu fī l-Adab wa-l-Naqd (Damascus: Dār al-Fikr, 2008), 66; Rāʾid al-Samhūrī, *ʿAlī al-Ṭanṭāwī wa-Aʿlām ʿAṣrih: Sayyid Quṭb wa-Ākharūn, Ṣadāqa, Khuṣūma, Naqd* (Beirut: Dār Madārik li-l-Nashr, 2012), 72.

44. An important distinction between the two is that al-Ṭanṭāwī's employment as a judge exceeded al-Jāsir's brief stint by many decades.
45. Thomas Pierret, *Religion and State in Syria: The Sunni Ulama from Coup to Revolution* (Cambridge: Cambridge University Press, 2013), 42.
46. Lacroix, *Awakening Islam*, 44–45.
47. al-Samhūrī, *ʿAlī al-Ṭanṭāwī wa-Aʿlām.*
48. He was believed to have been among the first religious scholars to phone into television and radio programs in Saudi Arabia. See al-Samhūrī, *ʿAli al-Ṭanṭāwī wa-Ārāʾuhu*, 74–75.
49. For this term, see ʿAbdallāh al-Ghadhdhāmī, *al-Faqīh al-Faḍāʾī: Taḥawwul al-Khiṭāb al-Dīnī min al-Minbar ilā l-Shāsha* (Casablanca: al-Markaz al-Thaqāfī al-ʿArabī, 2011).
50. For a discussion of the development of the kingdom's educational institutions, see Sarah Yizraeli, *Politics and Society in Saudi Arabia*, 227–63.
51. Lacroix's important study overlooks the significance of mass literacy for the emergence of a broad-based, grassroots religious revivalist movement in the modern kingdom.
52. Bernard Haykel, "On the Nature of Salafi Thought and Practice," in *Global Salafism: Islam's New Religious Movement*, ed. Roel Meijer (London: Hurst and Company, 2009), 33–57.
53. As Haykel notes, ". . . a principal definitional distinction between the traditional Wahhabis and the *ijtihad*-minded Salafis has to do with the former group's adherence to the views of the Hanbali school of law, and the extent to which *ijtihad* [i.e., independent interpretation] is not stressed in the formulation of legal opinions." Ibid., 42.
54. Ibid., 35, n. 5.
55. Interview with Nāṣir al-Dīn al-Albānī, "al-Taḥdhīr min ʿAlī al-Ṭanṭāwī," *YouTube*, https://www.youtube.com/watch?v=PBZ46TWWA_k.
56. On important points of Salafi principle, including the legitimacy of adherence to Islam's legal schools, the Ḥanafī jurist al-Ṭanṭāwī equivocated. On Sufism and the veneration of saints, another key Salafi issue, al-Ṭanṭāwī (like al-Jāsir) expressed a more firm disapproval. ʿAlī al-Ṭanṭāwī, *Fatāwā ʿAlī al-Ṭanṭāwī*, ed. Mujāhid Dayrāniyya (Jeddah: Dār al-Manāra, 1985), 49–51, 77–78.
57. Author interview, January 2012, Riyadh. One might draw a link here between al-Jāsir's private critique of the Ṣaḥwa and his critical attitude toward the half-educated, early twentieth-century *muṭawwaʿūn*, whom he blamed for the excesses of the Ikhwān movement.
58. Author interview, January 2012, Riyadh.
59. In a 1993 letter from a prominent Bāhilī, al-Jāsir was informed of a wedding sermon, delivered by the popular Saudi religious scholar ʿĀʾidh al-Qarnī, in

which al-Qarnī invoked Bāhila's low status and referenced the example of Qutayba b. Muslim to prove the futility of kinship-based chauvinisms. Al-Qarnī, who is from the historically peripheral south, admired al-Ṭanṭāwī. In his introduction to a recent volume about the late scholar, he described being moved to tears upon first reading *Rijāl min al-Tārīkh*. (Uncataloged)—Incoming, February 17, 1993, Maktabat al-ʿArab, Riyadh; Aḥmad b. ʿAlī Āl Marīʿ, *ʿAlī al-Ṭanṭāwī, Kāna Yawm Kuntu: Ṣināʿat al-Fiqh wa-l-Adab* (Riyadh: al-ʿUbaykān, 2007), 20.

60. al-Jāsir, *Bāhila*, 9.
61. Ibid., 26.
62. Ibid., 16; Ibid., 666. *Bāhila* found al-Jāsir also dabbling in Hadith criticism, another common Salafi practice in which Traditions of the Prophet Muḥammad, even those whose veracity is attested by a broad consensus of Muslim jurists, are subject to scrutiny and sometimes rejected as unsound. Specifically, al-Jāsir argued against the authenticity of a purported Tradition in which the Prophet was said to have affirmed Bāhila's low status.
63. Ibid., 662. Al-Jāsir's criticism of al-Ṭanṭāwī's reliance on the opinions of latter-day Ḥanafī scholars (*mutaʾakhkhirūn*) instead of those of their predecessors (*mutaqaddimūn*) is itself a Salafi move that echoes one of the strategies of textual criticism employed by influential Salafi scholar Yūsuf al-Qaraḍāwī. Muhammad Qasim Zaman, *Modern Islamic Thought in a Radical Age: Religious Authority and Internal Criticism* (Cambridge: Cambridge University Press, 2012), 305.
64. For discussions of some of the social implications of *kafāʾa* in diverse Arabian historical contexts, see Ho, *Graves of Tarim*, 147–51; Bernard Haykel, *Revival and Reform in Islamic Law: The Legacy of Muhammad al-Shawkani* (Cambridge: Cambridge University Press, 2003), 204–14; Samin, "*Kafāʾa fī l-Nasab* in Saudi Arabia."
65. The thirteenth-century jurist Ibn Qudāma (d. 1223), whose views on *kafāʾa fī l-nasab* were faithfully transcribed by Muḥammad b. ʿAbd al-Wahhāb and adopted as his own, allowed that the principle of *kafāʾa fī l-nasab* was valid as a minority opinion in the Ḥanbalī tradition. This opinion was invoked by twentieth-century Najdi legal authorities such as Muḥammad b. Ibrāhīm Āl al-Shaykh, and was endorsed by local judges, including Ḥamad al-Ḥuqayl. In 2006, lineal compatibility became the subject of public controversy with the case of Fāṭima and Manṣūr, a happily married couple who were forcibly divorced on the grounds that the husband had misrepresented his lineage at the time of his proposal. Muwaffaq al-Dīn ʿAbdallāh b. Aḥmad Ibn Qudāma, *al-Mughnī*, vol. 9 (Cairo: Dār al-Ḥadīth, 1996), 190–93; Ibn ʿAbd al-Wahhāb, *Muʾallafāt al-Shaykh*, vol. 1, 651; *Fatāwā al-Shaykh Ibn Ibrāhīm*, ed. Muḥammad b. ʿAbd al-Raḥmān b. Qāsim, "*2736: al-kafāʾa fī l-nasab*," vol. 10 (Mecca: Maṭbaʿat al-Ḥukūma, 1978), 82; al-Ḥuqayl, *Kanz al-Ansāb*, 179; Ḥanān Ḥasan ʿAṭāllāh, "Fāṭima wa-Manṣūr," *al-Riyāḍ*, September 21, 2006.

66. Al-Jāsir likened al-Ṭanṭāwī's missteps to those of the classical historians and genealogists who lacked familiarity with Arabia, including al-Thaʿlabī and al-Samʿānī. al-Jāsir, *Bāhila*, 708.
67. (401)—Outgoing, March 18, 1999, Maktabat al-ʿArab, Riyadh.
68. *Bāhila*, 708.
69. Ibid., 716.
70. The sense that *Bāhila* possessed a higher import was echoed in a news article by an al-Jāsir supporter, who considered that the book was not simply a defense of one tribe, but "a defense of Arab history and the realities of the histories of the tribes of the Arabian Peninsula." ʿAbd al-ʿAzīz al-Sunayd, "Karramu ʿAllāmatna al-Shaykh Ḥamad al-Jāsir fī Ḥayātihi," *al-Masāʾiyya*, November 5, 1992, Supplement, 26.
71. "Maqṭaʿ Muʾaththir li-l-Shaykh ʿAlī al-Ṭanṭāwī," *YouTube*, www.youtube.com/watch?v=CDkwTFid5cU.
72. al-Jāsir, *Bāhila*, 718.
73. *Bayān Nasab Āl ʿĪsā b. ʿAlī b. ʿAṭiyya*, ms. Riyadh, Dārat al-Malik ʿAbd al-ʿAzīz, ʿAbd al-Raḥmān al-ʿĪsā/24. The document is a copy made by Ibn ʿĪsā's student Muḥammad al-Bayz.
74. Amélie Le Renard, *Femmes et espaces publics en Arabie Saoudite* (Paris: Dalloz, 2011); Madawi al-Rasheed, *A Most Masculine State: Gender, Politics, and Religion in Saudi Arabia* (Cambridge: Cambridge University Press, 2013).
75. *Shajarat Nasab Āl ʿĪsā b. ʿAlī b. ʿAṭiyya*, ms. Riyadh, Dārat al-Malik ʿAbd al-ʿAzīz, ʿAbd al-Raḥmān al-ʿĪsā/23.
76. Similarly, while the names of the women of al-Ghāṭ are mentioned in the al-Ghāṭ documents—as witnesses, sellers/purchasers of land, or inheritors/bequeathers—they are absent from modern al-Ghāṭ family trees.
77. al-Rasheed, *Masculine State*, 254–55.
78. An example is the institution of the *mahr* or dower.
79. The recent Saudi film *Wadjda*, the first by a female director, comments poignantly on this phenomenon.
80. An exception would be elite or ruling lineages. For more on this point, see Gabriele vom Bruck, "Names as Bodily Signs," in *Anthropology of Names*, 225–50.
81. This issue had a place in the Bāhila controversy, Bāhila being originally the name of a woman. In his volume, al-Jāsir dismissed chauvinistic interpretations of Bāhila's origins by calling attention to the many ancient Arab tribes (and modern bedouin allies of the Āl Saʿūd) who were known to descend from a woman or whose names took an Arabic feminine form. al-Jāsir, *Bāhila*, 45–47.
82. For more on this case, see Samin, "*Kafāʾa fī l-Nasab*."
83. Her father was a Hijazi *sharīf*, and though he had divorced her Najdi mother and returned to the Hijaz without his daughter, this made her a *sharīf* as well. The ruler of Mecca at the time, ʿAwn al-Rafīq, held a group of Najdi pilgrims hostage until his demands for her divorce from her Najdi husband and return

to the guardianship of her father were met. Ḥamad al-Jāsir, "Ayyām fī Baʿḍ Bilād al-Shām," *al-ʿArab* 15, no. 3/4 (1980): 171.

CHAPTER FIVE. PARALLEL MIGRATIONS, DIVERGENT DESTINATIONS

1. Ḥasan al-Nuʿaymī is an invented name created to disguise the identities of the al-ʿUlā families who claim him as their ancestor. The names and personal details of these families have also been modified accordingly.
2. ʿĀtiq al-Bilādī, *Nasab Ḥarb: Qabīlat Ḥarb, Ansābuhā, Furūʿuhā, Tārīkhuhā wa-Diyāruhā* (Mecca: Dār Makka, 1984), 263–67; ʿUsaylān, *Ḥamad al-Jāsir wa-Juhūduhu.*
3. Al-Bilādī's *Nasab Ḥarb*, for example, is largely silent about the connection of the people of al-ʿUlā to the Ḥarb tribe. For one exception, see al-Bilādī, *Nasab Ḥarb*, 91.
4. ʿAbdallāh b. Ādām Ṣāliḥ Naṣīf, *al-ʿUlā: Dirāsa fī l-Turāth al-Ḥaḍārī wa-l-Ijtimāʿī* (Riyadh: ʿAbdallāh Naṣīf, 1995), 46.
5. Charles Doughty, *Travels in Arabia Deserta* (New York: Random House, 1936), 194; Jaussen and Savignac, *Mission archéologique*, vol. 2, 44.
6. Another ʿAnaza branch, the Walad ʿAlī, were also present south of al-ʿUlā.
7. For the motive behind this rebellion, see Kostiner, *Making of Saudi Arabia*, 161.
8. The first month of the Islamic calendar is Muḥarram, during which the holiday of ʿAshūra is celebrated. The identification of Muḥarram with ʿAshūra in the al-ʿUlā region is perhaps a legacy of the lasting influence of the Zaydī Shia theological views of the Ashrāf rulers of Medina and Mecca, ʿAshūra being principally a Shia holiday. For Shiʿism and the Ashrāf of the holy cities, see Richard Mortel, "Zaydi Shiism and the Hasanid Sharifs of Mecca," *International Journal of Middle East Studies* 19, no. 4 (1987): 455–72.
9. Uncataloged document from the collection of Muḥammad b. Ḥamad b. Khulayṣ al-Ḥarbī, al-ʿUlā; Jaussen and Savignac, *Mission archéologique*, supplement to vol. 2, 63.
10. Charles Huber, *Voyage dans l'Arabie centrale* (Paris: 1884–85), 522, 530.
11. Jaussen and Savignac, *Mission archéologique*, vol. 2, 30, n. 2.
12. Zabn b. Maʿzī b. Ṣāliḥ al-ʿAnazī, *Muʿjam wa-Tārīkh al-Qurā fī Wādī al-Qurā* (Riyadh: Zabn al-ʿAnazī, 1996), 217. According to the author, when Tabūk governor Fahd b. Sulṭān b. ʿAbd al-ʿAzīz heard this story, he ordered that the man be sent an annual monetary gift.
13. For more on the tale of Thamūd, see Jaroslav Stetkevych, *Muḥammad and the Golden Bough: Reconstructing Arabian Myth* (Bloomington: Indiana University Press, 2000).
14. The best known of these Traditions is "*Lā tadkhulū ʿalā hāʾulāʾ al-qawm, illā an takūnū bākīn*" ("Do not enter that nation's abode unless you are crying [tears of anguish]"). Muḥammad b. Rizq b. al-Ṭarhūnī, *al-Ṣayḥa al-Ḥazīna fī*

l-Balad al-Laʿīna: Risāla fī Ḥukm Ziyārat Madāʾin Ṣāliḥ wa-mā Shābahahā. (Dammam: Dār Ibn al-Qayyim, 1987), 14–15.

15. Interview with al-ʿUlā teacher, December 2011, al-ʿUlā.
16. After the 1930s, Kostiner observes, "the northern rural region of the Hijaz became a neglected and deprived area." Kostiner, *Making of Saudi Arabia*, 155, 173.
17. Wallin, *Travels in Arabia*, 126; Jaussen and Savignac, *Mission archéologique*, supplement to vol. 2, 7.
18. For an example of bedouin disturbance of the al-ʿUlā town economy in the early Saudi state period, see (191)—August 30, 1938, IPA Archive, Riyadh.
19. Zabn al-ʿAnazī, *Muʿjam al-Qurā*, 73.
20. Ibid., 75–77.
21. As Kostiner notes, in 1920, the ʿAnaza branches of the Madāʾin Ṣāliḥ region made common cause with the alliance of local Arabian leaders who opposed the expansion of Saudi rule. Kostiner, *Making of Saudi Arabia*, 47–48.
22. Ṣāliḥ b. Aḥmad ʿAbd al-Raḥmān al-Imām, *Tārīkh Wādī al-Qurā*, vol. 2 (Riyadh: Maṭābiʿ al-ʿUlā, 2000), 162–63.
23. Ḥarb historian ʿĀtiq al-Bilādī described vast territories of Ḥarb tribesmen cleared of their inhabitants in the post-World War Two period, as bedouin migration transformed Medina from a heterogeneous ethnic enclave into "Ḥarb's city." al-Bilādī, *Nasab Ḥarb*, 37–39; Yizraeli, *Politics and Society in Saudi Arabia*, 166.
24. ʿAbdallāh Muḥammad al-Ghadhdhāmī, *al-Qabīla wa-l-Qabāʾiliyya, aw Huwīyāt mā baʿda al-Ḥadātha* (Casablanca: al-Markaz al-Thaqāfī al-ʿArabī, 2009).
25. Interview with al-ʿUlā teacher, December 2011, al-ʿUlā.
26. "The Alowna are noted, by the Aarab [i.e., the bedouin], to be of tyrannical humour within their own palms, and faint hearts in the field," Doughty, *Travels*, 181; see also Naṣīf, *al-ʿUlā*, 74.
27. Visiting a number of northern Saudi villages, Sowayan noted how their inhabitants affiliated lineally with the dominant bedouin tribe of the area (Shammar), a residue of the time when Shammar exerted control over these settlements and extracted their surpluses in exchange for protection. It is interesting therefore that many people in al-ʿUlā claim origins from Ḥarb, as ʿAnaza and Balī and not Ḥarb are the dominant tribes in the al-ʿUlā area. Sowayan, *al-Ṣaḥrā al-ʿArabiyya*, 358.
28. Doughty, *Travels*, 181.
29. Interview with Mushayliḥ al-Blūwwī and Mālik Āl Ḥasan, March 2011, al-ʿUlā.
30. For example, the document implied that the al-ʿUlā branches might qualify to receive shares of inheritances from deceased members of the Slifa, or might be asked to contribute to blood payments involving members of the Slifa.
31. The rest house, *istirāḥa*, or *shabba*—as it is known in northern Saudi Arabia—is, among most adult Saudis, the primary venue for socializing. Saudi friends

and relatives often join together to rent an *istirāḥā*, where they can gather on a nightly or weekly basis for conversation (*sālifa*) and entertainment.

32. Naṣīf, *al-ʿUlā*, 74. ʿAwda's friends belonged to a number of different ʿAlāwna families.
33. Huber, *Voyage*, 518. Huber's observation reflected the cutting edge of European racial thought. His primary field guide was a set of general instructions for field investigation issued by the *Société d'anthropologie de Paris*, whose skin tone chart he used to estimate the hues of the town's inhabitants.
34. Wallin, *Travels in Arabia*, 115–16; Jaussen and Savignac, *Mission archéologique*, supplement to vol. 2, 34. Northwest Arabian bedouin communities also included members of African origin, both individuals linked to larger bedouin clans (sometimes in positions of leadership) and entire groups. Yet intermarriage was not permitted between these two segments of the bedouin population. Muḥammad al-ʿAbīd, a deputy leader of the Fuqarā bedouin who escorted the French travelers' Jaussen and Savignac during part of their archaeological expedition in northwest Arabia (1909–1910), was prohibited from marrying himself or his children into the tribe on account of his African ancestry.
35. The *qahwā* was a large interior room inside a family patriarch's home. After al-ʿUlā was absorbed into the Saudi state, the political function of the *qāhāwī* declined, and they were sometimes used as primary schools. For more on the *qahāwī*, see Ibrāhīm Salmān al-Maḥfūẓ, *Maqāhī al-ʿAshāʾir fī l-ʿUlā bi-Minṭaqat al-Madīna al-Munawwara* (Jeddah: Ibrāhīm al-Maḥfūẓ, 2001).
36. For textual evidence of this desired shift away from toponymic affiliation in al-ʿUlā, see Muḥammad b. Ḥamad Khulayṣ al-Ḥarbī's biography of his father. In the appendix, the author includes a 1971 Saudi Interior Ministry document (relating to his father's retirement from military service) in which his father's *nisba* is listed as al-ʿAlāwī, after the town of al-ʿUlā. The author has of course abandoned this *nisba* in favor of al-Ḥarbī. Muḥammad b. Ḥamad Khulayṣ al-Ḥarbī, *Hādhā l-Rajul* (Mecca: Muḥammad al-Ḥarbī, 2007), 305–8.
37. Interview with doctor of Ḥarb origin, January 2012, Riyadh.
38. The abolition of slavery constituted Article 10 of King Fayṣal's 1962 Ten Point Program. Approximately $1.25 million dollars was allocated to former slave-owners as compensation. Yizraeli, *Politics and Society in Saudi Arabia*, 112.
39. Wallin reported that some of the manumitted slaves and deserters from Muhammad Ali's army later served in the bodyguard of Ḥāʾil ruler ʿAbdallāh b. Rashīd, and would play an important role in consolidating Rashidi rule. Al-Rasheed, *Politics in an Arabian Oasis*, 130, 136.
40. Emad Ahmed Helal, "Muhammad Ali's First Army: The Experiment in Building an Entirely Slave Army," in *Race and Slavery in the Middle East: Histories of Trans-Saharan Africans in Nineteenth-Century Egypt, Sudan, and the Ottoman Mediterranean*, ed. Terence Walz and Kenneth M. Cuno (Cairo: American University in Cairo Press, 2010), 36; for the history of this Ottoman campaign, see Winder, *Saudi Arabia in the Nineteenth Century*.

41. Anita L. P. Burdett, ed., *The Slave Trade Into Arabia: 1820–1973*, vol. 2 (Slough: Archive Editions, 2006), 161–64; for the broader context of this prohibition, see Ehud R. Toledano, *Slavery and Abolition in the Ottoman Middle East* (Seattle: University of Washington Press, 1998), 10–11.
42. Possibly as a result of pressure from the British, the Pasha of Jeddah was asked the following year by Istanbul to take measures to curtail the importation of slaves into the Hijaz; despite this, the trade went largely uninterrupted. *Slave Trade*, vol. 2, 166.
43. *Slave Trade*, vol. 5, 547.
44. ʿAbd al-ʿĀlim ʿAbd al-Wahhāb Abū Haykal, "al-Raqīq al-Afrīqī bi-l-Ḥijāz khilāl al-Niṣf al-Awwal min al-Qarn al-ʿIshrīn," *al-Majalla al-Tārīkhiyya al-Miṣriyya* 36 (1989): 327–28.
45. *Slave Trade*, vol. 3, 455–56, 659, 720.
46. Pilgrim brokers would play a role in the deception, the document relates. *Slave Trade*, vol. 5, 599–600, 667.
47. Ibid., 563.
48. Ibid., 721.
49. Abū Haykal, "al-Raqīq al-Afrīqī bi-l-Ḥijāz," 338–40.
50. Interview with ʿAbdallāh b. Ḥākim Āl Ḥasan, December 2011, al-ʿUlā.
51. For more on the meaning of slavery in post-emancipation Saudi Arabia (c. 1972–3), see William Lancaster, *The Rwala Bedouin Today* (Cambridge: Cambridge University Press, 1981), 12–13.
52. Abū Haykal, "al-Raqīq al-Afrīqī bi-l-Ḥijāz," 338–39.
53. Engseng Ho, "Hadhramis Abroad in Hadhramaut: The *Muwalladīn*," in *Hadhrami Traders, Scholars, and Statesmen in the Indian Ocean, 1750s–1960s*, ed. Ulrike Freitag and William G. Clarence-Smith (Leiden: Brill, 1997), 131–146.
54. Wallin, *Travels in Arabia*, 135. Wallin did not visit the town, but transmitted information from his local informants and guides.
55. *Slave Trade*, vol. 2, 390.
56. It is likely that the elite of al-ʿUlā also owned slaves. One marriage contract described to me by a town resident required as part of the bride's dower (*mahr*) that she be furnished with a servant.
57. Huber, *Voyage*, 518; see also ibid., n. 1.
58. Author interview, January 2012, Riyadh.
59. Interview with Mushayliḥ al-Blūwwī and Mālik Āl Ḥasan, March 2011, al-ʿUlā.
60. Ḥamad al-Jāsir, "Riḥlatun ilā Bilād al-ʿUlā," *al-ʿArab* 12, no. 3/4 (1977): 161–85.
61. (2/670)—Outgoing, April 26, 1996, Maktabat al-ʿArab, Riyadh.
62. The author requested al-Jāsir's authentication "despite our certainty about our deep-rooted history."
63. (384)—Incoming and Outgoing, March 11, 1999, Maktabat al-ʿArab, Riyadh.
64. As al-Rasheed notes, the shaykhs of the neighboring Shammar tribe also

owned land in northwest Arabia's oases and sometimes employed slave labor to cultivate it. al-Rasheed, *Politics in an Arabian Oasis*, 76, 96.

65. Ḥamad al-Jāsir, *Fī Shimāl Gharb al-Jazīra* (Riyadh: Dār al-Yamāma li-l-Baḥth wa-l-Tarjama wa-l-Nashr, 1970), 290.
66. (374)—Incoming March 9, 1999, Maktabat al-ʿArab, Riyadh. The letter also disputes al-Jāsir's insistence that the ʿAnaza bedouin were the owners of the Khaybar oasis's date plantations. Al-Jāsir's depiction is contradicted further in the detailed and nuanced account provided by Doughty. See Doughty, *Travels*, 133–35. The history of land ownership in al-ʿUlā and other Hijazi oases and its influence on modern bedouin-sedentary relations is an important subject, and requires further study.
67. Muḥammad Ḥamad Khulayṣ al-Ḥarbī, a native of al-ʿUlā, complains about the unwillingness of al-ʿUlā families to share their *qawāʿid al-ansāb*. Muḥammad al-Ḥarbī, *Riḥla ilā Wādī al-Qurā* (Mecca: Muḥammad Ḥamad Khulayṣ al-Ḥarbi, 2006), 118; other prominent members of the Ḥarb tribe, historians among them, believe the very existence of these *qawāʿid* to be a fiction. For an example of this view, see: "Liqāʾ Ṣāḥīfat al-Madīna bi-Muʾarrikh Ḥarb," *Multaqā Qabīlat Ḥarb al-Rasmī*, www.m-harb.net/vb/showthread.php?t=80596.
68. Naṣīf, *al-ʿUlā*, 73–75.
69. Interview with Ḥākim Āl Ḥasan, December 2011, al-ʿUlā.
70. Roger S. Bagnall, *The Oxford Handbook of Papyrology* (Oxford: Oxford University Press, 2009), 453.
71. Vom Bruck and Bodenhorn, *Anthropology of Names*, 10.
72. Ibid., 4.
73. ʿAbdallāh ʿUsaylān, a former member of the Majlis al-Shūrā from Medina who is also of Ḥarb origin, lists al-Jāsir's *nisba* as al-Ḥarbī, a formulation al-Jāsir never used during his own lifetime. ʿUsaylān, *Ḥamad al-Jāsir wa-Juhūduhu*, 13.
74. Fāyiz b. Mūsā al-Badrānī, ed., *Mulāḥaẓāt ʿalā l-Muʾallifīn wa-l-Kuttāb ḥawl al-Tārīkh wa-l-Ansāb* (Riyadh: Dār al-Badrānī, 1996).
75. Burckhardt, *Notes on the Bedouins*, vol. 2 (London: H. Colburn and R. Bentley, 1831), 31.
76. Like most Arabian tribes, elements of Ḥarb migrated outside of the Arabian Peninsula. The famous al-Ẓawāhirī family of Cairo, for example, are noted by al-Bilādī to descend from Ḥarb. al-Bilādī, *Nasab Ḥarb*, 37.
77. After migrating to the urban centers of the Hijaz in the twentieth century, Ḥarbīs were said to have monopolized the auto repair industry in Mecca and Medina. Ibid., 38.
78. Burckhardt, *Notes on the Bedouins*, vol. 2, 32.
79. By contrast to the approach of most Ḥarb historians, a recent study by a member of the Nakhāwila Shia community of Medina calls explicit attention to the sectarian dimension of local history, drawing on Burckhardt's observa-

tions to argue that the Ḥarb landowners of Medina and the Nakhāwila farmers they "protected" were likely to have shared a common Shia sectarian identity. Ḥasan b. Marzūq al-Nakhlī, *al-Nakhāwila (al-Nakhlīyūn) fī l-Madīna al-Munawwara: al-Takwīn al-Ijtimāʿī wa-l-Thaqāfī* (Beirut: Muʾassasat al-Intishār al-ʿArabī, 2012), 70–71. I thank Werner Ende for this reference.

80. Al-ʿAwālī, now a neighborhood in the southern part of Medina, was previously a village inhabited by Shia. Werner Ende, "Pilgerfahrt und Glaubensstreit. Die 'Zehn Argumentationen' des Sayyid ʿAbdallāh Shirāzī," in *Fremde, Feinde Und Kurioses: Innen- Und Au Enansichten Unseres Muslimischen*, ed. Benjamin Jokisch, Ulrich Rebstock et al. (Berlin: Walter de Gruyter, 2009), 335.
81. Werner Ende, "The Nakhawila, a Shiite Community in Medina Past and Present," *Die Welt des Islams* 37, no. 3 (1997): 272–79.
82. Kostiner, *Making of Saudi Arabia*, 135.
83. Commins, *Wahhabi Mission*, 79.
84. Ḥamad al-Jāsir, "Banū Ḥarb wa-Ṣilatuhum bi-Wulāt al-Madīna,"in *Mulāḥaẓāt ʿalā l-Muʾallifīn*, 136.
85. Ḥarb historian Fāyiz al-Badrānī's numerous studies of the tribe similarly focus on Ḥarb's historical loyalty to the Āl Saʿūd. According to Ḥarb oral tradition, al-Badrānī writes, after the Ottoman destruction of the first Saudi state (1818), Ḥarb tribal leaders were brought as captives to Cairo and executed there along with members of the Āl Saʿūd and Āl al-Shaykh. These leaders had made a last stand with the Saudis in defense of their capital al-Dirʿiyya, he writes, thus proving their faithfulness to "their state and land during the most trying stages of the conflict, at a time when many of the leaders of other tribes had abandoned their posts and switched from the ranks of the Āl Saʿūd to the ranks of their enemies." Fāyiz al-Badrānī, *Fuṣūl min Tārīkh Qabīlat Ḥarb fī l-Ḥijāz wa-Najd* (Riyadh: Dār al-Badrānī, 1996), 366–68.
86. al-Bilādī, *Nasab Ḥarb*, 165–66; al-Badrānī, *Fuṣūl*, 248–51.
87. Philby, *Heart of Arabia*, vol. 1, 258.
88. They were settled at strategic remove from Medina, the base for their natural constituency, it would seem. For another strategic resettlement of bedouin populations by Ibn Saʿūd, see Philby, *Heart of Arabia*, vol. 1, 137.
89. al-Juhany, *Salafi Reform Movement*, 62–65.
90. al-Bilādī, *Nasab Ḥarb*, 103.
91. Ibid., 8.
92. al-Jāsir, *Baldat al-Burūd*, 15–16.
93. Al-Burūd is also in range of two other historically significant *hujar*, ʿArwā and Arṭāwiyya.
94. al-Jāsir, *Baldat al-Burūd*, 169. Al-Jāsir states that the *khuwwā* payment was intermittent, reflecting the generally harmonious relations between the people of al-Burūd and the surrounding bedouin.
95. Ibn Ghannām, *Tārīkh Najd*, 176.
96. Ibn Bishr, *ʿUnwān al-Majd*, vol. 1, 173–74.

97. George Rentz, "Hutaym," *Encyclopaedia of Islam, Second Edition*, ed. P. Bearman, Th. Bianquis et al. (Brill Online, 2013); Musil, *Manners and Customs*, 136.
98. al-Bilādī, *Nasab Ḥarb*, 165–66; al-Badrānī, *Fuṣūl*, 248–49.
99. al-Jāsir, *al-Burūd*, 205–7.
100. Ibn ʿĪsā, *Tārīkh Baʿḍ al-Ḥawādith*, 94.
101. al-Jāsir, *al-Burūd*, 163, n. 1.
102. al-Jāsir, *al-Burūd*, 187.
103. Ibid., 208.
104. (629) Outgoing—June 14, 1999, Maktabat al-ʿArab, Riyadh.
105. (27) Outgoing—November 1, 1998, Maktabat al-ʿArab, Riyadh.
106. In a reply to a 1989 article in *al-ʿArab* concerning the Banū Rashīd, al-Jāsir criticized the author for considering that the name Banū Rashīd was a recent invention with no actual provenance. Banū Rashid was the correct name for the tribe, he argued, as it is the name recognized and used by the tribe itself. Ḥamad al-Jāsir, "Banū Rashīd Laysū Hutayman," *al-ʿArab* 24, no. 3/4 (1989): 272–74.
107. By contrast with most other al-Sirr families mentioned in the volume, al-Jāsir is silent on the question of this family's marital relations with other area families.
108. al-Jāsir, *al-Burūd*, 390–2.
109. Ibid., 439–40.
110. Al-Badrānī, however, rejected al-Jāsir's interpretation of the documents and their presumed relevance for the scholar's family history. Fāyiz al-Badrānī, *Baʿḍ al-Aʿyān wa-Aʿlām al-Qabāʾil fī Wathāʾiq al-Maḥkama al-Sharʿiyya bi-l-Madīna al-Munawwara* (Kuwait: Fāyiz b. Mūsā al-Badrānī al-Ḥarbī, 2002), 683.
111. al-Jāsir, *al-Burūd*, 410.
112. Interview with al-ʿUlā historian, December 2011, al-ʿUlā.

CHAPTER SIX. TOWARD A GENEALOGICAL RULE OF GOVERNANCE

1. "The Boundary between Saudi Arabia and the Shaikhdoms of Qatar and Abu Dhabi and the Sultanate of Muscat and Oman: A Summary of the History of the Dispute Together with a Statement of the Evidence in Support of the Claims of Qatar, Abu Dhabi and Muscat." Jane Priestland, ed., *The Buraimi Dispute: Contemporary Documents*, vol. 1 (Cambridge: Archive Editions, 1992), 625.
2. (2/1445)—Outgoing, February 22, 1994, Maktabat al-ʿArab, Riyadh.
3. For more on Shryock's influential concept, consult his *Nationalism and the Genealogical Imagination*.
4. Wahba, *Arabian Days*; Habib, *Ibn Saʿud's Warriors*; Kostiner, *Making of Saudi Arabia*.
5. Vitalis, *America's Kingdom*; Steffen Hertog, *Princes, Brokers, and Bureaucrats: Oil and the State in Saudi Arabia* (Ithaca: Cornell University Press, 2010); Yizraeli, *Politics and Society in Saudi Arabia*.

6. al-Rasheed, *History of Saudi Arabia*, 84.
7. This is the Ibn Rifāda revolt. See Kostiner, *Making of Saudi Arabia*, 163.
8. (04/5942)—August 23, 1938, IPA Archive, Riyadh.
9. (No number)—June 25, 1935, IPA Archive, Riyadh. For a similar case that explicitly concerns taxation, see (11/6344)—February 14, 1939, IPA Archive, Riyadh.
10. (04/5747)—June 22, 1938, IPA Archive, Riyadh.
11. The Majlis al-Shūrā of the early twentieth century was comprised of thirteen Hijazi notables appointed by the Hijaz governor, Ibn Saʿūd's son Fayṣal b. ʿAbd al-ʿAzīz. The Majlis's role was to advise Fayṣal on affairs of state. Kostiner, *Making of Saudi Arabia*, 101.
12. (04/49411)—December 6, 1938, IPA Archive, Riyadh.
13. William Ochsenwald, *Religion, Society, and the State in Arabia: The Hijaz under Ottoman Control, 1840–1908* (Columbus: Ohio State University Press, 1984), 212.
14. The term *tābiʿiyya* derived from the word *tābiʿ* or follower. It could also have religious connotations, as in a follower of an imam or religious leader/commander. See Lane, *Arabic-English Lexicon*, 295–96.
15. Gianluca P. Parolin, *Citizenship in the Arab World: Kin, Religion, and Nation-State* (Amsterdam: University of Amsterdam Press, 2009), 24.
16. (11/572)—November 15, 1927; (11/648)—January 11, 1928, IPA Archive, Riyadh.
17. A 1938 decree exempted holders of a Saudi *tābiʿiyya* from the Ottoman-era *Kawshān* transit tax. (09/52110)—January 6, 1938, IPA Archive, Riyadh.
18. This rule applied as long as they held only Saudi citizenship papers. (04/3671)—March 18, 1934, IPA Archive, Riyadh.
19. (04/3499)—September 21, 1933, IPA Archive, Riyadh.
20. For example, as a condition for selling property. (04/3097)—December 5, 1932; (04/3671)—March 18, 1934, IPA Archive, Riyadh.
21. (11/5822)—July 4, 1938, IPA Archive, Riyadh.
22. In the more heterogeneous Hijazi towns, the authentication of documents and testimonials was performed by district representatives, or *ʿummād* (sing. *ʿumda*). (11/6631)—June 29, 1938, IPA Archive, Riyadh.
23. (04/13388)—June 7, 1961, IPA Archive, Riyadh.
24. Ibn Saʿūd allowed his provinces to be governed as semi-autonomous fiefdoms, a policy echoed in his 1930 upbraiding of the defeated Ikhwān leader Fayṣal al-Dawīsh: "Did you want to be King? But each of you were kings in the areas over which you were stationed." Habib, *Ibn Saʿud's Warriors*, 151.
25. Al-Aḥsāʾ was exempted as well. (02/10295)—May 27, 1947, IPA Archive, Riyadh.
26. Saʿūd al-Muṭayrī, "al-Tābiʿiyya: al-Jahl Yuwaththiq al-Tārīkh!" *al-Riyāḍ*, December 24, 2010.
27. *Buraimi Dispute*, vol. 1, 586–87.
28. For further discussion of this point, see Abdel Razzaq Takriti, *Monsoon Revolu-*

tion: Republicans, Sultans, and Empires in Oman, 1965–1976 (Oxford: Oxford University Press, 2013), 15.

29. Kostiner argues that it was his rival Ibn Rashīd's recognition of Ibn Saʿūd's authority over disputed tribes such as ʿUtayba, ʿAjmān, and Ḥarb that paved the way for the Saudi ruler's subsequent conquest of Arabia. Kostiner, *Making of Saudi Arabia*, 30.
30. In fact, by that point, Ibn Saʿūd had acquired lengthy experience in border negotiations with European and regional powers, and had entrusted his interests in these matters to a coterie of Westernized Arab advisors such as Fuʾād Ḥamza and Yūsuf Yasīn, as well as British and American sympathizers such as St. John (ʿAbdallāh) Philby and Aramco's George Rentz. For background, see Gary Troeller, *The Birth of Saudi Arabia: Britain and the Rise of the House of Saʿud* (Oxon: Routledge, 2013), 159–88.
31. *Buraimi Dispute*, vol. 1, 586. British officialdom's embrace of the tribal and genealogical dimension of the Buraymī dispute well into the 1950s belies Wilkinson's opposing claim. J. C. Wilkinson, "Nomadic Territory as a Factor in Defining Arabia's Boundaries," in *The Transformation of Nomadic Society in the Arab East*, ed. Martha Mundy and Basim Musallam (Cambridge: Cambridge University Press, 2000), 61.
32. As early as 1937, the Saudis had been working with American surveyors from Aramco to assess the maximal extent of their tribal supporters in the southeast. Wilkinson, "Nomadic Territory," 55.
33. William Mulligan to William Burleigh, "Meeting with Yusuf Yasin," April 29, 1954. Box 2, Folder 31, Mulligan Papers, Georgetown University.
34. Ibn Saʿūd later sent Rentz and other advisors to Jeddah and London to negotiate with the British government over Buraymī. "Arabian Research Division Fourth Quarterly Report," January 9, 1954. Box 2, Folder 31, Mulligan Papers, Georgetown University.
35. *Buraimi Dispute*, vol. 1, 588. The first four tribes listed inhabited territories more widely recognized to be under Saudi control.
36. It is telling that Aramco researchers included Līwā in a volume titled "The Eastern Reaches of al-Ḥāsa Province," al-Ḥāsa being the easternmost region of Saudi Arabia. *Aramco Reports on al-Hasa and Oman: 1950–1955*, vol. 1 (Cambridge: Archive Edition, 1990).
37. The current ruling family of Abu Dhabi, the Āl Nahyān, belong to the Al Bū Falāḥ.
38. *Aramco Reports on al-Hasa*, vol. 1, 1, 9, 10, 100. The denial of the Banī Yās's legitimacy extended to other aspects of the report as well. For example, while Aramco's Manāṣīr informants were praised, the knowledge and capacity of the research division's sole Banī Yās informant was repeatedly minimized. In addition, the report's authors adopt al-Jiwa (*Yiwa*) as the standard spelling for Līwā, the former being the Manāṣīr convention, the latter that of the Banī Yās.
39. The Manāṣīr's abundant presence in "al-Jiwa," Rentz concluded, "entitles them to be regarded as the predominant tribe" in the broader region. *Aramco Re-*

ports, vol. 1, 100. British records suggest that the Manāṣīr were already in the process of being lost to the Saudis due to Shaykh Shakhbūt of Abu Dhabi's unpopularity. Alan Rush, ed., *Ruling Families of Arabia: The United Arab Emirates* (Slough: Archive Editions, 1991), 169.

40. In a report meant for private consumption, Aramco researchers seemed to have less qualms about viewing the Banī Yās as one of a number of tribes that "roamed" around the vicinity of Buraymī and parts further north. "Saudi Arabian Boundary Proposal of 1949," Box 2, Folder 15, Mulligan Papers, Georgetown University.
41. Vitalis, *America's Kingdom*, 108–11.
42. *Buraimi Dispute*, vol. 1, 607.
43. Ibid., 586.
44. Ibid., 590.
45. *Aramco Reports*, vol. 1, 39–44. Several villages had mixed inhabitants.
46. The British felt that Rentz had greatly overstated the number of permanent dwelling structures in the oasis.
47. *Buraimi Dispute*, vol. 1, 625.
48. Ibid., 630.
49. The rulers of Abu Dhabi claimed to originate from the neighboring oasis of Līwā, and had often counted on the support of allied tribal groups from the Buraymī area. Christopher Davidson, *Abu Dhabi: Oil and Beyond* (New York: Columbia University Press, 2009), 5.
50. Pushing a Wahhabi line, the Saudis denied that tributes paid historically by the Banī Yās inhabitants of Līwā to the Āl Nahyān ruling family in Abu Dhabi constituted *zakāt*, claiming instead that they were merely gifts. *Aramco Reports*, vol. 1, 105; Wilkinson, "Nomadic Territory," 59. Wilkinson seems to concur with the Saudi interpretation.
51. Once arrived, Ibn ʿUṭayshān distributed Saudi *tābiʿiyya* papers to any tribesman who would accept them. Within two months of his arrival he had reportedly handed out 900 such documents. *Buraimi Dispute*, vol. 1, 747–49; for similar developments in more recent decades near the Saudi border with Hadramawt, see Ho, *Graves of Tarim*, p. 15.
52. Ibid., 743–44.
53. Davidson, *Abu Dhabi*, 40.
54. Aramco's Arabian Research Division produced the intelligence that identified the third local leader, ʿUbayd b. Jumʿa of the Banī Kaʿb, as a candidate for cultivation by the Āl Saʿūd at that moment. "Saudi Arabian Boundary Proposal of 1949," Box 2, Folder 15, Mulligan Papers, Georgetown University.
55. *Aramco Reports*, vol. 4, 135–36.
56. ". . . the main numerical strength of the Bani Yas derives from the Dhawahir, a division whose connections with the tribe are somewhat tenuous," Ibid., 148, 150–51, 174.
57. Buraymī is on the far right center of the map. In Līwā as well (al-Jiwa on the map), the Banī Yās appear surrounded by Manāṣīr.

58. The Omani dimension of the Buraymī dispute, while not discussed here, is significant. As Takriti explains, the October 1955 British push into Buraymī was part of a larger takeover of Imamate territories that followed on the heels of the accession of a new Omani Imam, the pro-Saudi Ghālib b. Hināʾī (d. 2009). Takriti, *Monsoon Revolution*, 23; Wilkinson, "Nomadic Territory," 61.
59. The three local leaders were ʿUbayd b. Jumʿa, Saqr b. Sulṭān, and Rāshid b. Ḥamad. The last two belonged to Nuʿaym, a tribe that during the nineteenth century was a frequent opponent of the Banī Yās and had made common cause with the Saudis during previous episodes of conflict. Davidson, *Abu Dhabi*, 119.
60. *Buraimi Dispute*, vol. 1, 653–57.
61. The newly conceded borderline still preserved Buraymī and most of Līwā for the rulers of Abu Dhabi, however. Alexander Mellamid, "The Buraimi Oasis Dispute," *Middle Eastern Affairs* 7, no. 2 (1956): 62.
62. *Buraimi Dispute*, vol. 1, 584–85.
63. This is notwithstanding Lorimer's ethnographic collection efforts on behalf of the British Indian government, which preceded those described here by almost half a century.
64. Al-Jāsir later published Aramco's studies of the tribes of the Eastern Province in *al-ʿArab*, with the view of "correcting what needs to be corrected" in them. "Qabīlat al-Manāṣīr: Aṣluhā wa-Furūʿuhā wa-Bilāduhā," *al-ʿArab* 4, no. 11 (1970), 1039.
65. For examples, see ibid., 656.
66. Yizraeli, *Politics and Society in Saudi Arabia*, 120.
67. This rhetoric of striving and self-improvement reflected the influence of American management-speak on the emergent Saudi elite. The influence of Aramco's corporate culture in the postwar kingdom is well documented in Vitalis, *America's Kingdom*.
68. Yizraeli, *Politics and Society in Saudi Arabia*, 113, 153–54.
69. Whereas Hertog, following Chaudhry, disputes the notion that the structure of Saudi society remained unchanged during the first decades of the oil era, he affirms Yizraeli's widely held view regarding the neat subordination of tribal structures and tribal authority by the centralizing Saudi state. Hertog, *Princes, Brokers, and Bureaucrats*, 17, 80.
70. By 1968, bedouin and other rural migrants comprised over fifty percent of the urban population of Riyadh. Pascal Menoret, *Joyriding in Riyadh: Oil, Urbanism, and Road Revolt* (Cambridge: Cambridge University Press, 2014), 83.
71. Ibid., 86.
72. al-Jāsir, "al-Bādiya: ʿIrḍ wa-Amal," 7; the same is true, though to a lesser extent, of John Habib, whose valuable book on the Ikhwān movement nonetheless contains a number of typographical and factual errors.
73. (20/1381)—October 30, 1961, IPA Archive, Riyadh; Saudi welfare rolls would later be expanded dramatically, no less so than in the wake of the Arab Spring uprisings of 2011.

74. Ugo Fabietti, "State Policies and Bedouin Adaptations," in *Transformation of Nomadic Society*, 84.
75. Hertog, *Princes, Brokers, and Bureaucrats*, 52.
76. *Aramco Reports*, vol. 2, 101; at the symbolic level, lineal association with the royal family became a point of pride for tribes such as Dawāsir and ʿAnaza, both of whom claimed genealogical connections to the Āl Saʿūd. al-Jāsir, *Jamharat Ansāb*, First Ed., 68–70; al-Ḥuqayl, *Kanz al-Ansāb*, 28.
77. Taha Osman M. el-Farra, "The Effects of Detribalizing the Bedouins on the Internal Cohesion of an Emerging State: The Kingdom of Saudi Arabia," (PhD diss., University of Pittsburgh, 1973), 184, n. 12.
78. Ṣunaytān, *al-Saʿūdiyya*, 90.
79. Hertog, *Princes, Brokers, and Bureaucrats*, 90.
80. (11/7472)—March 17, 1940, IPA Archive, Riyadh.
81. (01/14936)—February 16, 1963, IPA Archive, Riyadh; Hertog, *Princes, Brokers, and Bureaucrats*, 59; Madawi al-Rasheed and Loulouwa al-Rasheed, "The Politics of Encapsulation: Saudi Policy Towards Tribal and Religious Opposition," *Middle Eastern Studies* 32, no. 1 (1996): 104. Al-Rasheed discusses the case of the descendants of the defeated Rashidi opponents of the Āl Saʿūd, who were paid modest monthly salaries designed to limit their ability to entertain large numbers of guests and supporters in the manner of the Āl Saʿūd or other more loyal tribal shaykhs.
82. Ibid., 105.
83. Scott, *Seeing Like a State*, 65.
84. Kiren Aziz Chaudhry, *The Price of Wealth: Economies and Institutions in the Middle East* (Ithaca: Cornell University Press, 1997), 80.
85. Parolin, *Citizenship in the Arab World*, 89.
86. (04/13388)—June 7, 1961, IPA Archive, Riyadh; this decree seemed part of Fayṣal's effort to wrestle Ibn Jilūwwī's Eastern Province ministate away from him. See Hertog, *Princes, Brokers, and Bureaucrats*, 62; for background on how such ministates emerged in pre-oil Arabian politics, see Herb, *All in the Family*, 25.
87. Eickelman, *Middle East and Central Asia*, 126.
88. Historically, the *naqīb al-ashrāf* was the leader of the community of the Descendants of the Prophet in Egypt. The position was reestablished by Hosni Mubarak in 1991 due to changed political circumstances. Michael Winter, "The *Ashrāf* and the *Naqīb al-Ashrāf* in Ottoman Egypt and Syria: A Comparative Analysis," in *Sayyids and Sharifs in Muslim Societies: The Living Links to the Prophet*, ed. Kazuo Morimoto (London: Routledge, 2012), 139–158; Nicholas S. Hopkins, *Upper Egypt: Life Along the Nile* (Højbjerg: Moesgård Museum 2003), 74.
89. My investigation of the administrative dimension of naming practices owes its impetus to a recent study by Abdulaziz H. Al Fahad. "Rootless Trees: Genealogical Politics in Saudi Arabia," in *Saudi Arabia in Transition: Insights on Social, Political, Economic and Religious Change*, ed. Bernard Haykel,

Thomas Hegghammer et al. (Cambridge: Cambridge University Press, 2014), 263–91.

90. (11/21905)—May 26, 1969, IPA Archive, Riyadh.
91. For a discussion of the four-part name in Yemen, see Ho, *Graves of Tarim*, 142, n. 18.
92. Michel Foucault, *Discipline and Punish: The Birth of the Prison* (New York: Vintage, 1995).
93. Interview with Saad Sowayan, March 2011, Riyadh.
94. Author interview, January 2012, Riyadh.
95. Author interview, January 2012, Riyadh.
96. Author interview, January 2012, Riyadh.
97. al-Rasheed, "Politics of Encapsulation," 106.
98. When a person is killed in a car accident, for example, the Ministry of Labor and Social Affairs facilitates the payment of the *diya*, or blood money, from the party at fault to the victim's family. In one example I observed, ninety-four male members of a tribal subbranch paid 93,000 riyal (approximately $24,797) to the family of a car accident victim.
99. A conversation with a genealogy hobbyist from the Dawāsir tribe is perhaps illustrative of this preoccupation. Discussing the Saudi anthropologist Saad Sowayan and his knowledge of tribal structures, the genealogist sketched out a diagram that depicted his tribal ancestry. "Sowayan understands this," he said, pointing to the lower portion of the diagram, in which the most recent branches were represented; "and this," he said, pointing to the large tribal confederations whose histories are known popularly or from the classical Arabic genealogical texts; "but not this," he concluded, pointing to everything in the middle. Author interview, January 2011, Riyadh.
100. al-Rasheed, *Politics in an Arabian Oasis*, 10.
101. (09/52452)—February 4, 1985, IPA Archive, Riyadh.
102. (04/15975)—February 5, 1964, IPA Archive, Riyadh.
103. (04/36821)—December 28, 1978; (04/38651)—March 11, 1981, IPA Archive, Riyadh.
104. (04/38651)—March 11, 1981, IPA Archive, Riyadh.
105. As Hertog shows, every Saudi ministry was working to achieve such exemptions for itself, though the Ministry of Interior had wider latitude than most in claiming them. Hertog, *Princes, Brokers, and Bureaucrats*, 90.
106. The term *muʿarrif* is unknown in the classical Arabic lexicon, but derives from the verb *ʿarrafa*, to make something or someone known to someone else. See Lane, *Arabic–English Lexicon*, 2013.
107. Author interview, January 2012, Riyadh.
108. The *muʿarrif* is in certain respects similar to the Islamic legal institution of the *ʿadl* or professional witness, who identifies the plaintiff, the defendant, and other court attendees for the judge.
109. Ayubi, *Overstating the Arab State*, 224–55.
110. (20/1381)—October 30, 1961, IPA Archive, Riyadh.

111. (09/52884)—July 27, 1992, IPA Archive, Riyadh.
112. "30.11.1996: SAUDI ROYAL WEALTH: WHERE DO THEY GET ALL THAT MONEY?" *Aftenposten*, April 15, 2011.
113. (No number)—June 16, 2001, IPA Archive, Riyadh.
114. *al-Lajna al-Khāṣṣa Li-Ḍabṭ wa-Tawthīq Ansāb al-Ashrāf fī l-Mamlaka al-ʿArabiyya al-Saʿūdiyya.*
115. Ibn Rifāda's insurrection had been supported from Jordan by the exiled Hashemites. Kostiner, *Making of Saudi Arabia*, 160.
116. (02/5076)—June 22, 1937, IPA Archive, Riyadh.
117. Whereas many of the leading Hijazi Ashrāf families relocated to Jordan, Egypt, or India following the Saudi conquest, other Ashrāf families, such as the ʿAbdalīs, became functionaries in the emerging Saudi government.
118. (02/2519)—August 5, 1931, IPA Archive, Riyadh. Such insistence on local security and the complicity of the tribes was crucial during a period in which the Saudi government derived the majority of its revenue from fees associated with the annual pilgrimage to the holy cities of Mecca and Medina, as well as from taxes on tribal shaykhs.
119. (393)—Incoming, December 28, 1999, Maktabat al-ʿArab, Riyadh.
120. Author interview, February 2011, Jeddah. Shākir b. Hazzāʿ's son Hazzāʿ b. Shākir is the president of the Special Council.
121. *al-Idāra al-ʿĀmma li-l-Muqarrarāt wa-l-Qawāʿid.*
122. "30.11.1996:SAUDI ROYAL WEALTH"
123. (Uncataloged)—Outgoing, August 29, 1996, Maktabat al-ʿArab, Riyadh. In 1995, al-Jāsir fielded a similar query from a young woman who believed herself to descend from the Ḥasan line of the family of Muḥammad b. ʿAbd al-Wahhāb. (3/195)—Outgoing, October 16, 1995, Maktabat al-ʿArab, Riyadh.
124. (27)—Incoming and Outgoing, November 1, 1998, Maktabat al-ʿArab, Riyadh.
125. Author interview, February 2011, Jeddah; (11/5822)—July 4, 1938, IPA Archive, Riyadh.
126. Ali Mashhor al-Seflan, "The Essence of Tribal Leaders' Participation, Responsibilities, and Decisions in Some Local Government Activities in Saudi Arabia: A Case Study of the Ghamid and Zahran Tribes" (PhD diss., Claremont Graduate School, 1981), 183.
127. (04/12902)—January 22, 1961; (09/53274)—July 20, 1980; (09/49572)—May 8, 1985; (No number)—March 10, 1997; (09/51981)—November 17, 1997; (No number)—August 23, 1999, IPA Archive, Riyadh.
128. (2/857)—Incoming, May 12, 1993, Maktabat al-ʿArab, Riyadh.
129. ʿAbd al-ʿAzīz al-Khiḍr, *al-Saʿūdiyya: Sīrat Dawla wa-Mujtamaʿ* (Beirut: Arab Network for Research and Publishing, 2009), 19.
130. Herb, *All in the Family*, 7.
131. al-Rasheed, "Historical Imagination," 193.
132. A notable example, discussed in chapter three, is (10)—Incoming, June 17, 1997, Maktabat al-ʿArab, Riyadh.

133. Juhaymān al-ʿUtaybī, *Risālat al-Imāra wa-l-Bayʿa wa-l-Ṭāʿa wa-Ḥukm Talbīṣ al-Ḥukkām ʿalā Ṭalabat al-ʿIlm wa-l-ʿĀmma*, www.tawhed.ws/r?i=fcchouzr.
134. Robert Lacey, *Inside the Kingdom* (New York: Penguin, 2009), 18.
135. Nāṣir al-Ḥuzaymī, *Ayyām Maʿa Juhaymān: Kuntu Maʿa al-Jamāʿa al-Salafiyya al-Muḥtasiba* (Beirut: Arab Network for Research and Publishing, 2011), 39. The Quraysh condition was repeated in the sermon delivered by the group soon after it seized control of the Great Mosque. Ibid., 144. Juhaymān's Mahdī-designate, Muḥammad al-Qaḥṭānī, was revealed to possess the correct genealogical credentials for that office, whereas Juhaymān himself did not. For a discussion of al-Qaḥṭānī's implausible genealogy and how this cemented al-Ḥuzaymī's break from the group, see ibid., 75.
136. For details, see Hegghammer and Lacroix, "Rejectionist Islamism in Saudi Arabia," 108.
137. Herb, *All In the Family*, 27.
138. al-Rasheed, *History of Saudi Arabia*, 15–19.
139. Rāshid b. ʿAlī al-Ḥanbalī, *Muthīr al-Wajd fī Ansāb Mulūk Najd* (Riyadh: Dārat al-Malik ʿAbd al-ʿAzīz, 1979). The publication of the volume was described as "a first step" in the Dāra's mission to "preserve the country's history" and "revive its eternal heritage."
140. Ibid., 11.
141. T. E. Lawrence, *Seven Pillars of Wisdom* (Ware: Wordsworth Editions, 1991), 163.
142. Munīr al-ʿAjlānī, *Tārīkh al-Bilād al-ʿArabiyya al-Saʿūdiyya* (Beirut: Dār al-Kātib al-ʿArabī, 1966), 79, quoted in Rāshid b. ʿAlī b. Jurays al-Ḥanbalī, *Muthīr al-Wajd fī Ansāb Mulūk Najd* (Riyadh: Dārat al-Malik ʿAbd al-ʿAzīz, 1999).
143. al-Ḥuqayl, *Kanz al-Ansāb*, 28.
144. Ibn Saʿūd was said to have played up his ʿAnaza ancestry when encountering ʿAnaza tribesmen during his travels. Wahba, *Arabian Days*, 101.
145. al-Jāsir, *Jamharat Ansāb*, First Ed., 387–88.
146. For a critical and insightful analysis of this arbitrary anniversary, see al-Rasheed, "Historical Imagination."
147. *Muthīr al-Wajd* (1999), 14, 16.
148. Fāyiz al-Badrānī and Rāshid al-ʿAsākir, *Nasab Āl Saʿūd* (Riyadh: Dārat al-Malik ʿAbd al-ʿAzīz, 2012), 69. King Salmān b. ʿAbd al-ʿAzīz is the major proponent of the Banī Ḥanīfa turn in the family, having taken over this role from his uncle ʿAbdallāh b. ʿAbd al-Raḥmān.
149. Nadav Samin, "Our Ancestors, Our Heroes: Saudi Tribal Campaigns to Suppress Historical Docudramas," *British Journal of Middle East Studies* 41, no. 3 (2014): 285.
150. The cabinet is known as The Council of Ministers.
151. This as opposed to their dependency on a nonruling commercial or sedentary elite. Herb, *All in the Family*, 245–46.
152. Habib, *Ibn Saʿud's Warriors*, 154.

153. As Hertog explains, "the military was perceived as the most dangerous section of the new bureaucratic stratum," the threat of which was checked by dispersing it geographically and institutionally. Hertog, *Princes, Brokers, and Bureaucrats*, 82. So, while the National Guard has a heavy presence in Hijaz, Najd, and the Eastern Province, it has less of a permanent presence in the north and the south of the kingdom, where the Ministry of Defense's armed forces are concentrated (e.g., Tabūk, Khamīs Mushayt).
154. Yousif Makki, "Not What It Seems: The Role of the Tribe in State-Society Relations in Saudi Arabia," *Contemporary Arab Affairs* 4, no. 4 (2012): 459.
155. Author interview, January 2012, al-ʿUlā.
156. Ṣunaytān, *al-Saʿūdiyya*, 40.
157. SANG has expanded rapidly in recent years, having added at least one new active brigade to the eight already in existence. Author interview by phone, May 2013, Riyadh.
158. The other was Fayṣal al-Dawīsh of the Muṭayr tribe, whose descendants are actively involved in the Guard.
159. *al-Ḥaras al-Waṭanī*, September 2005.
160. (No number)—June 16, 2001, IPA Archive, Riyadh.
161. Author interview by phone, May 2013, Riyadh.
162. The same is not the case with the *Afwāj* (sing. *fawj*) or reserve squadrons, which are more likely to be constituted around preexisting tribal and kinship ties. *Fawj* reservists can earn a month's pay for a weekend of informal training and target practice near their homes. Ibid.; Yizraeli, *Politics and Society in Saudi Arabia*, 177, n. 44.
163. Author interview, January 2012, Riyadh. The same principle applies to enrollment in the military's officer schools.
164. Scott, *Seeing Like a State*, 82.

CONCLUSION

1. Anderson, *Imagined Communities*, 26, n. 39.
2. "Interview with ʿAbd al-ʿAzīz al-Muqrin," *Ṣawt al-Jihād*, 1 (2003).
3. "Qabīlat al-ʿUtayba Tazuff Aḥad Abnāʾihā Shahīdan," *Ṣawt al-Jihād*, 4 (2003).
4. Author interview, January 2012, Riyadh.
5. Private correspondence with Waḥīd Ragab, January 2012; author interview, March 2012, Riyadh.
6. This volume was funded and published by the government of Abu Dhabi, but was withdrawn from circulation on account of its controversial conclusions about various Emirati lineages.
7. *Al-Jazīra (al-ʿArabiyya)* is also the term for the Arabian Peninsula, suggesting a double meaning.
8. al-Khāṭirī, *Awthaq al-Maʿāyīr*, 23.

Bibliography

ARCHIVAL SOURCES

Institute of Public Administration (IPA), Riyadh
King Abdulaziz Foundation for Research and Archives, Riyadh
Maktabat al-ʿArab (Ḥamad al-Jāsir Library), Riyadh
Mulligan Papers, Georgetown University, Washington, DC

NEWSPAPERS AND MAGAZINES

Aftenposten (Oslo)
Agence France-Presse (Paris)
al-ʿArab (Riyadh)
Arab News (Jeddah)
al-Ḥaras al-Waṭanī (Riyadh)
al-Madīna (Medina)
Majallat Jidda (Jeddah)
al-Masāʾiyya (Riyadh)
al-Nadwa (Mecca)
al-Riyāḍ (Riyadh)
al-Sharq al-Awsaṭ (London and Jeddah)
ʿUkāẓ (Jeddah)
al-Yamāma (Riyadh)

SOURCES IN ARABIC

Abū Haykal, ʿAbd al-ʿĀlim ʿAbd al-Wahhāb. “Al-Raqīq al-Afrīqī bi-l-Ḥijāz khilāl al-Niṣf al-Awwal min al-Qarn al-ʿIshrīn.” *al-Majalla al-Tārīkhiyya al-Miṣriyya* 36 (1989): 317–52.

al-ʿAjlānī, Munīr. *Tārīkh al-Bilād al-ʿArabiyya al-Saʿūdiyya.* Beirut: Dār al-Kātib al-ʿArabī, 1966.

al-Albānī, Nāṣir al-Dīn. Interview with Nāṣir al-Dīn al-Albānī, “al-Taḥdhīr min ʿAlī al-Ṭanṭāwī,” *YouTube,* https://www.youtube.com/watch?v=PBZ46TWWA_k.

al-Amīr, Ibrāhīm b. Manṣūr al-Hāshimī. *al-Ishrāf fī Maʿrifat al-Muʿtanīyīn bi-Tadwīn Ansāb al-Ashrāf (Ahl al-Ḥijāz).* Beirut: Muʾassasat al-Rayyān, 2000.

al-ʿAnazī, Zabn b. Maʿzī b. Ṣāliḥ. *Muʿjam wa-Tārīkh al-Qurā fī Wādī al-Qurā.* Riyadh: Zabn al-ʿAnazī, 1996.

al-Asad, Nāṣir al-Dīn. "al-ʿAllāma al-Shaykh Ḥamad al-Jāsir: al-Nassāba, al-Jughrāfī, al-Lughawī." In *Ḥamad al-Jāsir: ʿAllāmat al-Jazīra al-ʿArabiyya.* Beirut: Maṭbaʿat ʿAlī Mūsā, 2002.

al-Asad, Nāṣir al-Dīn. "Ḥamad al-Jāsir wa-Abū ʿAlī al-Hajarī fī ʿal-Taʿlīqāt wa-l-Nawādir.'" In *al-Sijill al-ʿIlmī li-Nadwat al-Shaykh Ḥamad al-Jāsir wa-Juhūduhu al-ʿIlmiyya,* 1–14. Riyadh: Kulliyyat al-Ādāb [King Saud University], 2003.

al-Badrānī, Fāyiz b. Mūsā. *Baʿḍ al-Aʿyān wa-Aʿlām al-Qabāʾil fī Wathāʾiq al-Maḥkama al-Sharʿiyya bi-l-Madīna al-Munawwara.* Kuwait: Fāyiz b. Mūsā al-Badrānī al-Ḥarbī, 2002.

al-Badrānī, Fāyiz b. Mūsā. *Fuṣūl min Tārīkh Qabīlat Ḥarb fī l-Ḥijāz wa-Najd.* Riyadh: Dār al-Badrānī, 1996.

al-Badrānī, Fāyiz b. Mūsā, ed. *Mulāḥaẓāt ʿalā al-Muʾallifīn wa-l-Kuttāb ḥawl al-Tārīkh wa-l-Ansāb.* Riyadh: Dār al-Badrānī, 1996.

al-Badrānī, Fāyiz b. Mūsā and Rāshid al-ʿAsākir. *Nasab Āl Saʿūd.* Riyadh: Dārat al-Malik ʿAbd al-ʿAzīz, 2012.

al-Badrānī, Fāyiz b. Mūsā, ed. *Wathāʾiq min al-Ghāṭ.* Riyadh: ʿAbd al-Raḥmān al-Sudayrī Charitable Foundation, 2010.

al-Badrānī, Fāyiz b. Mūsā. *Ẓāhirat al-Taʾlīf fī l-Qabāʾil wa-l-Ansāb: al-Asbāb wa-l-Ḍawābiṭ al-Maṭlūba.* Riyadh: Fāyiz al-Ḥarbī, 2006.

Āl Bassām, ʿAbdallāh b. ʿAbd al-Raḥmān. *ʿUlamāʾ Najd Khilāl Thamāniyat Qurūn.* Riyadh: Dār al-ʿĀṣima li-l-Nashr wa-l-Tawzīʿ, 1998.

al-Bilādī, ʿĀtiq b. Ghayth. *Nasab Ḥarb: Qabīlat Ḥarb, Ansābuhā, Furūʿuhā, Tārīkhuhā wa-Diyāruhā.* Mecca: Dār Makka, 1984.

al-Dawsarī, Shuʿayb b. ʿAbd al-Ḥamīd. *Imtāʿ al-Sāmir bi-Takmilat Mutʿat al-Nāẓir.* Riyadh: Dārat al-Malik ʿAbd al-ʿAziz, 1998.

al-Ghadhdhāmī, ʿAbdallāḥ Muḥammad. *al-Faqīh al-Faḍāʾī: Taḥawwul al-Khiṭāb al-Dīnī min al-Minbar ilā l-Shāsha.* Casablanca: al-Markaz al-Thaqāfī al-ʿArabī, 2011.

al-Ghadhdhāmī, ʿAbdallāh Muḥammad. *al-Qabīla wa-l-Qabāʾiliyya, aw Huwīyāt mā baʿda al-Ḥadātha.* Casablanca: al-Markaz al-Thaqāfī al-ʿArabī, 2009.

Ḥamza, Fuʾād. *Qalb Jazīrat al-ʿArab.* Cairo: al-Maṭbaʿa al-Salafiyya, 1933.

al-Ḥanbalī, Rāshid b. ʿAlī b. Jurays. *Muthīr al-Wajd fī Ansāb Mulūk Najd.* Riyadh: Dārat al-Malik ʿAbd al-ʿAzīz, 1979.

al-Ḥanbalī, Rāshid b. ʿAlī b. Jurays. *Muthīr al-Wajd fī Ansāb Mulūk Najd.* Riyadh: Dārat al-Malik ʿAbd al-ʿAzīz, 1999.

al-Ḥarbī, Muḥammad b. Ḥamad Khulayṣ. *Hādhā l-Rajul.* Mecca: Muḥammad al-Ḥarbī, 2007.

al-Ḥarbī, Muḥammad b. Ḥamad Khulayṣ. *Riḥla ilā Wādī al-Qurā.* Mecca: Muḥammad Ḥamad Khulayṣ al-Ḥarbi, 2006.

al-Ḥuqayl, Ḥamad. *Kanz al-Ansāb wa-Majmaʿ al-Ādāb.* Ḥamad al-Ḥuqayl, 1967.

al-Ḥuzaymī, Nāṣir. *Ayyām Maʿa Juhaymān: Kuntu Maʿa al-Jamāʿa al-Salafiyya al-Muḥtasiba*. Beirut: Arab Network for Research and Publishing, 2011.
Ibn ʿAbd al-Wahhāb, Muḥammad. *Masāʾil allatī Khālafa fīhā Rasūl Allāh Ahl al-Jāhiliyya*. Edited by Yūsif b. Muḥammad al-Saʿīd. Saudi Arabia: Dār al-Muʾayyad, 1996.
Ibn ʿAbd al-Wahhāb, Muḥammad. *Muʾallafāt al-Shaykh al-Imām Muḥammad b. ʿAbd al-Wahhāb*. Riyadh: Jāmiʾat al-Imām Muḥammad b. Saʿūd, 1981.
Ibn Bayz, Muḥammad. *Bayān Nasab Āl ʿĪsā b. ʿAlī b. ʿAṭiyya*. ms. Riyadh, Dārat al-Malik ʿAbd al-ʿAzīz, ʿAbd al-Raḥmān al-ʿĪsā/24.
Ibn Bayz, Muḥammad. *Shajarat Nasab Āl ʿĪsā b. ʿAlī b. ʿAṭiyya*. ms. Riyadh, Dārat al-Malik ʿAbd al-ʿAzīz, ʿAbd al-Raḥmān al-ʿĪsā/23.
Ibn Bishr, ʿUthmān. *ʿUnwān al-Majd fī Tārīkh Najd*. Riyadh: Dārat al-Malik ʿAbd al-ʿAzīz, 1982.
Ibn Ghannām, Ḥusayn. *Tārīkh Najd*. Beirut: Dār al-Shurūq, 1985.
Ibn Ḥanbal, Aḥmad. *Musnad al-Imām Aḥmad b. Ḥanbal*. Edited by Samīr Ṭāhā al-Majzūb. Beirut: al-Maktab al-Islāmī, 1993.
Ibn ʿĪsā, Ibrāhīm b. Ṣāliḥ. *ʿIqd al-Durar fīmā Waqaʿa fī Najd min al-Ḥawādith fī Ākhir al-Qarn al-Thālith ʿAshar wa-Awwal al-Rābiʿ ʿAshar*. Riyadh: Dārat al-Malik ʿAbd al-ʿAzīz, 1999.
Ibn ʿĪsā, Ibrāhīm b. Ṣāliḥ. *Tārīkh Baʿḍ al-Ḥawādith al-Wāqiʿa fī Najd*. Riyadh: Dārat al-Malik ʿAbd al-ʿAzīz, 1999.
Ibn Junayd, Yaḥyā. *Ḥamad al-Jāsir: Dirāsa li-Ḥayātihi Maʿa Bibliyūjrāfiyya Shāmila li-Aʿmālihi al-Manshūra*. Riyadh: Maṭābiʿ al-Farazdaq al-Tijāriyya, 1995.
Ibn Laʿbūn, Ḥamad b. Muḥammad. *Tārīkh Ḥamad b. Muḥammad b. Laʿbūn al-Wāʾilī al-Ḥanbalī al-Najdī*. Ṭāʾif: Maktabat al-Maʿārif, 1988.
Ibn Qudāma, Muwaffaq al-Dīn ʿAbdallāh b. Aḥmad. *al-Mughnī*. Cairo: Dār al-Ḥadīth, 1996.
Ibn Saḥmān, Sulaymān. *Irshād al-Ṭālib ilā Ahamm al-Maṭālib wa-Minhāj Ahl al-Ḥaqq wa-l-Aṭbāʿ fī Mukhālafat Ahl al-Juhl wa-l-Ibtidāʿ*. Cairo: Maṭbaʿat al-Manār, 1926/7.
Ibn Salama, ʿAbd al-ʿAzīz b. Ṣāliḥ. *Ḥamad al-Jāsir wa-Maṣīrat al-Ṣiḥāfa wa-l-Ṭibāʿa wa-l-Nashr fī Madīnat al-Riyāḍ*. Riyadh: ʿAbd al-ʿAzīz b. Salama, 2002.
Ibn Ṣunaytān, Muḥammad. *al-Saʿūdiyya: al-Siyāsī wa-l-Qabīla*. Beirut: Arab Network for Research and Publishing, 2008.
Ibn al-Ṭarhūnī, Muḥammad b. Rizq. *al-Ṣayḥa al-Ḥazīna fī l-Balad al-Laʿīna: Risāla fī Ḥukm Ziyārat Madāʾin Ṣāliḥ wa-mā Shābahahā*. Dammam: Dār Ibn al-Qayyim, 1987.
al-Imām, Ṣāliḥ b. Aḥmad ʿAbd al-Raḥmān. *Tārīkh Wādī al-Qurā*. Riyadh: Maṭābiʿ al-ʿUlā, 2000.
Āl Ismāʿīl, Muḥammad b. ʿAbd al-Raḥmān. *al-Shaykh Muḥammad b. Ibrāhīm Āl al-Shaykh wa-Atharu Madrasatihi fī al-Nahḍa al-ʿIlmiyya wa-l-Adabiyya*. Beirut: Dār al-Bashāʾir al-Islāmiyya, 1999.

al-Jabūrī, A. D. Yaḥyā. *Maʿa al-Makhṭūṭāt al-ʿArabiyya: Dhikrayāt wa-Asfār wa-Ṣilāt bi-Muḥibbī al-Turāth.* Amman: Dār al-Majdalāwī, 2012.

al-Jāsir, Ḥamad. *Abū ʿAlī al-Hajarī wa-Abḥāthahu fī Taḥdīd al-Mawāḍiʿ.* Riyadh: Dār al-Yamāma li-l-Baḥth wa-l-Tarjama wa-l-Nashr, 1968.

al-Jāsir, Ḥamad. *Bāhila: al-Qabīla al-Muftarā ʿAlayhā.* Riyadh: Dār al-Yamāma li-l-Baḥth wa-l-Tarjama wa-l-Nashr, 1990.

al-Jāsir, Ḥamad. *Baldat al-Burūd: Mawqiʿan, wa-Tārīkhan, wa-Sukkānan.* Riyadh: Majalat al-ʿArab, 2000.

al-Jāsir, Ḥamad. *Fī Sarāt Ghāmid wa-Zahrān: Nuṣūs, Mushāhadāt, Inṭibāʿāt.* Riyadh: Dār al-Yamāma li-l-Baḥth wa-l-Tarjama wa-l-Nashr, 1971.

al-Jāsir, Ḥamad. *Fī Shimāl Gharb al-Jazīra.* Riyadh: Dār al-Yamāma li-l-Baḥth wa-l-Tarjama wa-l-Nashr, 1970.

al-Jāsir, Ḥamad. *Jamharat Ansāb al-Usar al-Mutaḥaḍḍira fī Najd.* Riyadh: Dār al-Yamāma li-l-Baḥth wa-l-Tarjama wa-l-Nashr, 2001 [1981].

al-Jāsir, Ḥamad. *Madīnat al-Riyāḍ ʿabra Aṭwār al-Tārīkh.* Riyadh: Dār al-Yamāma li-l-Baḥth wa-l-Tarjama, 1966.

al-Jāsir, Ḥamad. *Min Sawāniḥ al-Dhikrayāt.* Riyadh: Dār al-Yamāma li-l-Baḥth wa-l-Tarjama wa-l-Nashr, 2006.

al-Jāsir, Ḥamad. *al-Muʿjam al-Jughrāfī li-l-Bilād al-ʿArabiyya al-Saʿūdiyya: al-Minṭaqa al-Sharqiyya (al-Baḥrayn Qadīman).* Riyadh: Dār al-Yamāma li-l-Baḥth wa-l-Tarjama wa-l-Nashr, 1979.

al-Jāsir, Ḥamad. *al-Muʿjam al-Jughrāfī li-l-Bilād al-ʿArabiyya al-Saʿūdiyya, Shimāl al-Mamlaka: Imārāt Ḥāʾil wa-l-Jawf wa-Tabūk wa-ʿArʿar wa-l-Qurayyāt.* Riyadh: Dār al-Yamāma li-l-Baḥth wa-l-Tarjama wa-l-Nashr, 1979.

al-Jāsir, Ḥamad. *Muʿjam Qabāʾil al-Mamlaka al-ʿArabiyya al-Saʿūdiyya.* Riyadh: Dār al-Yamāma li-l-Baḥth wa-l-Tarjama wa-l-Nashr, 1981.

al-Jazāʾirī, ʿAbd al-Qādir. *A Poem Concerning Nomads and Townsfolk.* ms. Timbuktu, L'Organisation non gouvernementale pour la sauvegarde et la valorisation des manuscrits pour la défense de la culture Islamique (ONG SAVAMA-DCI).

al-Jiraysī, Khālid b. ʿAbd al-Raḥmān. *al-ʿAṣabiyya al-Qabalīyya min al-Manẓūr al-Islāmī.* Riyadh: al-Jiraysī Foundation, 2007.

al-Khāṭirī, Ḥamād b. ʿAbdallāh. *Awthaq al-Maʿāyīr fī Nasab Banī Yās wa-l-Manāṣīr.* Abu Dhabi: Center for Research and Documentation, 2007.

al-Khiḍr, ʿAbd al-ʿAzīz. *al-Saʿūdiyya: Sīrat Dawla wa-Mujtamaʿ.* Beirut: Arab Network for Research and Publishing, 2009.

al-Kuntī, Aḥmad al-Bakkāʾī b. Muḥammad b. al-Mukhtār. *Rawḍat al-Ḥamāʾil li-l-Khayyār wa-Shafrat al-Ṣawārim ʿalā al-Ashrār.* ms. Timbuktu, L'Organisation non gouvernementale pour la sauvegarde et la valorisation des manuscrits pour la défense de la culture Islamique (ONG SAVAMA-DCI).

al-Maḥfūẓ, Ibrāhīm Salmān. *Maqāhī al-ʿAshāʾir fī l-ʿUlā bi-Minṭaqat al-Madīna al-Munawwara.* Jeddah: Ibrāhīm al-Maḥfūẓ, 2001.

al-Māniʿ, ʿAbd al-Raḥmān b. ʿAbd al-ʿAzīz. *Muqtaṭafāt min al-Qiṣaṣ wa-l-Nawādir wa-l-Amthāl wa-l-Ashʿār al-Najdiyya*. Riyadh: ʿAbd al-Raḥmān b. ʿAbd al-ʿAzīz al-Māniʿ, 2004.

Āl Marīʿ, Aḥmad b. ʿAlī. *ʿAlī al-Ṭanṭāwī, Kāna Yawm Kuntu: Ṣināʿat al-Fiqh wa-l-Adab*. Riyadh: al-ʿUbaykān, 2007.

Markaz Ḥamad al-Jāsir al-Thaqāfī, ed. *Ḥamad al-Jāsir fī l-Ṣuḥuf al-Saʿūdiyya: Kashshāf bi-mā Nushira Lahu wa-ʿAnhu*. Riyadh: Markaz Ḥamad al-Jāsir al-Thaqāfī, 2007.

Markaz Ḥamad al-Jāsir al-Thaqāfī, ed. *Ḥamad al-Jāsir fī ʿUyūn al-Ākharīn*. Riyadh: Markaz Ḥamad al-Jāsir al-Thaqāfī, 2003.

al-Mughīrī, ʿAbd al-Raḥmān b. Ḥamad b. Zayd. *al-Muntakhab fī Dhikr Nasab Qabāʾil al-ʿArab*. Damascus: al-Maktab al-Islāmī, 1966.

al-Nakhlī, Ḥasan b. Marzūq. *al-Nakhāwila (al-Nakhlīyūn) fī al-Madīna al-Munawwara: al-Takwīn al-Ijtimāʿī wa-l-Thaqāfī*. Beirut: Muʾassasat al-Intishār al-ʿArabī, 2012.

Naṣīf, ʿAbdallāh b. Ādām Ṣāliḥ. *al-ʿUlā: Dirāsa fī l-Turāth al-Ḥaḍārī wa-l-Ijtimāʿī*. Riyadh: ʿAbdallāh Naṣīf, 1995.

al-Qabbānī, Aḥmad b. ʿAlī. *Naqd Qawāʿid al-Ḍalāl wa-Rafḍ ʿAqāʾid al-Ḍullāl*. ms. Princeton, Yahuda 2636.

al-Raddādī, ʿĀʾidh. *ʿInāyat al-Shaykh Ḥamad al-Jāsir bi-l-Ansāb*. Riyadh: ʿĀʾidh al-Raddādī, 2003.

al-Ṣafadī, Khalīl b. Aybak. *Kitāb al-Wāfī bi-l-Wafayāt*. Beirut: al-Nasharāt al-Islāmiyya, 1997.

al-Salmān, Muḥammad b. ʿAbdallāh b. Sulaymān. *al-Taʿlīm fī Najd fī ʿAhd al-Malik ʿAbd al-ʿAzīz*. Burayda: Nādī al-Qaṣīm al-Adabī bi-Burayda, 1999.

al-Samʿānī, ʿAbd al-Karīm b. Muḥammad. *Kitāb al-Ansāb*. Beirut: Dār Iḥyāʾ al-Turāth al-ʿArabī, 1999.

al-Samhūrī, Rāʾid. *ʿAlī al-Ṭanṭāwī wa-Aʿlām ʿAṣrih: Sayyid Quṭb wa-Ākharūn, Ṣadāqa, Khuṣūma, Naqd*. Beirut: Dār Madārik li-l-Nashr, 2012.

al-Samhūrī, Rāʾid. *ʿAli al-Ṭanṭāwī wa-Ārāʾuhu fī l-Adab wa-l-Naqd*. Damascus: Dār al-Fikr, 2008.

Āl al-Shaykh, Muḥammad b. Ibrāhīm. *Fatāwā al-Shaykh Ibn Ibrāhīm*. Edited by Muḥammad b. ʿAbd al-Raḥmān b. Qāsim. Mecca: Maṭbaʿat al-Ḥukūma, 1978.

al-Shubaylī, ʿAbd al-Raḥmān. *al-Shaykh Ḥamad al-Jāsir fī Ḥiwār Tilfizyūnī Tawthīqī*. Riyadh: ʿAbd al-Raḥmān al-Shubaylī, 2003.

Sowayan, Saad Abdullah. *al-Ṣaḥrāʾ al-ʿArabiyya: Thaqāfatuhā wa-Shiʿruhā ʿabra al-ʿUṣūr*. Beirut: al-Markaz al-Thaqāfī al-ʿArabī, 2010.

al-Ṭanṭāwī, ʿAlī. *Fatāwā ʿAlī al-Ṭanṭāwī*. Edited by Mujāhid Dayrāniyya. Jeddah: Dār al-Manāra, 1985.

al-Ṭanṭāwī, ʿAlī. *Rijāl min al-Tārīkh*. Damascus: Muʾassasat al-Salām li-l-Ṭibāʿa wa-l-Nashr, 1958.

Ṭulaymāt, Ghāzī and ʿIrfān al-Ashqar. *al-Shuʿarāʾ fī al-ʿAṣr al-Umawī*. Damascus: Dār al-Fikr, 2009.

al-ʿUbayyid, ʿAbd al-Raḥmān b. ʿAbd al-Karīm. *Qabīlat al-ʿAwāzim: Dirāsa ʿan Aṣlihā wa-Mujtamaʿihā wa-Diyārihā*. Kuwait: Maktabat al-Ādāb, 1971.

al-ʿUbūdī, Muḥammad. *Muʿjam Usar Burayda.* Riyadh: al-Thulūthiyya Press, 2010.

al-ʿUbūdī, Muḥammad. "al-Shaykh Ḥamad al-Jāsir wa-Juhūduhu al-Jughrāfiyya." In *al-Sijill al-ʿIlmī li-Nadwat al-Shaykh Ḥamad al-Jāsir wa-Juhūduhu al-ʿIlmiyya,* 65–81. Riyadh: Kulliyyat al-Ādāb [King Saud University], 2003.

ʿUsaylān, ʿAbdallāh b. ʿAbd al-Raḥīm. *Ḥamad al-Jāsir wa-Juhūduhu al-ʿIlmiyya.* Medina: Nādī al-Madīna al-Munawwara al-Adabī, 2010.

al-ʿUtaybī, Juhaymān b. Sayf. *al-Fitan wa-Akhbār al-Mahdī wa-Nuzūl ʿĪsā ʿAlayhi al-Salām wa-Ashrāṭ al-Sāʿa.* www.tawhed.ws/r?i=jsgm8fzr.

al-ʿUtaybī, Juhaymān b. Sayf. *al-Bayān wa-l-Tafṣīl fī Maʿrifat al-Dalīl.* www.tawhed.ws/dl?i=5iicoqrb.

al-ʿUtaybī, Juhaymān b. Sayf. *Risālat al-Imāra wa-l-Bayʿa wa-l-Ṭāʿa wa-Ḥukm Talbīṣ al-Ḥukkām ʿalā Ṭalabat al-ʿIlm wa-l-ʿĀmma.* www.tawhed.ws/r?i=fcchouzr.

al-Zāmil, Ṣalāḥ b. Ibrāhīm. *al-Muʾarrikh wa-l-Nassāba Ḥamad b. Ibrāhīm al-Ḥuqayl: Shaykh al-Udabāʾ wa-Adīb al-Shuyūkh.* Riyadh: al-Dār al-Waṭaniyya al-Saʿūdiyya, 2006.

al-Ziriklī, Khayr al-Dīn. *al-Wajīz fī Sīrat al-Malik ʿAbd al-ʿAzīz.* Beirut: Dār al-ʿIlm li-l-Malāyīn, 1971.

SOURCES IN EUROPEAN LANGUAGES

Altorki, Soraya. *Women in Saudi Arabia: Ideology and Behavior Among the Elite.* New York: Columbia University Press, 1986.

Anderson, Benedict. *Imagined Communities.* London: Verso, 2006.

Ayubi, Nazih. *Overstating the Arab State: Politics and Society in the Middle East.* London: I. B. Tauris, 1995.

Bagader, Abubaker Aḥmed. "Literacy and Social Change: The Case of Saudi Arabia." PhD diss., University of Wisconsin, 1978.

Bagnall, Roger S. *The Oxford Handbook of Papyrology.* Oxford: Oxford University Press, 2009.

Bayly, Susan. *Caste, Society and Politics in India from the Eighteenth Century to the Modern Age.* Cambridge: Cambridge University Press, 1999.

Beck, Lois. "Tribes and the State in Nineteenth- and Twentieth-Century Iran." In *Tribes and State Formation in the Middle East,* edited by Phillip S. Khoury and Joseph Kostiner, 185–225. Berkeley: University of California Press, 1990.

Belge, Ceren. "State Building and the Limits of Legibility: Kinship Networks and Kurdish Resistance in Turkey." *International Journal of Middle East Studies* 43, no. 1 (2011): 95–114.

Berkey, Jonathan. "Madrasas Medieval and Modern: Politics, Education, and the Problem of Muslim Identity." In *Schooling Islam,* edited by Robert W. Hefner and Muhammad Qasim Zaman, 40–60. Princeton: Princeton University Press, 2007.

Berlin, Isaiah. *Liberty.* Oxford: Oxford University Press, 2002.

Bonte, Pierre and Edouard Conte, eds. *al-Ansâb: La quête des origines. Anthropolo-*

gie historique de la société tribale Arabe. Paris: Fondation de la Maison des Sciences de l'Homme, 1991.

Bosworth, Clifford Edmund. "Ṣakk." *Encyclopaedia of Islam, Second Edition,* edited by P. Bearman, Th. Bianquis, C. E. Bosworth, E. van Donzel, and W. P. Heinrichs. Brill Online, 2013.

Bourdieu, Pierre. *Outline of a Theory of Practice.* Cambridge: Cambridge University Press, 1995.

Burckhardt, John Lewis. *Notes on the Bedouins and Wahábys.* London: H. Colburn and R. Bentley, 1831.

Burdett, Anita L. P., ed., *The Slave Trade Into Arabia: 1820–1973.* Slough: Archive Editions, 2006.

Charrad, Mounira M. *States and Women's Rights: The Making of Postcolonial Tunisia, Algeria, and Morocco.* Berkeley: University of California Press, 2001.

Carlson, Keith Thor, Kristina Fagan, and Natalia Khanenko-Friesen, eds. *Orality and Literacy: Reflections across Disciplines.* Toronto: University of Toronto Press, 2011.

Caton, Steven. *"Peaks of Yemen I Summon": Poetry as Cultural Practice in a North Yemeni Tribe.* Berkeley: University of California Press, 1990.

Cole, Donald P. *Nomads of the Nomads: The Al Murrah Bedouin of the Empty Quarter.* Lancaster: AHM Publishing, 1975.

Commins, David Dean. *The Wahhabi Mission and Saudi Arabia.* New York: I. B. Tauris, 2006.

Confidential U.S. State Department Central Files. Saudi Arabia. Internal Affairs and Foreign Affairs, 1950–54. Frederick: University Publications of America, 1985.

Cook, Michael. "The Historians of Pre-Wahhabi Najd." *Studia Islamica* no. 76 (1992): 163–76.

Cook, Michael. "The Expansion of the First Saudi State: The Case of Washm." In *The Islamic World from Classical to Modern Times: Essays in Honor of Bernard Lewis,* edited by C. E. Bosworth, Charles Issawi, Roger Savory, and A. L. Udovitch, 661–99. Princeton: The Darwin Press, 1989.

Crawford, M. J. "Civil War, Foreign Intervention, and the Question of Political Legitimacy: A Nineteenth-Century Saʿudi Qadi's Dilemma." *International Journal of Middle East Studies* 14, no. 3 (1982): 227–48.

Crone, Patricia. *Meccan Trade and the Rise of Islam.* Princeton: Princeton University Press, 1987.

Davidson, Christopher. *Abu Dhabi: Oil and Beyond.* New York: Columbia University Press, 2009.

Determann, Jörg Matthias. *Historiography in Saudi Arabia: Globalization and the State in the Middle East.* London: I. B. Tauris, 2014.

Dirks, Nicholas B. *Castes of Mind: Colonialism and the Making of Modern India.* Princeton: Princeton University Press, 2001.

Doughty, Charles. *Travels in Arabia Deserta.* New York: Random House, 1936.

Dresch, Paul. *A Modern History of Yemen.* Cambridge: Cambridge University Press, 2000.

Dresch, Paul. *Tribes, Government, and History in Yemen.* Oxford: Oxford University Press, 1989.

Eickelman, Dale F. *The Middle East and Central Asia: An Anthropological Approach.* Upper Saddle River: Prentice Hall, 1998.

Eickelman, Dale F. "Traditional Islamic Learning and Ideas of the Person in the Twentieth Century." In *Middle Eastern Lives: The Practice of Biography and Self-Narrative,* edited by Martin Kramer, 35–59. Syracuse: Syracuse University Press, 1991.

Eickelman, Dale F. and James Piscatori. *Muslim Politics.* Princeton: Princeton University Press, 1996.

Eickelman, Dale F. "Communication and Control in the Middle East: Publication and Its Discontents." In *New Media in the Muslim World: The Emerging Public Sphere,* edited by Dale F. Eickelman and John W. Anderson, 29–40. Bloomington: Indiana University Press, 2003.

Ende, Werner. "The Nakhawila, a Shiite Community in Medina Past and Present." *Die Welt des Islams* 37, no. 3 (1997): 263–348.

Ende, Werner. "Pilgerfahrt und Glaubensstreit. Die 'Zehn Argumentationen' des Sayyid ʿAbdallāh Shirāzī." In *Fremde, Feinde Und Kurioses: Innen- Und Au Enansichten Unseres Muslimischen,* edited by Benjamin Jokisch, Ulrich Rebstock, and Lawrence Conrad, 323–38. Berlin: Walter de Gruyter, 2009.

Enderwitz, Susanne. "al-Shuʿūbiyya." *Encyclopaedia of Islam, Second Edition,* edited by P. Bearman, Th. Bianquis, C. E. Bosworth, E. van Donzel, and W. P. Heinrichs. Brill Online, 2013.

Evans-Pritchard, Edward Evan. *The Nuer: A Description of the Modes of Livelihood and Political Institutions of a Nilotic People.* Oxford: The Clarendon Press, 1947.

Al Fahad, Abdulaziz H. "The ʿImama vs. the ʿIqal: Hadari-Bedouin Conflict and the Formation of the Saudi State." In *Counter-Narratives: History, Contemporary Society, and Politics in Saudi Arabia and Yemen,* edited by Madawi al-Rasheed and Robert Vitalis, 35–76. New York: Palgrave Macmillan, 2004.

Al Fahad, Abdulaziz H. "Rootless Trees: Genealogical Politics in Saudi Arabia." In *Complexity and Change in Saudi Arabia,* edited by Bernard Haykel, Thomas Hegghammer, and Stéphane Lacroix, 263–91. Cambridge: Cambridge University Press, 2013.

el-Farra, Taha Osman M. "The Effects of Detribalizing the Bedouins on the Internal Cohesion of an Emerging State: The Kingdom of Saudi Arabia." PhD diss., University of Pittsburgh, 1973.

Fortes, Meyer and Edward Evan Evans-Pritchard, eds. *African Political Systems.* London: Oxford University Press, 1940.

Foucault, Michel. *Discipline and Punish: The Birth of the Prison.* New York: Vintage, 1995.

Fox, James. "Sister's Child as Plant: Metaphors in an Idiom of Consanguinity." In *Rethinking Kinship and Marriage,* edited by Rodney Needham, 219–52. London: Tavistock, 1971.

Geary, Patrick. *The Myth of Nations: The Medieval Origins of Europe.* Princeton: Princeton University Press, 2002.
Goody, Jack. *The Development of the Family and Marriage in Europe.* Cambridge: Cambridge University Press, 1983.
Goody, Jack. *The Interface between the Written and the Oral.* Cambridge: Cambridge University Press, 1987.
Goody, Jack, ed. *Literacy in Traditional Societies.* Cambridge: Cambridge University Press, 1968.
Goody, Jack. *The Power of the Written Tradition.* Washington: Smithsonian Institution Press, 2000.
Gould, Stephen J. *Wonderful Life: The Burgess Shale and the Nature of History.* New York: W. W. Norton, 1989.
Gullette, David. *The Genealogical Construction of the Kyrgyz Republic: Kinship, State, and 'Tribalism'.* Folkestone: Global Oriental, 2010.
Habib, John S. *Ibn Saʿud's Warriors of Islam: The Ikhwan of Najd and Their Role in the Creation of the Saʿudi Kingdom, 1910–1930.* Brill: Leiden, 1978.
Havelock, Eric. *Preface to Plato.* Cambridge: Harvard University Press, 1963.
Hawting, G. R. "The Origin of Jeddah and the Problem of al-Shuʿayba." *Arabica* 31, no. 3 (1984): 318–26.
Haykel, Bernard. "On the Nature of Salafi Thought and Practice." In *Global Salafism: Islam's New Religious Movement,* edited by Roel Meijer, 33–57. London: Hurst and Company, 2009.
Haykel, Bernard. *Revival and Reform in Islamic Law: The Legacy of Muhammad al-Shawkani.* Cambridge: Cambridge University Press, 2003.
Hegghammer, Thomas and Stéphane Lacroix. "Rejectionist Islamism in Saudi Arabia: The Story of Juhayman al-ʿUtaybi Revisited." *International Journal of Middle East Studies* 39, no. 1 (2007): 103–22.
Helal, Emad Ahmed. "Muhammad Ali's First Army: The Experiment in Building an Entirely Slave Army." In *Race and Slavery in the Middle East: Histories of Trans-Saharan Africans in Nineteenth-Century Egypt, Sudan, and the Ottoman Mediterranean,* edited by Terence Walz and Kenneth M. Cuno, 17–42. Cairo: American University in Cairo Press, 2010.
Hertog, Steffen. *Princes, Brokers, and Bureaucrats: Oil and the State in Saudi Arabia.* Ithaca: Cornell University Press, 2010.
Herb, Michael. *All in the Family: Absolutism, Revolution, and Democracy in Middle Eastern Monarchies.* Albany: State University of New York Press, 1999.
Ho, Engseng. *The Graves of Tarim: Genealogy and Mobility across the Indian Ocean.* Berkeley: University of California Press, 2006.
Ho, Engseng. "Hadhramis Abroad in Hadhramaut: The *Muwalladīn.*" In *Hadhrami Traders, Scholars, and Statesmen in the Indian Ocean, 1750s–1960s,* edited by Ulrike Freitag and William G. Clarence-Smith, 131–46. Leiden: Brill, 1997.
Ho, Engseng. "Names Beyond Nations: The Making of Local Cosmopolitans." *Études rurales* 3, no. 163/4 (2002): 215–31.

Holmes, J. Teresa. "When Blood Matters: Making Kinship in Colonial Kenya." In *Kinship and Beyond: The Genealogical Model Reconsidered*, edited by Sandra Bamford and James Leach, 50–83. Oxford: Berghahn Books, 2009.

Holy, Ladislav. *Anthropological Perspectives on Kinship*. Ann Arbor: Pluto Press, 1996.

Hopkins, Nicholas S. *Upper Egypt: Life along the Nile*. Højbjerg: Moesgård Museum 2003.

Hoyland, Robert. Review of *Muhammad and the Believers: At the Origins of Islam*, by Fred M. Donner. *International Journal of Middle East Studies* 44, no. 3 (2012): 573–6.

Huber, Charles. *Voyage dans l'Arabie centrale*. Paris: 1884–85.

Hurgronje, C. Snouck. *Mekka in the Latter Part of the 19th Century*. Leiden: Brill, 2006.

Ibn Khaldūn. *The Muqaddimah: An Introduction to History*. Translated by Franz Rosenthal. Princeton: Princeton University Press, 1967.

Jaussen, Antonin and Raphaël Savignac. *Mission archéologique en Arabie*. Paris: E. Leroux, 1909.

Jones, Toby Craig. *Desert Kingdom: How Oil and Water Forged Modern Saudi Arabia*. Cambridge: Harvard University Press, 2011.

Jones, Toby Craig. "State of Nature: The Politics of Water in the Making of Saudi Arabia." In *Water on Sand: Environmental Histories of the Middle East and North Africa*, edited by Alan Mikhail, 231–50. Oxford: Oxford University Press, 2012.

al-Juhany, Uwaidah M. *Najd before the Salafi Reform Movement: Social, Political, and Religious Conditions during the Three Centuries Preceding the Rise of the Saudi State*. Reading: Ithaca Press, 2002.

Khomeini, Ruhollah. *Islam and Revolution*. Translated by Hamid Algar. Berkeley: Mizan Press, 1981.

Kingdom of Saudi Arabia, Ministry of Foreign Affairs. "Our Vision." www.mofa.gov.sa/sites/mofaen/aboutMinistry/Pages/MinistryVision.aspx.

Kostiner, Joseph. *The Making of Saudi Arabia, 1916–1936: From Chieftancy to Monarchical State*. Oxford: Oxford University Press, 1993.

Kraidy, Marwan. "Saudi Arabia, Lebanon and the Changing Arab Information Order." *International Journal of Communication* 1 (2007): 139–56.

Kuper, Adam. *The Invention of Primitive Society: Transformations of an Illusion*. London: Routledge, 1988.

Kurpershoek, P. Marcel. *Oral Poetry and Narratives from Central Arabia, Volume IV, A Saudi Tribal History: Honour and Faith in the Traditions of the Dawāsir*. Leiden: Brill, 2002.

Kurpershoek, P. Marcel. *Oral Poetry and Narratives from Central Arabia, Volume II: The Story of a Desert Knight*. Leiden: Brill, 1995.

Lacey, Robert. *Inside the Kingdom*. New York: Penguin, 2009.

Lacroix, Stéphane. *Awakening Islam*. Cambridge: Harvard University Press, 2011.

Lancaster, William. *The Rwala Bedouin Today*. Cambridge: Cambridge University Press, 1981.

Lane, Edward W. *An Account of the Manners and Customs of the Modern Egyptians.* Cairo: American University in Cairo Press, 2003.

Lane, Edward W. *An Arabic-English Lexicon.* London: Williams and Norgate, 1863–93.

Lawrence, T. E. *Seven Pillars of Wisdom.* Ware: Wordsworth Editions, 1991.

Le Renard, Amélie. *Femmes et espaces publics en Arabie Saoudite.* Paris: Dalloz, 2011.

Lewin, Bernhard. "al-Aṣmaʿī." *Encyclopaedia of Islam, Second Edition,* edited by P. Bearman, Th. Bianquis, C. E. Bosworth, E. van Donzel, and W. P. Heinrichs. Brill Online, 2013.

Lewis, Bernard. *Race and Slavery in the Middle East.* Oxford: Oxford University Press, 1990.

Lorimer, J. G. *Gazetteer of the Persian Gulf, Oman, and Central Arabia.* Calcutta: Superintendent Government Printing, 1915.

Makki, Yousif. "Not What It Seems: The Role of the Tribe in State-Society Relations in Saudi Arabia." *Contemporary Arab Affairs* 4, no. 4 (2012): 445–62.

Massad, Joseph. "Reviving the Discredited." Review of *Nationalism and the Genealogical Imagination: Oral History and Textual Authority in Tribal Jordan,* by Andrew Shryock. *Journal of Palestine Studies* 27, no. 1 (1997): 103–06.

Maudoodi, Syed Abul ʿAla. *The Islamic Movement: Dynamics of Values, Power and Change.* London: The Islamic Foundation, 1984.

Mellamid, Alexander. "The Buraimi Oasis Dispute." *Middle Eastern Affairs* 7, no. 2 (1956): 56–62.

Menoret, Pascal. *Joyriding in Riyadh: Oil, Urbanism, and Road Revolt.* Cambridge: Cambridge University Press, 2014.

Messick, Brinkley. *The Calligraphic State: Textual Domination and History in a Muslim Society.* Berkeley: University of California, 1993.

Messick, Brinkley. "Legal Documents and the Concept of 'Restricted Literacy' in a Traditional Society." *International Journal of the Sociology of Language* no. 42 (1983): 41–52.

Mortel, Richard. "Zaydi Shiism and the Hasanid Sharifs of Mecca." *International Journal of Middle East Studies* 19, no. 4 (1987): 455–72.

Mottahedeh, Roy P. "The Shuʿūbīyah Controversy and the Social History of Early Islamic Iran." *International Journal of Middle East Studies* 7, no. 2 (1976): 161–82.

Mundy, Martha. *Domestic Government: Kinship, Community and Polity in Northern Yemen.* London: I. B. Tauris, 1995.

Musil, Alois. *The Manners and Customs of the Rwala Bedouins.* New York: American Geographical Society, 1928.

Musil, Alois. *Northern Negd: A Topographical Itinerary.* New York: AMS Press, 1978.

Niebuhr, Carsten. *Travels through Arabia and Other Countries in the East.* Reading: Garnet, 1994.

Ochsenwald, William. "Arab Nationalism in the Hijaz." In *The Origins of Arab Nationalism*, edited by Rashid Khalidi, Lisa Anderson, Muhammad Muslih, and Reeva S. Simon, 189–203. New York: Columbia University Press, 1991.

Ochsenwald, William. "Islam and Loyalty in the Saudi Hijaz, 1926–1939." *Die Welt des Islams* 47, no. 1 (2007): 7–32.

Ochsenwald, William. *Religion, Society, and the State in Arabia: The Hijaz under Ottoman Control, 1840–1908*. Columbus: Ohio State University Press, 1984.

Ong, Walter. *Orality and Literacy: The Technologizing of the Word*. London: Methuen, 1982.

Palgrave, William G. *Personal Narrative of a Year's Journey through Central and Eastern Arabia (1862–63)*. London: Macmillan and Co., 1869.

Parolin, Gianluca P. *Citizenship in the Arab World: Kin, Religion, and Nation-State*. Amsterdam: University of Amsterdam Press, 2009.

Peters, Francis E. *Mecca: A Literary History of the Muslim Holy Land*. Princeton: Princeton University Press, 1994.

Philby, H. St. J. B. *The Heart of Arabia: A Record of Travel and Exploration*. London: Constable, 1922.

Philby, H. St. J. B. *The Land of Midian*. London: Ernest Benn Limited, 1957.

Pierret, Thomas. *Religion and State in Syria: The Sunni Ulama from Coup to Revolution*. Cambridge: Cambridge University Press, 2013.

Pike, Ruth. *Linajudos and Conversos in Seville: Greed and Prejudice in Sixteenth- and Seventeenth-Century Spain*. New York: Peter Lang, 2000.

Priestland, Jane, ed. *The Buraimi Dispute: Contemporary Documents*. Cambridge: Archive Editions, 1992.

Procházka Sr., Theodore. "Alois Musil and Prince Nūrī b. Shaʿlān." *Proceedings of the Fifteenth Seminar for Arabian Studies* 12 (1982): 61–67.

Qutb, Sayyid. *Milestones*. Indianapolis: American Trust Publications, 1990.

al-Rasheed, Madawi. *Contesting the Saudi State: Islamic Voices from a New Generation*. Cambridge: Cambridge University Press, 2007.

al-Rasheed, Madawi. *A History of Saudi Arabia*. Cambridge: Cambridge University Press, 2002.

al-Rasheed, Madawi. *A Most Masculine State: Gender, Politics, and Religion in Saudi Arabia*. Cambridge: Cambridge University Press, 2013.

al-Rasheed, Madawi. *Politics in an Arabian Oasis: The Rashidis of Saudi Arabia*. London: I. B. Tauris, 1991.

al-Rasheed, Madawi and Loulouwa al-Rasheed. "The Politics of Encapsulation: Saudi Policy Towards Tribal and Religious Opposition." *Middle Eastern Studies* 32, no. 1 (1996): 96–119.

Rentz, George and William Mulligan. *Aramco Reports on al-Hasa and Oman: 1950–1955*. Cambridge: Archive Edition, 1990.

Rentz, George. "Hutaym." *Encyclopaedia of Islam, Second Edition*, edited by P. Bearman, Th. Bianquis, C. E. Bosworth, E. van Donzel, and W. P. Heinrichs. Brill Online, 2013.

Round, J. Horace. *Peerage and Pedigree: Studies in Peerage Law and Family History.* London: James Nisbet & Co., 1910.

Rush, Alan, ed. *Ruling Families of Arabia: The United Arab Emirates.* Slough: Archive Editions, 1991.

Salibi, Kamal. *The Bible Came from Arabia.* London: Jonathan Cape, 1985.

Samin, Nadav. "*Kafāʾa fī l-Nasab* in Saudi Arabia: Islamic Law, Tribal Custom, and Social Change." *Journal of Arabian Studies* 2, no. 2 (2012): 109–26.

Samin, Nadav. "Our Ancestors, Our Heroes: Saudi Tribal Campaigns to Suppress Historical Docudramas." *British Journal of Middle East Studies* 41, no. 3 (2014): 266–86.

Schneider, David. *A Critique of the Study of Kinship.* Ann Arbor: University of Michigan, 1984.

Scott, James C. *Seeing Like a State: How Certain Schemes to Improve the Human Condition Have Failed.* New Haven: Yale University Press, 1998.

al-Seflan, Ali Mashhor. "The Essence of Tribal Leaders' Participation, Responsibilities, and Decisions in Some Local Government Activities in Saudi Arabia: A Case Study of the Ghamid and Zahran Tribes." PhD diss., Claremont Graduate School, 1981.

Shahshahani, Soheila. "The Tribal Schools of Iran: Sedentarisation through Education." In *Contemporary Society, Tribal Studies Volume Five: The Concept of Tribal Society,* edited by George Pfeffer and Deepak Kumar Behera, 308–22. New Delhi: Concept Publishing, 2002.

Shryock, Andrew. *Nationalism and the Genealogical Imagination: Oral History and Textual Authority in Tribal Jordan.* Berkeley: University of California Press, 1997.

Sneath, David. *The Headless State: Aristocratic Orders, Kinship Society, and Misrepresentations of Nomadic Inner Asia.* New York: Columbia University Press, 2007.

Sowayan, Saad Abdullah. *The Arabian Oral Historical Narrative: An Ethnographic and Linguistic Analysis.* Wiesbaden: O. Harrassowitz, 1992.

Sowayan, Saad Abdullah. *Nabati Poetry: The Oral Poetry of Arabia.* Berkeley: University of California Press, 1985.

Steinberg, Guido. "Ecology, Knowledge, and Trade in Central Arabia (Najd) during the Nineteenth and Early Twentieth Centuries." In *Counter-Narratives: History, Contemporary Society, and Politics in Saudi Arabia and Yemen,* edited by Madawi al-Rasheed and Robert Vitalis, 77–102. New York: Palgrave Macmillan, 2004.

Stetkevych, Jaroslav. *Muḥammad and the Golden Bough: Reconstructing Arabian Myth.* Bloomington: Indiana University Press, 2000.

Stewart, Devin J. "Family." *The Princeton Encyclopedia of Islamic Political Thought,* edited by Gerhard Böwering, 167–69. Princeton: Princeton University Press, 2013.

Szombathy, Zoltán. *The Roots of Arabic Genealogy: A Study in Historical Anthropology.* Piliscsaba: The Avicenna Institute of Middle Eastern Studies, 2003.

Takriti, Abdel Razzaq. *Monsoon Revolution: Republicans, Sultans, and Empires in Oman, 1965–1976.* Oxford: Oxford University Press, 2013.

Tapper, Melbourne. "Blood/Kinship, Governmentality, and Cultures of Order in Colonial Africa." In *Relative Values: Reconfiguring Kinship Studies*, edited by Sarah Franklin and Susan McKinnon, 329–55. Durham: Duke University Press, 2001.

Tarlo, Emma. *Unsettling Memories: Narratives of the Emergency in Delhi.* Berkeley: University of California Press, 2003.

Toledano, Ehud R. *Slavery and Abolition in the Ottoman Middle East.* Seattle: University of Washington Press, 1998.

Thomas, Rosalind. *Literacy and Orality in Ancient Greece.* Cambridge: Cambridge University Press, 1992.

Troeller, Gary. *The Birth of Saudi Arabia: Britain and the Rise of the House of Saʿud* Oxon: Routledge, 2013.

Valensi, Lucette. *Tunisian Peasants in the Eighteenth and Nineteenth Centuries.* Cambridge: Cambridge University Press, 1985.

Varisco, Daniel. *Reading Orientalism: Said and the Unsaid.* Seattle: University of Washington Press, 2007.

Vitalis, Robert. *America's Kingdom: Myth-Making on the Saudi Oil Frontier.* Stanford: Stanford University Press, 2007.

Vom Bruck, Gabriele. "Names as Bodily Signs." In *The Anthropology of Names and Naming*, edited by Gabriele vom Bruck and Barbara Bodenhorn, 225–50. Cambridge: Cambridge University Press, 2006.

Wagner, Mark. *Like Joseph in Beauty: Yemeni-Vernacular Poetry and Arab-Jewish Symbiosis.* Leiden: Brill, 2009.

Wahba, Hafiz. *Arabian Days.* London: A. Barker, 1864.

Wallin, Georg August. *Travels in Arabia 1845 and 1848.* Cambridge: Oleander Press, 1979.

Winder, R. Bayly. *Saudi Arabia in the Nineteenth Century.* London: Macmillan, 1965.

Winter, Michael. "The *Ashrāf* and the *Naqīb al-Ashrāf* in Ottoman Egypt and Syria: A Comparative Analysis." In *Sayyids and Sharifs in Muslim Societies: The Living Links to the Prophet*, edited by Kazuo Morimoto, 139–158. London: Routledge, 2012.

Yizraeli, Sarah. *Politics and Society in Saudi Arabia: The Crucial Years of Development, 1960–1982.* New York: Columbia University Press, 2012.

Yamani, Mai. *The Hijaz and the Quest for an Arabian Identity.* London: I. B. Tauris, 2004.

Zaman, Muhammad Qasim. *Modern Islamic Thought in a Radical Age: Religious Authority and Internal Criticism.* Cambridge: Cambridge University Press, 2012.

Zaman, Muhammad Qasim. *The Ulama in Contemporary Islam: Custodians of Change.* Princeton: Princeton University Press, 2002.
Zerubavel, Eviatar. *Ancestors and Relatives: Genealogy, Identity, and Community.* New York: Oxford University Press, 2012.

Index

PRINCETON STUDIES IN MUSLIM POLITICS

Diane Singerman, *Avenues of Participation: Family, Politics, and Networks in Urban Quarters of Cairo*

Tone Bringa, *Being Muslim the Bosnian Way: Identity and Community in a Central*

Bosnian Village

Dale F. Eickelman and James Piscatori, *Muslim Politics*

Bruce B. Lawrence, *Shattering the Myth: Islam beyond Violence*

Ziba Mir-Hosseini, *Islam and Gender: The Religious Debate in Contemporary Iran*

Robert W. Hefner, *Civil Islam: Muslims and Democratization in Indonesia*

Muhammad Qasim Zaman, *The 'Ulama in Contemporary Islam: Custodians of Change*

Michael G. Peletz, *Islamic Modern: Religious Courts and Cultural Politics in Malaysia*

Oskar Verkaaik, *Migrants and Militants: Fun and Urban Violence in Pakistan*

Laetitia Bucaille, *Growing Up Palestinian: Israeli Occupation and the Intifada Generation*

Robert W. Hefner, ed., *Remaking Muslim Politics: Pluralism, Contestation, Democratization*

Lara Deeb, *An Enchanted Modern: Gender and Public Piety in Shi'i Lebanon*

Roxanne L. Euben, *Journeys to the Other Shore: Muslim and Western Travelers in Search of Knowledge*

Robert W. Hefner and Muhammad Qasim Zaman, eds., *Schooling Islam: The Culture and Politics of Modern Muslim Education*

Loren D. Lybarger, *Identity and Religion in Palestine: The Struggle between Islamism and Secularism in the Occupied Territories*

Augustus Norton, *Hezbollah: A Short History*

Bruce K. Rutherford, *Egypt after Mubarak: Liberalism, Islam, and Democracy in the*

Arab World

Emile Nakhleh, *A Necessary Engagement: Reinventing America's Relations with the*

Muslim World

Roxanne L. Euben and Muhammad Qasim Zaman, eds., *Princeton Readings in Islamist Thought: Texts and Contexts from al-Banna to Bin Laden*

Irfan Ahmad, *Islamism and Democracy in India: The Transformation of Jamaat-e-Islami*

Kristen Ghodsee, *Muslim Lives in Eastern Europe: Gender, Ethnicity, and the Transformation of Islam in Postsocialist Bulgaria*

John R. Bowen, *Can Islam Be French? Pluralism and Pragmatism in a Secularist State*

Thomas Barfield, *Afghanistan: A Cultural and Political History*

Sara Roy, *Hamas and Civil Society in Gaza: Engaging the Islamist Social Sector*

Michael Laffan, *The Makings of Indonesian Islam: Orientalism and the Narration of a Sufi Past*

Jonathan Laurence, *The Emancipation of Europe's Muslims: The State's Role in Minority Integration*

Jenny White, *Muslim Nationalism and the New Turks*

Lara Deeb and Mona Harb, *Leisurely Islam: Negotiating Geography and Morality in Shi'ite South Beirut*

Ësra Özyürek, *Being German, Becoming Muslim: Race, Religion, and Conversion in the New Europe*

Ellen McLarney, *Soft Force: Women in Egypt's Islamic Awakening*

Avi Max Spiegel, *Young Islam: The New Politics of Religion in Morocco and the Arab World*

Nadav Samin, *Of Sand or Soil: Genealogy and Tribal Belonging in Saudi Arabia*

GPSR Authorized Representative: Easy Access System Europe - Mustamäe tee 50, 10621 Tallinn, Estonia, gpsr.requests@easproject.com

www.ingramcontent.com/pod-product-compliance
Lightning Source LLC
Chambersburg PA
CBHW022303280326
41932CB00010B/959
* 9 7 8 0 6 9 1 1 8 3 3 8 1 *